AMERICAN ISSUES

AMERICAN ISSUES

A Primary Source Reader
in United States History

Volume I

Edited by

IRWIN UNGER

New York University

Prentice Hall, Englewood Cliffs, New Jersey 07632

Library of Congress Cataloging-in-Publication Data

American issues : a primary source reader in United States history /
    edited by Irwin Unger.
        p.   cm.
    Includes bibliographical references.
    ISBN 0–13–031956–2 (v. 1).—ISBN 0–13–031964–3 (v. 2)
    1. United States—History—Sources.   I. Unger, Irwin.
E173.A73   1994
973—dc20

                                                                    93–10920
                                                                        CIP

Acquisitions editor: Steve Dalphin
Editorial assistant: Caffie Risher
Production Coordinator: Kelly Behr
Editorial / production supervision and
    interior design: Mary McDonald
Copy editor: Sherry Babbitt
Cover design: Violet Lake Studio

 © 1994 by Prentice-Hall, Inc.
A Paramount Communications Company
Englewood Cliffs, New Jersey 07632

Printed in the United States of America
10   9   8   7   6   5   4   3   2   1

ISBN 0-13-031956-2

Prentice-Hall International (UK) Limited, *London*
Prentice-Hall of Australia Pty. Limited, *Sydney*
Prentice-Hall Canada Inc., *Toronto*
Prentice-Hall Hispanoamericana, S.A., *Mexico*
Prentice-Hall of India Private Limited, *New Delhi*
Prentice-Hall of Japan, Inc., *Tokyo*
Simon & Schuster Asia Pte. Ltd., *Singapore*
Editora Prentice-Hall do Brasil, Ltda., *Rio de Janeiro*

Brief Contents

Contents

Chapter 18   The Last West   347

Preface

Americans worry about the state of education in the United States today. Recently we have been told how little students know about science, geography, mathematics, and history; we fear that our country will be unprepared to compete against the other advanced industrial societies in years to come. We are also concerned that the new generation will lack the shared civic knowledge essential for a functioning democratic system.

There is indeed reason to be dismayed by how small a stock of historical information young Americans possess. But it is important also to realize that education is not just transmission of data. It is also the fostering of critical thinking. The most encyclopedic knowledge do students little good if they cannot use it to reach valid and useful conclusions. It is this belief that has inspired *American Issues*. This two-volume work will stimulate critical thinking about American history—leading students to reject received ideas when appropriate, relate the past to their own experience, and reach conclusions on the basis of evidence. At times, no doubt, students will have to do additional reading beyond this textbook; that, of course, is all to the good.

American Issues is not a compendium of scholars' views. It is constructed out of *primary documents*, the raw material of history. In its pages participants and contemporary observers express their opinions, make their observations, and reach their conclusions about events and issues of their own day that affected the nation and American society. The selections do not point in one direction on any given issue. On the contrary, they were chosen to raise questions and force the student to confront disparity, complexity, and apparent contradiction. *American Issues* avoids giving students the "straight poop." Rather, it compels them to grapple with the same ambiguous raw materials that historians process to reach their conclusions. To further the engagement process, each selection asks specific questions of the student. The approach resembles that of the 1950 Japanese movie *Rashomon*, in which an event was depicted from the perspectives of several participants and viewers were expected to reach their own conclusions. That approach, I believe, is an incomparable way to enlighten students about the rich complexity and fullness of historical reality.

The selections in Volume I and Volume II range widely in subject matter across the American past. Besides the key political questions, they deal with the social, cultural, economic, and gender problems our predecessors faced. *American Issues* is guided by the sense that America has always been a heterogeneous society whose inhabitants led their lives in many ways. Yet it does not abandon the view that all of our forebears were also part of the same American experience and shared many concerns of their era.

What can we expect from conscientious use of *American Issues?* No single text can turn a passive human sponge into an active seeker and thinker. But *American Issues* can, I believe, engage college students' natural curiosity and tendency to differ and encourage the habit of critical appraisal. Instructors and students alike will find *American Issues* a stimulating and challenging introduction to informed and discriminating thinking about the American past.

Irwin Unger

1

The Settlement Enterprise

No one today has to encourage people from other lands to invest their money or their lives in America. Indeed, judging by current immigration pressures, half the world seems eager to share in the "American dream," and some Americans worry that the nation may lose control of its borders and its cultural future under the pressure of newcomers.

But this was not always so. At the very beginning the risks to life and fortune of settlement in North America seemed daunting. And even the supposed advantages often turned out to be false. Europeans were initially ignorant of the climate, resources, and human environment of the New World, and often miscalculated the pros and cons of settlement. And yet somehow the necessary personnel and capital required for successful colonization were forthcoming. How was this result accomplished? What moved people, both literally and figuratively? In any enterprise that involved so many human beings over so long a stretch of time, individual motives were inevitably widely diverse. Still, can you identify the most important factors behind the transfer of capital and people from the Old World to the New?

The documents that follow describe some of the forces that induced people to take their chances on America. Which of the forces depicted, would you suppose, were the most powerful overall? Is it likely that the primary forces varied from colony to colony? Is it possible that they changed over time?

1.1: Richard Hakluyt on the Colonizing of North America (1584)

Richard Hakluyt, a young Anglican minister, was one of many well educated Englishmen who caught "plantation fever" during the reign of

Good Queen Bess (1558–1603). In 1584 he wrote a report, "Discourse of Western Planting," urging Queen Elizabeth to place the human and financial resources of the English nation behind the settlement and exploitation of North America.

It is not easy to penetrate the sixteenth-century English that Hakluyt, like Shakespeare, used. Yet if read carefully, the meaning of the "Discourse" comes through. How would you classify Hakluyt's inducements to establishing colonies? Are they primarily economic? Are the economic motives themselves varied? How important to Hakluyt are the political considerations? What European rival of England does Hakluyt target? Does he play on additional themes besides the political and the economic? Do you know if Hakluyt represents any school of thought during this period regarding the role of the state in economic life?

Why England Should Settle North America

RICHARD HAKLUYT

A brefe collection of certaine reasons to induce her Majestie and the state to take in hande the westerne voyadge and the plantinge there.—Chapter XX. of Hakluyt's Discourse.

1. The soyle yeldeth, and may be made to yelde, all the severall comodities of Europe, and of all kingdomes, domynions, and territories that England tradeth withe, that by trade of marchandize cometh into this realme.

2. The passage thither and home is neither to longe nor to shorte, but easie, and to be made twise in the yere.

3. The passage cutteth not nere the trade of any prince, nor nere any of their contries or territories, and is a safe passage, and not easie to be annoyed by prince or potentate whatsoever.

4. The passage is to be perfourmed at all times of the yere, and in that respecte passeth our trades in the Levant Seas within the Straites of Juberalter, and the trades in the seas within the Kinge of Denmarkes Straite, and the trades to the portes of Norwey and of Russia, &c.; for as in the south weste Straite there is no passage in somer by lacke of windes, so within the other places there is no passage in winter by yse and extreme colde.

5. And where England nowe for certen hundreth yeres last passed, by the peculiar comoditie of wolles, and of later yeres by clothinge of the same, hath raised it selfe from meaner state to greater wealthe and moche higher honour, mighte, and power then before, to the equallinge of the princes of the same to the greatest potentates of this parte of the worlde; it cometh

"England's Title to North America," *Old South Leaflets* (Boston: Directors of the Old South Work, 1902), vol. 5, pp. 444–449.

nowe so to passe, that by the greate endevour of the increase of the trade of wolles in Spaine and in the West Indies, nowe daily more and more multi-plienge, that the wolles of England, and the clothe made of the same, will become base, and every day more base then other; which, prudently weyed, yt behoveth this realme, yf it meane not to returne to former olde meanes and basenes, but to stande in present and late former honour, glorye, and force, and not negligently and sleepingly to slyde into beggery, to foresee and to plante at Norumbega or some like place, were it not for any thing els but for the hope of the vent of our woll indraped, the principall and in effecte the onely enrichinge contynueinge naturall comoditie of this realme. And effectually pursueinge that course, wee shall not onely finde on that tracte of lande, and especially in that firme northwarde (to whome warme clothe shalbe righte wellcome), an ample vente, but also shall, from the north side of that firme, finde oute knowen and unknowen ilandes and domynions replenished with people that may fully vent the aboundaunce of that our comoditie, that els will in fewe yeres waxe of none or of small value by forreine aboundaunce, &c.; so as by this enterprice wee shall shonne the ymmynent mischefe hanginge over our heades, that els muste nedes fall upon the realme, without breache of peace or sworde drawen againste this realme by any forreine state; and not offer our auncient riches to scornefull neighboures at home, nor sell the same in effecte for nothinge, as wee shall shortly, if presently it be not provaided for. The increase of the wolles of Spaine and America is of highe pollicie, with greate desire of our over-throwe, endevoured; and the goodnes of the forren wolles our people will not enter into the consideration of, nor will not beleve aughte, they be so sotted with opinion of their owne; and, yf it be not foresene and some such place of vent provided, farewell the goodd state of all degrees in this realme.

6. This enterprise may staye the Spanishe Kinge from flowinge over all the face of that waste firme of America, yf wee seate and plante there in time, in tyme I say, and wee by plantinge shall lett him from makinge more shorte and more safe returnes oute of the noble portes of the purposed places of our plantinge, then by any possibilitie he can from the parte of the firme that nowe his navies by ordinary courses come from, in this that there is no comparison betwene the portes of the coastes that the Kinge of Spaine dothe nowe possesse and use, and the portes of the coastes that our nation is to possesse by plantinge at Norumbéga, and on that tracte faste by, more to the northe and northeaste, and in that there is from thence a moche shorter course, and a course of more temperature, and a course that possesseth more contynuaunce of ordinary windes, then the present course of the Spanishe Indian navies nowe dothe. And England possessinge the purposed place of plantinge, her Majestie may, by the benefete of the seate, havinge wonne goodd and royall havens, have plentie of excellent trees for mastes, of goodly timber to builde shippes and to make greate navies, of pitche, tarr, hempe, and all thinges incident for a navie royall, and that for no price, and

withoute money or request. Howe easie a matter may yt be to this realme, swarminge at this day with valiant youthes, rustinge and hurtfull by lacke of employment, and havinge goodd makers of cable and of all sortes of cordage, and the best and moste connynge shipwrights of the worlde, to be lordes of all those sees, and to spoile Phillipps Indian navye, and to deprive him of yerely passage of his treasure into Europe, and consequently to abate the pride of Spaine and of the sup-porter of the greate Antechriste of Rome, and to pull him downe in equallitie to   his neighbour princes, and consequently to cutt of the common mischefes that come to all Europe by the peculiar aboundaunce of his Indian treasure, and thiss withoute difficultie.

7. This voyadge, albeit it may be accomplished by barke or smallest pynnesse for advise or for a necessitie, yet for the distaunce, for burden and gaine in trade, the marchant will not for profitts sake use it but by shippes of greate burden; so as this realme shall have by that meane shippes of greate burden and of greate strengthe for the defence of this realme, and for the defence of that newe seate, as nede shall require, and withall greate increase of perfecte seamen, which greate princes in time of warres wante, and which kinde of men are neither nourished in fewe daies nor in fewe yeres.

8. This newe navie of mightie newe stronge shippes, so in trade to that Norumbega and to the coastes there, shall never be subjecte to arreste of any prince or potentate, as the navie of this realme from time to time hath bene in the portes of thempire, in the portes of the Base Contries, in Spaine, Fraunce, Portingale, &c., in the tymes of Charles the Emperour, Fraunces the Frenche kinge, and others; but shall be alwayes free from that bitter mischeefe, withoute grefe or hazarde to the marchaunte or to the state, and so alwaies readie at the comaundement of the prince with mariners, artillory, armor, and munition, ready to offende and defende as shalbe required.

9. The greate masse of wealthe of the realme imbarqued in the marchantes shippes, caried oute in this newe course, shall not lightly, in so farr distant a course from the coaste of Europe, be driven by windes and tempestes into portes of any forren princes, as the Spanishe shippes of late yeres have bene into our portes of the West Contries, &c.; and so our marchantes in respecte of private state, and of the realme in respecte of a generall safetie from venture of losse, are by this voyadge oute of one greate mischefe.

10. No forren commoditie that comes into England comes withoute payment of custome once, twise, or thrise, before it come into the realme, and so all forren comodities become derer to the subjectes of this realme; and by this course to Norumbega forren princes customes are avoided; and the forren comodities cheapely purchased, they become cheape to the subjectes of England, to the common benefite of the people, and to the savinge of greate treasure in the realme; whereas nowe the realme becomethe poore by the purchasinge of forreine comodities in so greate a masse at so excessive prices.

11. At the firste traficque with the people of those partes, the subjectes of this realme for many yeres shall chaunge many cheape comodities of these partes for thinges of highe valor there not estemed; and this to the greate inrichinge of the realme, if common use faile not.

12. By the greate plentie of those regions the marchantes and their factors shall lye there cheape, buye and repaire their shippes cheape, and shall returne at pleasure withoute staye or restrainte of forreine prince; whereas upon staies and restraintes the marchaunte raiseth his chardge in sale over of his ware; and, buyenge his wares cheape, he may mainteine trade with smalle stocke, and withoute takinge upp money upon interest; and so he shalbe riche and not subjecte to many hazardes, but shalbe able to afforde the comodities for cheape prices to all subjectes of the realme.

13. By makinge of shippes and by preparinge of thinges for the same, by makinge of cables and cordage, by plantinge of vines and olive trees, and by makinge of wyne and oyle, by husbandrie, and by thousandes of thinges there to be done, infinite nombers of the Englishe nation may be set on worke, to the unburdenynge of the realme with many that nowe lyve chardgeable to the state at home.

14. If the sea coste serve for makinge of salte, and the inland for wine, oiles, oranges, lymons, figges, &c., and for makinge of yron, all which with moche more is hoped, withoute sworde drawen, wee shall cutt the combe of the Frenche, of the Spanishe, of the Portingale, and of enemies, and of doubtfull frendes, to the abatinge of their wealthe and force, and to the greater savinge of the wealthe of the realme.

15. The substaunces servinge, wee may oute of those partes receave the masse of wrought wares that nowe wee receave out of Fraunce, Flaunders, Germanye, &c.; and so wee may daunte the pride of some enemies of this realme, or at the leaste in parte purchase those wares, that nowe wee buye derely of the Frenche and Flemynge, better cheape; and in the ende, for the parte that this realme was wonte to receave, dryve them oute of trade to idlenes for the settinge of our people on worke.

16. Wee shall by plantinge there inlarge the glory of the gospell, and from England plante sincere relligion, and provide a safe and a sure place to receave people from all partes of the worlde that are forced to flee for the truthe of Gods worde.

17. If frontier warres there chaunce to aryse, and if thereupon wee shall fortifie, yt will occasion the trayninge upp of our youthe in the discipline of warr, and make a nomber fitt for the service of the warres and for the defence of our people there and at home.

18. The Spaniardes governe in the Indies with all pride and tyranie; and like as when people of contrarie nature at the sea enter into gallies, where men are tied as slaves, all yell and crye with one voice, *Liberta, liberta*, as desirous of libertie and freedome, so no doubte whensoever the Queene of England, a prince of such clemencie, shall seate upon that firme of America,

and shalbe reported throughe oute all that tracte to use the naturall people there with all humanitie, curtesie, and freedome, they will yelde themselves to her governement, and revolte cleane from the Spaniarde, and specially when they shall understande that she hathe a noble navie, and that she aboundeth with a people moste valiaunte for theyr defence. And her Majestie havinge Sir Fraunces Drake and other subjectes already in credite with the Symerons, a people or greate multitude alreadye revolted from the Spanishe governemente, she may with them and a fewe hundreths of this nation, trayned upp in the late warres of Fraunce and Flaunders, bringe greate thinges to passe, and that with greate ease; and this broughte so aboute, her Majestie and her subjectes may bothe enjoye the treasure of the mynes of golde and silver, and the whole trade and all the gaine of the trade of marchandize, that nowe passeth thither by the Spaniardes onely hande, of all the comodities of Europe; which trade of marchandize onely were of it selfe suffycient (withoute the benefite of the riche myne) to inriche the subjectes, and by customes to fill her Majesties coffers to the full. And if it be highe pollicie to mayneteyne the poore people of this realme in worke, I dare affirme that if the poore people of England were five times so many as they be, yet all mighte be sett on worke in and by workinge lynnen, and suche other thinges of marchandize as the trade into the Indies dothe require.

19. The present shorte trades causeth the maryner to be cast of, and ofte to be idle, and so by povertie to fall to piracie. But this course to Norumbega beinge longer, and a contynuaunce of themploymente of the maryner, dothe kepe the maryner from ydlenes and from necessitie; and so it cutteth of the principal actions of piracie, and the rather because no riche praye for them to take cometh directly in their course or any thing nere their course.

20. Many men of excellent wittes and of divers singuler giftes, overthrown by suertishippe, by sea, or by some folly of youthe, that are not able to live in England, may there be raised againe, and doe their contrie goodd service; and many nedefull uses there may (to greate purpose) require the savinge of greate nombers, that for trifles may otherwise be devoured by the gallowes.

21. Many souldiers and servitours, in the ende of the warres, that mighte be hurtfull to this realme, may there be undladen, to the common profite and quiet of this realme, and to our forreine benefite there, as they may be employed.

22. The frye of the wandringe beggars of England, that growe upp ydly, and hurtefull and burdenous to this realme, may there by unladen, better bredd upp, and may people waste contries to the home and forreine benefite, and to their owne more happy state.

23. If Englande crie oute and affirme, that there is so many in all trades that one cannot live for another, as in all places they doe, this Norumbega (if it be thoughte so goodd) offreth the remedie.

1.2:   John Winthrop Advises Puritans to Emigrate (1629)

John Winthrop was a gentleman of Suffolk in East Anglia, a corner of England where, in the early seventeenth century, many of the people, including Winthrop, were Puritan dissenters against the established Church of England. In 1629 Winthrop and a group of fellow Puritans concluded that the England of Charles I was an inhospitable place for people of their views and circumstances, and resolved to emigrate to a portion of North America for which they had secured a royal charter. That year Winthrop circulated the letter below among influential Puritans, explaining why the time to leave England had arrived.

Winthrop was a lawyer, not a clergyman, yet like most Puritans he was intensely devout, a man for whom religion was virtually the core of existence. Does his argument for leaving England emphasize religious reasons? Why should people like him have found the English religious scene so deplorable in 1629? What other arguments for a Puritan exodus does Winthrop make? How do you explain these other arguments?

(In 1630 Winthrop followed his own advice and led the first Puritan contingent to Massachusetts Bay. For the next nineteen years, until his death in 1649, he served the colony successfully as governor and deputy governor.)

Why We Should Leave England

JOHN WINTHROP

Reasons to be considered for justifying the undertakers of the intended plantation in New England and for encouraging such whose hearts God shall move to join with them in it.

1. First, it will be a service to the church of great consequence to carry the gospel into those parts of the world, to help on the coming in of fullness of the Gentiles, and to raise a bulwark against the kingdom of anti-Christ which the Jesuits labor to rear up in those parts.

2. All other churches of Europe are brought to desolation, and our sins, for which the Lord begins already to frown upon us, do threaten us fearfully, and who knows but that God hath provided this place to be a refuge for many whom he means to save out of the general calamity. And seeing the church hath no place left to fly into but the wilderness, what better work can there be than to go before and provide tabernacles and food for her, against she cometh thither?

Massachusetts Historical Society Proceedings, vol. 8 (1864–65), pp. 420–427.

3. This land grows weary of her inhabitants, so as man who is the most precious of all creatures is here more vile and base than the earth we tread upon, and of less price among us than a horse or a sheep; masters are forced by authority to entertain servants, parents to maintain their own children. All towns complain of the burthen of their poor, though we have taken up many unnecessary, yea unlawful, trades to maintain them. And we use the authority of the law to hinder the increase of people, as urging the execution of the state against cottages and inmates, and thus it is come to pass that children, servants, and neighbors (especially if the[y] be poor) are counted the greatest burthen, which if things were right it would be the chiefest earthly blessing.

4. The whole earth is the Lord's garden, and He hath given it to the sons of men with a general condition, Gen. 1:28, "Increase and multiply, replenish the earth and subdue it," which was again renewed to Noah. The end is double moral and natural: that man might enjoy the fruits of the earth, and God might have his due glory from the creature. Why then should we stand here striving for places of habitation (many men spending as much labor and cost to recover or keep sometimes an acre or two of land as would procure them many hundred as good or better in an other country) and in the meantime suffer a whole continent as fruitful and convenient for the use of man to lie waste without any improvement?

5. We are grown to that height of intemperance in all excess of riot, as no man's estate almost will suffice to keep sail with his equals, and he who fails herein must live in scorn and contempt. Hence it comes that all arts and trades are carried in that deceitful and unrighteous course, as it is almost impossible for a good and upright man to maintain his charge and live comfortably in any of them.

6. The fountains of learning and religion are so corrupted (as beside the unsupportable charge of the education) most children (even the best wits and fairest hopes) are perverted, corrupted, and utterly overthrown by the multitude of evil examples and the licentious government of those seminaries, where men strain at gnats and swallow camels, use all severity for maintenance of capes and other complements, but suffer all ruffian-like fashion and disorder in manners to pass uncontrolled.

7. What can be a better work and more honorable and worthy a Christian than to help raise and support a particular church while it is in the infancy, and to join his forces with such a company of faithful people as by a timely assistance may grow strong and prosper, and for want of it may be put to great hazard, if not wholly ruined.

8. If any such who are known to be godly, and live in wealth and prosperity here, shall forsake all this to join themselves to this church, and to run a hazard with them of a hard and mean condition, it will be an example of great use both for removing the scandal of worldly and sinister respects which is cast upon the adventurers, to give more life to the faith of God's people in their prayers for the plantation, and to encourage others to join the more willingly in it.

9. It appears to be a work of God for the good of His church, in that He hath disposed the hearts of so many of His wise and faithful servants (both ministers and others) not only to approve of the enterprise but to interest themselves in it, some in their persons and estates, others by their serious advice and help otherwise. And all by their prayers for the welfare of it, Amos 3. The Lord revealeth His secrets to His servants the prophets; it is likely He hath some great work in hand which He hath revealed to His prophets among us, whom He hath stirred up to encourage His servants to this plantation, for He doth not use to seduce His people by His own prophets but commits that office to the ministry of false prophets and lying spirits.

Divers objections which have been made against this plantation with their answers and resolutions.

Objection 1:   We have no warrant to enter upon that land which hath been so long possessed by others.

Answer 1:   That which lies common and hath never been replenished or subdued is free to any that will possess and improve it, for God hath given to the sons of men a double right to the earth: there is a natural right and a civil right. The first right was natural when men held the earth in common, every man sowing and feeding where he pleased, and then as men and the cattle increased they appropriated certain parcels of ground by enclosing, and peculiar manurance, and this in time gave them a civil right. Such was the right which Ephron the Hittite had in the field of Machpelah, wherein Abraham could not bury a dead corpse without leave, though for the out parts of the country which lay common he dwelt upon them and took the fruit of them at his pleasure. The like did Jacob, which fed his cattle as bold in Hamor's land (for he is said to be the lord of the country) and other places where he came as the native inhabitants themselves. And that in those times and places men accounted nothing their own but that which they had appropriated by their own industry appears plainly by this: that Abimelech's servants in their own country, when they oft contended with Isaac's servants about wells which they had digged, yet never strove for the land wherein they were. So likewise between Jacob and Laban: he would not take a kid of Laban's without his special contract, but he makes no bargain with him for the land where they feed, and it is very probable if the country had not been as free for Jacob as for Laban, that covetous wretch would have made his advantage of it and have upbraided Jacob with it, as he did with his cattle. And for the natives in New England, they enclose no land, neither have any settled habitation, nor any tame cattle to improve the land by, and so have no other but a natural right to those countries. So as if we leave them sufficient for their use, we may lawfully take the rest, there being more than enough for them and us.

Secondly, we shall come in with the good leave of the Natives, who find benefit already by our neighborhood and learn of us to improve part to more use than before they could do the whole. And by this means we come in by valuable purchase, for they have of us that which will yield them more benefit than all the land which we have from them.

Thirdly, God hath consumed the Natives with a great plague in those parts so as there be few inhabitants left.

Objection 2: It will be a great wrong to our church to take away the good people, and we shall lay it the more open to the judgment feared.

Answer 1: The departing of good people from a country doth not cause a judgment but foreshew it, which may occasion such as remain to turn from their evil ways that they may prevent it, or to take some other course that they may escape it.

Secondly, such as go away are of no observation in respects of those who remain, and they are likely to do more good there than here. And since Christ's time, the church is to be considered as universal without distinction of countries, so as he who doeth good in any one place serves the church in all places in regard of the unity.

Thirdly, it is the revealed will of God that the gospel should be preached to all nations, and though we know not whether those barbarians will receive it at first or not, yet it is a good work to serve God's providence in offering it to them; and this is fittest to be done by God's own servants, for God shall have glory by it though they refuse it, and there is good hope that the posterity *shall by this means be gathered into Christ's sheepfold.*

Objection 3: We have feared a judgment a great while, but yet we are safe. It were better therefore to stay till it come, and either we may fly then, or if we be overtaken in it, we may well content ourselves to suffer with such a church as ours is.

Answer: It is likely this consideration made the churches beyond the seas, as the Palatinate, Rochelle, etc., to sit still at home and not to look out for shelter while they might have found it. But the woeful spectacle of their ruin may teach us more wisdom, to avoid the plague when it is foreseen, and not to tarry as they did till it overtake us. If they were now at their former liberty, we might be sure they would take other courses for their safety, and though half of them had miscarried in their escape, yet had it not been so miserable to themselves nor scandalous to religion as this desperate backsliding, and abjuring the truth, which many of the ancient professors among them, and the whole posterity which remain, are now plagued into.

Objection 4: The ill success of other plantations may tell us what will become of this.

Answer 1: None of the former sustained any great damage but Virginia; which happened through their own sloth and security.[1]

---

[1] Winthrop was aware of the tribulations of the early Virginia settlement at Jamestown, including hunger resulting from the sloth of the settlers—ED.

2. The argument is not good, for thus it stands: some plantations have miscarried, therefore we should not make any. It consists in particulars and so concludes nothing. We might as well reason thus: many houses have been burnt by kilns, therefore we should use none; many ships have been cast away, therefore we should content ourselves with our home commodities and not adventure men's lives at sea for those things which we might live without; some men have been undone by being advanced to great places, therefore we should refuse our preferment, etc.

3. The fruit of any public design is not to be discerned by the immediate success; it may appear in time that former plantations were all to good use.

4. There were great and fundamental errors in the former which are like to be avoided in this, for first their main end was carnal and not religious; secondly, they used unfit instruments—a multitude of rude and misgoverned persons, the very scum of the people; thirdly, they did not establish a right form of government.

Objection 5:   It is attended with many and great difficulties.

Answer: So is every good action. The heathen could say *ardua virtutis via.* And the way of God's kingdom (the best way in the world) is accompanied with most difficulties. Straight is the gate and narrow is the way that leadeth to life. Again, the difficulties are no other than such as many daily meet with and such as God hath brought others well through them.

Objection 6:   It is a work above the power of the undertakers.

Answer 1:   The welfare of any body consists not so much in quantity as in due portion and disposition of parts, and we see other plantations have subsisted divers years and prospered from weak means.

2. It is no wonder, for great things may arise from weak, contemptible beginnings; it hath been oft seen in kingdoms and states and may as well hold in towns and plantations. The Waldenses[2] were scattered into the Alps and mountains of Piedmont by small companies, but they became famous churches whereof some remain to this day; and it is certain that the Turks, Venetians, and other states were very weak in their beginnings.

Objection 7:   The country affords no natural fortifications.

Answer: No more did Holland and many other places which had greater enemies and nearer at hand, and God doth use to place His people in the midst of perils that they may trust in Him and not in outward means and safety; so when He would choose a place to plant His beloved people in, He seateth them not in an island or other place fortified by nature, but in a plain country beset with potent and bitter enemies round about, yet so long as they served Him and trusted in His help they were safe. So the Apostle

---

[2] A heretical medieval sect persecuted by the Catholic Church. By scattering to remote places the Waldenses survived until after the Reformation—ED.

Paul saith of himself and his fellow laborers, that they were compassed with dangers on every side and were daily under the sentence of death that they might learn to trust in the living God.

Objection 8:   The place affordeth no comfortable means to the first planters, and our breeding here at home have made us unfit for the hardship we are like to endure.

Answer 1:   No place of itself hath afforded sufficient to the first inhabitants; such things as we stand in need of are usually supplied by God's blessing upon the wisdom and industry of man, and whatsoever we stand in need of is treasured in the earth by the Creator and is to be fetched thence by the sweat of our brows.

2. We must learn with Paul to want as well as to abound; if we have food and raiment (which are there to be had), we ought to be contented. The difference in quality may a little displease us, but it cannot hurt us.

3. It may be by this means God will bring us to repent of our former intemperance, and so cure us of that disease which sends many amongst us untimely to their graves and others to hell; so He carried the Israelites into the wilderness and made them forget the flesh pots of Egypt, which was sorry pinch to them at first, but He disposed to their good in the end. Deut. 30: 3, 16.

Objection 9:   We must look to be preserved by miracle if we subsist, and so we shall tempt God.

Answer 1:   They who walk under ordinary means of safety and supply do not tempt God, but such will be our condition in this plantation therefore, etc. The proposition cannot be denied; the assumption we prove thus: that place is as much secured from ordinary dangers as many hundred places in the civil parts of the world, and we shall have as much provision beforehand as such towns do use to provide against a siege or dearth, and sufficient means for raising a succeeding store against that is spent. If it be denied that we shall be as secure as other places, we answer that many of our sea towns, and such as are upon the confines of enemies' countries in the continent, lie more upon and nearest to danger than we shall. And though such towns have sometimes been burnt or spoiled, yet men tempt not God to dwell still in them, and though many houses in the country amongst us lie open to thieves and robbers (as many have found by sad experience), yet no man will say that those which dwell in such places must be preserved by miracle.

2. Though miracles be now ceased, yet men may expect more than ordinary blessing from God upon all lawful means, where the work is the Lord's and He is sought in it according to His will, for it is usual with Him to increase or weaken the strength of the means as He is pleased or displeased with the instruments and the action, else we must conclude that God hath left the government of the world and committed all power to the creature, that the success of all things should wholly depend upon the second causes.

3. We appeal to the judgment of the soldiers if five hundred men may not in one month raise a fortification which with sufficient munition and victual they may make good against 3,000 for many months, and yet without miracle.

4. We demand an instance if any prince or state hath raised 3,000 soldiers and victualed for six or eight months, with shipping and munition answerable, to invade a place so far distant as this is from any foreign enemy, and where they must run a hazard of repulse and no booty or just title of sovereignty to allure them. . . .

1.3:   A Cavalier Goes into Exile (1649)

Twenty years after Winthrop and his fellow Puritans first made plans to leave the realm of England, their royalist-Anglican opponents found reasons themselves to consider America a refuge. Between 1629 and 1649 the Roundheads, Puritan followers of parliamentary leader Oliver Cromwell, had defeated the king and his supporters in a bloody civil war and imposed their own political and religious regime on England. In January 1649 the victors tried Charles I for high treason and soon after beheaded him. With the Roundheads in control of England, many royalists, often called Cavaliers, sought a safe haven elsewhere for themselves and their families.

The following document is by a Colonel Norwood who chose Virginia as his refuge. Why did Norwood choose Virginia? Do you know if the Cavalier emigration to that colony had an effect on its social structure or values? Was Virginia settled predominantly by Cavaliers?

A Voyage to Virginia

COLONEL NORWOOD

Time of Setting Out

The month of *August, Anno* 1649, being the time I engag'd to meet my two comrades, Major *Francis Morrison*, and Major *Richard Fox*, at *London*, in order to a full accomplishment of our purpose to seek our fortunes in *Virginia*, (pursuant to our agreement the year before in *Holland*) all parties very punctually appear'd at the time and place assign'd, and were all still in the same mind, fully bent to put in practice what we had so solemnly agreed upon, our inclinations that way being nothing abated, but were rather quicken'd, by the new changes that we saw in the state of things, and that very much for the worse: For if our spirits were somewhat depress'd in contemplation of a barbarous restraint upon the person of our king in the *Isle of*

"A Voyage to Virginia," in Peter Force, ed., vol. 3, no, 10, *Tracts and Other Papers Relating Principally to the Origin, Settlement and Progress of the Colonies in North America*, p. 1844.

Wight; to what horrors and despairs must our minds be reduc'd at the bloody and bitter stroke of his assassination, at his palace of *Whitehall*?

This unparallel'd butchery made the rebels cast away the scabbards of their swords with both their hands, in full resolution never to let them meet again, either by submission or capitulation; so that the sad prospect of affairs in this juncture, gave such a damp to all the royal party who had resolved to persevere in the principle which engaged them in the war, that a very considerable number of nobility, clergy, and gentry, so circumstanc'd, did fly from their native country, as from a place infected with the plague, and did betake themselves to travel any where to shun so hot a contagion, there being no point on the compass that would not suit with some of our tempers and circumstances, for transportation into foreign lands.

Of the number who chose to steer their course for *America*, such of them as inclin'd to try their fortunes at *Surinam, Barbados, Antigua,* and the *Leeward Islands*, were to be men of the first rate, who wanted not money or credit to balance the expence necessary to the carrying on the sugar works: And this consideration alone was enough to determine our choice for *Virginia*, had we wanted other arguments to engage us in the voyage. The honour I had of being nearly related to Sir *William Barkeley* the governor, was no small incitation to encourage me with a little stock to this adventure: Major *Morrison* had the king's commission to be captain of the fort; and Mr. *Fox* was to share in our good or bad success: But my best cargaroon[1] was his majesty's gracious letter in my favour, which took effect beyond my expectation, because it recommended me (above whatever I had or could deserve) to the governor's particular care.

1.4:   The Common Folk Come to America (1683)

Both Richard Hakluyt and John Winthrop were promoters of colonies, although Winthrop also emigrated to America himself. But what brought ordinary men and women to the new European settlements? We can assume that the religious factor was important in the founding of some colonies, especially in New England. Obviously politics could also be important, witness Colonel Norwood and Virginia. But were there other motives, especially in the case of the "common sort?"

The following document is an excerpt from a letter of 1683 written by William Penn, the founder of Pennsylvania, to a group of business people interested in trading with his new colony and speculating in its land. Penn had just returned from his first visit to Pennsylvania, and the inducements offered to prospective settlers that he describes were based on his recent experiences.

---

[1] A passport, in effect; actually, a sort of bill of lending—ED.

Penn obviously emphasizes the attractive economic environment for men and women of the laboring class, but he also talks about "younger Brothers of small Inheritances." What is he referring to here? And what sort of people were "Men of universal Spirits"? Why might the American colonies provide the common people with superior economic advantages compared to their native land?

Who Should Go to Pennsylvania?

WILLIAM PENN

IV. These persons that providence seems to have most fitted for Plantations are,

1st. Industrious Husbandmen and Day-Labourers, that are hardly able (with ex-treme Labour) to maintain their Families and portion their Children.

2dly. Laborious Handicrafts, especially Carpenters, Masons, Smiths, Weavers, Taylors, Tanners, Shoemakers, Shipwrights, etc. where they may be spared or are low in the World: And as they shall want no encouragement, so their Labour is worth more there than here, and there provision cheaper.

3dly. A Plantation seems a fit place for those Ingenious Spirits that being low in the World, are much clogg'd and oppress'd about a Livelyhood, for the means of subsisting being easie there, they may have time and opportunity to gratify their inclinations, and thereby improve Science and help Nurseries of people.

4thly. A fourth sort of men to whom a Plantation would be proper, takes in those that are younger Brothers of small Inheritances; yet because they would live in sight of their Kindred in some proportion to their Quality, and can't do it without a labour that looks like Farming, their condition is too strait for them; and if married, their Children are often too numerous for the Estate, and are frequently bred up to no Trades, but are a kind of Hangers on or Retainers to the elder Brothers Table and Charity: which is a mischief, as in it self to be lamented, so here to be remedied; For Land they have for next to nothing, which with moderate Labour produces plenty of all things necessary for Life, and such an increase as by Traffique may supply them with all conveniences.

Lastly, There are another sort of persons, not only fit for, but necessary in Plantations, and that is, Men of universal Spirits, that have an eye to the Good of Posterity, and that both understand and delight to promote good Discipline and just Government among a plain and well intending people; such persons may find Room in Colonies for their good Counsel and Contrivance, who are shut out from being of much use or service to great Nations under settl'd Customs: These men deserve much esteem, and would be harken'd to. Doubtless 'twas this (as I observ'd before) that put some of

Albert Cook Myers, ed., *Narratives of Early Pennsylvania, West Jersey, and Delaware* (New York: Charles Scribner's Sons, 1912), pp. 209–210.

the famous Greeks and Romans upon Transplanting and Reg- ulating Colonies of People in divers parts of the World; whose Names, for giving so great proof of their Wisdom, Virtue, Labour and Constancy, are with Justice honour-ably delivered down by story to the praise of our own times; though the World, after all its higher pretences of Religion, barbarously errs from their excellent Example.

1.5:   Coercion: The West African Slave (1729)

Thousands of the men and women who crossed the Atlantic during the colonial period came to America against their will. Some of these coerced immigrants were from the British Isles: youths kidnapped by unscrupulous ship captains; convicted felons "transported" as seven-year indentured servants; Irish rebels exiled for defying English rule in Ireland. The largest group of these unwilling newcomers by far, however, consisted of men and women plucked by slavers from their homes along the Atlantic coast of the African continent.

Many thousands of West Africans were brought as slaves to the Western Hemisphere in the sixteenth, seventeenth, and eighteenth centuries. Most were put to work on the sugar plantations of the Caribbean and South America. Relatively few came directly to the British mainland colonies. One who did was Venture Smith, a young man from Guinea who was seized by slavers in 1735 and brought to Connecticut to work as a house servant and farm hand.

Do you think Venture Smith's experiences, as described in the document below, were typical? What was the typical experience of the transplanted African in mainland British North America? Where did most go? What did most do? Do you know if the treatment of slaves on the mainland colonies was more humane than on the Caribbean sugar plantations?

An Eighteenth-Century African Describes His Enslavement[1]

VENTURE SMITH

Chapter I. Containing an Account of His Life, From His Birth to the Time of His Leaving His Native Country.

I was born at Dukandarra, in Guinea, about the year 1729. My father's name was Saungm Furro, Prince of the tribe of Dukandarra. My father had three

---

Venture Smith, *A Narrative of the Life and Adventures of Venture, A Native of Africa, But Resident Above Sixty Years in the United States of America* (Middletown, CT: J. S. Stewart, 1897), pp. 5–22.
[1] Footnotes renumbered.

wives. Polygamy was not uncommon in that country, especially among the rich, as every man was allowed to keep as many wives as he could maintain. By his first wife he had three children. The eldest of them was myself, named by my father, Broteer. The other two were named Cundazo and Soozaduka. My father had two children by his second wife, and one by his third. I descended from a very large, tall and stout race of beings, much larger than the generality of people in other parts of the globe, being commonly considerable above six feet in height, and every way well proportioned.

·   ·   ·   ·   ·   ·   ·   ·   ·   ·   ·   ·   ·

Before I dismiss [my] country, I must first inform my reader what I remember concerning this place. A large river runs through this country in a westerly course. The land for a great way on each side is flat and level, hedged in by a considerable rise in the country at a great distance from it. It scarce ever rains there, yet the land is fertile; great dews fall in the night which refresh the soil. About the latter end of June or first of July, the river begins to rise, and gradually increases until it has inundated the country for a great distance, to the height of seven or eight feet. This brings on a slime which enriches the land surprisingly. When the river has subsided, the natives begin to sow and plant, and the vegetation is exceeding rapid. Near this rich river my guardian's[2] land lay. He possessed, I cannot exactly tell how much, yet this I am certain of respecting it, that he owned an immense tract. He possessed likewise a great many cattle and goats. During my stay with him I was kindly used, and with as much tenderness, for what I saw, as his only son, although I was an entire stranger to him, remote from friends and relatives. The principal occupations of the inhabitants there were the cultivation of the soil and the care of their flocks. They were a people pretty similar in every respect to that of mine, except in their persons, which were not so tall and stout. They appeared to be very kind and friendly. I will now return to my departure from that place.

My father sent a man and horse after me. After settling with my guardian for keeping me, he took me away and went for home. It was then about one year since my mother brought me here. Nothing remarkable occurred to us on our journey until we arrived safe home. I found then that the difference between my parents had been made up previous to their sending for me. On my return, I was received both by my father and mother with great joy and affection, and was once more restored to my paternal dwelling in peace and happiness. I was then about six years old.

Not more than six weeks had passed after my return, before a message was brought by an inhabitant of the place where I lived the preceding year to my father, that that place had been invaded by a numerous army, from a nation not far distant, furnished with musical instruments, and all kinds of

[2] Why Venture had a guardian is not clear—ED.

arms then in use; that they were instigated by some white nation who equipped and sent them to subdue and possess the country; that his nation had made no preparation for war, having been for a long time in profound peace; that they could not defend themselves against such a formidable train of invaders, and must, therefore, necessarily evacuate their lands to the fierce enemy, and fly to the protection of some chief; and that if he would permit them they would come under his rule and protection when they had to retreat from their own possessions. He was a kind and merciful prince, and therefore consented to these proposals.

He had scarcely returned to his nation with the message before the whole of his people were obliged to retreat from their country and come to my father's dominions. He gave them every privilege and all the protection his government could afford. But they had not been there longer than four days before news came to them that the invaders had laid waste their country, and were coming speedily to destroy them in my father's territories. This affrighted them, and therefore they immediately pushed off to the south-ward, into the unknown countries there, and were never more heard of.

Two days after their retreat, the report turned out to be but too true. A detachment from the enemy came to my father and informed him that the whole army was encamped not far from his dominions, and would invade the territory and deprive his people of their liberties and rights, if he did not comply with the following terms. These were, to pay them a large sum of money, three hundred fat cattle, and a great number of goats, sheep, asses, etc.

My father told the messenger he would comply rather than that his subjects should be deprived of their rights and privileges, which he was not then in circumstances to defend from so sudden an invasion. Upon turning out those articles, the enemy pledged their faith and honor that they would not attack him. On these he relied, and therefore thought it unnecessary to be on his guard against the enemy. But their pledges of faith and honor proved no better than those of other unprincipled hostile nations, for a few days after, a certain relation of the king came and informed him that the enemy who sent terms of accommodation to him, and received tribute to their satisfaction, yet meditated an attack upon his subjects by surprise, and that probably they would commence their attack in less than one day, and concluded with advising him, as he was not prepared for war, to order a speedy retreat of his family and subjects. He complied with this advice.

The same night which was fixed upon to retreat, my father and his family set off about the break of day. The king and his two younger wives went in one company, and my mother and her children in another. We left our dwellings in succession, and my father's company went on first. We directed our course for a large shrub plain, some distance off, where we intended to conceal ourselves from the approaching enemy, until we could refresh ourselves a little. But we presently found that our retreat was not secure. For having struck up a little fire for the purpose of cooking victuals, the enemy, who happened to be encamped a little distance off, had sent out a scouting party who discovered us by the smoke of the fire, just as we were extinguishing it and about to eat. As soon as we had finished eating, my father discovered the party and immediately began to discharge arrows at them. This was what I first saw, and it alarmed both me and the women, who, being unable to make any resistance, immediately betook ourselves to the tall, thick reeds not far off, and left the old king to fight alone. For some time I beheld him from the reeds defending himself with great courage and firmness, till at last he was obliged to surrender himself into their hands.

They then came to us in the reeds, and the very first salute I had from them was a violent blow on the head with the fore part of a gun, and at the same time a grasp round the neck. I then had a rope put about my neck, as had all the women in the thicket with me, and were immediately led to my father, who was likewise pinioned and haltered for leading. In this condition we were all led to the camp. The women and myself, being submissive, had tolerable treatment from the enemy, while my father was closely interrogated respecting his money, which they knew he must have. But as he gave them no account of it, he was instantly cut and pounded on his body with great inhumanity, that he might be induced by the torture he suffered to make the discovery. All this availed not in the least to make him give up his money, but he despised all the tortures which they inflicted, until the continued exercise and increase of torment obliged him to sink and expire. He thus died without informing his enemies where his money lay. I saw him while he was thus tortured to death. The shocking scene is to this day fresh in my memory, and I have often been overcome while thinking on it. He was a man of remarkable stature. I should judge as much as six feet and six or seven inches high, two feet across the shoulders, and every way well proportioned. He was a man of remarkable strength and resolution, affable, kind and gentle, ruling with equity and moderation.

The army of the enemy was large, I should suppose consisting of about six thousand men. Their leader was called Baukurre. After destroying the old prince, they decamped and immediately marched towards the sea, lying to the west, taking with them myself and the women prisoners. In the march, a scouting party was detached from the main army. To the leader of this party I was made waiter, having to carry his gun, etc. As we were a-scouting, we came across a herd of fat cattle consisting of about thirty in number. These we set upon and immediately wrested from their keepers, and afterwards converted them into food for the army. The enemy had remarkable success in destroying the country wherever they went. For as far as they had penetrated they laid the habitations waste and captured the people. The distance they had now brought me was about four hundred miles. All the march I had very hard tasks imposed on me, which I must perform on pain of punishment. I was obliged to carry on my head a large flat stone used for grinding our corn, weighing, as I should suppose, as much as twenty-five pounds; besides victuals, mat and cooking utensils. Though I was pretty large and stout of my age, yet these burdens were very grievous to me, being only six years and a half old.

We were then come to a place called Malagasco. When we entered the place, we could not see the least appearance of either houses or inhabitants, but on stricter search found that instead of houses above ground they had dens in the sides of hillocks, contiguous to ponds and streams of water. In these we perceived they had all hid themselves, as I suppose they usually did on such occasions. In order to compel them to surrender, the enemy contrived to smoke them out with faggots. These they put to the entrance of the caves and set them on fire. While they were engaged in this business, to their great surprise some of them were desperately wounded with arrows which fell from above on them. This mystery they soon found out. They perceived that the enemy discharged these arrows through holes on the top of the dens directly into the air. Their weight brought them back, point downwards, on their enemies' heads, whilst they were smoking the inhabitants out. The points of their arrows were poisoned, but their enemy had an antidote for it which they instantly applied to the wounded part. The smoke at last obliged the people to give themselves up. They came out of their caves, first spatting the palms of their hands together, and immediately after extended their arms, crossed at their wrists, ready to be bound and pinioned. I should judge that the dens above mentioned were extended about eight feet horizontally into the earth, six feet in height, and as many wide. They were arched overhead and lined with earth, which was of the clay kind and made the surface of their walls firm and smooth.

The invaders then pinioned the prisoners of all ages and sexes indiscriminately, took their flocks and all their effects, and moved on their way towards the sea. On the march, the prisoners were treated with clemency, on account of their being submissive and humble. Having come to the next tribe, the enemy laid siege and immediately took men, women, children, flocks, and all their valuable effects. They then went on to the next district, which was contiguous to the sea, called in Africa, Anamaboo. The enemies' provisions were then almost spent, as well as their strength. The inhabitants, knowing what conduct they had pursued, and what were their present intentions, improved the favorable opportunity, attacked them, and took enemy, prisoners, flocks and all their effects. I was then taken a second time. All of us were then put into the castle and kept for market. On a certain time, I and other prisoners were put on board a canoe, under our master, and rowed away to a vessel belonging to Rhode Island, commanded by Captain Collingwood, and the mate, Thomas Mumford. While we were going to the vessel, our master told us to appear to the best possible advantage for sale. I was bought on board by one Robertson Mumford, steward of said vessel, for four gallons of rum and a piece of calico, and called VENTURE, on account of his having purchased me with his own private venture. Thus I came by my name. All the slaves that were bought for that vessel's cargo were two hundred and sixty.

Chapter II. Containing an Account of His Life from the Time of His Leaving Africa to That of His Becoming Free.

The first of the time of living at my master's own place, I was pretty much employed in the house, carding wool and other household business. In this situation I continued for some years, after which my master put me to work out of doors. After many proofs of my faithfulness and honesty, my master began to put great confidence in me. My behavior had as yet been submissive and obedient. I then began to have hard tasks imposed on me. Some of these were to pound four bushels of ears of corn every night in a barrel for the poultry, or be rigorously punished. At other seasons of the year, I had to card wool until a very late hour. These tasks I had to perform when only about nine years old. Some time after, I had another difficulty and oppression which was greater than any I had ever experienced since I came into this country. This was to serve two masters. James Mumford, my master's son, when his father had gone from home in the morning and given me a stint to perform that day, would order me to do *this* and *that* business different from what my master had directed me. One day in particular, the authority which my master's son had set up had like to have produced melancholy effects. For my master having set me off my business to perform that day and then left me to perform it, his son came up to me in the course of the day, big with authority, and commanded me very arrogantly to quit my present business and go directly about what he should order me. I replied to him that my master had given me so much to perform that day, and that I must faithfully complete it in that time. He then broke out into a great rage, snatched a pitchfork and went to lay me over the head therewith, but I as soon got another and defended myself with it, or otherwise he might have murdered me in his outrage. He immediately called some people who were within hearing at work for him, and ordered them to take his hair rope and come and bind me with it. They all tried to bind me, but in vain, though there were three assistants in number. My upstart master then desisted, put his pocket handkerchief before his eyes and went home with a design to tell his mother of the struggle with young VENTURE. He told that their young VENTURE had become so stubborn that he could not control him, and asked her what he should do with him. In the meantime I recovered my temper, voluntarily caused myself to be bound by the same men who tried in vain before, and carried before my young master, that he might do what he pleased with me. He took me to a gallows made for the purpose of hanging cattle on, and suspended me on it. Afterwards he ordered one of his hands to go to the peach orchard and cut him three dozen of whips to punish me with. These were brought to him, and that was all that was done with them, as I was released and went to work after hanging on the gallows about an hour.

.   .   .   .

Not a long time passed after that before Heddy[3] was sent by my master to New London [jail]. At the close of that year I was sold to a Thomas Stanton, and had to be separated from my wife and one daughter, who was about one month old. He resided at Stonington Point. To this place I brought with me from my late master's, two johannes, three old Spanish dollars, and two thousand of coppers, besides five pounds of my wife's money. This money I got by cleaning gentlemen's shoes and drawing-boots, by catching muskrats and minks, raising potatoes and carrots, etc., and by fishing in the night, and at odd spells.

.   .   .   .

Towards the close of the time that I resided with this master, I had a falling out with my mistress. This happened one time when my master was gone to Long Island a-gunning. At first the quarrel began between my wife and her mistress. I was then at work in the barn, and hearing a racket in the house, induced me to run there and see what had broken out. When I entered the house, I found my mistress in a violent passion with my wife, for what she informed me was a mere trifle—such a small affair that I forbear to put my mistress to the shame of having it known. I earnestly requested my wife to beg pardon of her mistress for the sake of peace, even if she had given no just occasion for offence. But whilst I was thus saying, my mistress turned the blows which she was repeating on my wife to me. She took down her horse whip, and while she was glutting her fury with it, I reached out my great black hand, raised it up and received the blows of the whip on it which were designed for my head. Then I immediately committed the whip to the devouring fire.

When my master returned from the island, his wife told him of the affair, but for the present he seemed to take no notice of it, and mentioned not a word of it to me. Some days after his return, in the morning as I was putting on a log in the fireplace, not suspecting harm from any one, I received a most violent stroke on the crown of my head with a club two feet long and as large around as a chair post. This blow very badly wounded my head, and the scar of it remains to this day. The first blow made me have my wits about me you may suppose, for as soon as he went to renew it I snatched the club out of his hands and dragged him out of the door. He then sent for his brother to come and assist him, but I presently left my master, took the club he wounded me with, carried it to a neighboring justice of the peace, and complained of my master. He finally advised me to return to my master and live contented with him till he abused me again, and then complain. I consented to do accordingly. But before I set out for my master's, up he came and his brother Robert after me. The Justice improved this convenient opportunity to caution my master. He asked him for what he treated his slave thus hastily and unjustly, and told him what would be the consequence

---

[3] Venture's wife, who he met when they were both owned by the Mumfords.

if he continued the same treatment towards me. After the justice had ended his discourse with my master, he and his brother set out with me for home, one before and the other behind me. When they had come to a by-place, they both dismounted their respective horses and fell to beating me with great violence. I became enraged at this and immediately turned them both under me, laid one of them across the other, and stamped them both with my feet what I would.

This occasioned my master's brother to advise him to put me off. A short time after this, I was taken by a constable and two men. They carried me to a blacksmith's shop and had me handcuffed. When I returned home my mistress enquired much of her waiters whether VENTURE was handcuffed. When she was informed that I was, she appeared to be very contented and was much transported with the news. In the midst of this content and joy, I presented myself before my mistress, showed her my handcuffs, and gave her thanks for my gold rings. For this my master commanded a negro of his to fetch him a large ox chain. This my master locked on my legs with two padlocks. I continued to wear the chain peaceably for two or three days, when my master asked me with contemptuous hard names whether I had not better be freed from my chains and go to work. I answered him, "No." "Well, then," said he, "I will send you to the West Indies, or banish you, for I am resolved not to keep you." I answered him, "I crossed the waters to come here and I am willing to cross them to return."

For a day or two after this not anyone said much to me, until one Hempstead Miner of Stonington asked me if I would live with him. I answered that I would. He then requested me to make myself discontented and to appear as unreconciled to my master as I could before that he bargained with him for me, and that in return he would give me a good chance to gain my freedom when I came to live with him. I did as he requested me. Not long after, Hempstead Miner purchased me of my master for fifty-six pounds lawful. He took the chain and padlocks from off me immediately after.

At Age 31, Venture Is Sold to Colonel Smith.

As I never had an opportunity of redeeming myself whilst I was owned my Miner, though he promised to give me a chance, I was then very ambitious of obtaining it. I asked my master one time if he would consent to have me purchase my freedom. He replied that he would.

. . . .

The next summer I again desired he would give me a chance of going to work. But he refused and answered that he must have my labor this summer, as he did not have it the past winter. I replied that I considered it as hard that I could not have a chance to work out when the season became advantageous, and that I must only be permitted to hire myself out in the poorest season of the year. He asked me after this what I would give him for the privilege per month. I replied that I would leave it wholly to his own generosity to determine what I should return him a month. Well then, said he, if so, two pounds a month. I answered him that if that was the least he would take I would be contented.

Accordingly I hired myself out at Fisher's Island, earning twenty pounds; thirteen pounds six shillings of which my master drew for the privilege and the remainder I paid for my freedom. This made fifty-one pounds two shillings which I paid him. In October following I went and wrought six months at Long Island. In that six month's time I cut and corded four hundred cords of wood, besides threshing out seventy-five bushels of grain, and received of my wages down only twenty pounds, which left remaining a larger sum. Whilst I was out that time, I took up on my wages only one pair of shoes. At night I lay on the hearth, with one coverlet over and another under me. I returned to my master and gave him what I received of my six months' labor. This left only thirteen pounds eighteen shillings to make up the full sum of my redemption. My master liberated me, saying that I might pay what was behind if I could ever make it convenient, otherwise it would be well. The amount of the money which I had paid my master towards redeeming my time, was seventy-one pounds two shillings. The reason of my master for asking such an unreasonable price, was, he said, to secure himself in case I should ever come to want. Being thirty-six years old, I left Colonel Smith once more for all. I had already been sold three different times, made considerable money with seemingly nothing to derive it from, had been cheated out of a large sum of money, lost much by misfortunes, and paid an enormous sum for my freedom.

2

America: Paradise or Hell?

After considering why people from the Old World came to America, we should also consider how well they fared once here. One can assume that enslaved Africans, ripped from their families, cultures, and familiar environment, were worse off in the American colonies than at home. But what about the others? Did settlers from Europe prosper once in America?

Obviously their experiences depended on their personal resources and, in the case of settlers in early colonies, on the skills and experience of their leaders and the colony promoters. The selections below describe the experiences of several groups and individuals as they encountered the new environment of North America.

It is always difficult to generalize from individual cases. Were these typical? Were they exceptional? There was, of course, no Gallup poll in seventeenth-century America, and so we cannot know whether the early settlers were glad or sorry that they had come to the New World. But is there any way we can estimate how most European settlers felt about their decision to cross the Atlantic? What facts can we use to make such an evaluation?

2.1: The "Starving Time" in Virginia (1609)

Jamestown, Virginia, the first permanent English colony in North America, was founded in May 1607, when three ships arrived from England and set ashore 105 European males on a spit of land near a malarial swamp. The settlement did not thrive, and, especially during the "Starving Time," as the winter of 1609 was known, the settlers suf-

fered terribly from hunger and disease. The selection below (which was actually written in 1624) vividly describes these early afflictions.

Does the document offer clues to why the early Virginia settlers experienced such hardships? Consider the fact that this was one of the first English attempts to establish a permanent colony in America. Also note the reliance on the Native Americans for help. What does this dependence suggest about the competence of this group of Europeans? Did this dependence persist? Or was it a temporary phase in the settlement process?

The Generall Historie of Virginia: The Fourth Booke[1]

JOHN SMITH

To make plaine the True Proceedings of the Historie for 1609.

We must follow the examinations of Doctor Simons, and two learned Orations published by the Companie; with the relation of the Right Honourable the Lord De la Ware.

What happened in the first government after the alteration, in the time of Captaine George Piercie their Governor.

The day before Captaine Smith returned[2] for England with the ships, Captaine Davis arrived in a small Pinace, with some sixteene proper men more: To these were added a company from James towne, under the command of Captaine John Sickelmore alias Ratliffe, to inhabit Point Comfort. Captaine Martin and Captaine West, having lost their boats and neere halfe their men among the Salvages, were returned to James towne; for the Salvages no sooner understood Smith was gone, but they all revolted, and did spoile and murther all they incountered.

Now wee were all constrained to live onely on what Smith had onely for his owne Companie,[3] for the rest had consumed their proportions. And now they had twentie Presidents with all their appurtenances: Master Piercie, our new President, was so sicke hee could neither goe nor stand. But ere all was consumed, Captaine West and Captaine Sickelmore, each with a small ship and thirtie or fortie men well appointed, sought abroad to trade. Sickelmore upon the confidence of Powhatan,[4] with about thirtie others as carelesse as himselfe, were all slaine; onely Jeffrey Shortridge escaped; and Pokahontas the Kings daughter saved a boy called Henry Spilman, that lived many yeeres after, by her meanes, amongst the Patawomekes. Powhatan still, as he found

John Smith, "The Generall Historie of Virginia," Lyon Gardner Tyler, ed., *Narratives of Early Virginia, 1606–1625* (New York: Charles Scribner's Sons, 1930), pp. 294–96.
[1] Footnotes renumbered.
[2] About October 4, 1609.
[3] I.e., the portion of the settlers retained at Jamestown.
[4] Chief of the Powhatan Confederacy—ED.

meanes, cut off their Boats, denied them trade: so that Captaine West set saile for England. Now we all found the losse of Captaine Smith, yea his greatest maligners could now curse his losse: as for corne provision and contribution from the Salvages, we had nothing but mortall wounds, with clubs and arrowes; as for our Hogs, Hens, Goats, Sheepe, Horse, or what lived, our commanders, officers and Salvages daily consumed them, some small proportions sometimes we tasted, till all was devoured; then swords, armes, pieces, or any thing, wee traded with the Salvages, whose cruell fingers were so oft imbrewed in our blouds, that what by their crueltie, our Governours indiscretion, and the losse of our ships, of five hundred within six moneths after Captaine Smiths departure, there remained not past sixtie men, women and children, most miserable and poore creatures; and those were preserved for the most part, by roots, herbes, acornes, walnuts, berries, now and then a little fish: they that had startch in these extremities, made no small use of it; yea, even the very skinnes of our horses. Nay, so great was our famine, that a Salvage we slew and buried, the poorer sort tooke him up againe and eat him; and so did divers one another boyled and stewed with roots and herbs: And one amongst the rest did kill his wife, powdered[5] her, and had eaten part of her before it was knowne; for which hee was executed, as hee well deserved: now whether shee was better roasted, boyled or carbonado'd, I know not; but of such a dish as powdered wife I never heard of. This was that time, which still to this day[6] we called the starving time; it were too vile to say, and scarce to be beleeved, what we endured: but the occasion was our owne, for want of providence industrie and government, and not the barrennesse and defect of the Countrie, as is generally supposed; for till then in three yeeres, for the numbers were landed us, we had never from England provision sufficient for six moneths, though it seemed by the bils of loading sufficient was sent us, such a glutton is the Sea, and such good fellowes the Mariners; we as little tasted of the great proportion sent us, as they of our want and miseries, yet notwithstanding they ever overswayed and ruled the businesse, though we endured all that is said, and chiefly lived on what this good Countrie naturally afforded. Yet had wee beene even in Paradice it selfe with these Governours, it would not have beene much better withe us; yet there was amongst us, who had they had the government as Captaine Smith appointed, but that they could not maintaine it, would surely have kept us from those extremities of miseries. This in ten daies more, would have supplanted us all with death.

But God that would not this Countrie should be unplanted, sent Sir Thomas Gates, and Sir George Sommers with one hundred and fiftie people most happily preserved by the Bermudas to preserve us: strange it is to say how miraculously they were preserved in a leaking ship, as at large you may reade in the insuing Historie of those Ilands.

[5]Salted.
[6]1924.

2.2:   The Plaint of an English Bondsman (1623)

The settlement at Jamestown managed to survive, and the Virginia colony as a whole eventually even prospered, especially after the introduction of tobacco culture in 1612. But that did not mean that every settler throve even then. The following selection is a pitiful cry from Richard Ffrethorne, a young man who was brought to Virginia to work as an indentured servant for the planters, probably for the typical period of four years.

As an indentured servant, Ffrethorne had volunteered to come to America. What seems to have gone wrong with his plans? Was his fate the result of bad luck or personal fecklessness? Or did the still primitive, infant society make demands that Europeans found difficult? Do you think his fate was typical of indentured servants in colonial America?

(We do not know if Richard Ffrethorne's plea for rescue was heard by his parents in England, to whom he addressed this letter.)

A Virginia Settler Regrets Coming

RICHARD FFRETHORNE

I have nothing to Comfort me, nor ther is nothing to be gotten here but sicknes, and death, except that one had money to lay out in some thinges for profit; But I have nothing at all, no not a shirt to my backe, but two Ragges nor no Clothes, but one poore suite, nor but one paire of shooes, but one paire of stockins, but one Capp, but two bands, my Cloke is stollen by one of my owne fellowes, and to his dying hower would not tell mee what he did with it but some of my fellows saw him have butter and beife out of a ship, which my Cloke I doubt [not] paid for, so that I have not a penny, nor a penny Worth to helpe me to either spice, or sugar, or strong Waters, without the which one cannot lyve here, for as strong beare in England doth fatten and strengthen them so water here doth wash and weaken theis here, onelie keepe life and soule togeather. but I am not halfe a quarter so strong as I was in England, and all is for want of victualls, for I doe protest unto you, that I have eaten more in a day at home then I have allowed me here for a Weeke. you have given more then my dayes allowance to a beggar at the doore; and if Mr Jackson had not releived me, I should bee in a poore Case, but he like a ffather and shee like a loveing mother doth still helpe me, for when wee goe up to James Towne that is 10 myles of us, there lie all the ships that Come to the land, and there they must deliver their goods, and when wee went up to Towne as it may bee on Moonedaye, at noone, and come there by night, then load the next day by noone, and goe home in the afternoone, and unload, and then away againe in the night, and bee up

Susan Myra Kingsbury, ed., *The Records of the Virginia Company of London* (1906) (Washington, D.C.: U.S. Government Printing Office, 1938), vol. 5, pp. 59, 62.

about midnight, then if it rayned, or blowed never so hard wee must lye in the boate on the water, and have nothing but alitle bread, for when wee go into the boate wee have a loafe allowed to two men, and it is all if we staid there 2 dayes, which is hard, and must lye all that while in the boate, but that Goodman Jackson pityed me & made me a Cabbin to lye in alwayes when I come up, and he would give me some poore Jacks home with me which Comforted mee more then pease, or water gruell. Oh they bee verie godlie folkes, and love me verie well, and will doe anie thing for me, and he much marvailed that you would send me a servaunt to the Companie, he saith I had beene better knockd on the head, and Indeede so I fynd it now to my greate greife and miserie, and saith, that if you love me you will redeeme me suddenlie, for wch I doe Intreate and begg. . . .

O that you did see may daylie and hourelie sighes, grones, and teares, and thumpes that I afford mine owne brest, and rue and Curse the time of my birth with holy Job. I thought no head had beene able to hold so much water as hath and doth dailie flow from mine eyes, But this is Certaine I never felt the want of ffather and mother till now, but now deare ffrends full well I knowe and rue it although it were too late before I knew it.

2.3: A Former Indentured Servant Praises the System (1666)

Clearly not every indentured servant in America found his experience intolerable. George Alsop, who came to Maryland in the 1660s, was one bondsman who considered his years in the colony a rewarding experience, as he states in the following selection. Does Alsop's description seem believable? We today would surely find the restrictions imposed on bond servants galling. But this was an era when many poor men and women were forced to defer to their "betters" and when economic freedom was hedged with harsh restrictions. Note as well that the work from which this excerpt is drawn was addressed to Lord Baltimore, the "Absolute Lord and Proprietary of the Provinces of Mary-Land and Avelon in America." Does this tell us anything about the motives behind Alsop's observations?

A Settler in Maryland Endorses His Experience[1]

GEORGE ALSOP

They whose abilities cannot extend to purchase their own transportation [from England] over into Mary-Land, (and surely he that cannot command

Clayton Colman Hall, ed., *Narratives of Early Maryland, 1633–1684* (New York: Charles Scribner's Sons, 1910), pp. 356–59.
[1] Footnotes renumbered.

so small a sum for so great a matter, his life must needs be mighty low and dejected) I say they may for the debarment of a four years sordid liberty, go over into this Province and there live plentiously well. And what's a four years Servitude to advantage a man all the remainder of his dayes, making his predecessors happy in his sufficient abilities, which he attained to partly by the restrainment of so small a time?

Now those that commit themselves unto the care of the Merchant to carry them over, they need not trouble themselves with any inquisitive search touching their Voyage; for there is such an honest care and provision made for them all the time they remain aboard the Ship, and are sailing over, that they want for nothing that is necessary and convenient.

The Merchant commonly before they go aboard the Ship, or set themselves in any forwardness for their Voyage, has Conditions of Agreements drawn between him and those that by a voluntary consent become his Servants, to serve him, his Heirs or Assigns, according as they in their primitive acquaintance have made their bargain, some two, some three, some four years; and whatever the Master or Servant tyes himself up to here in England by Condition, the Laws of the Province will force a performance of when they come there: Yet here is this Priviledge in it when they arrive, If they dwell not with the Merchant they made their first agreement withall, they may choose whom they will serve their prefixed time with; and after their curiosity has pitcht on one whom they think fit for their turn, and that they may live well withall, the Merchant makes an Assignment of the Indenture over to him whom they of their free will have chosen to be their Master, in the same nature as we here in England (and no otherwise) turn over Covenant Servants or Apprentices from one Master to another. Then let those whose chaps are always breathing forth those filthy dregs of abusive exclamations, which are Lymbeckt from their sottish and preposterous brains, against this Country of Mary-Land, saying, That those which are transported over thither, are sold in open Market for Slaves, and draw in Carts like Horses; which is so damnable an untruth, that if they should search to the very Center of Hell, and enquire for a Lye of the most antient and damned stamp, I confidently believe they could not find one to parallel this: For know, That the Servants here in Mary-Land of all Colonies, distant or remote Plantations, have the least cause to complain, either for strictness of Servitude, want of Provisions, or need of Apparel: Five dayes and a half in the Summer weeks is the alotted time that they work in; and for two months, when the Sun predominates in the highest pitch of his heat, they claim an antient and customary Priviledge, to repose themselves three hours in the day within the house, and this is undeniably granted to them that work in the Fields.

In the Winter time, which lasteth three months (*viz.*) December, January, and February, they do little or no work or imployment, save cutting of wood to make good fires to sit by, unless their Ingenuity will prompt them to hunt the Deer, or Bear, or recreate themselves in Fowling, to slaughter the Swans, Geese, and Turkeys (which this Country affords in a most plentiful manner:) For every Servant has a Gun, Powder and Shot allowed him, to sport him withall on all Holidayes and leasurable times, if he be capable of using it, or be willing to learn.

Now those Servants which come over into this Province, being Artificers, they never (during their Servitude) work in the Fields, or do any other imployment save that which their Handicraft and Mechanick endeavours are capable of putting them upon, and are esteem'd as well by their Masters, as those that imploy them, above measure. He that's a Tradesman here in Mary-Land (though a Servant), lives as well as most common Handicrafts do in London, though they may want something of that Liberty which Freemen have, to go and come at their pleasure; yet if it were rightly understood and considered, what most of the Liberties of the several poor Tradesmen are taken up about, and what a care and trouble attends that thing they call Liberty, which according to the common translation is but Idleness, and (if weighed in the Ballance of a just Reason) will be found to be much heavier and cloggy then the four years restrainment of a Mary-Land Servitude. He that lives in the nature of a Servant in this Province, must serve but four years by the Custom of the Country; and when the expiration of his time speaks him a Freeman, there's a Law in the Province, that enjoyns his Master whom he hath served to give him Fifty Acres of Land, Corn to serve him a whole year, three Sutes of Apparel, with things necessary to them, and Tools to work withall; so that they are no sooner free, but they are ready to set up for themselves, and when once entred, they live passingly well.

The Women that go over into this Province as Servants, have the best luck here as in any place of the world besides; for they are no sooner on shoar, but they are courted into a Copulative Matrimony, which some of them (for aught I know) had they not come to such a Market with their Virginity, might have kept it by them untill it had been mouldy, unless they had let it out by a yearly rent to some of the Inhabitants of Lewknors-lane,[2] or made a Deed of Gift of it to Mother Coney, having only a poor stipend out of it, untill the Gallows or Hospital called them away. Men have not altogether so good luck as Women in this kind, or natural preferment, without they be good Rhetoricians, and well vers'd in the Art of perswasion, then (probably) they may ryvet themselves in the time of their Servitude into the private and reserved favour of their Mistress, if Age speak their Master deficient.

In short, touching the Servants of this Province, they live well in the time of their Service, and by their restrainment in that time, they are made capable of living much better when they come to be free; which in several other parts of the world I have observed, That after some servants have brought their indented and limited time to a just and legal period by Servitude, they

---

[2]A disreputable neighborhood in London.

have been much more incapable of supporting themselves from sinking into the Gulf of a slavish, poor, fettered, and intangled life, then all the fastness of their prefixed time did involve them in before.

2.4:   A Well-Blessed Land (1725)

For some Europeans, clearly the move to colonial America was a success. The document below, a letter by an Irish Quaker immigrant to Pennsylvania friends and relatives back home, reflects a happy experience. Why was Robert Parke so pleased with Pennsylvania? Note the date. How long had the colony been settled by the time the letter was written? Might the time factor help explain the positive response? Parke was a free man rather than an indentured servant. Might his status, as compared to Richard Ffrethorne's, have affected how he fared?

Pennsylvania Is a Good Country

ROBERT PARKE

Chester Township the—of the 10th Mo. 1725.

Dear Sister Mary Valentine:

This goes with a Salutation of Love to thee, Brother Thomas and the children & in a word to all friends, Relations & well Wishers in Generall as if named, hoping it may find you all in good health, as I with all our family in Generall are in at this present writing & has been since our arival, for we have not had a day's Sickness in the Family Since we came into the Country, blessed be God for it. My father in Particular has not had his health better these ten years than Since he Came here, his ancient age considered. Our Irish Acquaintance in general are well Except Thoe: Lightfoot who Departed this Life at Darby in a Good old age About 4 weeks Since. Thee writes in thy Letter that there was a talk went back to Ireland that we were not Satisfyed in coming here, which was Utterly false: now let this Suffice to Convince you. In the first place he that carried back this Story was an Idle fellow, & one of our Ship-Mates, but not thinking this country Suitable to his Idleness, went back. . . . He is Sort of a Lawyer, or Rather a Lyar as I may term him, therefore I wod not have you give credit to Such false reports for the future, for there is not one of the family but what likes the country very well & wod If we were in Ireland again come here Directly it being the best country for working folk & tradesmen of any in the world. But for Drunkards and Idlers, they cannot live well any where. It is likewise an Extradin. healthy country. . . . Land is of all Prices Even from ten Pounds, to one hundred Pounds a hundred, according to the goodness or else the situation thereof, & Grows dearer every year

Charles A. Hanna, *The Scotch-Irish in North Britain, North Ireland, and North America* (New York: G. P. Putnam's Sons, 1902), pp. 64–67.

by Reason of Vast Quantities of People that come here yearly from Several Parts of the world, therefore thee & thy family or any that I wish well I wod desire to make what Speed you can to come here the Sooner the better. We have traveled over a Pretty deal of this country to seek the Land, & [though] we met with many fine Tracts of Land here & there in the country, yet my father being curious & somewhat hard to Please Did not buy any Land until the Second day of 10th mo: Last and then he bought a Tract of Land consisting of five hundred Acres for which he gave 350 pounds. It is Excellent good land but none cleared, Except about 20 Acres, with a small log house and Orchard Planted, we are going to clear some of it Directly, for our next Sumer's fallow. We might have bought Land much Cheaper but not so much to our Satisfaction. We stayed in Chester 3 months & then we Rented a Place 1 mile from Chester, with a good brick house & 200 Acres of Land for [—] pound a year, where we continue till next May. We have sowed about 200 Acres of wheat & 7 acres of rye this season. We sowed but a bushel on an acre, 3 pecks is Enough on new ground. I am grown an Experienced Plowman & my brother Abell is Learning. Jonathan & thy Son John drives for us. He is grown a Lusty fellow Since thou Saw him. We have the finest plows here that Can be. We plowed up our Sumer's fallows in May & June, with a Yoak of Oxen & 2 horses & they goe with as much Ease as Double the number in Ireland. We sow our wheat with 2 horses. A boy of 12 or 14 years old Can hold Plow here, a man Comonly holds & Drives himself. They plow an Acre, nay some Plows 2 Acres a day. They sow Wheat & Rye in August or September. We have had a crop of oats, barley & very good flax & hemp, Indian Corn & buckwheat all of our own Sowing & Planting this last summer. We also planted a bushel of white Potatoes Which Cost us 5 Shills. & we had 10 or 12 bushels Increase. This country yields Extraordinary Increase of all sorts of Grain Likewise—for nicholas hooper had of 3 Acres of Land & at most 3 bushels of Seed above 80 bushels Increase so that it is as Plentiful a Country as any Can be if people will be Industrious. . . . All Sorts of Provisions are Extraordinary Plenty in Philadelphia market, where Country people bring in their comodities. Their markets are on 4th day and 7th day. This country abounds in fruit, Scarce an house but has an Apple, Peach & cherry orchard. As for chestnuts, Wallnuts, & hasel nuts, Strawberrys, Billberrys & Mulberrys they grow wild in the woods and fields in Vast Quantities. They also make great Preparations against harvest; both Roast & boyled, Cakes & Tarts & Rum, stand at the Lands End, so that they may Eat and Drink at Pleasure. A Reaper has 2 Shills. & 3 pence a day, a mower has 2 Shills. & 6 pence & a pint of Rum beside meat & drink of the best; for no workman works without their Victuals in the bargain throughout the Country. A Laboring man has 18 or 20 pence a day in Winter. The Winters are not so cold as we Expected nor the Sumers so Extreme hot as formerly, for both Sumer and Winter are moderater than they ever were known. In Sumer time they wear nothing but a Shirt & Linnen drawers Trousers, which are breeches and stockings all in one made of Linnen; they are fine Cool wear in Sumer. As to what thee writt about the Governours Opening Letters it is Utterly false & nothing but a Lye & any one Except bound Servants may go out of the Country when they will & Servants when they Serve their time may Come away If they please but it is rare any are such fools to leave the Country Except men's business require it. They pay 9 Pounds for their Passage (of this money) to go to Ireland. There is 2 fairs, yearly & 2 markets weekly in Philadelphia also 2 fairs yearly in Chester & Likewise in new castle, but they Sell no Cattle nor horses, no living Creatures, but altogether Merchant's Goods, as hatts, Linnen & woolen Cloth, handkerchiefs, knives, Scizars, tapes & treds buckels, Ribonds & all Sorts of necessarys fit for our wooden Country & here all young men and women that wants wives or husbands may be Supplyed. Lett this Suffice for our fairs. As to meetings they are so plenty one may ride to their choice. I desire thee to bring or Send me a bottle of good Oyle fit for guns, thee may buy it in Dublin. . . . Dear Sister I wod not have thee Doupt the truth of what I write, for I know it to be true Tho I have not been long here. I wod have you Cloath yourselves well with Woolen & Linnen, Shoes & Stockings & hats for Such things are dear hear, & yet a man will Sooner Earn a suit of Cloths here than in Ireland, by Reason workman's Labour is so Dear. . . . I wod have you bring for your own Use 2 or 3 good falling Axes, a pair of beetle rings & 3 Iron wedges, for they are of good Service here. Your Plow Irons will not answer here, therefore you had better bring 1 or 2 hundred Iron. You may bring your Plow Chains as they are also a good—Iron. . . . Dear Sister I desire thee may tell my old friend Samuel Thornton that he could give so much credit to my words & find no Iffs nor ands in my Letter, that in Plain terms he could not do better than to Come here, for both his & his wife's trade are Very good here. The best way for him to do is to pay what money he Can Conveniently Spare at that side & Engage himself to Pay the rest at this Side & when he Comes here if he Can get no friend to lay down the money for him, when it Comes to the worst, he may hire out 2 or 3 children. & I wod have him Cloath his family as well as his Small Ability will allow. Thee may tell him what things are proper to bring with him both for his Sea Store & for his Use in this Country. I wod have him Procure 3 or 4 Lusty Servants & Agree to pay their passage at this Side he might sell 2 & pay the others' passage with the money. I fear my good will to him will be of Little Effect by reason he is So hard of beleif, but thou mayest Assure him from me that if I had not a particular Respect for him & his family I Should not have writ so much for his Encouragement.

2.5:   A Dutch Visitor to the Chesapeake (1679)

Jaspar Danckaerts was a native of Zeeland in Holland who came to America in 1679 as an agent of the Labadists, a small Protestant sect established by French mystic Jean de Labadie. Danckaerts and his companion, Peter Sluyter, were seeking a site for a Labadist colony, where this pious group could worship without official interference. The two agents traveled through the former Dutch colony of New Netherland, visited New England, and then scouted the Chesapeake region. The following document is an excerpt from Danckaerts's journal describing life on the Chesapeake in Maryland toward the end of the seventeenth century.

Danckaerts is critical of the Maryland planters' habits and is not impressed by the way they conducted their affairs. It is of course possible that objective observers would agree with his estimates of seventeenth-century Maryland society, but it is also possible that his views were governed by prejudice? Why might a man of his background have found the customs of the Chesapeake planters less than admirable? Can his judgment be accepted without question?

A Traveler Disapproves of the Chesapeake Planters[1]

JASPAR DANCKAERTS

All of Maryland that we have seen, is high land, with few or no meadows, but possessing such a rich and fertile soil, as persons living there assured me that they had raised tobacco off the same piece of land for thirty consecutive years. The inhabitants, who are generally English, are mostly engaged in this production. It is their chief staple, and the money with which they must purchase every thing they require, which is brought to them from other English possessions in Europe, Africa and America. There is, nevertheless, sometimes a great want of these necessaries, owing to the tobacco market being low, or the shipments being prevented by some change of affairs in some quarter, particularly in Europe, or indeed to both causes, as was the case at this time, whereby there sometimes arises a great scarcity of such articles as are most necessary, as we saw when there. So large a quantity of tobacco is raised in Maryland and Virginia, that it is one of the greatest sources of revenue to the crown by reason of the taxes which it yields. Servants and negroes are chiefly employed in the culture of tobacco, who are brought from other places to be sold to the highest bidders, the servants for a term of years only, but the negroes forever, and may be sold by their masters to other planters as many times as their masters choose, that is, the servants until their term is fulfilled, and the negroes for life. These men, one with another, each make, after they are able to work, from 2,500 pounds to 3,000 pounds and even 3,500 pounds of tobacco a year, and some of the masters

Jaspar Danckaerts, ed., *Journal of Jaspar Danckaerts, 1679–1680*, B. B. James and J. F. Jameson (New York: Charles Scribner's Sons, 1913), pp. 133–37.
[1] Footnotes renumbered.

and their wives who pass their lives here in wretchedness, do the same. The servants and negroes after they have worn themselves down the whole day, and come home to rest, have yet to grind and pound the grain, which is generally maize, for their masters and all their families as well as themselves, and all the negroes, to eat. Tobacco is the only production in which the planters employ themselves, as if there were nothing else in the world to plant but that, and while the land is capable of yielding all the productions that can be raised anywhere, so far as the climate of the place allows. As to articles of food, the only bread they have is that made of Turkish wheat or maize, and that is miserable. They plant this grain for that purpose everywhere. It yields well, not a hundred, but five or six hundred for one; but it takes up much space, as it is planted far apart like vines in France. This grain, when it is to be used for men or for similar purposes, has to be first soaked, before it is ground or pounded, because the grains being large and very hard, cannot be broken under the small stones of their light hand-mills; and then it is left so coarse it must sifted. They take the finest for bread, and the other for different kinds of groats, which, when it is cooked, is called *sapaen* or *homina*. The meal intended for bread is kneaded moist without leaven or yeast, salt or grease, and generally comes out of the oven so that it will hardly hold together, and so blue and moist that it is as heavy as dough; yet the best of it when cut and roasted, tastes almost like warm white bread, at least it then seemed to us so. This corn is also the only provender for all their animals, be it horses, oxen, cows, hogs, or fowls, which generally run in the woods to get their food, but are fed a little of this, mornings and evenings during the winter when there is little to be had in the woods; though they are not fed too much, for the wretchedness, if not cruelty, of such living, affects both man and beast. This is said not without reason, for a master having a sick servant, and there are many so, and observing from his declining condition, he would finally die, and that there was no probability of his enjoying any more service from him, made him, sick and languishing as he was, dig his own grave, in which he was to be laid a few days afterwards, in order not to busy any of the others with it, they having their hands full in attending to the tobacco.[2]

A few vegetables are planted, but they are of the coarsest kinds and are cultivated in the coarsest manner, without knowledge or care, and they are, therefore, not properly raised, and do not amount to much as regards the production, and still less as to their use. Some have begun to plant orchards, which all bear very well, but are not properly cultivated. The fruit is for the greater part pressed, and makes good cider, of which the largest portion becomes soured and spoiled through their ignorance or negligence, either

---

[2] Despite these criticisms as to slavery, it appears, if we can accept the hostile testimony of Dittelbach, *Verval en Val der Labadisten* (Amsterdam, 1692), that [Peter] Sluyter, when in control of the Labadist plantation at Bohemia Manor, employed slave labor without hesitation and with some harshness.

from not putting it into good casks, or from not taking proper care of the liquor afterwards. Sheep they have none, although they have what is requisite for them if they chose. It is a matter of conjecture whether you will find any milk or butter even in summer; we have not found any there at this season of the year. They bestow all their time and care in producing tobacco; each cask or hogshead, as they call it, of which pays two English shillings on exportation, and on its arrival in England, two pence a pound, besides the fees for weighing and other expenses here, and freight and other charges beyond sea. When, therefore, tobacco only brings four or five pence, there is little or nothing left for the owner.

The lives of the planters in Maryland and Virginia are very godless and profane. They listen neither to God nor his commandments, and have neither church nor cloister. Sometimes there is some one who is called a minister, who does not as elsewhere, serve in one place, for in all Virginia and Maryland there is not a city or a village[3]—but travels for profit, and for that purpose visits the plantations through the country, and there addresses the people; but I know of no public assemblages being held in these places; you hear often that these ministers are worse than anybody else, yea, are an abomination.

When the ships arrive with goods, and especially with liquors, such as wine and brandy, they attract everybody, that is, masters, to them, who then indulge so abominably together, that they keep nothing for the rest of the year, yea, do not go away as long as there is any left, or bring anything home with them which might be useful to them in their subsequent necessities. It must therefore go hard with the household, and it is a wonder if there be a single drop left for the future. They squander so much in this way, that they keep no tobacco to buy a shoe or a stocking for their children, which sometimes causes great misery. While they take so little care for provisions, and are otherwise reckless, the Lord sometimes punishes them with insects, flies, and worms, or with intemperate seasons, causing great famine, as happened a few years ago in the time of the last Dutch war with the English,[4] when the Lord sent so many weevils that all their grain was eaten up as well as almost all the other productions of the field, by reason of which such a great famine was caused that many persons died of starvation, and a mother killed her own child and ate it, and then went to her neighbors, calling upon them to come and see what she had done, and showing them the remains of her child, whereupon she was arrested and condemned to be hung. When she sat or stood on the scaffold, she cried out to the people, in the presence of the governor, that she was now going to God, where she would render an

[3] No cities, of course, but some villages.
[4] The war of 1672–1674. But the attack on the Hoere-kill (Whorekill, now Lewes, Delaware) was not an act of war against the Dutch, but an attack by Marylanders on inhabitants who were under the jurisdiction of the Duke of York, in a territory disputed between him and Lord Baltimore.

account, and would declare before him that what she had done she did in the mere delirium of hunger, for which the governor alone should bear the guilt; inasmuch as this famine was caused by the weevils, a visitation from God, because he, the governor, undertook in the preceding summer an expedition against the Dutch residing on the South River, who maintained themselves in such a good posture of defense, that he could accomplish but little; when he went to the Hoere-kill on the west side of that river, not far from the sea, where also he was not able to do much; but as the people subsisted there only by cultivating wheat, and had at this time a fine and abundant harvest in the fields—and from such harvests the people of Maryland generally, and under such circumstances as these particularly, were fed—he set fire to it, and all their other fruits, whether of the trees or the field; whereby he committed two great sins at the same time, namely, against God and his goodness, and against his neighbors, the Dutch, who lost it, and the English who needed it; and had caused more misery to the English in his own country, than to the Dutch in the enemy's country. This wretched woman protesting these words substantially against the governor, before Heaven and in the hearing of every one, was then swung up.

In addition to what the tobacco itself pays on exportation, which produces a very large sum, every hundred acres of land, whether cultivated or not, has to pay one hundred pounds of tobacco a year, and every person between sixteen and sixty years of age must pay three shillings a year. All animals are free of taxation, and so are all productions except tobacco.

It remains to be mentioned that those persons who profess the Roman Catholic religion have great, indeed, all freedom in Maryland, because the governor makes profession of that faith, and consequently there are priests and other ecclesiastics who travel and disperse themselves everywhere, and neglect nothing which serves for their profit and purpose. The priests of Canada take care of this region, and hold correspondence with those here, as is supposed, as well as with those who reside among the Indians. It is said there is not an Indian fort between Canada and Maryland, where there is not a Jesuit who teaches and advises the Indians, who begin to listen to them too much; so much so, that some people in Virginia and Maryland as well as in New Netherland, have been apprehensive lest there might be an outbreak, hearing what has happened in Europe,[5] as well as among their neighbors at Boston; but they hope the result of the troubles there will determine many things elsewhere. The Lord grant a happy issue there and here, as well as in other parts of the world, for the help of His own elect, and the glory of His name.

---

[5] The reference is to the Popish Plot in England; in respect to Boston, it is probably to King Philip's War, 1675–1676, and the hostilities along the Maine coast in 1677, though there is no reason to attribute these to French or Jesuit instigation. Yet possibly the great fire of August 8–9, 1679, is meant.

2.6:   Slaves' Reactions to America (1712)

Surviving statements by colonial slaves about their lives are exceedingly rare. After all, few could write, and their oppressors had little incentive to preserve their opinions or any protest they might make. But during the colonial period, as later, slaves at times expressed their feelings about their circumstances in a way that could not be hidden or ignored—by organized revolt.

There were a number of slave revolts during the colonial era. The most serious was the Stono rebellion in South Carolina in 1739, when thirty whites and forty-four blacks lost their lives. Earlier, in 1712, an armed uprising of slaves in New York City had been put down by the militia, and twenty-one of the rebels hanged.

The following selection is from a letter by a New York Governor Robert Hunter to the Lords of Trade, who exercised oversight of the American colonies, about the bloody 1712 New York uprising. Hunter touches only lightly on the motives for the revolt, but what can you conclude about the way New York's slaves were probably treated, given the savagery of the punishment? What does the document say about the humanity of the city's white authorities? In light of the 1712 outcome, do you think that armed revolt could have been a common recourse of colonial slaves?

The New York City Slave Revolt, 1712

ROBERT HUNTER

I must now give your Lordships an account of a bloody conspiracy of some of the slaves of this place, to destroy as many of the Inhabitants as they could. It was put in execution in this manner: when they had resolved to revenge themselves for some hard usage they apprehended to have received from their masters (for I can find no other cause), they agreed to meet in the orchard of Mr. Crook the middle of the Town—some provided with fire arms, some with swords and others with knives and hatchets. This was the sixth day of April; the time of meeting was about twelve or one o'clock in the night, when about three and twenty of them were got togeather. One Coffee an negroe slave to one Vantiburgh set fire to an out house of his Master's, and then repairing to the place where the rest were they all sallyed out togeather with their arms and marched to the fire. By this time, the noise of fire spreading through the town, the people began to flock to it; upon the approach of severall the slaves fired and killed them. The noise of the guns gave the allarm, and some, escaping their shot, soon published the cause of

E. B. O'Callaghan, ed., *Documents Relative to the Colonial History of the State of New York* (Albany: Weed, Parsons & Co., 1849), vol. 5, pp. 341–42.

the fire, which was the reason that not above nine Christians [whites] were killed, and about five or six wounded. Upon the first notice, which was very soon after the mischeif was begun, I order'd a detachment from the fort under a proper officer to march against them, but the slaves made their retreat into the woods by the favour of the night. Having ordered centries the next day in the most proper places on the Island to prevt their escape, I caused, the day following, the Militia of this town and of the county of west Chester to drive the Island; and by this means and strick searches in the town, we found all that put the design in execution. Six of these having first laid violent hands upon themselves, the rest were forthwith brought to their tryal before ye Justices of this place who are authorized by Act of Assembly to hold a Court in such cases. In that Court were twenty seven condemned, whereof twenty one were executed; one being a woman with child, her execution [was] by that means suspended. Some were burnt, others hanged, one broke on the wheele, and one hung a live in chains in the town, so that there has been the most exemplary punishment inflicted that could be possibly thought of, and which only this act of assembly could Justify. Among these guilty persons several others were apprehended and again acquitted by the Court for want of sufficient evidence. Among those was one Mars, a negroe man slave to one Mr Regnier, who was [taken] to his tryall and acquitted by the Jury—the Sheriffe the next day moving the Court for the discharge of such as were or should be soe acquitted, by reason hee apprehended they would attempt to make their excape [from jail]; but Mr Bickley, who yn [then] executed the office of the Atter: Generall, [out of hostility] for Mr Rayner [Regnier] opposed his [the sheriff's] motion, telling the Court that at that time, none but Mars being acquitted, the motion could be only intended in his [Mars'] favour, against whom he [Bickley] should have some thing further to object [charge], and therefore prayed he might not be discharg[ed]; so the sheriff did not obtain his motion. Mars was then indicted a second time and again acquitted but not discharg'd; and, being a third time presented, was transferr'd (the Court of Justices not designing to sit again) to the supream Court and there tryed and convicted on ye same evidence [as given] on his two former tryals. This prosecution was carryed on to gratify some private pique of Mr Bickleys against Mr Regnier, a gentleman of his own profession, which [trial] appearing so partial, and the evidence being represented to me as very defective, and [Mars] being wholly acquitted of ever having known any thing of the Conspiracy by the Negroe witnesses who were made use of in the tryals of all the criminals before the Justices (and without whose testimonies very few could have been punished), I thought fit to reprieve him till Her Majesties pleasure be known therein. In this supream court were likewise tryed one Husea belonging to Mrs Wenham, and one John belonging Mr Vantilbourgh—and convicted; these two are prisoners taken in a Spanish prize this war and brought into this Port by a Privateer about six or seven years agoe; and by reason of their colour, which is swarthy, they were said to be slaves and as such were sold

among many others of the same colour and country; these two I have likewise reprieved till Her Majesties pleasure be signified. Soon after my arrival
in this government I received petitions from several of these Spanish
Indians, as they are called here, representing to me that they were free men,
subjects to the King of Spain but sold here as slaves; I secretly pittyed their
condition but, haveing no other evidence of wt [what] they asserted then
[than] their own words, I had it not in my power to releive them. I am
informed that in the West Indies, where their laws against their slaves are
most severe, that in case of conspiracy in which many are engaged a few only
are executed for an example. In this case 21 are executed, and six having
done that Justice on themselves, more have suffered than we can find were
active in this bloody affair—which are reasons for my repreiving these; and if
your Lordships think them of sufficient weight, I beg you will procure Her
Majesty's pleasure to be signifyed to me for their pardon, for they lye now in
prison at their masters charge. I have likewise reprieved one Tom, a Negroe
belonging to mr Van Dam, and Coffee a Negroe belonging to Mr Walton;
these two I have repreived at the instance of the Justices of the Court, who
where of oppinion that the evidence against them was not sufficient to convict them.

3

Native Americans

Long before Europeans and Africans came to America, people from northeastern Asia had crossed to the Western Hemisphere by a land bridge that connected Siberia to Alaska. By the time of Columbus they numbered perhaps as many as 50 million people spread across the two American continents and the adjacent islands. Believing at first that the Americas were an eastern extension of Asia, Europeans called these people *Indians*. Many of their descendants, however, prefer the name *Native Americans*.

Europeans were ambivalent about the indigenous people of the New World. On the one hand the "natives" seemed uncivilized beings whose customs were alien and often "brutish." Even worse, they were heathens, ignorant of Christian revelation, and so, unless converted, consigned to eternal damnation.

But there was another side of the European response as well. Europeans could not help admiring many Native American qualities, although this admiration often rested on ascribed attributes they did not always have. Above all, many Europeans admired their supposed directness and simplicity, their closeness to nature. They were not really brutish creatures, these observers said, but "noble savages" (to use British poet John Dryden's expression) whose individual and collective characteristics put those of Europeans to shame.

The documents in this section present a range of European views of the Native American population during the years of early contact. Unfortunately we do not have any corresponding statements from Native American of this era about the Europeans. Keep in mind, however, the frequency of the bloody Indian wars of colonial America. They do more than hint at what the indigenous people felt toward the transatlantic invaders.

3.1:   A Professor Disparages the Native Americans of Virginia (1724)

In 1716 Hugh Jones, with a master's degree from Oxford University, came to Williamsburg, the capital of Virginia, to teach mathematics at the College of William and Mary. In 1721 he returned to England for three years and while there wrote The Present State of Virginia, *from which this selection is taken.*

Jones's observations were based on his actual contact with the Virginia Indians, but they are clearly imbued with the prejudices of a European. Can you detect "Euro-centered" opinions here? What are they? Is his description predominantly negative? Although Jones was a teacher, he was also an Anglican minister. Do any of his views reflect the fact that he was a Christian clergyman?

Characteristics of the Indians[1]

HUGH JONES

As to the government and life of the Indians they live in a kind of patriachal [sic] manner, variously diversifyed, not unlike the tribes and families mentioned in the Old Testament. Every small town is a petty kingdom governed by an absolute monarch, assisted and advised by his great men, selected out of the gravest, oldest, bravest, and richest; if I may allow their dear-skins, peak and roenoak (black and white shells with holes, which they wear on strings about their arms and necks) to be wealth.

Sometimes there are general emperors, who have several petty kingdoms in some measure under their protection and power.

They dwell in towns some twenty, some a hundred miles, and some farther from one another, each town having a particular jargon and peculiar customs; though for the most part they agree in certain signs, expressions, and manners.

They are frequently at war with all their neighbours, or most of them, and treat their captive prisoners very barbarously; either by scalping them (which I have seen) by ripping off the crown of the head, which they wear on a thong by their side as a signal trophee and token of victory and bravery, or sometimes they tie their prisoners, and lead them bound to their town,

Reprinted from *The Present State of Virginia: From When Is Inferred a Short View of Maryland and North Carolina*, by Hugh Jones. Edited by Richard L. Morton. Copyright © 1956 by The University of North Carolina Press.

[1] Footnotes deleted.

where with the most joyful solemnity they kill them, often by thrusting in several parts of their bodies scewers of light-wood which burn like torches. The poor victim all the while (which is sometimes two or three days) not shewing the least symptom of grief, nor sign of pain, but bearing it with a scornful sullenness.

In their rejoicings and wardances they with the most antick gestures, in the most frightful dress, with a hideous noise, enumerate the enemies, that they have murdered, and such like exploits.

They attack always by surprize, and will never stand their ground when discovered; but fly to ambush, whither the enemy may pursue with peril of his life.

They are made for running very swiftly, and are nicely dextrous at fishing, hunting, and fowling; whereby they support themselves and families with venison, fish, wild turkies, etc.

The women do all the hard labour, such as cutting down the trees, planting corn, etc. carrying burthens, and all their other work; the men only hunting, fishing and fowling, eating, drinking, dancing and sleeping.

The boys still use bows and arrows for exercise, with which they are very dextrous; but the men always use fire-arms, which with ammunition they buy of us with their dear-skins, going rarely out unarmed.

They are so wonderfully quick-sighted, that they will swiftly pursue by eye the track of any thing among the trees, in the leaves and grass, as an hound does by the scent, where we can't perceive the least mark or footstep.

They cohabit in some hundreds of families, and fix upon the richest ground to build their wooden houses, which they place in a circular form, meanly defended with pales, and covered with bark; the middle area (or forum) being for common uses and publick occasions. The women in order to plant their Indian corn and tobacco (to clear the ground of trees) cut the bark round; so that they die and don't shade the ground, and decay in time.

Wherever we meet with an old Indian field, or place where they have lived, we are sure of the best ground. They all remove their habitation for fear of their enemies, or for the sake of game and provision.

They have small sweating houses like ovens; out of which when they are almost smothered with heat, they run into a river, which they always contrive to build their towns near.

This practice in all distempers often kills vast numbers in sicknesses which are new to them.

They have no notion of providing for futurity; for they eat night and day whilst their provision lasts, falling to as soon as they awake, and falling asleep again as soon as they are well crammed.

Their fish, flesh, and fowl, they either barbacue on an high gridiron, or broil on sharp sticks before a fire, which they always keep in the middle of their cabbin; and they lie upon boards and skins raised like benches round about their room.

Their drink is water unless they can get rum; with which they make themselves the greatest beasts, never ceasing as long as they have liquor to drink, and can keep awake.

I have known, when cows have been given them, that they let them go dry for laziness in neglecting to milk them, and die in the winter for want of fodder.

They commonly wear a dear-skin, putting their arms through the holes of the shoulder, with a flap tyed before and behind to cover their nakedness; though they buy often matchcoats or blankets now, to defend them from the wet and cold, and think themselves very fine in such coats as our common soldiers wear, or of any taudry colours: besides this, some pin pieces of red or blue cloth about their legs, and make moccassons or leather purses for their feet, with which they can travel in the woods, without danger of thorns or stumps. For all the country is but one continued forest, with patches of some hundred acres here and there cleared; either being formerly seated by Indians, or the trees being burnt in fire-hunting, or cut down for plantations.

Their children almost as soon as born, are tyed flat on their backs to a board; and so may be flung on the ground or put to lean against any thing, or be slung over their neck in travelling, or hung upon a bough, as occasion requires.

This occasions them to be exactly strait; so that it is a miracle to see a crooked or deformed Indian.

Their hair is very black, coarse and long; and they are all over daubed frequently with bear's oil.

Each nation has some distinguishing mark, especially in the cut or tie of their hair, in which they are very whimsical and comical.

They often wear shells hanging upon their breasts with feathers or a deer's tail in their bored ears or hair, with a wolf or fox-skin for a snapsack; with other odd accoutrements.

In their opinion, they are finest when dressed most ridiculously or terribly. Thus some have their skins all over curiously wrought with blewish lines and figures, as if done with gun-powder and needles, and all of them delight in being painted; so that when they are very fine, you may see some of them with their hair cut off on one side, and a long lock on the other. The crown being crested and bedaubed with red lead and oil; their forehead being painted white, and it may be their nose black, and a circle of blue round one eye, with the cheek red, and all the other side of the face yellow, or in some such fantastical manner. These colours they buy of us, being persuaded to despise their own, which are common and finer.

They are treacherous, suspicious and jealous, difficult to be persuaded or imposed upon, and very sharp, hard in dealing, and ingenious in their way, and in things that they naturally know, or have been taught; though at the first they are very obstinate, and unwilling to apprehend or learn novelties, and seem stupid and silly to strangers.

An instance of their resolute stupidity and obstinacy in receiving a new custom, I have seen in the prodigious trouble of bringing them to sell their skins, and buy gunpowder by weight; for they could not apprehend the power and justice of the stilliard; but with the scales at lenth they apprehended it tolerably well; though at first they insisted upon as much gunpowder as the skin weighed, which was much more than their demand in measure. They have geographical notions, as to the situation of their own country, and will find the way to very remote places in a surprizing manner; steering by the course of the rivers, etc. or by the trees, whose north side is easily known by the moss.

Thus I know, that Wickmannatauchee (a great king among the southern Indians) whom I saw just before, and since, when he made his escape from his enemy Indians at Christanna, where his queen and abundance of his people were slain, and he tyed in order to be carried away prisoner; yet broke loose, and ran directly home several hundred miles stark-naked, without arms or provision, in the month of March, when the trees afforded no fruit; neither did he go near any other nation, till he got to his own; therefore I suppose roots were his provision, and water his liquor, unless by some cunning method (with which they abound) he caught fish, fowl, or venison; and as for fire I know they can kindle that by rubbing of certain sticks together.

They count their time by days, or by the return of the moon, and cohonks, a sort of wild geese. They walk one after another in a line, are very serious in debates, speak but one at a time; and in negotiations all agree to what either proposes or approves of, and are not easily imposed upon; and when affronted, they highly resent injuries, and being treacherous are no more to be trusted than tame lions, who can't wholly lose their savage hearts.

They have tolerable good notions of natural justice, equity, honour, and honesty, to the rules whereof the great men strictly adhere; but their common people will lye, cheat, and steal.

They seldom commit violence upon the English, but when provoked, or put on by others. . . .

The Indians have a blind worship and sacrifice, priests, and physicians, and expiation, with howling lamentations and purgation at their burials: all which I have seen at the funeral of their slain at Christanna, whom they buried thus; having made holes like sawpits, and lined them with bark and sticks, they wrapped the bodies in the best cloth they could buy with the skins of the deceased, and laid them in the graves, with all the cloths, skins and nicknacks of the dead: then they covered the body hollow with sticks, and flung in the earth with mournful noise; so the bodies lay as in coffins.

The priest or physician in curing the wounded, made an hideous noise, singing certain charms, with particular actions and forms of incantation, to which he ascribed the cure, though I believe this is done only to blind the common Indians; for I observed he did not begin his operation, till he had been in the woods. Then he shut us all out for an hour, and when we were readmitted, I perceived he had been using certain roots and herbs that I knew not.

Upon enquiry, we have from them these their notions of the state of the dead.

They believe that they go to Mohomny that lives beyond the sun, if they have not been wicked, nor like dogs nor wolves, that is, not unchast, then they believe that Mohomny sends them to a plentiful country abounding with fish, flesh, and fowls, the best of their kind, and easy to be caught; but if they have been naughty, then he sends them to a poor barren country, where be many wolves and bears, with a few nimble deer, swift fish and fowls, difficult to be taken; and when killed, being scarce any thing but skin and bones.

They allow polygamy if the man can maintain his family, as I have been informed.

They punish adultery in a woman by cutting off her hair, which they fix upon a long pole without the town; which is such a disgrace that the party is obliged to fly and becomes a victim to some enemy, a slave to some rover, or perishes in the woods.

3.2: A Pennsylvanian Calls the Native Americans "Devils" (1782)

From the seventeenth century onward, whites have implicitly denied Indians' rights to exclusive possession of the North American continent. At times they have made the case for the priority of the interests of the whites explicit, as in the selection below.[1] The statement is from a letter by Hugh Henry Brackenridge, a Pennsylvanian who wrote one of the first successful American novels.

Although himself a cultivated man, Brackenridge lived in Pittsburgh, then a crude frontier town. Do you think the fact that he was from the "west" of his day influenced Brackenridge's opinions? Does he make a convincing case for the right of Europeans to dispossess the Indians? Few of us would condone a "might makes right" moral code. But then we must ask whether Indian rights should have prevailed over those of the transatlantic intruders? Consider the implications for you and your family of a "yes" answer.

---

[1] Unfortunately, it is impossible to find a statement of this position that dates before the end of the eighteenth century, though it is clear that, judging by actions, the view goes back much further.

The Indians Have No Exclusive Claim to America

HUGH HENRY BRACKENRIDGE

With the narrative enclosed, I subjoin some observations with regard to the animals, vulgarly called Indians. It is not my intention to write any labored essay; for at so great a distance from the city, and so long unaccustomed to write, I have scarcely resolution to put pen to paper. Having an opportunity to know something of the character of this race of men, from the deeds they perpetrate daily round me, I think proper to say something on the subject. Indeed, several years ago, and before I left your city, I had thought different from some others with respect to the right of soil, and the propriety of forming treaties and making peace with them.

In the United States Magazine in the year 1777, I published a dissertation denying them to have a right in the soil. I perceive a writer in your very elegant and useful paper, has taken up the same subject, under the signature of "Caractacus," and unanswerably shown, that their claim to the extensive countries of America, is wild and inadmissible. I will take the liberty in this place, to pursue this subject a little.

On what is their claim founded?—Occupancy. A wild Indian with his skin painted red, and a feather through his nose, has set his foot on the broad continent of North and South America; a second wild Indian with his ears cut in ringlets, or his nose slit like a swine or a malefactor, also sets his foot on the same extensive tract of soil. Let the first Indian make a talk to his brother, and bid him take his foot off the continent, for he being first upon it, had occupied the whole, to kill buffaloes, and tall elks with long horns. This claim in the reasoning of some men would be just, and the second savage ought to depart in his canoe, and seek a continent where no prior occupant claimed the soil. Is this claim of occupancy of a very early date? When Noah's three sons, Shem, Ham, and Japhet, went out to the three quarters of the old world, Ham to Africa, Shem to Asia, Japhet to Europe, did each claim a quarter of the world for his residence? Suppose Ham to have spent his time fishing or gathering oysters in the Red Sea, never once stretching his leg in a long walk to see his vast dominions, from the mouth of the Nile, across the mountains of Ethiopia and the river Niger to the Cape of Good Hope, where the Hottentots, a cleanly people, now stay; or supposing him, like a Scots pedlar, to have traveled over many thousand leagues of that country; would this give him a right to the soil? In the opinion of some men it would establish an exclusive right. Let a man in more modern times take a journey or voyage like Patrick Kennedy and others to the heads of the Mississippi or Missouri rivers, would he gain a right ever after to exclude all persons from drinking the waters of these streams? Might not a second

Hugh Henry Brackenridge to the editor of the *Freeman's Journal,* in Wilcomb Washburn, ed. *Indian and White Man* (New York: New York University Press, 1964), pp. 111–27.

Adam make a talk to them and say, is the whole of this water necessary to allay your thirst, and may I also drink of it?

The whole of this earth was given to man, and all descendants of Adam have a right to share it equally. There is no right of primogeniture in the laws of nature and of nations. There is reason that a tall man, such as the chaplain in the American army we call the High Priest, should have a large spot of ground to stretch himself upon; or that a man with a big belly, like a goodly alderman of London, should have a larger garden to produce beans and cabbage for his appetite, but that an agile, nimble runner, like an Indian called the Big Cat, at Fort Pitt, should have more than his neighbors, because he has traveled a great space, I can see no reason.

I have conversed with some persons and found their mistakes on this subject, to arise from a view of claims by individuals in a state of society, from holding a greater proportion of the soil than others; but this is according to the laws to which they have consented; an individual holding one acre, cannot encroach on him who has a thousand, because he is bound by the law which secures property in this unequal manner. This is the municipal law of the state under which he lives. The member of a distant society is not excluded by the laws from a right to the soil. He claims under the general law of nature, which gives a right, equally to all, to so much of the soil as is necessary for subsistence. Should a German from the closely peopled country of the Rhine, come into Pennsylvania, more thinly peopled, he would be justifiable in demanding a settlement, though his personal force would not be sufficient to effect it. It may be said that the cultivation of melioration of the earth, gives a property in it. No—if an individual has engrossed more than is necessary to produce grain for him to live upon, his useless gardens, fields and pleasure walks, may be seized upon by the person who, not finding convenient ground elsewhere, choose to till them for his support.

It is a usual way of destroying an opinion by pursuing it to its consequence. In the present case we may say, that if the visiting one acre of ground could give a right to it, the visiting of a million would give a right on the same principle; and thus a few surly ill natured men, might in the earlier ages have excluded half the human race from a settlement, or should any have fixed themselves on a territory, visited before they had set a foot on it, they must be considered as invaders of the rights of others.

It is said that an individual, building a house or fabricating a machine has an exclusive right to it, and why not those who improve the earth? I would say, should man build houses on a greater part of the soil, than falls to his share, I would, in a state of nature, take away a proportion of the soil and the houses from him, but a machine or any work of art, does not lessen the means of subsistence to the human race, which an extensive occupation of the soil does.

Claims founded on the first discovery of soil are futile. When gold, jewels, manufactures, or any work of men's hands is lost, the finder is entitled to some reward, that is, he has some claims on the thing found, for a share of it.

When by industry or the exercise of genius, something unusual is invented in medicine or in other matters, the author doubtless has a claim to an exclusive profit by it, but who will say the soil is lost, or that any one can found a claim by discovering it. The earth with its woods and rivers still exist, and the only advantage I would allow to any individual for having cast his eye first on any particular part of it, is the privilege of making the first choice of situation. I would think the man a fool and unjust, who would exclude me from drinking the waters of the Mississippi river, because he had first seen it. He would be equally so who would exclude me from settling in the country west of the Ohio, because in chasing a buffalo he had been first over it.

The idea of an exclusive right to the soil in the natives had its origin in the policy of the first discoverers, the kings of Europe. Should they deny the right of the natives from their first treading on the continent, they would take away the right of discovery in themselves, by sailing on the coast. As the vestige of the moccasin in one case gave a right, so the cruise in the other was the foundation of a claim.

Those who under these kings, derived grants were led to countenance the idea, for otherwise why should kings grant or they hold extensive tracts of country. Men become enslaved to an opinion that has been long entertained. Hence it is that many wise and good men will talk of the right of savages to immense tracts of soil.

What use do these ring, streaked, spotted and speckled cattle make of the soil? Do they till it? Revelation said to man, "Thou shalt till the ground." This alone is human life. It is favorable to population, to science, to the information of a human mind in the worship of God. Warburton[1] has well said, that before you can make an Indian a christian you must teach him agriculture and reduce him to a civilized life. To live by tilling is *more humano*, by hunting is *more bestiarum*. I would as soon admit a right in the buffalo to grant lands, as in Killbuck, the Big Cat, the Big Dog, or any of the ragged wretches that are called chiefs and sachems. What would you think of going to a big lick or place where the beasts collect to lick saline nitrous earth and water, and addressing yourself to a great buffalo to grant you land? It is true he could not make the mark of the stone or the mountain reindeer, but he could set his cloven foot to the instrument like the great Ottomon, the father of the Turks, when he put his signature to an instrument, he put his large hand and spreading fingers in the ink and set his mark to the parchment. To see how far the folly of some would go, I had once a thought of supplicating some of the great elks or buffaloes that run through the woods, to make me a grant of a hundred thousand acres of land and prove he had brushed the weeds with his tail, and run fifty miles.

I wonder if Congress or the different States would recognize the claim? I am so far from thinking the Indians have a right to the soil, that not having

---

[1] Probably William Warburton, the Anglican Bishop of Gloucester, England—ED.

made a better use of it for many hundred years, I conceive they have forfeited all pretence to claim, and ought to be driven from it.

With regard to forming treaties or making peace with this race, there are many ideas:

They have the shapes of men and may be of the human species, but certainly in their present state they approach nearer the character of Devils; take an Indian, is there any faith in him? Can you bind him by favors? Can you trust his word or confide in his promise? When he makes war upon you, when he takes you prisoner and has you in his power will he spare you? In this he departs from the law of nature, by which, according to baron Montesquieu[2] and every other man who thinks on the subject, it is unjustifiable to take away the life of him who submits; the conqueror in doing otherwise becomes a murderer, who ought to be put to death. On this principle are not the whole Indian nations murderers?

Many of them may have not had an opportunity of putting prisoners to death, but the sentiment which they entertain leads them invariably to this when they have it in their power or judge it expedient; these principles constitute them murderers, and they ought to be prevented from carrying them into execution, as we would prevent a common homicide, who should be mad enough to conceive himself justifiable in killing men.

The tortures which they exercise on the bodies of their prisoners, justify extermination. Gelo of Syria made war on the Carthaginians because they oftentimes burnt human victims, and made peace with them on conditions they would cease from this unnatural and cruel practice. If we could have any faith in the promises they make we could suffer them to live, provided they would only make war amongst themselves, and abandon their hiding or lurking on the pathways of our citizens, emigrating unarmed and defenceless inhabitants; and murdering men, women and children in a defenceless situation; and on their ceasing in the meantime to raise arms no more among the American Citizens.

3.3:   William Penn Urges Kindness toward Native Americans (1683)

Until well into the eighteenth century, relations between whites and Native Americans were more peaceable in Pennsylvania than anywhere else. The following selection by William Penn, founder of the Pennsylvania colony, suggests why this was so.

Was it significant, in considering good Indian-white relations, that Pennsylvania was established under Quaker auspices? What was the

[2] Charles de Secondat Montesquieu, a prominent French philosopher of the early eighteenth century—ED.

Quaker view of power and authority? What was the Quaker view of racial differences? In the end, did it make a difference for the Indians of Pennsylvania that the colony's early rulers were Quakers? Or were they submerged there too?

William Penn Admires the Indians

WILLIAM PENN

XI. The *Natives* I shall consider in their Persons, Language, Manners, Religion and Government, with my sence of their Original. For their Persons, they are generally tall, streight, well-built, and of singular Proportion; they tread strong and clever, and mostly walk with a lofty Chin: Of Complexion, Black, but by design, as the Gypsies in England: They grease themselves with Bears-fat clarified, and using no defence against Sun or Weather, their skins must needs be swarthy; Their Eye is little and black, not unlike a straight-look't Jew: The thick Lip and flat Nose, so frequent with the East-Indians and Blacks, are not common to them; for I have seen as comely European-like faces among them of both, as on your side the Sea; and truly an Italian Complexion hath not much more of the White, and the Noses of several of them have as much of the Roman.

XII. Their Language is lofty, yet narrow, but like the Hebrew; in Signification full, like Short-hand in writing; one word serveth in the place of three, and the rest are supplied by the Understanding of the Hearer: Imperfect in their Tenses, wanting in their Moods, Participles, Adverbs, Conjunctions, Interjections: I have made it my business to understand it, that I might not want an Interpreter on any occasion: And I must say, that I know not a Language spoken in Europe, that hath words of more sweetness or greatness, in Accent and Emphasis, than theirs. . . .

XIII. Of their Customs and Manners there is much to be said; I will begin with Children. So soon as they are born, they wash them in Water, and while very young, in cold Weather to chuse, they Plunge them in the Rivers to harden and embolden them. Having wrapt them in a Clout, they lay them on a straight thin Board, a little more than the length and breadth of the Child, and swadle it fast upon the Board to make it straight; wherefore all Indians have flat Heads; and thus they carry them at their Backs. The Children will go very young, at nine Moneths commonly; they wear only a small Clout round their Waste, till they are big; if Boys, they go a Fishing till ripe for the Woods, which is about Fifteen; then they Hunt, and after having

Albert Cook Myers, ed., *Narratives of Early Pennsylvania, West Jersey, and Delaware* (New York: Charles Scribner's Sons, 1912), pp. 230–36.

given some Proofs of their Manhood, by a good return of Skins, they may Marry, else it is a shame to think of a Wife. The Girls stay with their Mothers, and help to hoe the Ground, plant Corn and carry Burthens; and they do well to use them to that Young, they must do when they are Old; for the Wives are the true Servants of their Husbands: otherwise the Men are very affectionate to them.

XIV. When the Young Women are fit for Marriage, they wear something upon their Heads for an Advertisement, but so as their Faces are hardly to be seen, but when they please: The Age they Marry at, if Women, is about thirteen and fourteen; if Men, seventeen and eighteen; they are rarely elder.

XV. Their Houses are Mats, or Barks of Trees set on Poles, in the fashion of an English Barn, but out of the power of the Winds, for they are hardly higher than a Man; they lie on Reeds or Grass. In Travel they lodge in the Woods about a great Fire, with the Mantle of Duffills they wear by day, wrapt about them, and a few Boughs stuck round them.

XVI. Their Diet is Maze, or Indian Corn, divers ways prepared: sometimes Roasted in the Ashes, sometimes beaten and Boyled with Water, which they call *Homine*; they also make Cakes, not unpleasant to eat: They have likewise several sorts of Beans and Pease that are good Nourishment; and the Woods and Rivers are their Larder.

XVII. If an European comes to see them, or calls for Lodging at their House or *Wigwam* they give him the best place and first cut. If they come to visit us, they salute us with an *Itah* which is as much as to say, Good be to you, and set them down, which is mostly on the Ground close to their Heels, their Legs upright; may be they speak not a word more, but observe all Passages: If you give them any thing to eat or drink, well, for they will not ask; and be it little or much, if it be with Kindness, they are well pleased, else they go away sullen, but say nothing.

XVIII. They are great Concealers of their own Resentments, brought to it, I believe, by the Revenge that hath been practised among them; in either of these, they are not exceeded by the Italians. A Tragical Instance fell out since I came into the Country; A King's Daughter thinking her self slighted by her Husband, in suffering another Woman to lie down between them, rose up, went out, pluck't a Root out of the Ground, and ate it, upon which she immediately dyed; and for which, last Week he made an Offering to her Kindred for Attonement and liberty of Marriage; as two others did to the Kindred of their Wives, that dyed a natural Death: For till Widdowers have done so, they must not marry again. Some of the young Women are said to take undue liberty before Marriage for a Portion; but when marryed, chaste; when with Child, they know their Husbands no more, till delivered; and during their Moneth, they touch no Meat, they eat, but with a Stick, least they should defile it; nor do their Husbands frequent them, till that time be expired.

XIX. But in Liberality they excell, nothing is too good for their friend; give them a fine Gun, Coat, or other thing, it may pass twenty hands, before it sticks; light of Heart, strong Affections, but soon spent; the most merry Creatures that live, Feast and Dance perpetually; they never have much, nor want much: Wealth circulateth like the Blood, all parts partake; and though none shall want what another hath, yet exact Observers of Property. Some Kings have sold, others presented me with several parcels of Land; the Pay or Presents I made them, were not hoarded by the particular Owners, but the neighbouring Kings and their Clans being present when the Goods were brought out, the Parties chiefly concerned consulted, what and to whom they should give them? To every King then, by the hands of a Person for that work appointed, is a proportion sent, so sorted and folded, and with that Gravity, that is admirable. Then that King sub-divideth it in like manner among his Dependents, they hardly leaving themselves an Equal share with one of their Subjects: and be it on such occasions, at Festivals, or at their common Meals, the Kings distribute, and to themselves last. They care for little, because they want but little; and the Reason is, a little contents them: In this they are sufficiently revenged on us; if they are ignorant of our Pleasures, they are also free from our Pains. They are not disquieted with Bills of Lading and Exchange, nor perplexed with Chancery-Suits and Exchequer-Reckonings. We sweat and toil to live; their pleasure feeds them, I mean, their Hunting, Fishing and Fowling, and this Table is spread every where; they eat twice a day, Morning and Evening; their Seats and Table are the Ground. Since the European came into these parts, they are grown great lovers of strong Liquors, Rum especially, and for it exchange the richest of their Skins and Furs: If they are heated with Liquors, they are restless till they have enough to sleep; that is their cry, Some more, and I will go to sleep; but when Drunk, one of the most wretchedst Spectacles in the world.

XX. In sickness impatient to be cured, and for it give any thing, especially for their Children, to whom they are extreamly natural; they drink at those times a *Teran* or Decoction of some Roots in spring Water; and if they eat any flesh, it must be of the Female of any Creature; If they dye, they bury them with their Apparel, be they Men or Women, and the nearest of Kin fling in something precious with them, as a token of their Love: Their Mourning is blacking of their faces, which they continue for a year; They are choice of the Graves of their Dead; for least they should be lost by time, and fall to common use, they pick off the Grass that grows upon them, and heap up the fallen Earth with great care and exactness.

XXI. These poor People are under a dark Night in things relating to Religion, to be sure, the Tradition of it; yet they believe a God and Immortality, without the help of Metaphysicks; for they say, There is a great King that made them, who dwells in a glorious Country to the Southward of them, and that the Souls of the good shall go thither, where they shall live again. Their Worship consists of two parts, Sacrifice and *Cantico*. Their Sacrifice is their first Fruits; the first and fattest Buck they kill, goeth to the fire, where he is all burnt with a Mournful Ditty of him that performeth the Ceremony, but with such marvellous Fervency and Labour of Body, that he will even sweat to a foam. The other part is their *Cantico*, performed by round-Dances, sometimes Words, sometimes Songs, then Shouts, two being in the middle that begin, and by Singing and Drumming on a Board direct the Chorus: Their Postures in the Dance are very Antick and differing, but all keep measure. This is done with equal Earnestness and Labour, but great appearance of Joy. In the Fall, when the Corn cometh in, they begin to feast one another; there have been two great Festivals already, to which all come that will: I was at one my self; their Entertainment was a green Seat by a Spring, under some shady Trees, and twenty Bucks, with hot Cakes of new Corn, both Wheat and Beans, which they make up in a square form, in the leaves of the Stem, and bake them in the Ashes: And after that they fell to Dance, But they that go, must carry a small Present in their Money, it may be six Pence, which is made of the Bone of a Fish; the black is with them as Gold, the white, Silver; they call it all *Wampum*.

XXII. Their Government is by Kings, which they call *Sachema*, and those by Succession, but always of the Mothers side; for Instance, the Children of him that is now King, will not succeed, but his Brother by the Mother, or the Children of his Sister, whose Sons (and after them the Children of her Daughters) will reign; for no Woman inherits; the Reason they render for this way of Descent, is, that their Issue may not be spurious.

XXIII. Every King hath his Council, and that consists of all the Old and Wise men of his Nation, which perhaps is two hundred People: nothing of Moment is undertaken, be it War, Peace, Selling of Land or Traffick, without advising with them; and which is more, with the Young Men too. 'Tis admirable to consider, how Powerful the Kings are, and yet how they move by the Breath of their People. I have had occasion to be in Council with them upon Treaties for Land, and to adjust the terms of Trade; their Order is thus: The King sits in the middle of an half Moon, and hath his Council, the Old and Wise on each hand; behind them, or at a little distance, sit the younger Fry, in the same figure. Having consulted and resolved their business, the King ordered one of them to speak to me; he stood up, came to me, and in the Name of his King saluted me, then took me by the hand,

and told me, That he was ordered by his King to speak to me, and that now it was not he, but the King that spoke, because what he should say, was the King's mind. He first pray'd me, To excuse them that they had not complyed with me the last time; he feared, there might be some fault in the Interpreter, being neither Indian nor English; besides, it was the Indian Custom to deliberate, and take up much time in Council, before they resolve; and that if the Young People and Owners of the Land had been as ready as he, I had not met with so much delay. Having thus introduced his matter, he fell to the Bounds of the Land they had agreed to dispose of, and the Price, (which now is little and dear, that which would have bought twenty Miles, not buying now two.) During the time that this Person spoke, not a man of them was observed to whisper or smile; the Old, Grave, the Young, Reverend in their Deportment; they do speak little, but fervently, and with Elegancy: I have never seen more natural Sagacity, considering them without the help, (I was agoing to say, the spoil) of Tradition; and he will deserve the Name of Wise, that Outwits them in any Treaty about a thing they understand. When the Purchase was agreed, great Promises past between us of Kindness and good Neighbourhood, and that the Indians and English must live in Love, as long as the Sun gave light. Which done, another made a Speech to the Indians, in the Name of all the *Sachamakers* or Kings, first to tell them what was done; next, to charge and command them, To Love the Christians, and particularly live in Peace with me, and the People under my Government: That many Governours had been in the River, but that no Governour had come himself to live and stay here before; and having now such a one that had treated them well, they should never do him or his any wrong. At every sentence of which they shouted, and said, Amen, in their way.

XXIV.   The Justice they have is Pecuniary: In case of any Wrong or evil Fact, be it Murther it self, they Attone by Feasts and Presents of their *Wampon*, which is proportioned to the quality of the Offence or Person injured, or of the Sex they are of: for in case they kill a Woman, they pay double, and the Reason they render, is, That she breedeth Children, which Men cannot do. 'Tis rare that they fall out, if Sober; and if Drunk, they forgive it, saying, It was the Drink, and not the Man, that abused them.

XXV.   We have agreed, that in all Differences between us, Six of each side shall end the matter: Don't abuse them, but let them have Justice, and you win them: The worst is, that they are the worse for the Christians, who have propagated their Vices, and yielded them Tradition for ill, and not for good things. But as low an Ebb as they are at, and as glorious as their Condition looks, the Christians have not out-liv'd their sight with all their Pretensions to an higher

Manifestation: What good then might not a good People graft, where there is so distinct a Knowledge left between Good and Evil? I beseech God to incline the Hearts of all that come into these parts, to out-live the Knowledge of the Natives, by a fixt Obedience to their greater Knowledge of the Will of God, for it were miserable indeed for us to fall under the just censure of the poor Indian Conscience, while we make profession of things so far transcending.

3.4: A Moravian Missionary Praises Native American Values (1777)

The Reverend John Heckewelder was a clergyman of the Moravian denomination, a pious Protestant sect that traced its roots to fifteenth-century Central Europe. Moravians came to America in the 1740s and settled in Pennsylvania. From Bethlehem, their hub, they soon dispatched missionaries to the Indians.

Heckewelder spent many years among the frontier tribes during the last half of the eighteenth century and wrote an account of his experiences. The following selection describes Indian hospitality and Indian attitudes toward private property. Do these views help explain why Native Americans and people of European ancestry often clashed? Is there a resemblance between Indian attitudes toward nature during the eighteenth century and views of modern environmentalists? Why might there be such a similarity? Would it be fair to describe the effort to convert the Indians to the Christian faith as an implicit act of disrespect?

Indians and Nature

JOHN HECKEWELDER

Not satisfied with paying this first of duties to the Lord of all, in the best manner they are able, the Indians also endeavour to fulfil the views which they suppose he had in creating the world. They think that he made the earth and all that it contains for the common good of mankind; when he stocked the country that he gave them with plenty of game, it was not for the benefit of a few, but of all. Every thing was given in common to the sons of men. Whatever liveth on the land, whatsoever groweth out of the earth, and all that is in the rivers and waters flowing through the same, was given jointly

John Heckewelder, *Account of the History, Manners and Customs of the Indian Nations, Who Once Inhabited Pennsylvania and the Neighboring States* (Philadelphia: The American Philosophical Society, 1819), pp. 85–87.

to all, and every one is entitled to his share. From this principle, hospitality flows as from its source. With them it is not a virtue but a strict duty. Hence they are never in search of excuses to avoid giving, but freely supply their neighbour's wants from the stock prepared for their own use. They give and are hospitable to all, without exception, and will always share with each other and often with the stranger, even to their last morsel. They rather would lie down themselves on an empty stomach, than have it laid to their charge that they had neglected their duty, by not satisfying the wants of the stranger, the sick or the needy. The stranger has a claim to their hospitality, partly on account of his being at a distance from his family and friends, and partly because he has honoured them by his visit, and ought to leave them with a good impression upon his mind; the sick and the poor because they have a right to be helped out of the common stock: for if the meat they have been served with, was taken from the woods, it was common to all before the hunter took it; if corn or vegetables, it had grown out of the common ground, yet not by the power of man, but by that of the Great Spirit. Besides, on the principle, that all are descended from one parent, they look upon themselves as but one great family, who therefore ought at all times and on all occasions, to be serviceable and kind to each other, and by that means make themselves acceptable to the head of the universal family, the great and good Mannitto. Let me be permitted to illustrate this by an example.

Some travelling Indians having in the year 1777, put their horses over night to pasture in my little meadow, at Gnadenhutten on the Muskingum, I called on them in the morning to learn why they had done so. I endeavoured to make them sensible of the injury they had done me, especially as I intended to mow the meadow in a day or two. Having finished my complaint, one of them replied: "My friend, it seems you lay claim to the grass my horses have eaten, because you had enclosed it with a fence: now tell me, who caused the grass to grow? Can *you* make the grass grow? I think not, and no body can except the great Mannitto. He it is who causes it to grow both for my horses and for yours! See, friend! the grass which grows out of the earth is common to all; the game in the woods is common to all. Say, did you never eat venison and bear's meat?—"Yes, very often."—Well, and did you ever hear me or any other Indian complain about that? No; then be not disturbed at my horses having eaten only once, of what you call *your* grass, though the grass my horses did eat, in like manner as the meat you did eat, was given to the Indians by the Great Spirit. Besides, if you will but consider, you will find that my horses did not eat *all* your grass. For friendship's sake, however, I shall never put my horses in your meadow again."

The Indians are not only just, they are also in many respects a generous people, and cannot see the sick and the aged suffer for want of clothing. To such they will give a blanket, a shirt, a pair of leggings, mocksens, &c. Otherwise, when they make presents, it is done with a view to receive an equivalent in return, and the receiver is given to understand what that ought to be. In making presents to strangers, they are content with some trifle in token of remembrance; but when they give any thing to a trader, they at least expect double the value in return, saying that he can afford to do it, since he had cheated them so often.

They treat each other with civility, and shew much affection on meeting after an absence. When they meet in the forenoon, they will compliment one another with saying, "a good morning to you!" and in the afternoon "a good evening." In the act of shaking hands with each other, they strictly attend to the distinguishing names of relations, which they utter at the time; as for instance, "a good morning, father, grandfather, uncle, aunt, cousin," and so down to a small grandchild. They are also in the habit of saluting old people no ways related to them, by the names of grandfather and grand-mother, not in a tone of condescending superiority or disguised contempt, but as a genuine mark of the respect which they feel for age. The common way of saluting where no relationship exists, is that of "friend;" when, howev-er, the young people meet, they make use of words suitable to their years or stage in life; they will say "a good morning, comrade, favourite, beloved, &c." Even the children salute each other affectionately. "I am glad to see you," is the common way in which the Indians express themselves to one another after a short absence; but on meeting after a long absence, on the return of a messenger or a warrior from a critical or dangerous expedition, they have more to say; the former is saluted in the most cordial manner with some such expression: "I thank the Great Spirit, that he has preserved our lives to this time of our happily meeting again. I am, indeed, very glad to see you." To which the other will reply: "you speak the truth; it is through the favour of the great and good Spirit that we are permitted to meet. I am equally glad to see you." To the latter will be said: "I am glad that the Great Spirit has pre-served your life and granted you a safe return to your family."

3.5: The Paxton Boys and Native American Extermination (1764)

In 1763 Pennsylvania, for many years the model of good Indian-white relations, witnessed one of the most deplorable incidents of white brutali-ty against Native Americans during the colonial era. The perpetrators were the so-called Paxton Boys, a group of hot-headed frontier farmers, mostly of Scotch-Irish stock, who deeply resented the refusal of the Quaker-dominated legislature in Philadelphia to protect them against Indian attack. Claiming that the Conestoga Indians, converts to Christianity, were selling guns to the hostile frontier tribes, in 1763 they descended on the unarmed Conestogas, and, despite the colonial authorities' attempt to provide protection, massacred most of them without regard to age or sex.

Benjamin Franklin, by now a prominent man of affairs in Philadelphia, penned the eloquent denunciation of the Paxton Boys' bru-

tal assault that follows. No figure in our history so closely approximates the American ideal of common decency as Franklin. Some would say his outrage does credit to our national tradition of fairness. Does it? Does the incident say anything about the differences between frontier attitudes toward Indians and those of the older, settled regions?

The perpetrators were never punished, in spite of Governor John Penn's offer of a reward for their capture. Does this failure reveal anything about white attitudes?

A Narrative of the Late Massacres, in Lancaster County, of a Number of Indians, Friends of This Province, by Persons Unknown. With Some Observations on the Same. Printed in the Year MDCCLXIV.

BENJAMIN FRANKLIN

These *Indians* were the Remains of a Tribe of the *Six Nations*, settled at *Conestogoe*, and thence called *Conestogoe Indians*. On the first Arrival of the *English* in *Pennsylvania*, Messengers from this Tribe came to welcome them, with Presents of Venison, Corn, and Skins; and the whole Tribe entered into a Treaty of Friendship with the first Proprietor, William Penn, which was to last "as long as the Sun should shine, or the Waters run in the Rivers."

This Treaty has been since frequently renewed, and the *Chain brightened*, as they express it, from time to time. It has never been violated, on their Part or ours, till now. As their Lands by Degrees were mostly purchased, and the Settlements of the White People began to surround them, the Proprietor assigned them lands on the Manor of *Conestogoe*, which they might not part with; there they have lived many years in Friendship with their White Neighbours, who loved them for their peaceable inoffensive Behaviour.

It has always been observed, that *Indians*, settled in the Neighbourhood of White People, do not increase, but diminish continually. This Tribe accordingly went on diminishing, till there remained in their Town on the Manor, but 20 persons, viz. 7 Men, 5 Women, and 8 Children, Boys and Girls.

Of these, *Shehaes* was a very old Man, having assisted at the second Treaty held with them, by Mr. Penn, in 1701, and ever since continued a faithful and affectionate Friend to the *English*; He is said to have been an exceeding good Man, considering his Education, being naturally of a most kind, benevolent Temper.

Peggy was *Shehaes's* Daughter; she worked for her aged Father, continuing to live with him, though married, and attended him with filial Duty and Tenderness.

John was another good old Man; his Son *Harry* helped to support him.

Benjamin Franklin, *The Writings of Benjamin Franklin*, ed. A. H. Smyth (New York: The Macmillan Company, 1905–7), vol. 4, pp. 289–93.

George and *Will Soc* were two Brothers, both young Men.

John Smith, a valuable young Man of the *Cayuga* Nation, who became acquainted with *Peggy*, *Shehaes's* Daughter, some few Years since, married her, and settled in that Family. They had one Child, about three Years old.

Betty, a harmless old Woman; and her son *Peter*, a likely young Lad.

Sally, whose *Indian* name was *Wyanjoy*, a Woman much esteemed by all that knew her, for her prudent and good Behaviour in some very trying situations of Life. She was a truly good and an amiable Woman, had no Children of her own, but, a distant Relation dying, she had taken a Child of that Relation's, to bring up as her own, and performed towards it all the Duties of an affectionate Parent.

The Reader will observe, that many of their Names are *English*. It is common with the *Indians* that have an affection for the *English*, to give themselves, and their Children, the Names of such *English* Persons as they particularly esteem.

This little Society continued the Custom they had begun, when more numerous, of addressing every new Governor, and every Descendant of the first Proprietor, welcoming him to the Province, assuring him of their Fidelity, and praying a Continuance of that Favour and Protection they had hitherto experienced. They had accordingly sent up an Address of this Kind to our present Governor, on his Arrival; but the same was scarce delivered, when the unfortunate Catastrophe happened, which we are about to relate.

On *Wednesday*, the 14th of *December*, 1763, Fifty-seven Men, from some of our Frontier Townships, who had projected the Destruction of this little Commonwealth, came, all well mounted, and armed with Firelocks, Hangers and Hatchets, having travelled through the Country in the Night, to *Conestogoe* Manor. There they surrounded the small Village of *Indian* Huts, and just at Break of Day broke into them all at once. Only three Men, two Women, and a young Boy, were found at home, the rest being out among the neighbouring White People, some to sell the Baskets, Brooms and Bowls they manufactured, and others on other Occasions. These poor defenceless Creatures were immediately fired upon, stabbed, and hatcheted to Death! The good *Shehaes*, among the rest, cut to Pieces in his Bed. All of them were scalped and otherwise horribly mangled. Then their Huts were set on Fire, and most of them burnt down. Then the Troop, pleased with their own Conduct and Bravery, but enraged that any of the poor *Indians* had escaped the Massacre, rode off, and in small Parties, by different Roads, went home.

The universal Concern of the neighbouring White People on hearing of this Event, and the Lamentations of the younger *Indians*, when they returned and saw the Desolation, and the butchered half-burnt Bodies of their murdered Parents and other Relations, cannot well be expressed.

The Magistrates of *Lancaster* sent out to collect the remaining *Indians*, brought them into the Town for their better Security against any farther Attempt; and it is said condoled with them on the Misfortune that had happened, took them by the Hand, comforted and *promised them Protection*. They were all put into the Workhouse, a strong Building, as the Place of greatest Safety.

When the shocking News arrived in Town, a Proclamation was issued by the Governor, in the following Terms, viz.

"Whereas I have received Information, that on *Wednesday*, the Fourteenth Day of this Month, a Number of People, armed, and mounted on Horseback, unlawfully assembled together, and went to the *Indian* Town in the *Conestogoe* Manor, in *Lancaster County*, and without the least Reason or Provocation, in cool Blood, barbarously killed six of the *Indians* settled there, and burnt and destroyed all their Houses and Effects: And whereas so cruel and inhuman an Act, committed in the Heart of this Province on the said *Indians*, who have lived peaceably and inoffensively among us, during all our late Troubles, and for many Years before, and were justly considered as under the Protection of this Government and its Laws, calls loudly for the vigorous Exertion of the civil Authority, to detect the Offenders, and bring them to condign Punishment; I have therefore, by and with the Advice and Consent of the Council, thought fit to issue this Proclamation, and do hereby strictly charge and enjoin all Judges, Justices, Sheriffs, Constables, Officers Civil and Military, and all other His Majesty's liege Subjects within this Province, to make diligent Search and Enquiry after the Authors and Perpetrators of the said Crime, their Abettors and Accomplices, and to use all possible Means to apprehend and secure them in some of the publick Gaols of this Province, that they may be brought to their Trials, and be proceeded against according to Law.

"And whereas a Number of other *Indians*, who lately lived on or near the Frontiers of this Province, being willing and desirous to preserve and continue the ancient Friendship, which heretofore subsisted between them and the good People of this Province, have, at their own earnest Request, been removed from their Habitations, and brought into the County of *Philadelphia* and seated for the present, for their better Security, on the *Province Island*, and in other places in the Neighbourhood of the City of *Philadelphia*, where Provision is made for them at the public Expence; I do therefore hereby strictly forbid all Persons whatsoever, to molest or injure any of the said *Indians*, as they will answer the contrary at their Peril.

"*Given under my Hand, and the Great Seal of the said Province, at* Philadelphia, *the Twenty-second Day of* December, *Anno Domini One Thousand Seven Hundred and Sixty-three, and in the Fourth Year of His Majesty's Reign.*

"JOHN PENN.

"*By his Honour's Command,*
"JOSEPH SHIPPEN, *Jun., Secretary.*
"God save the King."

Notwithstanding this Proclamation, those cruel Men again assembled themselves, and hearing that the remaining fourteen *Indians* were in the Workhouse at *Lancaster*, they suddenly appeared in that Town, on the 27th of *December*. Fifty of them, armed as before, dismounting, went directly to the Workhouse, and by Violence broke open the Door, and entered with the utmost Fury in their Countenances. When the poor Wretches saw they had *no Protection* nigh, nor could possibly escape, and being without the least Weapon for Defence, they divided into their little Families, the Children clinging to the Parents; they fell on their Knees, protested their Innocence, declared their Love to the *English*, and that, in their whole Lives, they had never done them Injury; and in this Posture they all received the Hatchet! Men, Women and little Children were every one inhumanly murdered!—in cold Blood!

The barbarous Men who committed the atrocious Fact, in defiance of Government, of all Laws human and divine, and to the eternal Disgrace of their Country and Colour, then mounted their Horses, huzza'd in Triumph, as if they had gained a Victory, and rode off—*unmolested!*

The Bodies of the Murdered were then brought out and exposed in the Street, till a Hole could be made in the Earth to receive and cover them.

But the Wickedness cannot be covered, the Guilt will lie on the whole Land, till Justice is done on the Murderers. THE BLOOD OF THE INNOCENT WILL CRY TO HEAVEN FOR VENGEANCE.

It is said that, *Shehaes* being before told, that it was to be feared some *English* might come from the Frontier into the Country, and murder him and his People; he replied, "It is impossible: there are *Indians*, indeed, in the Woods, who would kill me and mine, if they could get at us, for my Friendship to the *English*; but the *English* will wrap me in their Matchcoat, and secure me from all Danger." How unfortunately was he mistaken!

4

Colonial Religious Toleration

America's role as refuge for victims of religious persecution is a historical commonplace. Puritans, Quakers, Baptists, German Pietists, Catholics, Jews, and others fled from Europe to the New World during the colonial period to escape religious persecution and find freedom to worship as they wished. But was their quest successful? Was America a safe haven for those persecuted for religion's sake? Did the religious refugees find the freedom they sought?

Clearly religious outsiders from Europe who established their own colonies found genuine sanctuary. Orthodox Puritans were safe in Massachusetts; Quakers were not penalized in Pennsylvania. But what about the others? Did the American colonies as a whole provide room for religious diversity? Or did they prove to be just as intolerant as Europe toward those who did not conform to the local majority? Was colonial America generally, then, a religiously tolerant community?

4.1: Puritans Disagree: Anne Hutchinson (1637)

The Puritan settlers of Massachusetts Bay are the classic example of refugees from Europe's religious intolerance, and yet they themselves were persecutors. In 1635 they banished the Reverend Roger Williams from the colony for disagreeing with the authorities over relations between Puritans and the Church of England, over Indian claims, and over the right of the political authorities to coerce religious dissenters. In 1637–38 they drove Anne Hutchinson into exile for disagreeing with the majority of ministers and magistrates over the theological issue of salvation by "grace" or by "works."

Wife of a wealthy businessman and mother of eleven, Hutchinson was brilliant, forceful, and dauntless. Soon after coming to the Bay Colony in 1634, she became an active participant in the religious controversies coursing through the community. Inspired, she said, by the Reverend John Cotton, she began to conduct meetings in her home, where she discussed with other spiritual seekers the "covenant of grace" versus the "covenant of works." The first emphasized the dependence of salvation on God's free gift; the second stressed its dependence on worthy and pious deeds. This difference had originally separated all Protestants from Catholics, but, Hutchinson suggested, the concept had been lost sight of by the ministerial leaders of Massachusetts and was clearly espoused only by John Cotton and her own brother-in-law, the Reverend John Wheelwright. This claim deeply offended the Massachusetts Bay authorities. Convinced that she was sowing dissension within the colony, they brought her to trial in November 1637.

The document that follows is a highly condensed record of Anne Hutchinson's two-day hearing before the leading magistrates and ministers of the Bay Colony. The document is difficult both because of its language and its issues, and you may need to read it several times to extract its meaning. It is worth the effort.

What seem to be the objections of Governor John Winthrop and the other authorities to Hutchinson's views? Why are they so shocked by her claim to "an immediate revelation"? There are surely theological questions at stake here, but there are also political ones. What are they? Why might theological dissent be considered politically dangerous in a community like Massachusetts Bay? And what about Anne Hutchinson's sex? Are there any suggestions in the trial record that her actions were offensive to the authorities because she was a woman?

After the court banished her, Hutchinson moved with her family to the more tolerant settlement at Narragansett Bay in what later became Rhode Island. Following her husband's death in 1642, she moved to the Dutch colony of New Netherland. A year later she and most of her youngest children died in an Indian attack.

The Trial of Anne Hutchinson

Mr. [John] Winthrop, Governor: Mrs. Hutchinson, you are called here as one of those who have troubled the peace of the commonwealth and the church-

Reprinted by permission of the publishers from *The History of the Colony and Province of Massachusetts Bay*, by Thomas Hutchinson, Cambridge, Mass.: Harvard University Press, Copyright © 1936 by the President and Fellows of Harvard College.

es here; you are known as a woman that hath had a great share in the promoting and divulging of those opinions that are causes of this trouble, and to be nearly joined not only in affinity and affection with some of those the court had taken notice of and passed censure upon, but you have spoken divers things as we have been informed very pre-judicial to the honor of the churches and the ministers thereof, and you have maintained a meeting and an assembly in your house that hath been condemned by the general assembly[1] as a thing not tolerable nor comely in the sight of God nor fitting for your sex, and nothwithstanding that was cried down [i.e., condemned] you have continued the same. Therefore we have thought good to send for you to understand how things are, that if you be in an erroneous way we may reduce [i.e., reform] you that so you may become a profitable member here among us. Otherwise if you be obstinate in your course that then the court may take such course that you may trouble us no further. Therefore I would intreat you to express whether you do assent and hold in practice to those opinions and factions that have been handled in court already. . . .

[Anne] Hutchinson: I am called here to answer before you but I hear no things laid to my charge.

Governor: I have told you some already and more I can tell you. . . .

[At this point Winthrop chides Hutchinson for giving refuge to and encouraging groups of dissenters whose views jeopardized Massachusetts Bay.]

Mrs. Hutchinson: Must not I then entertain the saints because I must keep my conscience? . . . What law do [I] . . . transgress?

Governor: The law of God and of the state.

Hutchinson: In what particular?

Governor: Why in this among the rest, whereas the Lord doth say honor thy father and thy mother. . . . This honor you have broke in giving countenance to them.

Hutchinson: In entertaining those [i.e., the dissenters] did I entertain them against any act . . . or what God hath appointed?

Governor: You knew that Mr. [John] Wheelwright did preach this sermon and that those that countenance him in this do break the law?

Hutchinson: What law have I broken?

Governor: Why the fifth commandment. . . . [i.e., "honor thy father and thy mother. . . ."]

Hutchinson: What breach of law is that Sir?

---

[1] The Massachusetts Bay legislature—ED.

Governor: Why dishonoring of parents.

Hutchinson: But put the case, Sir, that I do fear the Lord and my parents. May not I entertain them that fear the Lord because my parents will not give me leave?

Governor: If they be the fathers of the commonwealth, and they [i.e, the others] of another religion, if you entertain them then you dishonor your parents and are just punishable. . . .

Hutchinson: I may put honor upon them as the children of God as they do honor the Lord.

Governor: We do not mean to discourse with those of your sex but only this: you do adhere unto them and do endeavor to set forward this faction and you do dishonor us.

Hutchinson: I do acknowledge no such thing. Neither do I think that I ever put any dishonor upon you.

Governor: Why do you keep such a meeting at your house as you do every week upon a set day? . . .

Hutchinson: It is lawful for me to do, as it is all your practices, and can you find a warrant for yourself and condemn me for the same thing? . . .

Governor: For this, that you appeal to practice you need no confutation [i.e, to be proved wrong]. . . . [But] I will say that there was no meeting of women alone, but your meeting is of another sort for there are sometimes men among you.

Hutchinson: There was never any man with us.

Governor: Well, admit that there was no man at your meeting and that you was sorry for it, [still] there is no warrant for your doings, and by what warrant do you continue such a course?

Hutchinson: I conceive there lies a clear rule in Titus[2] that the elder women should instruct the younger. . . .

Governor: All this I grant you, . . . but what is this to the purpose that you Mrs. Hutchinson must call a company together from their callings to be taught of you?

Hutchinson: Will it please you to answer me this and to give me a rule, for then I will willingly submit to any truth. If any come to my house to be instructed in the ways of God what rule do I hath to put them away? . . .

---

[2] An early Christian to whom Saint Paul addressed one of his epistles as recorded in the New Testament—ED.

Governor: Your course is not to be suffered. . . . [We] find that such a course as this to be greatly prejudicial to the state. . . . [The] occasion . . . is to seduce many honest persons that are called to these meetings and your opinions being known to be different from the word of God may seduce many simple souls that resort unto you. Besides that the occasion [i.e., difficulties] which hath come of late come from none but such as have frequented your meetings, so now they are flown off [i.e, have ceased to respect] from magistrates and ministers . . . since they have come to you. And [moreover] . . . it will not stand well with the commonwealth that families should be neglected for so many neighbors and dames and so much time spent. We see no rule of God for this. We see not that any should have authority to set up any other [religious] exercises besides what authority hath already set up and so what hurt comes of this you will be guilty of and we for suffering you.

Hutchinson: Sir, I do not believe that to be so.

Governor: Well, we see how it is. We must therefore put it away from you or restrain you from maintaining this course.

Hutchinson: If you have rule for it from God's word you may.

Governor: We are [your] judges, and not you ours and we must compel you to it. . . .

Deputy Governor [Thomas Dudley]:   I will go a little higher with Mrs. Hutchinson. About three years ago we were all in peace. Mrs. Hutchinson from that time she came hath made a disturbance, and some that came over with her on the ship did inform me what she was as soon as she was landed. I being then in place dealt with the pastors and teachers of Boston and asked them to enquire of her, and then I was satisfied that she held nothing different from us. But within half a year after, she had vented divers of her strange opinions and had made parties [i.e., factions] in the country. . . . [It] appears by this woman's meeting that Mrs. Hutchinson hath so forestalled [manipulated] the minds of many by their resort to her meetings that now she hath a potent party in the country. Now if all these things have endangered us from that foundation and if she in particular hath disparaged all our ministers in the land that they have preached a covenant of works, and only Mr. [John] Cotton a covenant of grace, why this is not to be suffered, and therefore being driven to the foundation [i.e., getting to the bottom of things] and it being found that Mrs. Hutchinson is she that hath depraved all the ministers and hath been the cause of what is falled out, why we must take away the foundation and the building will fall.

Hutchinson: I pray, Sir, prove it that I said that they preached nothing but a convenant of works. . . .

Deputy Governor: If they do not preach a covenant of grace clearly, then they preach a covenant of works.

Hutchinson: No, Sir, one may preach a covenant of grace more clearly than another, so I said. . . .

[*The examination continued the following day when Anne Hutchinson made the damaging statement below.*]

Hutchinson: If you please to give me leave I shall give you the ground of what I know to be true. Being much troubles to see the falseness of the constitution [i.e., the doctrines, structure, and practices] of the Church of England, I like to had turned Separatist [i.e., left the Church of England entirely, like the Pilgrims of Plymouth Colony]. Whereupon I kept a day of solemn humiliation and pondering of the thing, the scripture was brought unto me—he that denies Jesus Christ to be come in the flesh is antichrist. . . . The Lord knows that I could not open [i.e., decipher] scripture; he must by his prophetic office open it unto me. So that being unsatisfied in the thing, the Lord was pleased to bring this scripture out of the Hebrews. He that denies the testament denies the testator, and . . . this did open unto me and give me to see that those who did not teach the new covenant [i.e., the covenant of grace] had the spirit of antichrist . . . and ever since I bless the Lord. He hath let me see which was the clear ministry and which was the wrong. . . . Now if you do condemn me for speaking what in my conscience I know to be truth I must commit myself unto the Lord.

Mr. Nowell [a member of the colony assembly]:   How do you know that that was the spirit?

Hutchinson: How did Abraham know that it was God that bid him offer his son being a breach of the sixth commandment?[3]

Deputy Governor: By an immediate voice.

Hutchinson: So to me by an immediate revelation.

Deputy Governor: How! an immediate revelation.

Hutchinson: By the voice of his spirit to my soul. . . .

Deputy Governor: These disturbances that have come among the Germans[4] have all been grounded upon revelations, and so they have vented them and stirred up their hearers to take up arms against their prince and to cut the throats of one another, and these have been the fruits of them, and whether the devil may inspire the same into their hearts here I know not, for I am fully persuaded that Mrs. Hutchinson is deluded by the devil, because the spirit of God speaks truth to all his servants.

---

[3] Thou shalt not kill—ED.
[4] Possibly a reference to the Anabaptists, a German Protestant sect put down by force in the sixteenth century—ED.

Governor: I am persuaded that the revelation she brings forth is delusion. . . . The court hath already declared themselves satisfied concerning the things you hear, and concerning the troublesomeness of her spirit and the danger of her course amongst us, which is not to be suffered. Therefore if it be the mind of the court that Mrs. Hutchinson for these things that appear before us is unfit for our society, and if it be the mind of the court that she shall be banished out of our liberties and imprisoned till she be sent away, let them hold up their hands. . . .

[*In a show of hands on Hutchinson's banishment only three voted nay.*]

Hutchinson: I desire to know wherefor I am banished?

Governor: The court knows whereof and is satisfied.

4.2:   The Quakers (1657, 1658)

No Protestant group in America suffered such bloody persecution as the Society of Friends, popularly known as the Quakers. "Enthusiasts" whose preaching seemed to violate decorum, pacifists who refused to fight for the state, democrats whose behavior offended rulers, Quakers were mistreated in many colonies, especially in New England.

Yet they were also admired, and at times non-Quakers defended their right to worship as they wished, unmolested. The first document below is a petition for tolerance toward Quakers. It comes from the village of Flushing (Vlissingen) on Long Island, part of the Dutch New Netherland colony, and is addressed to Peter Stuyvesant, the governor of the colony. The petitioners are not themselves Quakers, but they present a powerful moral case for extending religious toleration to a group of Friends who had recently come among them. What is their case? In the second document, Stuyvesant reacts to this plea for toleration. How does Peter Stuyvesant respond? Why did Stuyvesant disdain the Quakers so much? Were his objections primarily doctrinal? Or were they political?

Remonstrance of the Inhabitants of Flushing, L. I., against the Law against Quakers and Subsequent Proceedings by the Government against Them and Others Favoring Quakers

Right Honorable. [Peter Stuyvesant]

You have been pleased to send up unto us a certain Prohibition or Command that we should not receive or entertain any of those people called *Quakers* because they are supposed to be, by some, seducers of the people.

B. Fernow, ed., *Documents Relating to the History of Early Colonial Settlements, Principally on Long Island* (Albany: Weed, Parsons and Company, 1883), vol. 14, pp. 402–9.

For our part we cannot condemn them. In this case neither can we stretch out our hands against them to punish, banish, or persecute them, for out of Christ God is a consuming fire and it is a fearful [thing] to fall into the hands of a living God. We desire therefore in this case not to judge lest we be judged; neither to Condemn lest we be condemned, but rather let every man stand and fall to his own. . . .

The law of love, peace, and liberty [extends] . . . to *Jews, Turks* and *Egyptians,* as they are considered the sons of Adam, which is the glory of the . . . state of *Holland.* So love, peace, and liberty, extending to all in Christ Jesus, condemns hatred, war, and bondage. And because our Savior saith it is impossible but that offenses will come, but woe be it unto him by whom they cometh, our desire is not to offend one of his little ones in whatsoever form, name, or title he appears, whether Presbyterian, Independent Baptist, or Quaker, but [we] shall be glad to see anything of God in any of them. Desiring to do unto all men as we desire all men should do unto us—which is the true law of both church and state— . . . therefore, if any of these said persons come in love unto us we cannot in conscience lay violent hands upon them but give them free egress and regress unto our town and houses as God shall persuade our consciences, and in all this we are true subjects both of Church and State for we are bound by the law of God and man to do good unto all men and evil to no man, and this is according to the patent and charter of our town given unto us in the name of the States General which we are not willing to infringe and violate but shall hold to our patent and shall remain your humble subjects.

The inhabitants of *Vlishing* [*Vlissingen*] Written this 27th of December in the year 1657 by me:

Tobias Freake	Edward Heart Clericus
The Mark of William Noble	Nicolas Blackford
William Thorne, seignor	The Mark of Micah Tue
The Mark of Wm. Thorne, Jr.	The Mark of Philipp Ud
Edward Tarne	Edward Ffarington
John Storer	Robert Ffield, senior
Nathaniel Heffered	Robert Ffield, junior
Benjamin Hubbard	Nick Colas Parsell
The Mark of William Pidgion	Michael Milner
The Mark of George Clere	Henry Townsend

[And Others]

Sentence of Tobias Freake, *Schout* of Vlissingen

Whereas *Tobias Freake,* a resident of *Vlissingen* on *Long Island,* now prisoner, has confessed and acknowledged, that he received an order from the Honorable Director-General [Peter Stuyvesant], not to admit, lodge and entertain in the said village any one of the heretical abominable sect called Quakers, but has nevertheless had the audacity, in contempt of the said

order and formerly published and renewed placats, to be a leader and insti-
gator in the conception of a seditious, mutinous and detestable letter of defiance . . . signed by himself and his accomplices and by him retained and
then delivered to the Director-General, wherein they justify and uphold the
abominable sect of Quakers, who vilify both the political authorities and the
Ministers of the Gospel and undermine the State and God's service, and
absolutely demand, that all sects, especially the said abominable and heretical sects of Quakers shall and must be tolerated and admitted; all of which is
directly contrary and repugnant to the above referred to orders and placats
of the Director-General and Council, which he pursuant to his oath, official
position and duty, as a subordinate officer of the [Director]-General and
Schout in the said village of *Vlissingen*, should by all means have upheld and
enforced.

But whereas he has herein not only failed, but has himself transgressed
and disobeyed, for which as an example to others he deserves severe punishment, yet considering the humble petition of the prisoner *Freake*, confessing
his wrongdoing and promising hereafter to avoid such errors.

Therefore the Director-General and Council of *New Netherland*, administering the law in the name of their High and Mighty, the Lords States
General of the *United Netherlands*, and the Lords Directors of the . . . W[est]
I[ndia] Company first dismiss the said *Tobias Freake* from his office as Schout
of the said village of *Vlissingen* and banish him from this Province of *New
Netherland* or to pay a fine of 200 fl. [florins] to be applied as directed by law,
if he will keep his promise, together with the costs and mises of law.

Done at *Fort Amsterdam* in *N[ew] N[etherland]* the 28th of January 1658

P. Stuyvesant
Pieter Tonneman

4.3:   The Catholics (1649, 1654, 1777)

*The religious diversity that so influenced the social, political, and intel-
lectual life of the American colonies derived from the momentous events
of the 1530s, when the English king Henry VIII broke with the Catholic
church and set in motion the Protestant Reformation in England. Henry
intended primarily to gain personal control of the church, but in fact he
unleashed a wave of religious innovation. Before long in Britain
Protestant would be battling Protestant in a free-for-all fight for religious
supremacy that would roil society for the next two centuries.*

*Oblique parties to the struggle were England's Catholics, loyal to the
faith that had preceded the Reformation. Attacked by English Protestants
as benighted "papists" for their continued allegiance to Rome and
accused of treason for the support they received from England's enemies*

among the Catholic monarchs of Europe, they found themselves, like the Puritans, hounded and harried by the English government and the Church of England.

In 1632 Cecelius Calvert, Lord Baltimore, an English Catholic nobleman, received a charter for Maryland, a colony he conceived as a refuge for his coreligionists. Relatively few Catholics came to the colony, however, and Protestants soon became the majority. Still, for a time, Maryland served as a haven for Catholic exiles.

Elsewhere in British North America, Catholics were even more heavily outnumbered. In many communities they retained their image as aliens whose faith raised doubts of their loyalty to the larger society.

What do the documents that follow tell us about the attitudes of American Protestants toward Catholics outside Maryland? Note the paired documents on Maryland itself. What seems to have happened eventually in the Catholic-founded colony? Finally, consider the letter of John Adams to his wife Abigail dated 1777, just after the Americans had proclaimed their independence from Great Britain. What does it reveal about the views of the founders toward Catholicism well into the "enlightened" eighteenth century?

Maryland's Act of Religious Toleration, April 21, 1649

[F]orasmuch as in a well governed and Xtian [Christian] Comon Weath matters concerning Religion and the honor or God ought in the first place to bee taken into serious consideraton and endeavoured to bee settled. Be it therefore ordered and enacted . . . That whatsoever pson or psons within this Province . . . shall from henceforth blaspheme God . . . or deny our Saviour Jesus Christ to bee the sonne of God, or shall deny the holy Trinity the ffather sonne and holy Ghost, or the Godhead of any of the said Three psons of the Trinity or the Unity of the Godhead . . . shalbe punished with death and confiscaton or forfeiture of all his or her lands and goods to the Lord Proprietary and his heires. . . . And bee it also Enacted by the Authority and with the advise and assent aforesaid. That whatsoever pson or psons shall from henceforth use or utter any reproachfull words or Speeches concerning the blessed Virgin Mary the Mother of our Saviour or the holy Apostles or Evangelists or any of them shall in such case for the first offence forfeit to the Lord Proprietary and his heires . . . the sume of ffive pound Sterling or the value thereof to be Leveyed on the goods and chattells of every such pson soe offending. . . . And be it also further Enacted by the

William Hande Brown, ed., *Archives of Maryland: Proceedings and Acts of the General Assembly of Maryland, January 1637/38–September 1664* (Baltimore: Maryland Historical Society, 1883), vol. 1, pp. 244–47.

same authority. . . . that whatsoever pson or psons shall from henceforth uppon any occasion of Offence or otherwise in a reproachful manner or Way declare call or denoniminate any pson or psons whatsoever inhabiting . . . within this Province . . . an heritick, Scismatick, Idolator, puritan, Independant, Prespiterian popish prest, Jesuite, Jesuited papist, Lutheran, Calvenist, Anabaptist, Brownist, Antinomian, Barrowist, Roundhead, Sepatist, or any other name or terme in a reproachfull manner relating to matter of Religion shall for every such Offence forfeit and loose sōme or tenne shillings sterling or the value thereof to bee leveyed on the goods and chattels of every such Offender. . . . And whereas the inforceing of the conscience in matters of Religion hath frequently fallen out to be of dangerous Consequence in those commonwealthes where it hath been practised, And for the more quiett and peaceable government of this Province, and the better to pserve mutuall Love and amity amongst the Inhabitants thereof. Be it Therefore . . . enacted (except as in this psent Act is before Declared and sett forth) that noe person or psons whatsoever within this Province, or the Islands, Ports, Harbors, Creekes, or havens thereunto belonging professing to beleive in Jesus Christ, shall from henceforth bee any waies troubled, Molested or discountenanced for or in respect of his or her religion nor in the free exercise therof within this Province or the Islands thereunto belonging nor any way compelled to the beleife or exercise of any other Religion against his or her consent, soe as they be not unfaithfull to the Lord Proprietary, or molest or conspire against the civill Governemt established or to bee established in this Province under him or his heires. And that all & every pson or psons that shall presume Contrary to this Act and the true intent and meaning thereof directly or indirectly either in person or estate willfully to wrong disturbe trouble or molest any person whatsoever within this Province professing to beleive in Jesus Christ for or in respect of his or her religion or the free exercise thereof within this Province other than is provided for in this Act that such pson or psons soe offending, shalbe compelled to pay trebble damages to the party soe wronged or molested, and for every such offence shall also forfeit 20^s sterling in money or the value therof. . . . Or if the ptie soe offending as aforesaid shall refuse or bee unable to recompense the party so wronged, or to satisfy such ffyne or forfeiture, then such Offender shalbe severly punished by publick whipping & imprisonmt during the pleasure of the Lord Proprietary, or his Lieuetenāt or cheife Governor of this Province for the tyme being without baile or maineprise.

The Disfranchisement of Catholics in Maryland, October 20, 1654

It is Enacted and Declared in the Name of his Highness the Lord Protector with the Consent and by the Authority of the present Generall Assembly That none who profess and Exercise the Popish Religion Commonly known

William Hande Brown, ed., *Archives of Maryland: Proceedings and Acts of the General Assembly of Maryland, January 1637/38–September 1664* (Baltimore: Maryland Historical Society, 1883), vol. 1, pp. 340–41.

by the Name of the Roman Catholick Religion can be protected in this Province by the Lawes of England formerly Established and yet unrepealed . . . but are to be restrained from the Exercise thereof, Therefore all and Every person or persons Concerned in the Law aforesaid are required to take notice.

Such as profess faith in God by Jesus Christ (though Differing in Judgment from the Doctrine worship & Discipline publickly held forth shall not be restrained from but shall be protected in the profession of the faith) & Exercise of their Religion so as they abuse not this Liberty to the injury of others The Disturbance of the publique peace on their part, Provided that this Liberty be not Extended to popery or prelacy nor to such as under the profession of Christ hold forth and practice Licentiousness before their faces: their books, furniture, and whatever was in the house, fell a prey to the robbers. With almost the entire loss of their property, private and domestic, together with great peril of life, they were secretly carried into Virginia; and in the greatest want of necessaries, scarcely, and with difficulty, do they sustain life. They live in a mean hut, low and depressed, not much unlike a cistern, or even a tomb, in which that great defender of the faith, St. Athanasius, lay concealed for many years. To their other miseries this inconvenience was added, that whatever comfort or aid this year, under name of stipend, from pious men in England, was destined for them, had been lost, the ship being intercepted in which it was carried. But nothing affects them more than that there is not a supply of wine, which is sufficient to perform the sacred mysteries of the altar. They have no servant, either for domestic use, or for directing their way through unknown and suspected places, or even to row and steer the boat, if at any time there is need. Often, over spacious and vast rivers, one of them, alone and unaccompanied, passes and repasses long distances, with no other pilot directing his course than Divine Providence. By and by the enemy may be gone and they may return to Maryland; the things which they have already suffered from their people, and the disadvantages which still threaten are not much more tolerable.

John Adams Expresses His Disdain for Catholicism

I am wearied to death with the life I lead. The business of the Congress is tedious beyond expression. . . .

This day I went to Dr. Allison's meeting in the forenoon and heard the Dr.; a good discourse upon the Lord's supper. . . . This is a Presbyterian meeting. I confess I am not fond of Presbyterian meetings in this town. . . . And I must confess that the Episcopal Church is quite as agreeable to my taste as the Presbyterian. They are both slaves to the domination of the priesthood. I like the Congregational way best, next to that Independent.

This afternoon, led by curiosity and good company, I strolled away to

John Adams to Abigail Adams, Philadelphia, 10/9/1771, in *Familiar Letters of John Adams and His Wife Abigail, during the Revolution*, ed., Charles Francis Adams (New York: Hurd and Houghton, 1876), pp. 45–46.

mother church, or rather grandmother church. I mean the Romish chapel. I heard a good, short moral essay upon the duty of parents to their children, founded in justice and charity, to take care of their interests, temporal and spiritual. This afternoon's entertainment was to me most awful and affecting; the poor wretches fingering their beads, chanting Latin, not a word of which they understood; their pater nosters and ave Marias; their holy water; their crossing themselves perpetually; their bowing to the name of Jesus, whenever they hear it; their bowings, kneelings, genuflections before the altar. The dress of the priest was rich white lace. His pulpit was velvet and gold. The altar-piece was very rich, little images and crucifixes about; wax candles lighted up. But how shall I describe the picture of our Saviour in a frame of marble over the altar, at full length, upon the cross in the agonies, and the blood dropping and streaming from his wounds! The music, consisting of an organ and a choir of singers, went all the afternoon except sermon time, and the assembly chanted most sweetly and exquisitely.

Here is everything which can lay hold of the eye, ear, and imagination— everything which can charm and bewitch the simple and ignorant. I wonder how Luther ever broke the spell. Adieu.

4.4:   The Jews (1654–56)

Jews first arrived in colonial America in the mid-seventeenth century as refugees from the former Dutch colony of Pernambuco in present-day Brazil after its reconquest by the intolerant Portuguese. Although originally from Portugal themselves, the Jews had lived in Holland for many years, and thus they turned to New Netherland, the Dutch colony in North America, for refuge. The responses of the New Netherland clergy, the colonial governor—the irascible Peter Stuyvesant—and the directors of the Dutch West India Company, the business firm that had founded and governed the colony, are indicated in the short documents below.

What were the sources of the Dutch animosity to the Jews in New Netherland? Were they practical ones? Were there deeper-seated reasons for their hostility? Was Holland itself a tolerant land for its day? Why did the Dutch West India Company favor admitting the Jewish refugees to New Netherland?

Letter from Peter Stuyvesant to the Dutch West India Company, September 22, 1654

The Jews who have arrived would nearly all like to remain here, but learning that they (with their customary usury and deceitful trading with the Christians) were very repugnant to the inferior magistrates, as also to the

Samuel Oppenheim, "Early History of the Jews in New York, 1654–1664," *American Jewish Historical Society Publications*, vol. 18 (1909), pp. 35–37.

people having the most affection for you; the Deaconry also fearing that owing to their present indigence they might become a charge in the coming winter, we have, for the benefit of this weak and newly developing place and the land in general, deemed it useful to require them in a friendly way to depart; praying also most seriously in this connection, for ourselves as also for the general community of your worships [i.e., the West India Company Directors], that the deceitful race,—such hateful enemies and blasphemers of the name of Christ,—be not allowed further to infect and trouble this new colony, to the detraction of your worships and the disatisfaction of your worships' most affectionate subjects.

Letter from the Directors of the Dutch West India Company to Peter Stuyvesant, April 26, 1655

We would have liked to agree to your wishes and request that the new territories should not be further invaded by people of the Jewish race, for we foresee from such immigration the same difficulties which you fear, but after having further weighed and considered this matter we observe that it would be unreasonable and unfair, especially because of the considerable loss sustained by the Jews in the taking of *Brasil* and also because of the large amount of capital which they have invested in shares of this Company. After many consultations we have decided and resolved upon a certain petition made by the said *Portuguese* Jews, that they shall have permission to sail and trade in *New Netherland* and to live and remain there, provided the poor among them shall not become a burden to the Company or the community, but be supported by their own nation. You will govern yourself accordingly.

Letter from the Directors of the Dutch West India Company to Peter Stuyvesant, March 13, 1656

The permission given to the *Jews* to go to *New Netherland* and enjoy there the same privileges as they have here, has been granted only as far as civil and political rights are concerned, without giving said *Jews* a claim to the privilege of exercising their religion in a synagogue or at a gathering; as long therefore as you receive no request for granting them this liberty of religious exercise, your considerations and anxiety about this matter are premature and when later something shall be said about it, you can do no better, than to refer them to us and await the order.

Letter from the Directors of the Dutch West India Company to Peter Stuyvesant, June 14, 1656

We have seen and heard with displeasure that against our orders of the 15th of February 1655, issued at the request of the *Jewish* or *Portuguese* nation, you

B. Fernow, ed., *Documents Relating to the Early Settlements Principally on Long Island* (Albany: Weed, Parson and Company, 1883), vol. 14, p. 315, p. 341, p. 351.

have forbidden them to trade to *Fort Orange* and the South river, also the purchase of real estate, which is granted to them without difficulty here in this country, and we wish it had not been done and that you had obeyed our orders, which you must always execute punctually and with more respect: *Jews* or *Portuguese* people however shall not be employed in public service (to which they are neither admitted in this city), nor allowed to have open retail shops, but they may quietly and peacefully carry on their business as before said and exercise in all quietness their religion within their houses, for which end they must without doubt endeavor to build their houses close together in a convenient place on one or another side of *New Amsterdam*,—at their own choice—as they have done here.

4.5:   America as the Land of Toleration (1782)

Writing just as America was making good its claim to independence, Hector St. John de Crèvecoeur, a long-time French-born resident, described the new republic as a Babel where many religious voices were heard and all were tolerated.

Clearly Crèvecoeur approves of American religious diversity and toler-ance, but what might be the drawbacks of the regime he describes from the point of view of the truly religious? Does he suggest the source of the toler-ance he observes? More than 160 years separate Anne Hutchinson from Crèvecoeur. Does the passage of time help explain the change in religious toleration in America? What experiences in that span of years might account for increasing toleration?

American Diversity: American Tolerance

HECTOR ST. JOHN DE CRÈVECOEUR

As I have endeavoured to shew you how Europeans become Americans; it may not be disagreable to shew you likewise how the various Christian sects introduced, wear out, and how religious indifference becomes prevalent. When any considerable number of a particular sect happen to dwell contigu-ous to each other, they immediately erect a temple, and there worship the Divinity agreeably to their own peculiar ideas. Nobody disturbs them. If any new sect springs up in Europe, it may happen that many of its professors will come and settle in America. As they bring their zeal with them, they are at liberty to make proselytes if they can, and to build a meeting and to follow the dictates of their consciences; for neither the government nor any other power interferes. If they are peaceable subjects, and are industrious, what is it to their neighbours how and in what manner they think fit to address their

Hector St. John de Crèvecoeur, *Letters from an American Farmer* (London: 1782), pp. 54–70.

prayers to the Supreme Being? But if the sectaries are not settled close together, if they are mixed with other denominations, their zeal will cool for want of fuel, and will be extinguished in a little time. Then the Americans become as to religion, what they are as to country, allied to all. In them the name of Englishman, Frenchman, and European is lost, and in like manner, the strict modes of Christianity as practised in Europe are lost also. This effect will extend itself still farther hereafter, and though this may appear to you as a strange idea, yet it is a very true one. I shall be able perhaps hereafter to explain myself better, in the meanwhile, let the following example serve as my first justification.

Let us suppose you and I to be travelling; we observe that in this house, to the right, lives a Catholic, who prays to God as he has been taught, and believes in transubstantion [sic]; he works and raises wheat, he has a large family of children, all hale and robust; his belief, his prayers offend nobody. About one mile farther on the same road, his next neighbour may be a good honest plodding German Lutheran, who addresses himself to the same God, the God of all, aggreably [sic] to the modes he has been educated in, and believes in consubstantiation [sic]; by so doing he scandalizes nobody; he also works in his fields, embellishes the earth, clears swamps, &c. What has the world to do with his Lutheran principles? He persecutes nobody, and nobody persecutes him, he visits his neighbours, and his neighbours visit him. Next to him lives a seceder, the most enthusiastic of all sectaries; his zeal is hot and fiery, but separated as he is from others of the same complexion, he has no congregation of his own to resort to, where he might cabal and mingle religious pride with worldly obstinacy. He likewise raises good crops, his house is handsomely painted, his orchard is one of the fairest in the neighbourhood. How does it concern the welfare of the country, or of the province at large, what this man's religious sentiments are, or really whether he has any at all? He is a good farmer, he is a sober, peaceable, good citizen: William Penn himself would not wish for more. This is the visible character, the invisible one is only guessed at, and is nobody's business. Next again lives a Low Dutchman, who implicitly believes the rules laid down by the synod of Dort.[1] He conceives no other idea of a clergyman than that of an hired man; if he does his work well he will pay him the stipulated sum; if not he will dismiss him, and do without his sermons, and let his church be shut up for years. But notwithstanding this coarse idea, you will find his house and farm to be the neatest in all the country; and you will judge by his waggon and fat horses, that he thinks more of the affairs of this world than of those of the next. He is sober and laborious, therefore he is all he ought to be as to the affairs of this life; as for those of the next, he must trust to the great Creator. Each of these people instruct their children as well as they can, but these instructions are feeble compared to those which are given to the youth of the poorest class in Europe. Their children will therefore grow

---

[1] A convocation of orthodox Dutch Calvinists in 1618–19 that condemned the views of Jacob Arminius and envisioned strict Calvinist views—ED.

up less zealous and more indifferent in matters of religion than their parents. The foolish vanity, or rather the fury of making Proselytes, is unknown here; they have no time, the seasons call for all their attention, and thus in a few years, this mixed neighbourhood will exhibit a strange religious medley, that will be neither pure Catholicism nor pure Calvinism. A very perceptible indifference even in the first generation, will become apparent; and it may happen that the daughter of the Catholic will marry the son of the seceder, and settle by themselves at a distance from their parents. What religious education will they give their children? A very imperfect one. If there happens to be in the neighbourhood any place of worship, we will suppose a Quaker's meeting; rather than not shew their fine clothes, they will go to it, and some of them may perhaps attach themselves to that society. Others will remain in a perfect state of indifference; the children of these zealous parents will not be able to tell what their religious principles are, and their grandchildren still less. The neighbourhood of a place of worship generally leads them to it, and the action of going thither, is the strongest evidence they can give of their attachment to any sect. The Quakers are the only people who retain a fondness for their own mode of worship; for be they ever so far separated from each other, they hold a sort of communion with the society, and seldom depart from its rules, at least in this country. Thus all sects are mixed as well as all nations; thus religious indifference is imperceptibly disseminated from one end of the continent to the other; which is at present one of the strongest characteristics of the Americans. Where this will reach no one can tell, perhaps it may leave a vacuum fit to receive other systems. Persecution, religious pride, the love of contradiction, are the food of what the world commonly calls religion. These motives have ceased here: zeal in Europe is confined; here it evaporates in the great distance it has to travel; there it is a grain of powder inclosed, here it burns away in the open air, and consumes without effect.

5

Patriot versus Loyalist

The patriot (Whig) cause that propelled the American colonies toward independence was not universally admired or embraced. Many colonists preferred the loyalist (Tory) view that considered British policy benign and dismissed the angry and unruly attacks against Britain after 1763 as undeserved. When the tensions of the imperial crisis finally sparked armed revolt in 1775, about a quarter of the American people chose the loyalist road.

The documents below record the discordant voices, British and American, patriot and loyalist, of the political debate that swirled through the empire in the years following England's peace with France in 1763. In evaluating them try to detect, beneath the debaters' formal logic, the different assumptions of each. Both sides often emphasize rights. But what about interests? What conflicting interests were at stake in the conflict over the future of America within the empire?

5.1: The Stamp Act Congress Denounces Taxation without Representation (1765)

Conflict over American political autonomy was probably inevitable as the English-speaking colonies matured and grew in population and wealth. Yet a significant incident was required to trigger a British-American imperial crisis. That incident came in March 1765 with the passage by

Parliament of the Stamp Act, placing taxes, in the form of a stamp, on legal and commercial documents, college diplomas, playing cards, dice, newspapers, advertisements, almanacs, and calendars.

The measure was intended to force the Americans to share the cost of defending the empire and to relieve the British taxpayer of a crushing burden. It produced an explosion of wrath in America. Reaction ranged from dignified petitions and remonstrances to riots and physical violence against defenders of British policies and the tax collectors appointed to administer the law. The most effective weapons against the tax were consumer boycotts of British goods and nonimportation agreements by the port merchants against British suppliers.

In October 1765, at the urging of the Massachusetts General Court, representatives of nine colonies met in New York as the Stamp Act Congress, and adopted the resolutions below addressed to the king and the British government. What are the Americans' chief arguments against the Stamp Act? Do the stated reasons for their objections include all the real reasons? Is the tone of the document respectful? Do the Americans seem to revere the empire and their status as Britons? Do you detect any signs of a desire for independence?

(The allusion at the end of the document to "any other acts of parliament" refers primarily to the Sugar Act of 1764, which placed new taxes on various imports into the colonies and established a corps of imperial officials to enforce the measure.)

Declarations of the Stamp Act Congress
STAMP ACT CONGRESS

The members of this congress, sincerely devoted, with the warmest sentiments of affection and duty to his Majesty's person and government; inviolably attached to the present happy establishment of the Protestant succession, and with minds deeply impressed by a sense of the present and impending misfortunes of the British colonies on this continent; . . . make the following declarations, of our humble opinion, respecting the most essential rights and liberties of the colonists, and of the grievances under which they labour, by reason of several late acts of Parliament.

I. That his Majesty's subjects in these colonies, owe the same allegiance to the Crown of Great Britain, that is owing from his subjects born within the realm, and all due subordination to that august body, the Parliament of Great Britain.

John Alman, ed., "The Declarations of the Stamp Act Congress," *Collection of Interesting, Authentic Papers Relative to the Disputes between Britain and America* (London, n.p., 1777), vol. 5, no. 1, pp. 11–13.

II. That his Majesty's liege subjects in these colonies are entitled to all the inherent rights and liberties of his natural born subjects within the kingdom of Great Britain.

III. That it is inseparably essential to the freedom of a people, and the undoubted right of Englishmen, that no taxes should be imposed on them, but with their own consent, given personally, or by their representatives.

IV. That the people of these colonies are not, and from their local circumstances, cannot be represented in the House of Commons in Great Britain.

V. That the only representatives of the people of these colonies, are persons chosen therein, by themselves; and that no taxes ever have been, or can be constitutionally imposed on them, but by their respective legislature.

VI. That all supplies to the Crown, being free gifts of the people, it is unreasonable and inconsistent with the principles and spirit of the British constitution, for the people of Great Britain to grant to his Majesty the property of the colonists.

VII. That trial by jury is the inherent and invaluable right of every British subject in these colonies.

VIII. That the late Act of Parliament, entitled, An Act for granting and applying certain Stamp Duties, . . . by imposing taxes on the inhabitants of these colonies, and the said Act, and several other Acts, by extending the jurisdiction of the courts of admiralty beyond its ancient limits, have a manifest tendency to subvert the rights and liberties of the colonists.

IX. That the duties imposed by several late Acts of Parliament, from the peculiar circumstances of these colonies, will be extremely burdensome and grievous, and from the scarcity of specie, the payment of them absolutely impracticable.

X. That as the profits of the trade of these colonies ultimately centre in Great Britain, to pay for the manufactures which they are obliged to take from thence, they eventually contribute very largely to all supplies granted there to the Crown.

XI. That the restrictions imposed by several late Acts of Parliament, on the trade of these colonies, will render them unable to purchase the manufactures of Great Britain.

XII. That the increase, prosperity and happiness of these colonies, depend on the full and free enjoyment of their rights and liberties, and an intercourse with Great Britain, mutually affectionate and advantageous.

XIII. That it is the right of the British subjects in these colonies, to petition the king or either house of Parliament.

Lastly, that it is the indispensable duty of these colonies to the best of sovereigns, to the mother country, and to themselves, to endeavor by a loyal and dutiful address to his Majesty, and humble applications to both houses of Parliament, to procure the repeal of the Act for granting and applying certain stamp duties, of all clauses of any other Acts of Parliament, whereby the jurisdiction of the admiralty is extended as aforesaid, and of the other late Acts for the restriction of American commerce.

5.2:   The Boston Town Meeting Presents the Patriot Case (1772)

Between 1765, when the Stamp Act Congress met, and 1772, when the Boston Town Meeting adopted the resolutions below, seven eventful, contentious years had intervened. Nevertheless, by 1772 many of the points of friction between Britain and America had been smoothed over, mostly by British concessions—including repeal of the Stamp Act—and the patriot cause had receded. This calm dismayed a group of Boston firebrands, headed by the militant Samuel Adams, who believed that a fundamental alteration of British-American political relationships was necessary. When the Massachusetts royal governor Thomas Hutchinson announced that the crown would be paying his salary, a change that freed him from financial dependence on the Massachusetts legislature, Adams saw his chance to reignite anti-British feelings and actions. The document below, written by Joseph Warren, a physician who would die fighting the redcoats at Bunker Hill, catches the mood of the patriot zealots.

What new complaints against British policy have been added to the charges of the Stamp Act Congress? What do the references to hats, slitting mills, and wool signify? What do the Boston patriots mean when they refer to an "American Episcopate"? Do the new complaints seem exaggerated?

A List of Infringements and Violations of Rights[1]

JOSEPH WARREN

We cannot help thinking, that an enumeration of some of the most open infringments of our rights, will by every candid person be judged sufficient to justify whatever measures have been already taken, or may be thought proper to be taken, in order to obtain a redress of the grievances under which we labour. . . .

1. The British Parliament have assumed the power of legislation for the colonists in all cases whatsoever, without obtaining the consent of the inhabitants, which is ever essentially necessary to the right establishment of such a legislative.

Boston Town Records, 1770–1777, Eighteenth Report of the Boston Record Commissioners, n.p. 1887, pp. 90–92.
[1]Footnotes deleted.

2. They have exerted that assumed power, in raising a revenue in the colonies without their consent; thereby depriving them of that right which every man has to keep his own earnings in his own hands until he shall in person, or by his Representative, think fit to part with the whole or any portion of it. . . .

3. A number of new officers, unknown in the charter of this Province, have been appointed to superintend this revenue, whereas by our charter the Great and General Court or Assembly of this Province has the sole right of appointing all civil officers, excepting only such officers, the election and constitution of whom is in said charter expressly excepted; among whom these officers are not included.

4. These officers are by their commission invested with powers altogether unconstitutional, and entirely destructive to that security which we have a right to enjoy; and to the last degree dangerous, not only to our property, but to our lives. For the Commissioners of His Majesty's Customs in America, or any three of them, are by their commission impowered, 'by writing under their hands and seales to constitute and appoint inferior officers in all and singular the ports within the limits of their commissions'. Each of these petty officers so made is intrusted with power more absolute and arbitrary than ought to be lodged in the hands of any man or body of men whatsoever. . . .

   Thus our houses and even our bed chambers are exposed to be ransacked, our boxes, chests, and trunks broke open, ravaged and plundered by wretches, whom no prudent man would venture to employ even as menial servants; whenever they are pleased to say *suspect* there are in the house wares, etc., for which the dutys have not been paid. Flagrant instances of the wanton exercise of this power, have frequently happened in this and other seaport towns. By this we are cut off from that domestick security which renders the lives of the most unhappy in some measure agreable. . . .

5. Fleets and armies have been introduced to support these unconstitutional officers in collecting and managing this unconstitutional revenue; and troops have been quarter'd in this metropolis for that purpose. Introducing and quartering standing armies in a free country in times of peace without the consent of the people either by themselves or by their representatives, is and always has been deemed a violation of their rights as freemen; and of the charter or compact made between the King of Great Britain, and the people of this province, whereby all the rights of British subjects are confirmed to us.

6. The Revenue arising from this tax unconstitutionally laid, and committed to the management of persons arbitrarily appointed and supported by an armed force quartered in a free city, has been in part applyed to the most destructive purposes. It is absolutely necessary in a mixt government like that of this Province, that a due proportion or balance of power should be established among the several branches of legislative. Our ancestors received from King William and Queen Mary a charter by which it was understood by both parties in the contract, that such a proportion or balance was fixed; and therefore everything which renders any one branch of the legislative more independent of the other two than it was originally designed, is an alteration of the constitution as settled by the charter; and as it has been untill the establishment of this revenue, the constant practise of the General Assembly to provide for the support of government, so it is an essential part of our constitution, as it is a necessary means of preserving an equilibrium, without which we cannot continue a free state.

   In particular it has always been held that the dependence of the Governor of this Province upon the General Assembly for his support, was necessary for the preservation of this equilibrium; nevertheless His Majesty has been pleased to apply fifteen hundred pounds sterling annually out of the American revenue, for the support of the Governor of this Province independent of the Assembly, whereby the ancient connection between him and this people is weakened, the confidence in the Governor lessened and the equilibrium destroyed, and the constitution essentially altered.

And we look upon it highly probable from the best intelligence we have been able to obtain, that not only our Governor and Lieuvetenant Governor, but the Judges of the Superior Court of Judicature, as also the King's Attorney and Solicitor General are to receive their support from this grievous tribute. This will if accomplished compleat our slavery. . . .

7. We find ourselves greatly oppressed by instructions sent to our Governor from the Court of Great Britain, whereby the first branch of our legislature is made merely a ministerial engine. And the Province has already felt such effects from these instructions, as we think justly intitle us to say that they threaten an entire destruction of our liberties, and must soon, if not checked, render every branch of our government a useless burthen upon the people. We shall point out some of the alarming effects of these instructions which have already taken place.

   In consequence of instructions, the Governor has called and adjourned our General Assemblies to a place highly inconvenient to the members, and grately disadvantageous to the interest of the Province, even against his own declared intention.

   In consequence of instructions, the Assembly has been prorogued from time to time, when the important concerns of the Province required their meeting.

   In obedience to instructions, the General Assembly was anno 1768 dissolved by Governor Bernard, because they would not consent to rescind the resolution of a former house, and thereby sacrifise the rights of their constituents.

   By an instruction, the honourable His Majesty's Council are forbid to meet and transact matters of publick concern as a Council of advice to the Governor, unless called by the Governor; and if they should from a zealous regard to the interest of the Province so meet at any time, the Governor is ordered to negative them at the next election of Councellors. . . .

   His Excellency has also pleaded instructions for giving up the provincial fortress, Castle William, into the hands of troops, over whom he had declared he had no controul, and that at a time when they were menaceing the Slaughter of the inhabitants of the Town, and our streets were stained with the blood which they had barbariously shed. . . .

8. The extending the power of the Courts of Vice Admirality to so enormous a degree as deprives the people in the colonies in a great measure of their inestimable right to tryals by juries: which has ever been justly considered as the grand bulwark and security of English property. . . .

9. The restraining us from erecting slitting mills for manufacturing our iron, the natural produce of this country, is an infringement of that right with which God and nature have invested us, to make use of our skill and industry in procuring the necessaries and conveniences of life. And we look upon the restraint laid upon the manufacture and transportation of hatts to be altogether unreasonable and grievous. Although by the charter all havens, rivers, ports, waters, etc., are expressly granted the inhabitants of the Province and their successors, to their only proper use and behoof forever, yet the British Parliament passed an Act, whereby they restrain us from carrying our wool, the produce of our own farms, even over a ferry; whereby the inhabitants have often been put to the expence of carrying a bag of wool near an hundred miles by land, when passing over a river or water of one quarter of a mile, of which the Province are the absolute proprietors, would have prevented all that trouble.

10. The Act passed in the last session of the British Parliament, intitled, An Act for the better preserving his Majestys Dock Yards, Magizines, Ships, Ammunition and Stores, is, as we apprehend a violent infringement of our rights. By this Act any

one of us may be taken from his family, and carried to any part of Great Britain, there to be tried whenever it shall be pretended that he has been concerned in burning or otherwise destroying any boat or vessel, or any materials for building, etc., any naval or victualling store, etc., belonging to His Majesty. . . .

11. As our Ancestors came over to this Country that they might not only enjoy their civil but their religious rights, and particularly desired to be free from the prelates, who in those times cruilly persecuted all who differed in sentiment from the established Church; we cannot see without concern the various attempts which have been made and are now making, to establish an American Episcopate. Our Episcopal brethren of the colonies do enjoy, and rightfully ought ever to enjoy, the free exercise of their religeon, we cannot help fearing that they who are so warmly contending for such an establishment, have views altogether inconsistent with the universal and peaceful enjoyment of our Christian privileges. And doing or attempting to do anything which has even the remotest tendency to endanger this enjoyment, is justly looked upon a great grievance, and also an infringement of our rights, which is not barely to exercise, but peaceably and securely to enjoy, that liberty wherewith Christ has made us free.

    And we are further of Opinion that no power on Earth can justly give either temporal or spiritual jurisdiction within this Province, except the Great and General Court. We think therefore that every design for establishing the jurisdiction of a bishop in this Province, is a design both against our civil and religeous rights. And we are well informed, that the more candid and judicious of our brethren of the Church of England in this and the other colonies, both clergy and laity, conceive of the establishing an American Episcopate both unnecessary and unreasonable.

12. Another grievance under which we labour is the frequent alteration of the bounds of the colonies by decisions before the King and Council, explanatory of former grants and charters. This not only subjects men to live under a constitution to which they have not consented, which in itself is a great grievance; but moreover under color that the right of soil is affected by such declarations, some governors, or ministers, or both in conjunction, have pretended to grant in consequence of a mandamus many thousands of acres of lands appropriated near a century past; and rendered valuable by the labors of the present cultivators and their ancestors. There are very notable instances of setlers, who having first purchased the soil of the natives, have at considerable expence obtained confermation of title from this Province; and on being transferred to the jurisdiction of the Province of New Hampshire have been put to the trouble and cost of a new grant or confermation from thence; and after all this there has been a third declaration of royal will, that they should henceforth be considered as pertaining to the Province of New York. The troubles, expences, and dangers which hundreds have been put to on such occasions, cannot here be recited; but so much may be said, that they have been most cruelly harrassed, and even threatned with a military force, to dragoon them into a compliance with the most unreasonable demands.

5.3:   The Declaration of Independence (1776)

Another four years brought the Declaration of Independence, the final political break with Britain. This followed the outbreak of actual hostilities and the loss of lives, both British and American, in several colonies.

Written primarily by Thomas Jefferson, delegate to the Continental Congress from Virginia, the document summarized the accumulated reasons for the drastic American action.

A part of the Declaration is an indictment of specific British "abuses and usurpations." It refers both to longstanding grievances and to immediate ones, especially the punitive measures adopted by Britain following the Boston Tea Party in late 1773. Objective scholars today would discount much of this section of the Declaration as exaggerated rhetoric. More important, however, is the second paragraph. In this section Jefferson presents, in a few dozen words, a theory of government that formed the philosophical foundation for the Revolution. What is this theory? Was it widely held in its day? From what sources did it derive? Has it influenced political thinking since that era?

The Declaration of Independence

THOMAS JEFFERSON

In Congress, July 4, 1776,

The Unanimous Declaration of theThirteen United States of America,

When in the Course of human events, it becomes necessary for one people to dissolve the political bands which have connected them with another, and to assume among the Powers of the earth, the separate and equal station to which the Laws of Nature and of Nature's God entitle them, a decent respect to the opinions of mankind requires that they should declare the causes which impel them to the separation.

We hold these truths to be self-evident, that all men are created equal, that they are endowed by their Creator with certain unalienable Rights, that among these are Life, Liberty and the pursuit of Happiness. That to secure these rights, Governments are instituted among Men, deriving their just powers from the consent of the governed, That whenever any Form of Government becomes destructive of these ends, it is the Right of the People to alter or to abolish it, and to institute new Government, laying its foundation on such principles and organizing its powers in such form, as to them shall seem most likely to effect their Safety and Happiness. Prudence, indeed, will dictate that Governments long established should not be changed for light and transient causes; and accordingly all experience hath shown, that mankind are more disposed to suffer, while evils are sufferable, than to right themselves by abolishing the forms to which they are accustomed. But when a long train of abuses and usurpations, pursuing invariably the same Object evinces a design to reduce them under absolute Despotism, it is their right, it is their duty, to throw off such Government, and to provide new Guards for their future security.—Such has been the patient sufferance of these Colonies; and such is now the necessity which constrains them to alter their former Systems of Government. The history of the present King of Great Britain is a history of repeated injuries and usurpations, all having in direct object the establishment of an absolute Tyranny over these States. To prove this, let Facts be submitted to a candid world.

He has refused his Assent to Laws, the most wholesome and necessary for the public good.

He has forbidden his Governors to pass Laws of immediate and pressing importance, unless suspended in their operation till his Assent should be obtained; and when so suspended, he has utterly neglected to attend to them.

He has refused to pass other Laws for the accommodation of large districts of people, unless those people would relinquish the right of Representation in the Legislature, a right inestimable to them and formidable to tyrants only.

He has called together legislative bodies at places unusual, uncomfortable, and distant from the depository of their Public Records, for the sole purpose of fatiguing them into compliance with his measures.

He has dissolved Representative Houses repeatedly, for opposing with manly firmness his invasions on the rights of the people.

He has refused for a long time, after such dissolutions, to cause others to be elected; whereby the Legislative Powers, incapable of Annihilation, have returned to the People at large for their exercise; the State remaining in the mean time exposed to all the dangers of invasion from without, and convulsions within.

He has endeavoured to prevent the population of these States; for that purpose obstructing the Laws of Naturalization of Foreigners; refusing to pass others to encourage their migration hither, and raising the conditions of new Appropriations of Lands.

He has obstructed the Administration of Justice, by refusing his Assent to Laws for establishing Judiciary Powers.

He has made Judges dependent on his Will alone, for the tenure of their offices, and the amount and payment of their salaries.

He has erected a multitude of New Offices, and sent hither swarms of Officers to harass our People, and eat out their substance.

He has kept among us, in times of peace, Standing Armies without the Consent of our legislature.

He has affected to render the Military independent of and superior to the Civil Power.

He has combined with others to subject us to a jurisdiction foreign to our constitution, and unacknowledged by our laws; giving his Assent to their acts of pretended legislation:

For quartering large bodies of armed troops among us:

For protecting them, by a mock Trial, from Punishment for any Murders which they should commit on the Inhabitants of these States:

For cutting off our Trade with all parts of the world:

For imposing taxes on us without our Consent:

For depriving us in many cases, of the benefits of Trial by Jury:

For transporting us beyond Seas to be tried for pretended offences:

For abolishing the free System of English Laws in a neighbouring Province, establishing therein an Arbitrary government, and enlarging its Boundaries so as to render it at once an example and fit instrument for introducing the same absolute rule into these Colonies:

For taking away our Charters, abolishing out most valuable Laws, and altering fundamentally the Forms of our Governments:

For suspending our own Legislature, and declaring themselves invested with Power to legislate for us in all cases whatsoever.

He has abdicated Government here, by declaring us out of his Protection and waging War against us.

He has plundered our seas, ravaged our Coasts, burnt our towns, and destroyed the lives of our people.

He is at this time transporting large armies of foreign mercenaries to compleat the works of death, desolation and tyranny, already begun with circumstances of Cruelty & perfidy scarcely paralleled in the most barbarous ages, and totally unworthy the Head of a civilized nation.

He has constrained our fellow Citizens taken Captive on the high Seas to bear Arms against their Country, to become the executioners of their friends and Brethren, or to fall themselves by their Hands.

He has excited domestic insurrections amongst us, and has endeavoured to bring on the inhabitants of our frontiers, the merciless Indian Savages, whose known rule of warfare, is an undistinguished destruction of all ages, sexes and conditions.

In every stage of these Oppressions We have Petitioned for Redress in the most humble terms: Our repeated Petitions have been answered only by repeated injury. A Prince, whose character is thus marked by every act which may define a Tyrant, is unfit to be the ruler of a free People.

Nor have We been wanting in attention to our Brittish brethren. We have warned them from time to time of attempts by their legislature to extend an unwarrantable jurisdiction over us. We have reminded them of the circumstances of our emigration and settlement here. We have appealed to their native justice and magnanimity, and we have conjured them by the ties of our common kindred to disavow these usurpations, which, would inevitably interrupt our connections and correspondence. They too have been deaf to the voice of justice and of consanguinity. We must, therefore, acquiesce in the necessity, which denounces our Separation, and hold them, as we hold the rest of mankind, Enemies in War, in Peace Friends.

We, therefore, the Representatives of the united States of America, in General Congress, Assembled, appealing to the Supreme Judge of the world for the rectitude of our intentions, do, in the Name, and by Authority of the good People of these Colonies, solemnly publish and declare, That these United Colonies are, and of Right ought to be Free and Independent States;

that they are Absolved from all Allegiance to the British Crown, and that all political connection between them and the State of Great Britain, is and ought to be totally dissolved; and that as Free and Independent States, they have full Power to levy War, conclude Peace, contract Alliances, establish Commerce, and to do all other Acts and Things which Independent States may of right do. And for the support of this Declaration, with a firm reliance on the Protection of Divine Providence, we mutually pledge to each other our Lives, our Fortunes and our sacred Honor.

JOHN HANCOCK.

New Hampshire
JOSIAH BARTLETT,
WM. WHIPPLE,
MATTHEW THORNTON.

Massachusetts-Bay
SAML. ADAMS,
JOHN ADAMS,
ROBT. TREAT PAINE,
ELBRIDGE GERRY.

Rhode Island
STEP. HOPKINS,
WILLIAM ELLERY.

Connecticut
ROGER SHERMAN,
SAM'EL HUNTINGTON,
WM. WILLIAMS,
OLIVER WOLCOTT.

Georgia
BUTTON GWINNETT,
LYMAN HALL,
GEO. WALTON.

Maryland
SAMUEL CHASE,
WM. PACA,
THOS. STONE,
CHARLES CARROLL.
of Carrollton.

Virginia
GEORGE WYTHE,
RICHARD HENRY LEE,
TH. JEFFERSON,
BENJA. HARRISON,
THS. NELSON, JR.,
FRANCIS LIGHTFOOT LEE,
CARTER BRAXTON.

New York
WM. FLOYD,
PHIL. LIVINGSTON,
FRANS. LEWIS,
LEWIS MORRIS.

Pennsylvania
ROBT. MORRIS,
BENJAMIN RUSH,
BENJA. FRANKLIN,
JOHN MORTON,
GEO. CLYMER,
JAS. SMITH,
GEO. TAYLOR,
JAMES WILSON,
GEO. ROSS.

Delaware
CAESAR RODNEY,
GEO. READ,
THO. M'KEAN.

North Carolina
WM. HOOPER,
JOSEPH HEWES,
JOHN PENN.

South Carolina
EDWARD RUTLEDGE,
THOS. HEYWARD, JUNR.,
THOMAS LYNCH, JUNR.,
ARTHUR MIDDLETON.

New Jersey
RICHD. STOCKTON,
JNO. WITHERSPOON,
FRAS. HOPKINSON,
JOHN HART,
ABRA. CLARK.

5.4:   A British Official Argues for Taxing Americans (1766)

The stamp tax and the other imperial measures to raise revenues in America appeared very different when viewed from the eastern side of the Atlantic. In 1766 Thomas Whately, a British treasury official, wrote Considerations on the Trade and Finances of This Kingdom, *excerpted below, to explain why both justice and necessity required the new imperial taxes and trade regulations after the end of the French and Indian War in 1763.*

Are Whately's arguments convincing? Did the Americans really bene-fit by the British military victory over France? Should the colonists have contributed more to the cost of the French and Indian War? Might there have been a better way for them to have contributed to common imperial needs than the methods the British government tried to impose?

British Policies Are Just

THOMAS WHATELY

[O]f all the Measures which were pursued for the Benefit of Trade, those were by far the most important which respected the Colonies, who have of late been the Darling Object of the Mother Country's Care: We are not yet recovered from a War undertaken solely for their Protection: Every Object for which it was begun, is accomplished; and still greater are obtained than at first were even thought of; but whatever may be the Value of the Acquisitions in *America*, the immediate Benefit of them is to the Colonies; and this Country [Britain] feels it only in their Prosperity; for though the Accessions of Trade and of Territory which were obtained by the Peace, are so many Additions to the Empire and the Commerce of *Great Britain* at large, yet they principally affect that Part of her Dominions, and that Branch of her Trade, to which they immediately relate [the American colonies]. To improve these Advantages, and to forward still further the peculiar Interests of the Colonies, was the chief Aim of the Administration in the Period now before me. . . .

Were there no other Ground to require a Revenue from the Colonies, than as a Return for these Obligations, it would alone be a sufficient Foundation: Add to these the Advantages obtained for them by the Peace; add the Debt incurred by [Britain in] a War undertaken in their Defense only; the Distress thereby brought upon the [British] Finances, upon the Credit both publick and private, upon the Trade, and upon the people of this Country; and it must be acknowledged that no Time was ever so season-

Thomas Whately, *Considerations on the Trade and Finances of This Kingdom* (London: G. Wilkie, 1766), pp. 66–72.

able for claiming their Assistance. The Distribution is too unequal, of Benefits only to the Colonies, and all the Burthens upon the Mother Country; and yet no more was desired than that they should contribute to the Preservation of the Advantages they have received, and take upon themselves a small Share of the [military] Establishment necessary for their own Protection: Upon these Principles several new Taxes were laid upon the Colonies: Many were indeed . . . rather Regulations of Trade than Funds of Revenue: But some were intended to answer both Purposes. . . .

But it was never intended to impose on them any Share of the National Debt: They were never called upon to defray any Part of our domestic civil Expenses: the Legislature [Parliament] only required of them to contribute to the Support of those Establishments, which are equally interesting to all the Subjects of *Great Britain*. The Charge of the Navy, Army, and Ordinance, of *Africa* and of *America*, is about £3,000,000 *per ann*. These, surely, are general; they are as important to the Colonies as to the Mother Country; as necessary to their Protection, as conducive to their Welfare, as to our own: If all share the Benefit, they should also share the Burthen; the whole ought not to be borne by a Part. . . .

. . . We have their All, they say; all that they can gain, all that they can raise is sent hither to purchase *British* Manufactures, and we must therefore be content to see their Demand diminish, by so much as any Revenue we require may amount to: But does their All really even center in *Great Britain?* Their illicit Trade was computed during the last Peace to be about a Third of their actual Imports; and the Money diverted from that to the Establishment is surely no national Loss. . . .

The Argument is nearly the same, it is only weaker, when instead of the Consumption of the Colonies, the Consequence of that Consumption, their Debt to this Country, is pleaded, and the new Duties are represented as depriving them of the Means of discharging it: the Complaint would be just if a Revenue had been exacted from them without furnishing of the means for raising it: But the Peace, and the measures taken since for improving the Advantages of it, have done much more: for it would be rating the Cessions made by *France* very low indeed, if the Security which is the Consequence of them; if the vast Accession of Territory; if the Intercourse [commerce] opened with the *Indians*, their greater Demand for Cloathing, Arms, Spirits, and other Commodities, and the Monopoly of their Return in Beaver, Furs, and all sorts of Peltry; if the Improvements of the Cod, Seal, and Sea-Cow Fishery, [and other major commercial gains to America derived from the victory over France and the treaty of 1763] . . . . By all these Means we have increased the Abilities of the Colonies to purchase our Manufactures, . . . and to discharge their Debts in *Great Britain*. All Objections therefore to the Taxing them, as affecting their Trade, are resolvable at last into a Complaint, that we have not done more for them. . . .

The only remaining Argument worth Notice is, that Restraints being laid upon the Trade of the Colonies, they ought therefore be exempted from contributing to the Revenue: A very general Argument indeed, equally applicable to all Times, and to all Taxes: but which would not be a just Inference even from a Supposition that they had no other Trade than to their Mother Country; and is preposterous when applied to a People whose Lands through all their various Soils and Climates are luxuriantly rich in almost all the Productions of the Earth, who besides their inexhaustible Fisheries, and besides their Intercourse with *Great Britain,* carry on a most exhaustive Traffick with the *West-Indies,* with *Africa,* and with all Parts of *Europe* to the Southward of Cape *Finisterre;* and whose Seas are from all these Causes throng'd with Ships, and their Rivers floating with Commerce. This flourishing State of their Commerce contradicts all the Complaints which have been made of the Restraints laid upon it. For such Restraints have subsisted from a very early Period, and under them that Trade has been established and enlarged, which is now pretended they oppress. . . .

If from what has been said it appears, that no Principle of Finance or of Commerce forbids the Taxing of the Colonies for the Purposes of Revenue only; it must on the other Hand be admitted that the Circumstances of this Country [Britain] call for every Aid which any of its Subjects can give: And there is a peculiar Propriety in requiring it from the *Americans,* who have contributed so little and for whom so much has been done. . . .

5.5:   A British View of "No Taxation without Representation" (1765)

Whately's argument for imperial taxes emphasized the need to share economic burdens. Other defenders of British policy took issue with the American claim that taxation without representation violated the age-old rights of English subjects. In the selection that follows Soame Jenyns, a member of Parliament, criticizes the American argument by an appeal to both history and precedent. In truth, Jenyns's facts are correct: few people in England, including most adult men, had the vote, and yet all had to submit to taxes. But was the American case different from that of the disfranchised English taxpayers? How would you have answered Jenyns?

"No Taxation without Representation" Is an Invalid Argument

SOAME JENYNS

The great capital argument, which I find on this subject, and which, like an elephant at the head of a Nabob's army, being once overthrown, must put the whole into confusion, is this: that no Englishman is, or can be taxed, but

Soame Jenyns, *The Works of Soame Jenyns,* ed. Charles N. Cole (London, n.p. 1790), vol. 2, pp. 191–94.

by his own consent: by which must be meant one of these three propositions; either that no Englishman can be taxed without his own consent as an individual; or that no Englishman can be taxed without the consent of the persons he chuses to represent him; or that no Englishman can be taxed without the consent of the majority of all those, who are elected by himself and others of his fellow-subjects to represent them. Now let us impartially consider, whether any one of these propositions are in fact true: if not, then this wonderful structure which has been erected upon them, falls at once to the ground, and like another Babel, perishes by a confusion of words, which the builders themselves are unable to understand.

First then, that no Englishman is or can be taxed but by his own consent as an individual: this is so far from being true, that it is the very reverse of truth, for no man that I know of is taxed by his own consent; and an Englishman, I believe, is as little likely to be so taxed, as any man in the world.

Secondly, that no Englishman is, or can be taxed, but by the consent of those persons, whom he has chose to represent him; for the truth of this I shall appeal only to the candid representatives of those unfortunate counties which produce cyder, and shall willingly acquiesce under their determination.

Lastly, that no Englishman is, or can be taxed, without the consent of the majority of those, who are elected by himself, and others of his fellow-subjects, to represent them. This is certainly as false as the other two; for every Englishman is taxed, and not one in twenty represented: copyholders, leaseholders, and all men possessed of personal property only, chuse no representatives: Manchester, Birmingham, and many more of our richest and most flourishing trading towns send no members to parliament, consequently cannot consent by their representatives, because they chuse none to represent them; yet are they not Englishmen? or are they not taxed?

I am well aware, that I shall hear Locke, Sidney, Seldon, and many other great names quoted, to prove that every Englishman, whether he has a right to vote for a representative or not, is still represented in the British parliament; in which opinion they all agree: on what principle of common sense this opinion is founded I comprehend not, but on the authority of such respectable names I shall acknowledge its truth; but then I will ask one question, and on that I will rest the whole merits of the cause: Why does not this imaginary representation extend to America as well as over the whole island of Great Britain? If it can travel three hundred miles, why not three thousand? if it can jump over rivers and mountains, why cannot it sail over the ocean? If the towns of Manchester and Birmingham sending no representatives to parliament, are notwithstanding there represented, why are not the cities of Albany and Boston equally represented in that assembly? Are they not alike British subjects? are they not Englishmen? or are they only Englishmen when they solicit for protection, but not Englishmen when taxes are required to enable this country to protect them? . . .

One method indeed has been hinted at, and but one, that might render the exercise of this power in a British parliament just and legal, which is the introduction of representatives from the several colonies into that body; but as this has never seriously been proposed, I shall not here consider the impracticability of this method, nor the effects of it, if it could be practiced; but only say, that I have lately seen so many specimens of the great powers of speech, of which these American gentlemen are possessed, that I should be much afraid, that the sudden importation of so much eloquence at once, would greatly endanger the safety of the government of this country; or in terms more fashionable, though less understood, this our most excellent constitution. If we can avail ourselves of these taxes on no other condition, I shall never look upon it as a measure of frugality; being perfectly satisfied, that in the end, it may be much cheaper for us to pay their army, than their orators.

5.6: American Loyalists Defend Britain (1774, 1775)

American Tories, who after 1776 preferred the name loyalists, were a large fraction of the entire population. Many belonged to certain specific categories: recent arrivals from Britain, colonial officeholders, Anglican ministers, and those who had retained close ties with the mother country, either emotional or economic.

Two of the most articulate Tories were the Anglican ministers Samuel Seabury and Jonathan Boucher, the first from New York, the second from Maryland. In the selections below they express their dismay at the defiant mood of their fellow Americans toward Parliament and the king. What are the underlying political and social assumptions shared by the two clergymen? Can you see a connection between their allegiance to the Anglican church, which in the new United States, would take the name "Episcopal," and their views of the proper relations of subject and ruler?

Anglican Ministers Defend Britain's Position

SAMUEL SEABURY AND JONATHAN BOUCHER

Samuel Seabury

In every government there must be a supreme, absolute authority lodged somewhere. In arbitrary governments this power is in the monarch; in aristo-

---

Samuel Seabury, *A View of the Controversy between Great Britain and Her Colonies* (New York, n.p. 1774), p. 6.

cratical governments, in the nobles; in democratical in the people; or the deputies of their electing. . . .

Upon supposition that every English colony enjoyed a legislative power independent of the parliament; and that the parliament has no just authority to make laws to bind them, this absurdity will follow—that there is no power in the British empire, which has authority to make laws for the whole empire; i. e. we have an empire, without government; or which amounts to the same thing, we have a government which has no supreme power. All our colonies are independent of each other: Suppose them independent of the British parliament,—what power do you leave to govern the whole? None at all. You split and divide the empire into a number of petty, insignificant states. This is the direct, the necessary tendency of refusing submission to acts of parliament. Every man who can see one inch beyond his nose, must see this consequence. And every man who endeavors to accelerate the independency of the colonies on the British parliament, endeavors to accelerate the ruin of the British empire.

To talk of being liege subjects to King George, while we disavow the authority of parliament is another piece of whiggish nonsense. I love my King as well as any whig in America or England either, and am as ready to yield him all lawful submission: But while I submit to the King, I submit to the authority of the laws of the state, whose guardian the King is. The difference between a good and a bad subject, is only this, that the one obeys, the other transgresses the law. The difference between a loyal subject and a rebel, is, that the one yields obedience to, and faithfully supports the supreme authority of the state, and the other endeavours to overthrow it. If we obey the laws of the King, we obey the laws of the parliament. If we disown the authority of the parliament, we disown the authority of the King. There is no medium without ascribing powers to the King which the constitution know nothing of:—without making him superior to the laws, and setting him above all restraint. These are some of the ridiculous absurdities of American whiggism. . . .

I will here, Sir, venture to deliver my sentiments upon the line that ought to be drawn between the supremacy of Great-Britain, and the dependency of the colonies. And I shall do it with the more boldness, because, I know it to be agreeable to the opinions of many of the warmest advocates for America, both in England and in the colonies, in the time of the stamp-act.—I imagine that if all internal taxation be vested in our own legislatures, and the right of regulating trade by duties, bounties, etc. be left in the power of the Parliament; and also the right of enacting all general laws for the good of all the colonies, that we shall have all the security for our rights, liberties and property, which human policy can give us: The dependence of the colonies on the mother country will be fixed on a firm foundation; the sovereign authority of Parliament, over all the dominions of the empire will be established, and the mother-country and all her colonies will be knit together, in one GRAND, FIRM, AND COMPACT BODY.

Jonathan Boucher

It can, I think, admit of no dispute, that an accommodation between the Colonies and the Mother Country, on almost any terms, is infinitely more to be desired by both countries than even the most signal successes in war. In the latter way, to succeed is to become a separate people; not as Abram and Lot became a separate people, whilst yet they continued to be friends; but having no longer any community either of interest or affection, as perfect aliens to each other, and, in short, as totally distinct and separate nations. There seems no possibility of any middle course. . . .

Were the question to be determined by present expediency, it is possible the arguments in favour of a separation might be found to be the strongest. But, as such a separation would be a new thing in the world, . . . and as also there are in this vast continent many thousands of respectable men, who, considering allegiance [to the British crown] as a duty, find it impossible to bring themselves to retain or relinquish it just as a mere convenience may seem to suggest, we hope at least to be permitted to pause before we determine.

There is an objection of no ordinary magnitude at the very threshold of this novel proposal. It has never been proved, nor, in my humble opinion, can it ever be proved, that the Parent State can do what is asked; that is to say, can, without a breach of the Constitution, voluntarily withdraw or forbear it's [*sic*] government over America. Allegiance and protection are not merely reciprocal duties, entirely dependent the one on the other. Each duty continues to be equally obligatory, and in force, whether the other be performed or not. . . .

The only rational idea of civil liberty, or (which is the same thing) of a legitimate and good government . . . is, when the great body of the people are trained and led habitually to submit to and acquiesce in some fixed and steady principles of conduct. It is essential, moreover, to Liberty, that such principles shall be of power sufficient to controul the arbitrary and capricious wills of mankind; which, whenever they are not so controuled, are found to be dangerous and destructive to the best interests of society. The primary aim, therefore, of all well-framed Constitutions is, to place man, as it were, out of the reach of his own power, and also out of the power of others as weak as himself, by placing him under the power of law. To counteract that aim (and to do so is the object of all self-constituted assemblies) is to carry back social man to his supposed original independence, and to throw him once more into what has been called a state of Nature. In our own case, it is violently pulling down an old, well-poised Constitution, arbitrarily to introduce, in its stead, what, if it be no anarchy, must at best be a democracy. Now, it ought never to be out of the recollection of mankind, that democra-

Jonathan Boucher, *A View of the Causes and Consequences of the American Revolution* (London, n.p. 1797), p. 16.

cies, even when established without either tumult or tyranny, and by the very general though perhaps not unanimous consent of the community, not contended with an equality of rights, in theory at least, naturally aim at an equality of possessions. . . .

This popular notion, that government was originally formed by the consent or by a compact of the people, rests on, and is supported by, another similar notion, not less popular, nor better founded. This other notion is, that the whole human race is born equal; and that no man is naturally inferior or or, an any respect, subjected to another; and that he can be made subject to another only by his own consent. . . . Man differs from man in every thing that can be supposed to lead to supremacy and subjection, *as one star differs from another star in glory.* . . . A musical instrument composed of chords, keys, or pipes, all perfectly equal in size and power, might as well be expected to produce harmony, as a society composed of members all perfectly equal to be productive of harmony and peace. If (according to the idea of the advocates of this chimerical scheme of equality) no man could rightfully *be compelled to come in* and be a member even of a government to be formed by a regular compact, but by his own individual consent; it clearly follows, from the same principles, that neither could he rightfully be made or compelled to submit to the ordinances of any government already formed, to which he has not individually or actually consented. On the principle of equality, neither his parents, nor even the vote of a majority of the society . . . can have any such authority over any man. . . . The same principle of equality that exempts him from being governed without his own consent, clearly entitles him to recall and resume that consent whenever he sees fit; and he alone has a right to judge when and for what reasons it may be resumed.

All government, whether lodged in one or in many, is, in its nature, absolute and irresistible. . . . Without some paramount and irresistible power, there can be no government. In our Constitution, this supremacy is vested in the King and the Parliament; and, subordinate to them, in our Provincial Legislatures. If you were now released from this constitutional power, you must differ from all others "of the human race," if you did not soon find yourselves under a necessity of submitting to a power no less absolute, though vested in other persons, and a government differently constituted.

6

The Constitution

We who live under the federal Constitution seldom question its wisdom and effectiveness. But its creation and adoption in 1787–88 provoked major battles among Americans. To some it seemed imprudent and unnecessary; the loose confederation of near sovereign states established by the Articles of Confederation during the Revolution was good enough. A stronger central government, such people worried, might tyrannize the states and the people themselves.

Supporters of the new frame of government, on the other hand—the "federalists"[1]—believed it essential to remedy American weakness at home and abroad. The new United States, they insisted, was in danger of becoming a collection of squabbling, petty states, a laughingstock among nations, unable to protect its sovereignty or further its people's interests and prosperity.

The delegates to the Constitutional Convention that met in Philadelphia during the summer of 1787 required that the system they created be submitted to the states. The state governments in turn, they assumed, would submit it to special state ratifying conventions. When nine of these had ratified, the Constitution would become operative. It was during the ratification process from late September 1787 to mid-summer 1788 that the public debate over adoption raged most vociferously.

Pro- or antiratification opinion was not distributed at random. Nor was it solely a matter of individual temperament, although personal attitudes toward freedom versus authority obviously played a part in determining people's positions. Citizens saw advantages or disadvantages for themselves or their group in the new Constitution however they defined

[1]"Federalist" at this point meant a supporter of the Constitution. By the mid-1790s it had come to mean a supporter of a new political party that was opposed to the Jeffersonian Republicans.

these benefits or drawbacks. Compared to the existing Confederation, a new, stronger central government promised to be more solvent, to be more effective internationally, to exert greater power over the economy, and to be more forceful in preventing threats to social order. Inevitably, expanded influence for the central government seemed likely to confer gains on some, losses on others.

There was also the matter of national pride. Thousands who had fought and sacrificed for independence had a stake in a government that could effectively express collective American aspirations, a role that the government of the Articles of Confederation seemed unable to play.

On the other hand, many Americans had no sense of national solidarity. Their chief loyalty was to their local communities, especially to their states. These, not some abstract entity controlled by a remote authority in some national capital, were their "countries." They also feared the effects of a strong central government on freedom. As originally composed, the Constitution had no guarantees of citizens' rights against the new federal government. Critics thought it might well become an instrument of tyranny.

See if you can detect the primary motivation of the writers in the selections that follow. What lay behind their arguments for or against the Constitution?

6.1: Patrick Henry Denounces the Constitution (1788)

By the time the Virginia convention came to debate the adoption of the Constitution on June 2, 1788, most of the nine states needed to put the document into effect had already ratified it. Still, the formation of a national government without Virginia was unthinkable: it was the largest state, and its leaders had been at the forefront of the patriot cause.

One of the most formidable opponents of the Constitution in Virginia was the patriot firebrand Patrick Henry. In a speech to the state ratification convention, Henry drew a dramatic contrast between power and liberty: government could either exercise power effectively or protect individual freedom; it could not do both. Was he right? Does a strong government inevitably endanger liberty? Is the preservation of liberty the most important goal of government? Did the consolidated government Henry feared actually trample on rights? on states' rights? on individual rights? What revisions of the original document may have reduced fears of federal power over individuals?

Interestingly, in the 1790s, possibly out of admiration for the

Federalist president George Washington, Henry became a member of the political party that favored expanding the new Constitution to maximize the power and authority of the government it had created.

Virginia Should Reject the Constitution

PATRICK HENRY

Mr. Chairman, the public mind, as well as my own, is extremely uneasy at the proposed change of government. Give me leave to form one of the number of those who wish to be thoroughly acquainted with the reasons of this perilous and uneasy situation, and why we are brought hither to decide on this great national question. I consider myself as the servant of the people of this commonwealth, as a sentinel over their rights, liberty, and happiness. I represent their feelings when I say that they are exceedingly uneasy at being brought from that state of full security, which they enjoyed, to the present delusive appearance of things. A year ago, the minds of our citizens were at perfect repose. Before the meeting of the late federal Convention at Philadelphia, a general peace and a universal tranquillity prevailed in this country; but, since that period, they are exceedingly uneasy and disquieted. When I wished for an appointment to this Convention, my mind was extremely agitated for the situation of public affairs. I conceived the republic to be in extreme danger. If our situation be thus uneasy, whence has arisen this fearful jeopardy? It arises from this fatal system; it arises from a proposal to change our government—a proposal that goes to the utter annihilation of the most solemn engagements of the states. . . .

. . . Make the best of this new government—say it is composed by any thing but inspiration—you ought to be extremely cautious, watchful, jealous of your liberty; for, instead of securing your rights, you may lose them forever. If a wrong step be now made, the republic may be lost forever. If this new government will not come up to the expectation of the people, and they shall be disappointed, their liberty will be lost, and tyranny must and will arise. I repeat it again, and I beg gentlemen to consider, that a wrong step, made now, will plunge us into misery, and our republic will be lost. It will be necessary for this Convention to have a faithful historical detail of the facts that preceded the session of the federal Convention, and the reasons that actuated its members in proposing an entire alteration of government, and to demonstrate the dangers that awaited us. If they were of such awful magnitude as to warrant a proposal so extremely perilous as this, I must assert, that this Convention has an absolute right to a thorough discovery of every circumstance relative to this great event. And here I would make this inquiry of those worthy characters who composed a part of the late federal

Jonathan Elliot, ed., *The Debates in the Several State Conventions on the Adoption of the Federal Constitution* (Washington, DC: J. Elliot, 1840), vol. 3, pp. 21–22, 44–46, 58–60, 65–66.

Convention. I am sure they were fully impressed with the necessity of forming a great consolidated government, instead of a confederation. That this is
a consolidated government is demonstrably clear; and the danger of such a
government is, to my mind, very striking. I have the highest veneration for
those gentlemen; but, sir, give me leave to demand, What right had they to
say, *We, the people?* My political curiosity, exclusive of my anxious solicitude
for the public welfare, leads me to ask: Who authorized them to speak the
language of, *We, the people,* instead of, *We, the states?* States are the characteristics and the soul of confederation. If the states be not the agents of this compact, it must be one great, consolidated, national government, of the people
of all the states. . . .

. . . Here is a resolution as radical as that which separated us from Great
Britain. It is radical in this transition; our rights and privileges are endangered, and the sovereignty of the states will be relinquished: and cannot we
plainly see that this is actually the case? The rights of conscience, trial by
jury, liberty of the press, all your immunities and franchises, all pretensions
to human rights and privileges, are rendered insecure, if not lost, by this
change, so loudly talked of by some, and inconsiderately by others. Is this
tame relinquishment of rights worthy of freemen? Is it worthy of that manly
fortitude that ought to characterize republicans? It is said eight states have
adopted this plan. I declare that if twelve states and a half had adopted it, I
would, with manly firmness, and in spite of an erring world, reject it. You are
not to inquire how your trade may be increased, nor how you are to become
a great and powerful people, but how your liberties can be secured; for liberty ought to be the direct end of your government. . . .

. . . We are come hither to preserve the poor commonwealth of Virginia,
if it can be possibly done: something must be done to preserve your liberty
and mine. The Confederation, this same despised government, merits, in my
opinion, the highest encomium: it carried us through a long and dangerous
war; it rendered us victorious in that bloody conflict with a powerful nation;
it has secured us a territory greater than any European monarch possesses:
and shall a government which has been thus strong and vigorous, be
accused of imbecility, and abandoned for want of energy? Consider what you
are about to do before you part with the government. Take longer time in
reckoning things; revolutions like this have happened in almost every country in Europe; similar examples are to be found in ancient Greece and
ancient Rome—instances of the people losing their liberty by their own care-
lessness and the ambition of a few. We are cautioned by the honorable gentleman, who presides, against faction and turbulence. I acknowledge that
licentiousness is dangerous, and that it ought to be provided against: I
acknowledge, also, the new form of government may effectually prevent it:
yet there is another thing it will as effectually do—it will oppress and ruin
the people. . . .

. . . An opinion has gone forth, we find, that we are contemptible people:
the time has been when we were thought otherwise. Under the same

despised government, we commanded the respect of all Europe: wherefore are we now reckoned otherwise? The American spirit has fled from hence: it has gone to regions where it has never been expected; it has gone to the people of France, in search of a splendid government—a strong, energetic government. Shall we imitate the example of those nations who have gone from a simple to a splendid government? Are those nations more worthy of our imitation? What can make an adequate satisfaction to them for the loss they have suffered in attaining such a government—for the loss of their liberty? If we admit this consolidated government, it will be because we like a great, splendid one. Some way or other we must be a great and mighty empire; we must have an army, and a navy, and a number of things. When the American spirit was in its youth, the language of America was different: liberty, sir, was then the primary object. We are descended from a people whose government was founded on liberty: our glorious forefathers of Great Britain made liberty the foundation of every thing. That country is become a great, mighty, and splendid nation; not because their government is strong and energetic, but, sir, because liberty is its direct end and foundation. We drew the spirit of liberty from our British ancestors: by that spirit we have triumphed over every difficulty. But now, sir, the American spirit, assisted by the ropes and chains of consolidation, is about to convert this country into a powerful and mighty empire. If you make the citizens of this country agree to become the subjects of one great consolidated empire of America, your government will not have sufficient energy to keep them together. Such a government is incompatible with the genius of republicanism. There will be no checks, no real balances, in this government. What can avail your specious, imaginary balances, your rope-dancing, chain-rattling, ridiculous ideal checks and contrivances? But, sir, we are not feared by foreigners; we do not make nations tremble. Would this constitute happiness, or secure liberty? I trust, sir, our political hemisphere will ever direct their operations to the security of those objects.

Consider our situation, sir: go to the poor man, and ask him what he does. He will inform you that he enjoys the fruits of his labor, under his own fig-tree, with his wife and children around him, in peace and security. Go to every other member of society,—you will find the same tranquil ease and content; you will find no alarms or disturbances. Why, then, tell us of danger, to terrify us into an adoption of this new form of government? And yet who knows the dangers that this new system may produce? They are out of the sight of the common people: they cannot foresee latent consequences. I dread the operation of it on the middling and lower classes of people: it is for them I fear the adoption of this system. I fear I tire the patience of the committee; but I beg to be indulged with a few more observations. When I thus profess myself an advocate for the liberty of the people, I shall be told I am a designing man, that I am to be a great man, that I am to be a demagogue; and many similar illiberal insinuations will be thrown out: but, sir, conscious rectitude outweighs those things with me. I see great jeopardy in this new government. I see none from our present one. . . .

This Constitution is said to have beautiful features; but when I come to examine these features, sir, they appear to me horribly frightful. Among other deformities, it has an awful squinting; it squints towards monarchy; and does not this raise indignation in the breast of every true American?

Your President may easily become king. Your Senate is so imperfectly constructed that your dearest rights may be sacrificed by what may be a small minority; and a very small minority may continue forever unchangeably this government, although horridly defective. Where are your checks in this government? Your strongholds will be in the hands of your enemies. It is on a supposition that your American governors shall be honest, that all the good qualities of this government are founded, but its defective and imperfect construction puts it in their power to perpetrate the worst of mischiefs, should they be bad men; and, sir, would not all the world, from the eastern to the western hemisphere, blame our distracted folly in resting our rights upon the contingency of our rulers being good or bad? Show me that age and country where the rights and liberties of the people were placed on the sole chance of their rulers being good men, without a consequent loss of liberty! I say that the loss of that dearest privilege has ever followed, with absolute certainty, every such mad attempt.

If your American chief be a man of ambition and abilities, how easy is it for him to render himself absolute! The army is in his hands, and if he be a man of address, it will be attached to him, and it will be the subject of long meditation with him to seize the first auspicious moment to accomplish his design; and sir, will the American spirit solely relieve you when this happens? I would rather infinitely—and I am sure most of this Convention are of the same opinion—have a king, lords, and commons, than a government so replete with such insupportable evils. If we make a king, we may prescribe the rules by which he shall rule his people, and interpose such checks as shall prevent him from infringing them; but the President, in the field, at the head of his army, can prescribe the terms on which he shall reign master, so far that it will puzzle any American ever to get his neck from under the galling yoke. I cannot with patience think of this idea. If ever he violates the laws, one of two things will happen: he will come at the head of his army, to carry every thing before him; or he will give bail, or do what Mr. Chief Justice will order him. If he be guilty, will not the recollection of his crimes teach him to make one bold push for the American throne? Will not the immense difference between being master of every thing, and being ignominiously tried and punished, powerfully excite him to make this bold push? But, sir, where is the existing force to punish him? Can he not, at the head of his army, beat down every opposition? Away with your President! we shall have a king: the army will salute him monarch: your militia will leave you, and assist in making him king, and fight against you: and what have you to oppose this force? What will then become of you and your rights? Will not absolute despotism ensue? . . .

I beg pardon of this house for having taken up more time than came to my share, and I thank them for the patience and polite attention with which I have been heard. If I shall be in the minority, I shall have those painful sensations which arise from a conviction of *being overpowered in a good cause.* Yet I will be a peaceable citizen. My head, my hand, and my heart, shall be at liberty to retrieve the loss of liberty, and remove the defects of that system in a constitutional way. I wish not to go to violence, but will wait with hopes that the spirit which predominated in the revolution is not yet gone, nor the cause of those who are attached to the revolution yet lost. I shall therefore patiently wait in expectation of seeing that government changed, so as to be compatible with the safety, liberty, and happiness, of the people.

6.2:   The Constitution as a Usurpation (1787)

Richard Henry Lee was another Virginian who opposed the Constitution. He and Patrick Henry had been closely allied in the struggle against Great Britain and continued to be allies in the fight to derail the Constitution. In the following essay, the first of his anti-Constitution series collected as Letters of the Federal Farmer, *Lee attacks both the motives and the methods of his opponents.*

What does he mean by "aristocratical men"? Who, for example, might be included in that group? Did the craftsmen, small shopkeepers, and "mechanics" of the cities vote for pro-Constitution delegates to the states' adoption conventions?

The Constitution Will Encourage Aristocracy

RICHARD HENRY LEE

The present moment discovers a new face in our affairs. Our object has been all along to reform our federal system, and to strengthen our governments—to establish peace, order, and justice in the community—but a new object now presents. The plan of government now proposed is evidently calculated totally to change, in time, our condition as a people. Instead of being thirteen republics, under a federal head, it is clearly designed to make us one consolidated government. Of this, I think, I shall fully convince you in my following letters on this subject. This consolidation of the states has been the object of several men in this country for some time past. Whether such a change can ever be effected, in any manner; whether it can be effected with-

Richard Henry Lee, *Letters of the Federal Farmer to a Republican, October 8, 1787,* (New York: Thomas Greenleaf, 1787), pp. 6–8.

out convulsions and civil wars; whether such a change will not totally destroy the liberties of this country—time only can determine.

To have a just idea of the government before us, and to show that a consolidated one is the object in view, it is necessary not only to examine the plan, but also its history, and the politics of its particular friends.

The Confederation was formed when great confidence was placed in the voluntary exertions of individuals, and of the respective states; and the framers of it, to guard against usurpation, so limited and checked the powers that, in many respects they are inadequate to the exigencies of the union. We find, therefore, members of Congress urging alterations in the federal system almost as soon as it was adopted. It was early proposed to vest Congress with powers to levy an impost, to regulate trade, &c., but such was that known to be the caution of the states in parting with power, the vestment even of these was proposed to be under several checks and limitations. During the war the general confusion and the introduction of paper money infused in the minds of people vague ideas respecting government and credit. We expected too much from the return of peace, and of course we have been disappointed. Our governments have been new and unsettled; and several legislatures, by making tender, suspension, and paper money laws, have given just cause of uneasiness to creditors. By these and other causes, several orders of men in the community have been prepared, by degrees, for a change of government; and this very abuse of power in the legislatures, which in some cases has been charged upon the democratic part of the community, has furnished aristocratical men with those very weapons, and those very means, with which in great measure they are rapidly effecting their favorite object. And should an oppressive government be the consequence of the proposed change, [posterity] may reproach not only a few overbearing, unprincipled men, but those parties in the states which have misused their powers.

The conduct of several legislatures, touching paper money and tender laws, has prepared many honest men for changes in government which otherwise they would not have thought of—when by the evils, on the one hand, and by the secret instigations of artful men, on the other, the minds of men were become sufficiently uneasy, a bold step was taken which is usually followed by a revolution or a civil war. A general convention for mere commercial purposes was moved for—the authors of this measure saw that the people's attention was turned solely to the amendment of the federal system; and that, had the idea of a total change been started, probably no state would have appointed members to the convention. The idea of destroying ultimately the state government and forming one consolidated system could not have been admitted. A convention, therefore, merely for vesting in Congress power to regulate trade was proposed. This was pleasing to the commercial towns, and the landed people had little or no concern about it. September, 1786, a few men from the middle states met at Annapolis and hastily proposed a convention to be held in May, 1787, for the purpose, generally, of amending the Confederation. This was done before the delegates of Massachusetts and of the other states arrived. Still not a word was said about destroying the old constitution and making a new one. The states still unsuspecting and not aware that they were passing the Rubicon, appointed members to the new convention, for the sole and express purpose of revising and amending the Confederation—and, probably not one man in ten thousand in the United States till within these ten or twelve days, had an idea that the old ship was to be destroyed, and he put to the alternative of embarking in the new ship presented, or of being left in danger of sinking. The States, I believe, universally supposed the convention would report alterations in the Confederation which would pass an examination in Congress, and after being agreed to there, would be confirmed by all the legislatures, or be rejected.

Virginia made a very respectable appointment and placed at the head of it the first man in America. In this appointment there was a mixture of political characters; but Pennsylvania appointed principally those men who are esteemed aristocratical. Here the favorite moment for changing the government was evidently discerned by a few men, who seized it with address. Ten other states appointed, and tho' they chose men principally connected with commerce and the judicial department, yet they appointed many good republican characters—had they all attended we should now see, I am persuaded, a better system presented. The nonattendance of eight or nine men who were appointed members of the convention, I shall ever consider as a very unfortunate event to the United States. Had they attended, I am pretty clear that the result of the convention would not have had that strong tendency to aristocracy now discernible in every part of the plan. There would not have been so great an accumulation of powers, especially as to the internal police of this country, in a few hands as the constitution reported proposes to vest in them—the young visionary men and the consolidating aristocracy would have been more restrained than they have been. Eleven states met in the convention and after four months close attention presented the new constitution, to be adopted or rejected by the people. The uneasy and fickle part of the community may be prepared to receive any form of government; but I presume the enlightened and substantial part will give any constitution presented for their adoption a candid and thorough examination; and silence those designing or empty men who weakly and rashly attempt to precipitate the adoption of a system of so much importance. We shall view the convention with proper respect—and, at the same time that we reflect there were men of abilities and integrity in it, we must recollect how disproportionately the democratic and aristocratic parts of the community were represented. Perhaps the judicious friends and opposers of the new constitution will agree that it is best to let it rely solely on its own merits, or be condemned for its own defects.

6.3:   "The Father of the Constitution" Defends His Offspring (1788)

*If any one person was the guiding hand behind the Philadelphia deliber-
ations that shaped the Constitution, it was James Madison of Virginia.
In June 1788, Madison was called on to defend his handiwork in the
Virginia adoption convention against the attack of Patrick Henry and
others.*

*In the section of Madison's defense excerpted below, he responds to
Henry's attacks on the taxing powers conferred on the proposed new government. He reviews the severe handicaps the Articles of Confederation
imposed on the ability of the general government to pay its bills. He also
describes the financial and economic plight of the nation under the
Confederation, as perceived by a nationalist.*

*In what ways, according to Madison, did the weak revenue-raising
power of the Confederation government hurt the American nation? Do
you see any connection between the antifederalists' fears of the taxing
power of the new general government and the opposition to Britain after
1763? Was the conferring of greater taxing power on the new federal
government in some ways a retreat from the "Spirit of '76"?*

The Constitution Should be Ratified

JAMES MADISON

Mr. Chairman, in considering this great subject, I trust we shall find that
part which gives the general government the power of laying and collecting
taxes indispensable, and essential to the existence of any efficient or well-
organized system of government: if we consult reason, and be ruled by its
dictates, we shall find its justification there: if we review the experience we
have had, or contemplate the history of nations, here we find ample reasons
to prove its expediency. There is little reason to depend for necessary supplies on a body which is fully possessed of the power of withholding them. If
a government depends on other governments for its revenues—if it must
depend on the voluntary contributions of its members—its existence must
be precarious. A government which relies on thirteen independent sover-
eignties for the means of its existence, is a solecism in theory and a mere
nullity in practice. Is it consistent with reason that such a government can
promote the happiness of any people? It is subversive of every principle of
sound policy, to trust the safety of a community with a government totally

Jonathan Elliot, ed., *The Debates in the Several State Conventions on the Adoption of the Federal
Constitution* (Washington, DC: J. Elliot, 1840), vol. 3, pp. 128–29, 135–36, 147–49.

destitute of the means of protecting itself or its members. Can Congress, after the repeated unequivocal proofs it has experienced of the utter inutili- ty and inefficacy of requisitions, reasonably expect that they would be here- after effectual or productive? Will not the same local interests, and other causes, militate against a compliance? Whoever hopes the contrary must ever be disappointed. The effect, sir, cannot be changed without a removal of the cause. Let each county in this commonwealth be supposed free and inde- pendent; let your revenues depend on requisitions of proportionate quotas from them; let application be made to them repeatedly:—is it to be pre- sumed that they would comply, or that an adequate collection could be made from partial compliances? It is now difficult to collect taxes from them: how much would that difficulty be enhanced, were you to depend solely on their generosity! I appeal to the reason of every gentleman here, whether he is not persuaded that the present Confederation is as feeble as the government of Virginia would be in that case: to the same reason I appeal, whether it be compatible with prudence to continue a government of such manifest and palpable debility. . . .

I agree with the honorable gentleman (Mr. Henry) that national splendor and glory are not our objects; but does he distinguish between what will ren- der us secure and happy at home, and what will render us respectable abroad? If we be free and happy at home, we shall be respectable abroad.

The Confederation is so notoriously feeble, that foreign nations are unwilling to form any treaties with us; they are apprized that our general government cannot perform any of its engagements, but that they may be violated at pleasure by any of the states. Our violation of treaties already entered into proves this truth unequivocally. No nation will, therefore, make any stipulations with Congress, conceding any advantages of importance to us: they will be the more averse to entering into engagements with us, as the imbecility of our government enables them to derive many advantages from our trade, without granting us any return. But were this country united by proper bands, in addition to other great advantages, we could form very ben- eficial treaties with foreign states. But this can never happen without a change in our system. Were we not laughed at by the minister of that nation, from which we may be able yet to extort some of the most salutary measures for this country? Were we not told that it was necessary to temporize till our government acquired consistency? Will any nation relinquish national advantages to us? You will be greatly disappointed, if you expect any such good effects from this contemptible system. Let us recollect our conduct to that country from which we have received the most friendly aid [France]. How have we dealt with that benevolent ally? Have we complied with our most sacred obligations to that nation? Have we paid the interest punctually from year to year? Is not the interest accumulating, while not a shilling is dis- charged of the principal? The magnanimity and forbearance of that ally are so great that she has not called upon us for her claims, even in her own distress and necessity. This, sir, is an additional motive to increase our exertions. At this moment of time a very considerable amount is due from us to that country and others.

[Here Mr. Madison mentioned the amount of the debts due to different foreign nations.]

We have been obliged to borrow money even to pay the interests of our debts. This is a ruinous and most disgraceful expedient. Is this a situation on which America can rely for security and happiness? How are we to extricate ourselves? The honorable member told us we might rely on the punctuality and friendship of the states, and that they will discharge their quotas for the future. The contributions of the states have been found inadequate from the beginning, and are diminishing instead of increasing. From the month of June, 1787, till June, 1788, they have only paid 276,641 dollars into the federal treasury for the purposes of supporting the national government, and discharging the interest of the national debts—a sum so very insufficient, that it must greatly alarm the friends of their country. Suggestions and strong assertions dissipate before these facts. I shall no longer fatigue the committee at this time, but will resume the subject as early as I can.

6.4:   Alexander Hamilton on Pro- and Anti-Constitution Forces (1787)

Alexander Hamilton was a New York delegate to the Constitutional Convention. An intense nationalist, he had condemned the document that emerged from the deliberations at Philadelphia as too weak, too tilted toward local rights. Despite such misgivings, however, he much preferred it to the Articles of Confederation, and fought hard for its adoption by his state. Together with James Madison and John Jay, Hamilton authored a set of brilliant newspaper articles designed to convince New Yorkers of the wisdom of adopting the new frame of government. These became the famous Federalist Papers, *one of the best commentaries on the Constitution to this day. Hamilton also participated in the actual New York convention debates.*

The following brief selection is a frank, private memo that Hamilton composed soon after the Philadelphia convention had adjourned that summarizes what he anticipated would be the alignment of pro- and anti-Constitution sentiment in the country. Are Hamilton's remarks biased? What is he referring to when he speaks of "the depredations which the democratic spirit is apt to make on property"? Who are the "Creditors of the United States" he mentions, and why are they supposedly interested in a stronger national government?

Conjectures about the New Constitution

ALEXANDER HAMILTON

The new constitution has in favour of its success these circumstances—a very great weight of influence of the persons who framed it, particularly in the universal popularity of General Washington—the good will of the commercial interest throughout the states which will give all its efforts to the establishment of a government capable of regulating protecting and extending the commerce of the Union—the good will of most men of property in the several states who wish a government of the union able to protect them against domestic violence and the depredations which the democratic spirit is apt to make on property; and who are besides anxious for the respectability of the nation—the hopes of the Creditors of the United States that a general government possessing the means of doing it will pay the debt of the Union—a strong belief in the people at large of the insufficiency of the present confederation to preserve the existence of the Union and of the necessity of the union to their safety and prosperity; of course a strong desire of a change and a predisposition to receive well the propositions of the Convention.

Against its success is to be put the dissent of two or three important men in the Convention; who will think their characters pleged to defeat the plan—the influence of many *inconsiderable* men in possession of considerable offices under the state governments who will fear a diminution of their consequence, power and emolument by the establishment of the general government and who can hope for nothing there—the influence of some *considerable* men in office possessed of talents and popularity who partly from the same motives and partly from a desire of *playing a part* in a convulsion for their own aggrandisement will oppose the quiet adoption of the new government—(some considerable men out of office, from motives of (am)bition may be disposed to act the same part)—add (to) these causes the disinclination of the people to taxes, and of course to a strong government—the opposition of all men much in debt who will not wish to see a government established one object of which is to restrain the means of cheating Creditors—the democratical jealousy of the people which may be alarmed at the appearance of institutions that may seem calculated to place the power of the community in few hands and to raise a few individuals to stations of great preeminence—and the influence of some foreign powers who from different motives will not wish to see an energetic government established throughout the states.

In this view of the subject it is difficult to form any judgment whether the plan will be adopted or rejected. It must be essentially [a] matter of conjec-

Alexander Hamilton, "Conjectures about the New Constitution," *The Papers of Alexander Hamilton*, ed. Harold Syrett (New York: Columbia University Press, 1962), vol. 4, pp. 275–77. © Columbia University Press, New York. Reprinted with the permission of the publisher.

ture. The present appearances and all other circumstances considered the probability seems to be on the side of its adoption.

But the causes operating against its adoption are powerful and there will be nothing astonishing in the Contrary.

If it do not finally obtain, it is probable the discussion of the question will beget such struggles animosities and heats in the community that this circumstance conspiring with the *real necessity* of an essential change in our present situation will produce civil war. Should this happen, whatever parties prevail it is probable governments very different from the present in their principles will be established. A dismemberment of the Union and monarchies in different portions of it may be expected. It may however happen that no civil war will take place; but several republican confederacies be established between different combinations of the particular states.

A reunion with Great Britain, from universal disgust at a state of commotion, is not impossible, though not much to be feared. The most plausible shape of such a business would be the establishment of a son of the present monarch in the supreme government of this country with a family compact.

If the government be adopted, it is probable general Washington will be the President of the United States. This will insure a wise choice of men to administer the government and a good administration. A good administration will conciliate the confidence and affection of the people and perhaps enable the government to acquire more consistency than the proposed constitution seems to promise for so great a Country. It may then triumph altogether over the state governments and reduce them to an intire subordination, dividing the larger states into smaller districts. The *organs* of the general government may also acquire additional strength.

If this should not be the case, in the course of a few years, it is probable that the contests about the boundaries of power between the particular governments and the general government and the *momentum* of the larger states in such contests will produce a dissolution of the Union. This after all seems to be the most likely result.

But it is almost arrogance in so complicated a subject, depending so intirely on the incalculable fluctuations of the human passions, to attempt even a conjecture about the event.

It will be Eight or Nine months before any certain judgment can be formed respecting the adoption of the Plan.

7

Federalist versus Republican

The founders of the United States planned well for a new national government, but they left out one vital piece: political parties. In every modern democracy voters with similar social, economic, political, ideological, and cultural views have combined into parties to win elections and enact programs that reflect their ideals and interests.

Yet the early leaders of the American republic deplored parties as divisive and likely to be corrupt and self-serving. They made no provision for them in their new frame of government. But parties soon appeared. They coalesced around a cluster of issues, domestic and foreign, that would divide the young nation.

At home the most urgent concerns of the new government led by President George Washington were the financial problems that had beset its predecessor: the lack of revenue, the unpaid government debts, the disarray in the nation's currency, and America's financial reputation abroad. The man Washington placed in charge of the nation's finances was Alexander Hamilton, the New York lawyer who had helped get the Constitution adopted in his home state, even though it was too weak for his tastes. As secretary of the Treasury, Hamilton would push a program of federal taxes, debt refunding, a protective tariff, and a national bank designed to transform the economic base of American society.

The new republic was also forced to reorder its relations with other nations. The United States faced problems with Spain over the navigation of the Mississippi and with Britain over Indian relations, unpaid debts, exclusion of Americans from traditional trade routes, and continued military occupation of American territory in the West.

Even more tangled were America's associations with France, which after 1789 experienced the shattering political, social, and ideological upheaval known as the French Revolution. Franco-American relations would become particularly nettlesome when France, under its revolutionary leaders, went to war with Austria, Prussia, and England in 1792–93 and sought to involve the United States on its side. In charge of the Washington administration's foreign policy was Secretary of State Thomas Jefferson, the chief author of the Declaration of Independence. Jefferson would take a pro-French, anti-British position, although he would refuse to sacrifice American interests for the sake of the French republic.

Fierce partisan differences over finance and foreign policy would become the bases for the first American political parties. Behind these policy differences would be philosophical differences over human nature and ideological disagreements over the best form of government. Hamilton and Jefferson would become the leaders of the two political organizations, the Federalists and Republicans,[1] respectively.

In the selections that follow, you should look beyond the disagreements over specific policies and programs to underlying conflicts of interest or ideology. What major economic changes in America did the successful enactment of Hamilton's program imply? What alternative did the Jeffersonian Republicans represent? Who stood to gain from Hamilton's financial and economic program? Who stood to lose? Why did some Americans favor France over Britain and vice versa?

[1]These Republicans should not be confused with the supporters of the Republican Party organized in the 1850s to oppose the spread of slavery. It is this later party that is the ancestor of the Republicans of today.

7.1:   Alexander Hamilton's Economic Reports (1790–91)

In 1790–91 Secretary of Treasury Alexander Hamilton, at Congress's bidding, prepared a series of reports recommending legislation to deal with pressing national economic issues. There were three major reports, two of which (excerpted here), the "First and Second Reports on Public Credit,"[1] formed the bases for immediate path-breaking legislation: the Funding Act of 1790 and the act establishing the Bank of the United States. A third, the Report on Manufactures, *did not produce a quick legislative response, but it expressed even more clearly than the other two documents the Hamiltonian attitude toward America's future economic and social course. In it Hamilton casts himself in the role of the first*

[1]"The Second Report on Public Credit" is also often called "The Report on a National Bank."

modern economic planner. This report became an arsenal of arguments for those determined to encourage the growth of domestic manufactures in the United States. Eventually its protectionist philosophy was also incorporated into specific legislation, although long after Hamilton was dead.

"The First Report on Public Credit" dealt with the unpaid debts of the Revolution. These were of three kinds: debts owed by the United States to foreign countries; debts owed by the United States to its own citizens; and debts owed by the thirteen states to American creditors. Some states had taxed their own citizens to pay their debts; others had not. All the debts of the national government, those owed both at home and abroad, had fallen into arrears, and many of the debt certificates had been sold by the original possessors to speculators for whatever they would bring.

Hamilton, in the first report, starts by making a case for the prompt and full payment of all the new nation's public debts. He then seeks to deal with the controversies over how to pay the domestic debt, both state and national. In his arguments are embedded certain attitudes toward creditors and debtors, toward the role of government in the economy, toward the business community, and toward America's future. What are these? The secretary of the Treasury strongly favored the federal "assumption" of the unpaid debts of the states. Why does he argue for this position? What would taxpayers in states that had already paid their debts probably feel about such an assumption plan?

The first report already hinted at Hamilton's view of the larger economic role of a "funded" debt, that is, a consolidated federal debt, backed by provisions to pay interest and principle, into which the old debts could be converted. In his second report he more explicitly links this new funded debt with certain larger economic goals through a federally chartered central bank that would accept the new securities as paid-in capital. The bank would then issue paper money backed by these securities. What hopes does Hamilton have for this paper money? What are his larger economic goals? How would the new national bank further them? In what ways would the national bank help the government itself as contrasted to the economy in general?

Given Hamilton's bias toward commerce and industry, how do you explain his tribute in his Report on Manufactures *to agriculture? Was he being realistic in his hope that sectional differences over manufactures need not be disruptive? Is his vision of a transformed American economic future an attractive one? Could America have avoided the outcome he anticipated? Which of the eleven methods to encourage manufactures he suggests did Americans ultimately use most widely?*

The First Report on Public Credit, January 9, 1790

ALEXANDER HAMILTON

In the opinion of the Secretary [Hamilton] . . . [we must consider certain] plain and undeniable truths.

That exigencies are to be expected to occur, in the affairs of nations, in which there will be a necessity for borrowing.

That loans in times of public danger, especially from foreign war, are found [to be] an indispensable resource even to the wealthiest of them.

And that in a country which, like this, is possessed of little active wealth, or in other words, little monied capital, the necessity for that resource, must, in such emergencies, be proportionately urgent. . . .

And as . . . the necessity for borrowing in particular emergencies cannot be doubtful, so . . . it is equally evident that to be able to borrow upon good terms, it is essential that the credit of a nation should be well established.

For, when the credit of a country is in any degree questionable, it will never fail to give an extravagant premium . . . upon all the loans it has occasion to make. . . .

If the maintenance of public credit, then, be truly so important, the next inquiry which suggests itself is: By what means is it to be effected? The ready answer to which question is, by good faith; by a punctual performance of contracts. . . .

To justify and preserve their confidence; to promote the increasing respectability of the American name; to answer the calls of justice; to restore landed property to its due value; to furnish new resources, both to agriculture and commerce; to cement more closely the union of the states; to add to their security against foreign attack; to establish public order on the basis of an upright and liberal policy;—these are the great and invaluable ends to be secured by a proper and adequate provision . . . for the support of the public credit. . . .

The advantage to the public creditors, from the increased value of that part of their property which constitutes the public debt, needs no explanation.

But there is a consequence of this, less obvious, though not less true, in which every citizen is interested. It is a well-known fact, that, in countries in which the national debt is properly funded, and an object of established confidence, it answers most of the purposes of money. Transfers of stock or public debt are there equivalent to payments in specie [i.e., gold and silver]. The same thing would, in all probability, happen here under the like circumstances.

Henry Cabot Lodge, ed., *The Works of Alexander Hamilton* (New York: G. P. Putnam's Sons, 1904), vol. 2, pp. 227–96.

The benefits of this are various and obvious:

First.—Trade is extended by it. . . .
Secondly.—Agriculture and manufactures are also promoted by it. . . .
Thirdly.—The interest of money will be lowered by it. . . .

And from a combination of these effects, additional aids will be furnished to labor, to industry, and to arts of every kind. . . .

Having now taken a concise view of the inducements to a proper provision of the public debt, the next inquiry which presents itself is: What ought to be the nature of such a provision . . . ?

It is agreed on all hands, that that part of the debt which . . . is denominated the foreign debt, ought to be provided for, according to the precise terms of the contracts relating to it. The discussions, which can arise, therefore, will have reference essentially to the domestic part of it. . . .

[The question has arisen] whether a discrimination ought not to be made between original holders of the public securities, and present possessors by purchase. Those who advocate a discrimination are for making a full provision for the securities of the former, at their nominal [i.e., face] value; but contend, that the latter ought to receive no more than the cost to them and the interest. . . .

In favor of this scheme, it is alleged, that it would be unreasonable to pay twenty shillings in the pound [i.e., full face value] to one who had not given more for it than three or four. And it is added, that it would be hard to aggravate the misfortune of the first owner, who, probably through necessity, parted with his property at so great a loss, by obliging him to contribute to the profit of the person, who has speculated on his distresses.

The Secretary . . . is induced to reject the doctrine [this argument] contains, as equally unjust and impolitic, as highly injurious, even to the original holders of public securities; as ruinous to public credit.

It is inconsistent with justice, because in the first place, it is a breach of contract; in violation of the rights of a fair purchaser.

The nature of the contract in its origin, is, that the public will pay the sum expressed in the security, to the first holder, or his *assignee.* The *intent* in making the security assignable, is, that the proprietor may be able to make use of his property, by selling it for as much as it *may be worth in the market,* and that the buyer be *safe* in the purchase.

Every buyer therefor stands exactly in the place of the seller, has the same right with him in the identical sum expressed in the security. . . .

That he is to be considered as a fair purchaser, results from this: Whatever necessity the seller may have been under, was occasioned by the government in not making proper provision for its debts. The buyer had no agency in it and therefore ought not to suffer. He is not even chargeable with having taken an undue advantage. He paid what the commodity was worth on the market and took the risks of reimbursement upon himself. . . .

That the case of those, who parted with their securities from necessity, is a hard one, cannot be denied. But . . . they knew, that by the terms of the contract . . . , the public were bound to pay those to whom they should convey their title, the sums stipulated to be paid to them; and that as citizens of the United States, they were to bear their proportion of the contribution to that purpose. This, by the act of assignment, they tacitly agreed to do. . . .

The impolicy of discrimination [between original holder and later speculative purchaser] results from two considerations; one, that it proceeds upon a principle destructive of the *quality* of the public debt . . . which is essential to the capacity for answering the purpose of money—that is the *security of transfer;* the other, as because it includes a breach of faith, it renders property in the funds [i.e., in the public securities] less valuable; consequently induces lenders to demand a higher premium [i.e., interest] for what they lend and produces every other inconvenience of a bad state of public credit. . . .

But there is still a point in view in which it will appear perhaps even more exceptionable than in either of the former. It would be repugnant to an express provision of the Constitution of the United States. This provision is that "all debts contracted and engagements entered into before the adoption of this Constitution shall be as valid against the United States under this Constitution, as under the confederation," which amounts to a constitutional ratification of the contract respecting the debt, in the state in which they existed under the confederation. And resorting to that standard, there can be no doubt, that the rights of assignees and original holders, must be considered equal. . . .

The Secretary . . . proceeds to examine whether a difference ought to be permitted [between United States creditors and] . . . those of the states. . . .

The Secretary . . . entertains a full conviction, that assumption of the debts of the particular states by the union, will be a measure of sound policy and substantial justice.

It would . . . contribute . . . to an orderly, stable and satisfactory arrangement of the national finances. . . .

If all the public creditors receive their dues from one source, distributed with an equal hand, their interest will be the same. And having the same interests, they will unite in support of the fiscal arrangements of the government. . . .

If on the contrary there are distinct provisions [for paying the federal and the state debts], there will be distinct interests, drawing different ways. That union and concert of views, among the [public] creditors, which in every government is of great importance to their security, and to that of the public credit, will not only not exist, but will likely give place to mutual jealousy and opposition. And from this cause, the operation of the system which may be adopted, both by the particular states, and by the union in relation to their respective debts, will be in danger of being counteracted. . . .

Persuaded, as the Secretary is, that the proper funding of the present debt, will render it a national blessing: Yet he is so far from acceding to the position . . . that "public debts are public benefits"—a position inviting to prodigality, and liable to dangerous abuse—that he ardently wishes to see it incorporated as a fundamental maxim . . . that the creation of debt should always be accompanied by the means of extinguishment. This he regards as the true secret for rendering public credit immortal.

The Second Report on Public Credit, December 13, 1790

ALEXANDER HAMILTON

The . . . Secretary further . . . reports that . . . a National Bank is an institution of primary importance to the proper administration of the finances, and would be of the greatest utility in the operations connected with the support of the public credit. . . .

The following are among the principle advantages of a bank.

First. The augmentation of the active or productive capital of a country. Gold and silver, when they are employed merely as the instruments of exchange . . . have not been improperly denoted dead stock [i.e., unproductive]: but when deposited in banks, to become the basis of a paper circulation, . . . they then acquire life, or, in other words, an active and productive quality. . . . It is evident, for instance, that the money, which a merchant keeps in his chest, waiting for a favorable opportunity to employ it, produces nothing 'till that opportunity arrives. But if . . . he either deposits it in a bank or invests it in the stock of a bank, it yields a profit, during the interval. . . . His money thus deposited or invested is a fund, upon which himself and others can borrow to a much larger amount. It is a well established fact, that banks in good credit can circulate a far greater sum than the actual quantum of their capital in gold and silver. The extent of the possible excess seems indeterminate; though it has been conjecturally stated at the proportions of three to one. . . .

Secondly. Greater facility to the government in obtaining pecuniary aids, especially in sudden emergencies. . . . The capitals of a great number of individuals are [through banks], collected to a point, and placed under one direction. . . . [T]his mass is always ready, and can at once be put in motion, in aid of the government. . . .

Thirdly. The facilitating of the payment of taxes. This advantage is produced in two ways. Those who are in a situation to have access to the bank can have the assistance of loans to answer with punctuality the public calls upon them. . . . The other way . . . is the increasing of the quantity of circulating medium and the quickening of circulation. . . . And it is evident, that, whatever enhances the quantity of circulating money adds to the ease with which every industrious member of the community may acquire that portion of it of which he stands in need; and enables him to better pay his taxes, as well as supply his other wants. Even where the circulation of the bank paper [i.e., paper money issued by the banks] is not general, it must still have the same effect, though in a less degree, for whatever furnishes additional supplies to the channels of circulation, in one quarter, naturally contributes to keep the streams fuller elsewhere. . . . Banks tend to facilitate the payment of taxes, and to exemplify their utility to business of every kind, in which money is an agent. . . .

Henry Cabot Lodge, ed., *The Works of Alexander Hamilton* (New York: G. P. Putnam's Sons, 1904), vol. 2, pp. 337–51.

The combination of a portion of the public debt in the formation of capital, is the principal thing, of which an explanation is requisite. The chief object of this is, to enable the creation of a capital sufficiently large to be the basis of an extensive circulation, and an adequate security for it. . . . [T]he original plan of the Bank of North America[1] contemplated a capital of ten millions of dollars. . . . But to collect such a sum in this country in gold and silver, into one depository, may, without hesitation, be pronounced impracticable. Hence the necessity of an auxiliary which the public debt at once presents.

This part of the fund will be always ready to come in aid of the specie. It will more and more command a ready sale; and can therefore expeditiously be turned into coin if an exigency of the bank should at any time require it. This quality of prompt convertibility into coin, renders it an equivalent for that necessary agent of bank circulation; and distinguishes it from a fund in land.[2]

The Report on Manufactures, December 5, 1791

ALEXANDER HAMILTON

The expediency of encouraging manufactures in the United States . . . appears at this time to be pretty generally admitted. . . . [T]he restrictive regulations which in foreign markets abridge the vent [i.e., export] of the increasing surplus of our Agricultural produce, serve to beget an earnest desire, that a more extensive demand for that surplus may be created at home. . . .

There . . . are . . . respectable patrons of opinions unfriendly to the encouragement of manufactures. The following are . . . the arguments by which these opinions are defended. [Hamilton summarizes the views of those opposed to encouraging manufactures, which are as follows: (1) especially in a country like the United States, with "immense tracts of fertile territory," no other occupation is as productive as agriculture; (2) for government to encourage manufactures is "to transfer the natural current of industry from a more to a less beneficial channel"; (3) America's abundant land relative to its small population makes it difficult to recruit workers for manufactures, since people will prefer the independence of farming to the "less independent condition of an artisan"; and (4) if somehow, despite

---

[1]The Bank of North America, the first private commercial bank in the United States, was chartered by the Confederation Congress in 1781 to help with the financing of the Revolution. It accomplished less than its organizers hoped—ED.

[2]The reference here is to the controversial land banks established in several colonies before 1776 to provide a circulating medium. These were generally not successful—ED.

Henry Cabot Lodge, ed., *The Works of Alexander Hamilton* (New York: G. P. Putnam's Sons, 1904), vol. 4, pp. 70–198.

these facts, government can by "heavy duties, prohibitions, bounties, or by other forced expedients" give a "premature spring" to manufactures, it "will only sacrifice the interests of the community to those of particular classes." He then resumes his own arguments.]

It ought readily to be conceded that the cultivation of the earth, as the primary and most certain source of national supply; as the immediate and chief source of sustenance to man; as the principal source of those materials which constitute the nutriment of other kinds of labor; as including a state most favourable to the freedom and independence of the human mind— one, perhaps, most conducive to the multiplication of the human species; has intrinsically a strong claim to pre-eminence over every other kind of industry.

But, that it has a title to any thing like an exclusive predilection, in any country, ought to be admitted with great caution. That it is even more productive than every other branch of Industry requires more evidence, than has yet been given in support of the position. . . .

It is now proper to . . . enumerate the principal circumstances from which it may be inferred that manufacturing establishments not only occasion a positive augmentation of the produce and revenue of the society, but that they contribute essentially to rendering them greater than they could possibly be, without such establishments. These circumstances are:

1. The division of labor.
2. An extension of the use of machinery.
3. Additional employment to classes of the community not ordinarily engaged in the business.
4. The promotion of emigration from foreign countries.
5. The furnishing greater scope for the diversity of talents and dispositions, which discriminate men from each other.
6. The affording a more ample and variable field for enterprise.
7. The creating, in some instances, a new, and securing, in all, a more certain and steady demand for the surplus produce of the soil. . . .

Not only the wealth; but the independence and security of a country, appear to be materially connected with the prosperity of manufactures. Every nation, with a view to those great objects, ought to endeavor to possess within itself all the essentials of national supply. These comprise the means of subsistence, habitation, clothing, and defence. . . .

It is not uncommon to meet with an opinion, that, though the promoting of manufactures may be the interest of a part of the Union, it is contrary to that of another part. The Northern and Southern regions are sometimes represented as having adverse interests in this respect. Those are called manufacturing, these agricultural States: and a species of opposition is imagined to subsist between the manufacturing and agricultural interests. . . .

Ideas of a contrariety of interests between the Northern and Southern regions of the Union are, in the main, as unfounded as they are mischievous. The diversity of circumstances on which such a contrariety is usually predicated, authorizes a directly contrary conclusion. Mutual wants constitute one of the strongest links of political connexion. . . .

If the Northern and Middle States should be the principal scenes of such [manufacturing] establishments, they would immediately benefit the more Southern, by creating a demand for productions. . . . These productions . . . are timber, flax, hemp, cotton, wool, raw silk, indigo, iron, lead, fur, hides, skins and coals. . . .

The extensive cultivation of cotton, can, perhaps, hardly be expected but from the previous establishment of domestic manufactories [i.e., workshops] of the article. . . .

A full view having now been taken of the inducements to the promotion of manufactures in the United States, . . . it is proper . . . to consider the means by which it may be effected. . . .

1. *Protecting duties—or duties on those foreign articles which are the rivals of the domestic ones intended to be encouraged. . . .*
2. *Prohibitions of rival articles, or duties equivalent to prohibitions. . . .*
3. *Prohibitions of the exportation of the materials of manufactures. . . .*
4. *Pecuniary Bounties. . . .*
5. *Premiums. . . .*
6. *The exemption of the materials of manufactures from duty. . . .*
7. *Drawbacks of the duties which are imposed on the materials of manufactures. . . .*
8. *The encouragement of new inventions and discoveries at home, and of the introduction into the United States of such as may have been made in other countries; particularly, those which relate to machinery. . . .*
9. *Judicious regulations for the inspection of manufactured commodities. . . .*
10. *The facilitating of pecuniary remittances from place to place. . . .*
11. *The facilitating of the transportation of commodities. . . .*

In countries where there is great private wealth, much may be effected by the voluntary contributions of patriotic individuals; but in a community situated like that of the United States, the public purse must apply the deficiency of private resource. In what can it be so useful, as in prompting and improving the efforts of industry?

7.2:   Thomas Jefferson and the American Arcadia (1784)

Thomas Jefferson himself never expressed his views of America's social and economic future as comprehensively as did Hamilton, his chief rival. But the following selection from his only full-length book, Notes on the State of Virginia, *written in 1784, captures his attitudes as expressed shortly after the peace with Britain confirming America's independence.*

Considering his origins and background, why might Jefferson, more than Hamilton, be a defender of agriculture over manufactures? Why does Jefferson oppose manufactures? Why does he seem fearful of cities? As president, did any of his major policies reinforce the vision of America's future he expressed here? Is Jefferson's view of human nature implicit in the document?

Query XIX: Manufactures[1]

THOMAS JEFFERSON

The Present State of Manufactures, Commerce, Interior and Exterior Trade?

We never had an interior trade of any importance. Our exterior commerce has suffered very much from the beginning of the present contest. During this time we have manufactured within our families the most necessary articles of cloathing. Those of cotton will bear some comparison with the same kinds of manufacture in Europe; but those of wool, flax and hemp are very coarse, unsightly, and unpleasant: and such is our attachment to agriculture, and such our preference for foreign manufactures, that be it wise or unwise, our people will certainly return as soon as they can, to the raising raw materials, and exchanging them for finer manufactures than they are able to execute themselves.

The political œconomists of Europe have established it as a principle that every state should endeavour to manufacture for itself: and this principle, like many others, we transfer to America, without calculating the difference of circumstance which should often produce a difference of result. In Europe the lands are either cultivated, or locked up against the cultivator. Manufacture must therefore be resorted to of necessity not of choice, to support the surplus of their people. But we have an immensity of land courting the industry of the husbandman. Is is best then that all our citizens should be employed in its improvement, or that one half should be called off from that to exercise manufactures and handicraft arts for the other? Those who labour in the earth are the chosen people of God, if ever he had a chosen people, whose breasts he has made his peculiar deposit for substantial and genuine virtue. It is the focus in which he keeps alive that sacred fire, which otherwise might escape from the face of the earth. Corruption of morals in the mass of cultivators is a phænomenon of which no age nor nation has furnished an example. It is the mark set on those, who not looking up to heaven, to their own soil and industry, as does the husbandman, for their subsistance [*sic*], depend for it on the casualties and caprice of customers. Dependance begets subservience and venality, suffocates the germ of virtue, and prepares fit tools for the designs of ambition. This, the natural progress and consequence of the arts, has sometimes perhaps been retarded by accidental circumstances: but, generally speaking, the proportion which the

Thomas Jefferson, *Notes on the State of Virginia*, in *The Writings of Thomas Jefferson*, ed. Paul Leicester Ford (New York: G. P. Putnam's Sons, 1894), vol. 3, pp. 268–69.
[1]Footnotes deleted.

aggregate of the other classes of citizens bears in any state to that of its husbandmen, is the proportion of its unsound to its healthy parts, and is a good-enough barometer whereby to measure its degree of corruption. While we have land to labour then, let us never wish to see our citizens occupied at a work-bench, or twirling a distaff. Carpenters, masons, smiths, are wanting in husbandry: but, for the general operations of manufacture, let our work-shops remain in Europe. It is better to carry provisions and materials to workmen there, than bring them to the provisions and materials, and with them their manners and principles. The loss by the transportation of commodities across the Atlantic will be made up in happiness and permanence of government. The mobs of great cities add just so much to the support of pure government, as sores do to the strength of the human body. It is the manners and spirit of a people which preserve a republic in vigour. A degeneracy in these is a canker which soon eats to the heart of its laws and constitution.

7.3:   Thomas Jefferson Attacks the Hamiltonian System (1790)

During the years 1785–89 Jefferson served as American minister to France. Appointed while abroad by Washington as the first secretary of state, he returned home in 1789 to find himself in the middle of the debate over the Hamiltonian program. The following document is an excerpt from "The Anas," a journal Jefferson kept at the time and later revised, in which he fiercely attacks the Hamiltonian system and the party, the Federalists, that coalesced around it.

One part of the indictment was that the Hamiltonians were "monarchists." In what sense could the funding system be considered monarchist? Another charge was that the Hamiltonians were corrupt men motivated largely by their lust for personal gain. How does this conflict with the arguments of Hamilton for his financial programs? Were Jefferson's claims of corruption valid, or were they primarily the charges of a political partisan unhappy at the successes of an opponent?

The Vile Hamiltonian System

THOMAS JEFFERSON

I returned from that mission [to France] in the 1st. year of the new government, having landed in Virginia in Dec. [17]89 & proceeded to N. York [the nation's first capital] in March [17]90 to enter on the office of Secretary of

Thomas Jefferson, *The Writings of Thomas Jefferson*, ed. Paul Leicester Ford (New York: G. P. Putnam's Sons, 1895), vol. 1, pp. 159–66.

State. Here certainly I found a state of things which, of all I had ever contemplated, I the least expected. I had left France in the first year of its revolution, in the fervor of natural rights, and zeal for reformation. My conscientious devotion to these rights could not be heightened, but it had been aroused and excited by daily exercise. The president [George Washington] received me cordially, and my Colleagues & the circle of principal citizens, apparently, with welcome. The courtesies of dinner parties given me as a stranger newly arrived among them placed me at once in their familiar society. But I cannot describe the wonder and mortification with which the table conversations filled me. Politics were the chief topic, and a preference for kingly, over republican, government, was evidently the favorite sentiment. An apostate I could not be; nor yet a hypocrite: and I found myself, for the most part, the only advocate on the republican side of the question, unless, among the guests, there chanced to be some member of that party from the legislative Houses [i.e., Congress]. Hamilton's financial system had then passed. It had two objects: 1st as a puzzle, to exclude popular understanding & inquiry. 2dly, as a machine for the corruption of the legislature; for he avowed the opinion that man could be governed by one of two motives only, force or interest: force he observed, in this country, was out of the question; and the interests therefore of the members must be laid hold of, to keep the legislature in unison with the Executive [i.e., the president]. And with grief and shame it must be acknowledged that his machine was not without effect. That even in this, the birth of our government, some members were found sordid enough to bend their duty to their interests, and to look after personal, rather than public good.

It is well-known that, during the [Revolutionary] war, the greatest difficulty we encountered was the want of money or means, to pay our soldiers who fought, or our farmers, manufacturers & merchants who furnished the necessary supplies of food & clothing for them. After the expedient of paper money had exhausted itself, certificates of debt were given to the individual creditors, with the assurance of payment, so soon as the U.S. be able. But the distresses of these people often obliged them to part with these for the half, the fifth, and even a tenth of their value; and speculators had made a trade of cozening them from the holders, by the most fraudulent practices and persuasions that they would never be paid. In the bill for funding & paying these, Hamilton made no difference between the original holders & the fraudulent purchasers of this paper. Great & just repugnance arose in putting these two classes of creditors on the same footing, and great exertions were used to pay to the former the full value, and to the latter the price only which he had paid, with interest.

But this would have prevented the game which was to be played, & for which the minds of greedy members were already tutored and prepared. When the trial of strength . . . had indicated the form in which the bill would finally pass, this being known within doors sooner than without, and especially than to those who were in distant parts of the Union, the base scramble began. Couriers & relay horses by land and swift sailing pilot boats by sea, were flying in all directions. Active partners & agents were associated & employed in every state, town, and country neighborhood, and this paper was bought up at 5 [shillings] and even low 2 [shillings] in the pound [i.e., from one-fourth to one-tenth of face value] before the holder knew that Congress had already provided for its redemption at par. Immense sums were thus filched from the poor & ignorant, and fortunes accumulated by those who had themselves been poor enough before.

[Jefferson attacks the assumption of state debts by the federal government as another example of the perfidy of the Hamiltonian funding program. He excuses his own role in inducing the southern states to accept assumption by claiming that he was new to the issue, having been abroad when it was first discussed and having yielded out of ignorance to Hamilton's plea that unless the assumption passed the union would be dissolved. His explanation downplays the deal he helped arrange between the Hamiltonians and the southern states to locate the future national capital on the Potomac River in exchange for accepting assumption.]

. . . [A]nd so the assumption was passed, and 20 millions of stock divided among favored states and thrown in as pabulum [i.e., food] to the stock-jobbing herd. This added to the number of votaries [i.e., supporters] to the treasury and made its Chief [Hamilton] the master of every vote in the legislature that might give the government the direction suited to his political views. I know well . . . that nothing like a majority in Congress had yielded to this corruption. Far from it. But a division, not very unequal, had already taken place in the honest part of that body, between the parties styled republican and federal. The latter being monarchists in principle, adhered to Hamilton of course, as their leader in that principle, and this mercenary phalanx added to them ensured always a majority in both houses: so that the whole action of the legislature was now under the direction of the treasury. Still the machine was not compleat. The effect of the funding system, & of the assumption, would be temporary. It would be lost with the loss of the individual members whom it had enriched, and some engine of influence more permanent must be contrived, while those myrmidons [i.e., henchmen] were yet in place to carry it thro' all opposition. This engine was the Bank of the U.S. . . . While the government remained at Philadelphia, a selection of members of both houses were constantly kept as Directors, who, on every question interesting to that institution, or to the views of the federal head, voted at the will of that head; and, together with the stockholding members, could always make the federal [Federalist] vote that of the majority. By this combination, legislative expositions [i.e., interpretations] were given to the constitution, and all the administrative laws were shaped on the model of England & so passed. . . .

Here then was the real ground of the [Republican] opposition which was

made to the course of the [Federalist] administration. Its object was to preserve the legislature pure and independent of the Executive, to restrain the
administration to republican forms and principles, and not permit the constitution to be construed into a monarchy, and to be warped in practice into
all the principles and pollutions of their favorite English model. Nor was this
an opposition to Gen'l Washington. He was true to the republican charge
confided to him; & has solemnly and repeatedly protested to me, in our private conversations, that he would lose the last drop of blood in support of it,
and he did this the oftener, and with the more earnestness because he knew
my suspicions of Hamilton's designs against it; & wished to quiet them. For
he was not aware of the drift, or of the effect of Hamilton's schemes.
Unversed in financial projects & calculations, & budgets, his approbation of
them was bottomed on his confidence in the man. But Hamilton was not
only a monarchist, but for a monarchy bottomed on corruption. . . .
Hamilton was indeed a singular character. Of acute understanding, disinterested, honest, and honorable in all private transactions, amiable in society,
and duly valuing virtue in private life, yet so bewitched & perverted by the
British example, as to be under thoro' conviction that corruption was essential to the government of a nation.

7.4:   The Jeffersonians Embrace the French (1793)

*In 1789 forces long repressed rose up to challenge the "Old Regime," the
ancient order of privilege that reigned in France. In 1790 the French
insurgents established a constitutional monarchy and abolished most of
the prerogatives and trappings of aristocracy. In 1792 the revolutionar-
ies deposed the French king and replaced the age-old monarchy with a
republic based on many of the same concepts of natural rights that had
inspired the Americans in 1776. The following year they tried Louis XVI
for treason and beheaded him. Marie Antoinette, his frivolous queen,
soon followed him to the guillotine.*

*France's conservative neighbors were appalled by the revolution and
its excesses. In 1792, even before Louis's execution, revolutionary France
found itself at war with Austria and Prussia and in the following year
with Great Britain. For the next twenty years the French and their allies
were embroiled in almost constant warfare in Europe and wherever
French influence reached, against a coalition of forces bitterly opposed to
their policies and principles.*

*From the outset the wars of the French Revolution had an important
ideological dimension. The leaders of France, at least until 1795, were
militant secular democrats who loathed organized religion as well as
social and political inequality. Yet at the same time they had little respect*

for civil liberties. The revolutionary leaders used terror to cow their opponents. Thousands of aristocrats and clergy fled France for exile in more hospitable lands, including America. Many who remained suffered the same fate as the king and queen. Before long the war between France and its enemies came to be seen as a struggle between two fundamentally different political philosophies, one that celebrated stability, hierarchy, and traditional religion, another that cherished change, equality, and secularism.

At first most Americans cheered the French Revolution. But as it became more radical, the French republic became a divisive force in American political life. This effect was magnified by the 1778 Franco-American treaty of alliance that the French claimed obliged the Americans to support them in their new war with Britain and their other enemies.

Thomas Jefferson himself had been in Paris as minister to France at the outbreak of the revolution and had applauded the sweeping political changes he witnessed. After he returned to America, he continued to give them his support.

The following letter from Secretary of State Jefferson to William Short, U.S. minister to the Netherlands, expresses his cordial feelings toward the French republic. Jefferson and his subordinate obviously disagreed over the Jacobins, the most militant faction among the French revolutionary leaders and the group most committed to using violent deeds against the revolution's enemies.

How does Jefferson condone the bloodshed unleashed by the Jacobins? Does he himself seem an extremist? Do his views support the principle that a good end justifies any means to achieve it?

In Praise of the French Jacobins

THOMAS JEFFERSON

To William Short

Philadelphia Jan 3. 1793.

Dear Sir,—My last private letter to you was of Oct. 16. since which I have received your No. 103, 107, 108, 109, 110, 112, 113 & 114 and yesterday your private one of Sep 15, came to hand. The tone of your letters had for some time given me pain, on account of the extreme warmth with which they censured the proceedings of the Jacobins of France. I considered that sect as

Thomas Jefferson, *The Writings of Thomas Jefferson*, ed. Paul Leicester Ford (New York: G. P. Putnam's Sons, 1895), vol. 1, pp. 153–56.

the same with the Republican patriots, & the Feuillants[1] as the Monarchical patriots, well known in the early part of the revolution, & but little distant in their views, both having in object the establishment of a free constitution, & differing only on the question whether their chief Executive should be hereditary or not. The Jacobins (as since called) yielded to the Feuillants & tried the experiment of retaining their hereditary Executive. The experiment failed completely, and would have brought on the reestablishment of despotism had it been pursued. The Jacobins saw this, and that the expunging that officer was of absolute necessity. And the Nation was with them in opinion, for however they might have been formerly for the constitution framed by the first assembly, they were come over from their hope in it, and were now generally Jacobins. In the struggle which was necessary, many guilty persons fell without the forms of trial, and with them some innocent. These I deplore as much as any body, & shall deplore some of them to the day of my death. But I deplore them as I should have done had they fallen in battle. It was necessary to use the arm of the people, a machine not quite so blind as balls and bombs, but blind to a certain degree. A few of their cordial friends met at their hands the fate of enemies. But time and truth will rescue & embalm their memories, while their posterity will be enjoying that very liberty for which they would never have hesitated to offer up their lives. The liberty of the whole earth was depending on the issue of the contest, and was ever such a prize won with so little innocent blood? My own affections have been deeply wounded by some of the martyrs to this cause, but rather than it should have failed, I would have seen half the earth desolated. Were there but an Adam & Eve left in every country, & left free, it would be better than as it now is. I have expressed to you my sentiments, because they are really those of 99. in an hundred of our citizens. The universal feasts, and rejoicings which have lately been had on account of the successes of the French shewed the genuine effusions of their hearts. You have been wounded by the sufferings of your friends, and have by this circumstance been hurried into a temper of mind which would be extremely disrelished if known to your countrymen. The *reserve of the President of the United States* had never permitted me to discover the light in which he viewed it, and as I was more anxious that you should satisfy him than me, I had still avoided explanations with you on the subject. But your 113. induced him to break silence and to notice the extreme acrimony of your expressions. He added that he had been informed the sentiments you expressed *in your conversations* were equally offensive to our allies, & that you should consider yourself as the representative of your country and that what you say might be imputed to your constituents. He desired me therefore to write to you on this subject. He added

---

[1]A moderate group, later suppressed by the Jacobins—ED.

that he considered *France as the sheet anchor of this country and its friendship as a first object.* There are in the U.S. some characters of opposite principles; some of them are high in office, others possessing great wealth, and all of them hostile to France and fondly looking to England as the staff of their hope. These I named to you on a former occasion. Their prospects have certainly not brightened. Excepting them, this country is entirely republican, friends to the constitution, anxious to preserve it and to have it administered according to it's [*sic*] own republican principles. The little party above mentioned have espoused it only as a stepping stone to monarchy, and have endeavored to approximate it to that in it's [sic]administration in order to render it's [*sic*] final transition more easy. The successes of republicanism in France have given the coup de grace to their prospects, and I hope to their projects.—I have developed to you faithfully the sentiments of your country, that you may govern yourself accordingly. I know your republicanism to be pure, and that it is no decay of that which has embittered you against it's [*sic*] votaries in France, but too great a sensibility at the partial evil which it's [*sic*] object has been accomplished there. I have written to you in the stile to which I have been always accustomed with you, and which perhaps it is time I should lay aside. But while old men are sensible enough of their own advance in years, they do not sufficiently recollect it in those whom they have seen young. In writing too the last private letter which will probably be written under present circumstances, in contemplating that your correspondence will shortly be turned over to I know not whom, but certainly to some one not in the habit of considering your interests with the same fostering anxieties I do, I have presented things without reserve, satisfied you will ascribe what I have said to it's true motive, use it for your own best interest, and in that fulfil completely what I had in view.

7.5:   The Federalists Denounce the French Revolution (1793)

One opponent of the French cause was Thomas Jefferson's successor as American minister to France, Gouverneur Morris. From a distinguished New York family, Morris had been a delegate to the Constitutional Convention, where he had supported a strong central government. Like Jefferson, he was in Paris when the revolution first erupted. But unlike the red-haired Virginian, he supported the besieged monarchy. He later became a Federalist senator from New York.

In the following letter to George Washington, Morris discloses his loathing for the tactics of the revolutionary leaders. How to you explain his sympathy for the queen? Was Morris correct in his prediction that France would end up being governed by "a single despot"?

Deploring the Excesses of the French Revolution

GOUVERNEUR MORRIS

To George Washington

Paris, October 18th, 1793

My Dear Sir,

You will see by the official correspondence, that your orders are complied with, and that your intentions are fulfilled. Permit me on this occasion to remark, that had the people of America been well informed of the state of things on this side of the Atlantic, no one would have dared to adopt the conduct which M. Genêt[1] has pursued. In reading the few gazettes which have reached me, I am surprised to see so little sound intelligence.

The present government is evidently a despotism both in principle and practice. The Convention[2] now consists of only a part of those, who were chosen to frame a constitution. These, after putting under arrest their fellows, claim all power, and have delegated the greater part of it to a *Committee of Safety.* You will observe, that one of the ordinary measures of government is to send out Commissioners with unlimited authority. They are invested with power to remove officers elected by the people, and put others in their places. This power, as well as that of imprisoning on suspicion, is liberally exercised. The revolutionary tribunal established here to judge on general principles, gives unbounded scope to will. It is an emphatic phrase in fashion among the patriots [i.e., the revolution's supporters] that *terror is the order of the day.* Some years have elapsed since Montesquieu[3] wrote that the principle of arbitrary government is *fear.*

The Queen was executed the day before yesterday. Insulted during her trial and reviled during her last moments, she behaved with dignity throughout. This execution will, I think, give to future hostilities a deeper dye, and unite more intimately the allied powers [at war with France]. It will silence

---

Jared Sparks, *The Life of Gouverneur Morris with Selections from His Correspondence* (Boston: Gray and Bowen, 1832), vol. 2, pp. 369–70.

[1]Edmond Charles Genêt was sent in 1792 as French minister to the United States, charged with inducing the Americans to aid the French republic against its enemies. He became the center of debate in America between the friends and the enemies of revolutionary France, and was eventually recalled at the request of the American government. To spare him punishment in France, however, he was allowed to stay in the United States—ED.

[2]The body created in 1791 to draw up a new constitution for France that would embody the changed political order. It represented a range of political views from royalists to Jacobins—ED.

[3]Charles de Secondat Montesquieu, a French political philosopher, is considered the source of the theory of checks and balances—ED.

the opposition of those, who would not listen to the dismemberment of this country, and, therefore it may be concluded that the blow by which she died was directed from a distance.

But whatever may be the lot of France in remote futurity, and putting aside the military events, it seems evident that she must be governed by a single despot. Whether she will pass through that point through the medium of a triumvirate, [a partnership of three leaders], or other small body of men, seems as yet undetermined. I think it most probable that she will. A great and awful crisis seems to be near at hand. A blow is, I am told, meditated which will shroud in grief and horror a guilty land. Already the prisons are surcharged with persons who consider themselves victims. Nature recoils, and I yet hope that these ideas are circulated only to inspire fear. I am, &c.

Gouverneur Morris

8

Pioneers and Native Americans

From the very outset the United States was a huge country. It became still larger through the Louisiana Purchase (1803), the purchase of Florida (1819), the Mexican Cession (1848), the acquisition of Oregon (1848), and the Gadsden Purchase (1853). By 1860, the nation had grown to almost 3 million square miles.

Beyond the coastal band of dense settlement in the early republic, most of this vast expanse was initially without many inhabitants of Old World extraction. To contemporary whites it seemed an empty,[1] bounteous resource that offered escape from troubles in the older East and new opportunities for attaining wealth. In the "West," Americans could earn a second chance.

One of the epochal developments of the early nation was the opening of the trans-Appalachian West to white settlement after the War of 1812. During the years between 1815 and the start of the Civil War, millions of acres of western lands were wrested from Indian control and carved into farms and plantations. Bustling cities rose where Indian villages or virgin forest had existed. By 1849 seventeen new states had been added to the original thirteen, almost all in the great interior valley drained by the Mississippi and its tributaries.

What was the fate of the thousands of people who pulled up stakes and headed west during these years? How well did they prosper in their new homes? What hardships did they face? What did those who stayed behind think of the new communities that sprang up in the "territories"? And what about the Indian inhabitants of the region? How did the pre-Civil War westward movement of whites[2] affect them?

[1] It was, of course, not empty, but inhabited by many Native American tribes. Few whites, however, took their claims seriously—as you will see—ED.

[2] And many blacks as well, mostly as slaves brought by their owners—ED.

134

Eastern Americans have always been ambivalent about the West. To some it has seemed the place that best expressed the American spirit. To others it has been the abode of savagery, the region where imported civilization quickly decayed. The documents below deal with this dialogue. In what ways do the antagonists' premises about civilization differ?

8.1: Timothy Dwight Attacks "Foresters" (1821)

Timothy Dwight epitomized the refined and cultivated easterner of the early republic. A descendant of Jonathan Edwards, the Massachusetts minister who sparked the religious revival known as the Great Awakening, he graduated from Yale at the age of seventeen and in 1795, after serving as pastor and teacher in Connecticut, became president of his alma mater. An ardent Federalist who despised the democratic trends of the day, Dwight was nonetheless a patriot who resented European attacks on America. His three-volume Travels in New England and New York, *written after he left Yale, is an able defense of his nation, or at least of the northeastern portion of it.*

Yet Dwight had little use for "foresters," as he termed the western types we call frontierspeople. In his ambitious travel account he included the following famous attack on the earliest settlers in new regions, whether in the West or, as in this case, in the newly settled backwoods areas of New England.

What might explain Dwight's harsh criticism? Was it class snobbery? Was it rooted in his Puritan work ethic? Does his description of at least two stages of settlement in new communities correspond with the reality of frontier settlement? Does Dwight suggest that the frontier might serve as a social safety valve? Why, as Dwight indicates, might the wife of the frontiersman be the repository of less shiftless attitudes than her husband?

The Shiftless Pioneers

TIMOTHY DWIGHT

In the formation of Colonies, those, who are first inclined to emigrate, are usually such, as have met with difficulties at home. These are commonly joined by persons, who, having large families, and small farms, are induced, for the sake of settling their children comfortably, to seek for newer and cheaper lands. To both are always added the discontented, the enterprising,

Timothy Dwight, *Travels in New England and New York* (New Haven, 1821), vol. 2, pp. 458–61.

the ambitious, and the covetous. Many, of the first, and some, of all these classes, are found in every new American country, within ten years after its settlement has commenced. From this period, kindred, friendship, and former neighbourhood, prompt others to follow them. Others, still, are allured by the prospect of gain, presented in every new country to the sagacious, from the purchase and sale of lands: while not a small number are influenced by the brilliant stories, which every where are told concerning new tracts during the early progress of their settlement. A considerable part of those, who *begin* the cultivation of the wilderness, may be denominated *foresters*, or *Pioneers*. The business of these persons is no other than to cut down trees, build log-houses, lay open forested grounds to cultivation, and prepare the ways for those who come after them. These men cannot live in regular society. They are too idle; too talkative; too passionate; too prodigal; and too shiftless; to acquire either property or character. They are impatient of the restraints of law, religion, and morality; grumble about taxes, by which Rulers, Ministers, and School-masters, are supported; and complain incessantly, as well as bitterly, of the extortions of mechanics, farmers, merchants, and physicians; to whom they are always indebted. At the same time, they are usually possessed, in their own view, of uncommon wisdom; understand medical science, politics, and religion, better than those, who have studied them through life; and, although they manage their own concerns worse than any other men, feel perfectly satisfied, that they could manage those of the nation far better than the agents, to whom they are committed by the public. After displaying their own talents, and worth; after censuring the weakness, and wickedness, of their superiours; after exposing the injustice of the community in neglecting to invest persons of such merit with public offices; in many an eloquent harangue, uttered by many a kitchen fire, in every blacksmith's shop, and in every corner of the streets; and finding all their efforts vain; they become at length discouraged: and under the pressure of poverty, the fear of a gaol [jail], and the consciousness of public contempt, leave their native places, and betake themselves to the wilderness.

Here they are obliged to work or starve. They accordingly cut down some trees, and girdle others; they furnish themselves with an ill-built log-house, and a worse barn; and reduce a part of the forest into fields, half-enclosed, and half-cultivated. The forests furnish browse [grazing]; and their fields yield a stinted herbage. On this scanty provision they feed a few cattle: and with these, and the penurious products of their labour, eked out by hunting and fishing, they keep their families alive.

A farm, thus far cleared, promises immediate subsistence to a better husbandman. A log-house, thus built, presents, when repaired with moderate exertions, a shelter for his family. Such a husbandman is therefore induced by these little advantages, where the soil and situation please him, to purchase such a farm; when he would not plant himself in an absolute wilderness. The proprietor is always ready to sell: for he loves this irregular, adventurous, half-working, and half-lounging life; and hates the sober industry, and prudent economy, by which his bush pasture might be changed into a farm, and himself raised to thrift and independence. The bargain is soon made. The forester, receiving more money for his improvements than he ever before possessed, and a price for the soil, somewhat enhanced by surrounding settlements, willingly quits his house, to build another like it, and his farm, to girdle trees, hunt, and saunter, in another place. His wife accompanies him only from a sense of duty, or necessity; and secretly pines for the quiet, orderly, friendly society, to which she originally bade a reluctant farewell. Her husband, in the mean time, becomes less and less a civilized man: and almost every thing in the family, which is amiable and meritorious, is usually the result of her principles, care, and influence.

The second proprietor is commonly called a *farmer;* and with industry and spirit, deserving no small commendation, changes the desert into a fruitful field. . . .

The class of men, who have been the principle subject of these remarks, have already straggled onward from New-England, as well as other parts of the Union, to Louisiana [i.e., to the Louisiana Purchase region]. In a political view, their emigration is of very serious utility to the ancient settlements. All countries contain restless inhabitants; men impatient of labour; men who will contract debts without intending to pay them; who would rather talk than work; whose vanity persuades them, that they are wise, and prevents them from knowing, that they are fools; who are delighted with innovation; who think places of power and profit due their peculiar merits; who feel, that every change from good order and established society will be beneficial to themselves; who have nothing to lose, and therefore expect to be gainers by every scramble; and, who, of course, spend life in disturbing others, with the hope of gaining something for themselves. Under despotic governments they are awed into quiet; but in every free community they create, to a greater or lesser extent, continual turmoil; and have often overturned the peace, liberty, and happiness of their fellow-citizens.

8.2:   Timothy Flint Defends the West (1826)

Like Timothy Dwight, Timothy Flint was also a New England–born clergyman. Unlike Dwight, however, he lived many years in the trans-Appalachian West as a traveling missionary. Although his missionary work was inspired by eastern worry about western "barbarism" and irreligion, and although Flint, like Dwight, was a proud Yankee, he respected and defended westerners. In the excerpt below he specifically seeks to refute the charges of Dwight and other easterners that western pioneers were shiftless, coarse, and uneducated brutes prone to drunkenness, gambling, crime, and personal violence.

Is Flint convincing? Both Dwight and Flint were Yankees, but were there other aspects of their origins or experiences that might explain the differences in their views? How would the typical westerner, as described by Flint, fit into a modern American suburb?

The Virtues of the Pioneers

TIMOTHY FLINT

The people in the Atlantic states have not yet recovered from the horror, inspired by the term "backwoodsman." This prejudice is particularly strong in New England, and is more or less felt from Maine to Georgia. When I first visited this country, I had my full share, and my family by far too much for their comfort. In approaching the country, I heard a thousand stories of gougings, and robberies, and shooting down with the rifle. I have travelled in these regions thousands of miles under all circumstances of exposure and danger. I have travelled alone, or in company only with such as needed protection, instead of being able to impart it; and this too, in many instances, where I was not known as a minister, or where such knowledge would have had no influence in protecting me. I never have carried the slightest weapon of defence. I scarcely remember to have experienced any thing that resembled insult, or to have felt myself in danger from the people. I have often seen men that had lost an eye. Instances of murder, numerous and horrible in their circumstances, have occurred in my vicinity. But they were such lawless rencounters, as terminate in murder every where, and in which the drunkenness, brutality, and violence were mutual. They were catastrophes, in which quiet and sober men would be in no danger of being involved. When we look round these immense regions, and consider that I have been in settlements three hundred miles from any court of justice, when we look at the position of the men, and the state of things, the wonder is, that so few outrages and murders occur. The gentlemen of the towns, even here, speak often with a certain contempt and horror of the backwoodsmen. I have read, and not without feelings of pain, the bitter representations of the learned and virtuous Dr. Dwight, in speaking of them. He represents these vast regions, as a grand reservoir for the scum of the Atlantic states. He characterizes in the mass the emigrants from New England, as discontented cob[b]lers, too proud, too much in debt, too unprincipled, too much puffed up with self-conceit, too strongly impressed that their fancied talents could not find scope in their own country, to stay there. It is true there are worthless people here, and the most so, it must be confessed, are from New England. It is true there are gamblers, and gougers, and outlaws; but there are fewer of them, than from the nature of things, and the character of the age and the world, we ought to expect. But it is unworthy of the excellent

Timothy Flint, *Recollections of the Last Ten Years Passed in Occasional Residences and Journeyings in the Valley of the Mississippi* (Boston: Cummings, Hilliard and Company, 1826), pp. 174–78.

man in question so to designate this people in the mass. The backwoodsman of the west, as I have seen him, is generally an amiable and virtuous man. His general motive for coming here is to be a freeholder, to have plenty of rich land, and to be able to settle his children about him. It is a most virtuous motive. And notwithstanding all that Dr. Dwight and Talleyrand[1] have said to the contrary, I fully believe, that nine in ten of the emigrants have come here with no other motive. You find, in truth, that he has vices and barbarisms, peculiar to his situation. His manners are rough. He wears, it may be, a long beard. He has a great quantity of bear or deer skins wrought into his household establishment, his furniture, and dress. He carries a knife, or a dirk in his bosom, and when in the woods has a rifle on his back, and a pack of dogs at his heels. An Atlantic stranger, transferred directly from one of our cities to his door, would recoil from an encounter with him. But remember, that his rifle and his dogs are among his chief means of support and profit. Remember, that all his first days here were passed in dread of the savages. Remember, that he still encounters them, still meets bears and panthers. Enter his door, and tell him you are benighted, and wish the shelter of his cabin for the night. The welcome is indeed seemingly ungracious: "I reckon you can stay," or "I suppose we must let you stay." But this apparent ungraciousness is the harbinger of every kindness that he can bestow, and every comfort that his cabin can afford. Good coffee, corn bread and butter, venison, pork, wild and tame fowls are set before you. His wife, timid, silent, reserved, but constantly attentive to your comfort, does not sit at the table with you, but like the wives of the patriarchs, stands and attends on you. You are shown to the best bed which the house can offer. When this kind of hospitality has been afforded you as long as you choose to stay, and when you depart, and speak about your bill, you are most commonly told with some slight mark of resentment, that they do not keep tavern. Even the flaxen-headed urchins will turn away from your money.

In all my extensive intercourse with these people, I do not recollect but one instance of positive rudeness and inhospitality. It was on the waters of the Cuivre of the upper Mississippi; and from a man to whom I had presented bibles, who had received the hospitalities of my house, who had invited me into his settlement to preach. I turned away indignantly from a cold and reluctant reception here, made my way from the house of this man,—who was a German and comparatively rich,—through deep and dark forests, and amidst the concerts of wolves howling on the neighbouring hills. Providentially, about midnight, I heard the barking of dogs at a distance, made my way to the cabin of a very poor man, who arose at midnight, took me in, provided supper, and gave me a most cordial reception.

With this single exception, I have found the backwoodsmen to be such as

---

[1]Charles Maurice de Talleyrand-Périgord was a French Statesman who had lived for a time in the United States and wrote about his experiences–ED.

I have described; a hardy, adventurous, hospitable, rough, but sincere and upright race of people. I have received so many kindnesses from them, that it becomes me always to preserve a grateful and affectionate remembrance of them. If we were to try them by the standard of New England customs and opinions, that is to say, the customs of a people under entirely different circumstances, there would be many things in the picture, that would strike us offensively. They care little about ministers, and think less about paying them. They are averse to all, even the most necessary restraints. They are destitute of the forms and observances of society and religion; but they are sincere and kind without professions, and have a coarse, but substantial morality, which is often rendered more striking by the immediate contrast of the graceful bows, civility, and professions of their French Catholic neighbours, who have the observances of society and the forms of worship, with often but a scanty modicum of the blunt truth and uprightness of their unpolished neighbours.

8.3:   The Pioneer Experience (1818)

Once past the initial pioneer phase, how did the emigrants to the West fare? One of our best sources on the early nineteenth-century frontier is the account of Morris Birkbeck, an Englishman who traveled through the West just after 1815. Birkbeck was not just a visitor. He came to America with his large family as a permanent immigrant and settled on land in Illinois. In the selection below he describes both the bright and the dark side of the pioneer farmer's experiences. Which do you think was the more typical? In the absence of opinion polls, how could you determine whether people probably gained or lost by their move west?

The Life of the Western Farmer

MORRIS BIRKBECK

June 8. We were detained at Washington [in western Pennsylvania] by the indisposition of one of our party, and to-day proceeded only twenty-two miles to Ninian Beall's Tavern. We now consider ourselves, though east of the Ohio, to have made an inroad on the western territory: a delightful region;—healthy, fertile, romantic.

Our host has a small and simple establishment, which his civility renders truly comfortable. His little history may serve as an example of the natural growth of property in this young country.

Morris Birkbeck, *Notes on a Journey in America from the Coast of Virginia to the Territory of Illinois* (London: James Ridgeway, 1818), pp. 50–51, 120–21.

He is about thirty; has a wife and three fine and healthy children: his father is a farmer; that is to say, a proprietor, living five miles distant. From him he received five hundred dollars, and "began the world," in true style of American enterprize, by taking a cargo of flour to New Orleans, about two thousand miles, gaining a little more than his expences, and a stock of knowledge. Two years ago he had increased his property to nine hundred dollars; purchased this place; a house, stable, &c. and two hundred and fifty acres of land (sixty-five of which are cleared and laid down to grass,) for three thousand five hundred dollars, of which he has already paid three thousand, and will pay the remaining five hundred next year. He is now building a good stable, and going to improve his house. His property is at present worth seven thousand dollars; having gained, or rather grown, five thousand five hundred dollars in two years, with prospects of future accumulation to his utmost wishes. Thus it is that people here grow wealthy without extraordinary exertion, and without anxiety.

.   .   .   .

August 1. Dagley's, twenty miles north of Shawnee Town [in Indiana]. After viewing several beautiful prairies, so beautiful with their surrounding woods as to seem like the creation of fancy, gardens of delight in a dreary wilderness; and after losing our horses and spending two days recovering them, we took a hunter as our guide, and proceeded across the Little Wabash, to explore the country between that river and the Skillet-fork.

Since we left the Fox [Indian] settlement . . . cultivation has been very scanty, many miles intervening between the little "clearings." This may therefore be truly called a new country.

These lonely settlers are poorly off;—their bread corn must be ground thirty miles off, requiring three days to carry to the mill, and bring back, the small horse-load of three bushels. Articles of family manufacture are very scanty, and what they purchase is of the meanest quality and excessively dear: yet they are friendly and willing to share their simple fare with you. . . . To struggle with privations has now become the habit of their lives, most of them having made several successive plunges into the wilderness; and they begin already to talk of selling their "improvements," and getting farther "back," on finding that emigrants of another description are thickening about them.

8.4:   Indian Removal (1825–35)

If the pre–Civil War westward movement was a mixed experience for white settlers from the East and Europe, it was a complete disaster for the Native Americans who lived beyond the Appalachians. These peoples, divided into numerous tribes, or nations, occupied land and resources coveted by the white settlers. Between 1815 and 1860 they were largely evicted from their ancestral lands and pushed further west into unfamiliar regions by a concerted government policy of Indian "removal."

At first the removal policy was ad hoc and piecemeal, designed to accommodate whites pressing against a given Indian-occupied tract. After 1825 it became a systematic effort to herd all the eastern Indians beyond the Mississippi so that their vacated land might be carved into farms and towns for white settlers.

In the four items that follow we see the process from the point of view of white settlers, the federal government, and the Native Americans themselves.

Most white settlers considered the Indians a savage, bloodthirsty race. In the first item below, Timothy Flint endorses this view and describes the way settlers dealt with Indian attack. His is the classic picture of brave pioneers and "wild" Indians that for many years colored our history. Are his stories of Indian attacks false? How would you explain those attacks? What would have to be added to Flint's account to make it a rounded picture of Indian-white relations?

The second item, an 1832 petition to Congress by Florida settlers, suggests the material reasons for Indian removal. What special factors might have influenced the petitioners' attitudes? What other sorts of material considerations would have influenced white expulsionists?

The federal government's removal plans are described in the third item, an 1825 statement by Secretary of War John C. Calhoun, later the preeminent champion of southern rights. Was Calhoun's program completely indifferent to the claims of justice or the needs of the so-called five civilized nations? Is he weeping Crocodile tears for the Indians? Does the secretary of war reveal cultural biases? If so, what were they?

The Indians themselves protested the removal policy. Especially eloquent and forceful were those of the so-called five civilized tribes, composed of the Choctaw, Chickasaw, Cherokee, Creeks, and Seminole, Indian nations that occupied choice lands in the Southeast. The Cherokees particularly had borrowed the best of white culture (and some of the worst as well) and combined it with their own. Possessing large herds of cattle, gristmills, sawmills, schools, a written language, and, alas, even slaves, they were able to put up a formidable legal struggle against the officials of Georgia and the federal government. The 1830 petition below was one step in their case against removal farther west.

Do the Indians make their case convincingly? President Andrew Jackson believed that the Indians occupied far too much land considering their numbers. Is this argument for the need for the Indians to surrender land to the whites valid?

The Indians Are Savages

TIMOTHY FLINT

In the immense extent of frontier, which I have visited, I have heard many an affecting tale of the horrible barbarities and murders of the Indians, precisely of a character with those, which used to be recorded in the early periods of New England history. I saw two children, the only members of a family—consisting of a father, mother, and a number of children—that were spared by the Indians. It was on the river Femme-Osage. A party of Sacs and Foxes, that had been burning and murdering in the vicinity, came upon the house, as the father was coming in from abroad. They shot him, and he fled, wounded, a little distance, and fell. They then tomahawked the wife, and mangled her body. She had been boiling the sap of the sugar-maple. The Indians threw two of the children into the boiling kettles. The younger of the two orphans that I saw, was but three years old. His sister two years older, drew him under the bed before they were seen by the Indians. It had, in the fashion of the country, a cotton counterpane that descended to the floor. The howling of these demons, the firing, the barking of the dogs, the shrieking of the children that became their victims, never drew from these poor things, that were trembling under the bed, a cry, or the smallest noise. The Indians thrust their knives through the bed, that nothing concealed there, might escape them, and went off, through fear of pursuit, leaving these desolate beings unharmed.

You will see the countenances of the frontier people, as they relate numberless tragic occurrences of this sort, gradually kindling. There seems, between them and the savages, a deep-rooted enmity, like that between the seed of the woman and the serpent. They would be more than human, if retaliation were not sometimes the consequence. They tell you, with a certain expression of countenance, that in former days when they met an Indian in the woods, they were very apt to see him suffer under the falling-sickness. This dreadful state of things has now passed away, and I have seldom heard of late of a murder committed by the whites upon the Indians. Twenty years ago, the Indians and whites both considered, when casual rencounters took place in the woods, that it was a fair shot upon both sides. A volume would not contain the cases of these unrecorded murders.

The narrations of a frontier circle, as they draw round their evening fire, often turn upon the exploits of the old race of men, the heroes of the past days, who wore hunting shirts, and settled the country. Instances of undaunted heroism, of desperate daring, and seemingly of more than mortal endurance, are recorded of these people. In a boundless forest full of panthers and bears, and more dreadful Indians, with not a white within a hun-

Timothy Flint, *Recollections of the Last Ten Years Passed in Occasional Residences and Journeyings in the Valley of the Mississippi* (Boston: Cummings, Hilliard and Company, 1826), pp. 160–62.

dred miles, a solitary adventurer penetrates the deepest wilderness, and begins to make the strokes of his axe resound among the trees. The Indians find him out, ambush, and imprison him. A more acute and desperate warrior than themselves, they wish to adopt him, and add his strength to their tribe. He feigns contentment, uses the savage's insinuations, outruns him in the use of his own ways of management, but watches his opportunity, and when their suspicion is lulled, and they fall asleep, he springs upon them, kills his keepers, and bounds away into unknown forests, pursued by them and their dogs. He leaves them all at fault, subsists many days upon berries and roots, and finally arrives at his little clearing, and resumes his axe. In a little palisade, three or four resolute men stand a siege of hundreds of assailants, kill many of them, and mount calmly on the roof of their shelter, to pour water upon the fire, which burning arrows have kindled there, and achieve the work amidst a shower of balls. A thousand instances of that stern and unshrinking courage which had shaken hands with death, of that endurance which defied all the inventions of Indian torture, are recorded of these wonderful men. The dread of being roasted alive by the Indians, called into action all their hidden energies and resources.

Memorial to Congress by Inhabitants of the Territory

[Referred March 26, 1832]

To the Hon. the Senate & House of Representatives of the United States In Congress Assembled

The Memorial of the undersigned humbly shewith; that your memorialists Inhabitants Florida, are and have been for a long time greatly annoyed by the Semenole or Florida Indians; who are constantly wandering from their own Country and trespassing upon the property of the Whites: Their depredations upon our stock; are so frequent and extensive, that we cannot for a moment, feel any thing like Security, in relation to this description of our property & unless some measures are adopted by the Government to give us protection, we see no alternative left, but to abandon the settlements we have made at much expence & toil & retire to situation affording greater safety & less troublesome neighbours. We apprehend that unless the Indians are entirely removed from our Territory to some distant position, the evil in view, can not be effectfully remedied. The wildness & unsettled character of the frontier, (being in extent more than three hundred miles) between the whites and Indians, afford much ample facility for them to indulge their national disposition to wander, that it will be next to impossible to confine them within their own Territorial limits:—But were it possible to restrain & keep them at home, there is still to be found a most weighty objection to

Clarence E. Carter, ed., *The Territorial Papers of the United States* (Washington, DC: Government Printing Office, 1959), vol. 24, pp. 678–79.

their continuing to occupy, (as they now do) a tract of Country, within the geographical boundaries, of our Territory: in the fact, that absconding Slaves, find ready security among the Indians & such aid as is amply sufficient, to enable them successfully to alude the best efforts of their masters to recover them. It is believed that their are at this time, fifty or more runaway negroes in the Indian nation, who have taken refuge their since the treaty of 1823; to whom the Indians give protection, (in the way of secrecy at least) notwithstanding they are in that treaty obligated by a solemn pledge to apprehend & surrender all Slaves who may seek shelter in their Country. So long as a state of things thus dangerous to the interests of the inhabitants of Florida continues she cannot hope for prosperity or improvement: It cannot be expected that people of property will settle in a Country where their is so little security in relation to their property. We humbly pray therefore that your honourable body will take the matter into consideration and award to us such relief as is in your opinion necessary & proper.

Justification for "Removal"

JOHN C. CALHOUN

Of the four southern tribes, two of them (the Cherokees and Choctaws) have already allotted to them a tract of country west of the Mississippi. That which has been allotted to the latter is believed to be sufficiently ample for the whole nation, should they emigrate; and if an arrangement, which is believed not to be impracticable, could be made between them and the Chickasaws, who are their neighbors, and of similar habits and dispositions, it would be sufficient for the accommodation of both. A sufficient country should be reserved to the west of the Cherokees on the Arkansas, as a means of exchange with those who remain on the east. To the Creeks might be allotted a country between the Arkansas and the Canadian river, which limits the northern boundary of the Choctaw possessions in that quarter. There is now pending with the Creeks a negotiation, under the appropriation of the last session, with a prospect that the portion of that nation which resides within the limits of Georgia may be induced, with the consent of the nation, to cede the country which they now occupy for a portion of the one which it is proposed to allot for the Creek nation on the west of the Mississippi. Should the treaty prove successful, its stipulations will provide for the means of carrying it into effect, which will render any additional provision, at present, unnecessary. It will be proper to open new communications with the Cherokees, Choctaws, and Chickasaws, for the purpose of explaining to them the views of the Government, and inducing them to remove beyond the Mississippi, on the principles and conditions which may be proposed to the other tribes. It is known that there are many individuals of each of the

American State Papers: Indian Affairs (Washington, DC: 1834), vol. 2, pp. 543–44.

tribes who are desirous of settling west of the Mississippi, and, should it be thought advisable, there can be no doubt that (if, by an adequate appropriation, the means were afforded the Government of bearing their expense) they would emigrate. Should it be thought that the encouragement of such emigration is desirable, the sum of $40,000, at least, would be required to be appropriated for this object, to be applied under the discretion of the President of the United States. The several sums which have been recommended to be appropriated, if the proposed arrangement should be adopted, amount to $95,000. The appropriation may be made either general or specific, as may be considered most advisable.

I cannot, however, conclude without remarking, that no arrangement ought to be made which does not regard the interest of the Indians as well as our own; and that, to protect the interest of the former, decisive measures ought to be adopted to prevent the hostility which must almost necessarily take place, if left to themselves, among tribes hastily brought together, of discordant character, and many of which are actuated by feelings far from being friendly towards each other. But the preservation of peace between them will not alone be sufficient to render their condition as eligible in their new situation as it is in their present. Almost all of the tribes proposed to be affected by the arrangement are more or less advanced in the arts of civilized life, and there is scarcely one of them which has not the establishments of schools in the nation, affording, at once, the means of moral, religious, and intellectual improvement. These schools have been established, for the most part, by religious societies, with the countenance and aid of the Government; and, on every principle of humanity, the continuance of similar advantages of education ought to be extended to them in their new residence. There is another point which appears to be indispensable to be guarded, in order to render the condition of this race less afflicting. One of the greatest evils to which they are subject is that incessant pressure of our population, which forces them from seat to seat, without allowing time for that moral and intellectual improvement, for which they appear to be naturally eminently susceptible. To guard against this evil, so fatal to the race, there ought to be the strongest and the most solemn assurance that the country given them should be theirs, as a permanent home for themselves and their posterity, without being disturbed by the encroachments of our citizens. To such assurance, if there should be added a system, by which the Government, without destroying their independence, would gradually unite the several tribes under a simple but enlightened system of government and laws formed on the principles of our own, and to which, as their own people would partake in it, they would, under the influence of the contemplated improvement, at no distant day, become prepared, the arrangements which have been proposed would prove to the Indians and their posterity a permanent blessing. It is believed that, if they could be assured that peace and friendship would be maintained among the several tribes; that the advantages of education, which they now enjoy, would be extended to them; that they should have a permanent and solemn guaranty for their possessions, and receive the countenance and aid of the Government for the gradual extension of its privileges to them, there would be among all the tribes a disposition to accord with the views of the Government. There are now, in most of the tribes, well educated, sober, and reflecting individuals, who are afflicted at the present condition of the Indians, and despondent at their future prospects. Under the operation of existing causes, they behold the certain degradation, misery, and even the final annihilation of their race, and, no doubt, would gladly embrace any arrangement which would promise to elevate them in the scale of civilization, and arrest the destruction which now awaits them. It is conceived that one of the most cheap, certain, and desirable modes of effecting the object in view, would be for Congress to establish fixed principles, such as have been suggested, as the basis of the proposed arrangement; and to authorize the President to convene, at some suitable point, all of the well-informed, intelligent, and influential individuals of the tribes to be affected by it, in order to explain to them the views of the Government, and to pledge the faith of the nation to the arrangements that might be adopted. Should such principles be established by Congress, and the President be vested with suitable authority to convene the individuals as proposed, and suitable provision be made to meet the expense, great confidence is felt that a basis of a system might be laid, which, in a few years, would entirely effect the object in view, to the mutual benefit of the Government and the Indians; and which, in its operations, would effectually arrest the calamitous course of events to which they must be subject, without a radical change in the present system. Should it be thought advisable to call such a convention, as one of the means of effecting the object in view, an additional appropriation of $30,000 will be required; making, in the whole, $125,000 to be appropriated.

All of which is respectfully submitted.

J. C. Calhoun

The Indians Protest Against Removal

CHEROKEE PETITIONERS

We are aware that some persons suppose it will be for our advantage to remove beyond the Mississippi. We think otherwise. Our people universally think otherwise. Thinking that it would be fatal to their interests, they have almost to a man sent their memorial to Congress, deprecating the necessity of a removal. This question was distinctly before their minds when they signed their memorial. Not an adult person can be found, who has not an opinion on the subject; and if the people were to understand distinctly, that

Ebenezer C. Tracy, *Memoir of the Life of Jeremiah Evarts* (Boston: Crocker and Brewster, 1845), pp. 149–58.

they could be protected against the laws of the neighboring States, there is probably not an adult person in the nation, who would think it best to remove; though possibly a few might emigrate individually. There are doubtless many who would flee to an unknown country, however beset with dangers, privations and sufferings, rather than be sentenced to spend six years in a Georgia prison for advising one of their neighbors not to betray his country. And there are others who could not think of living as outlaws in their native land, exposed to numberless vexations, and excluded from being parties or witnesses in a court of justice. It is incredible that Georgia should ever have enacted the oppressive laws to which reference is here made, unless she had supposed that something extremely terrific in its character was necessary, in order to make the Cherokees willing to remove. We are not willing to remove; and if we could be brought to this extremity, it would be, not by argument; not because our judgment was satisfied; not because our condition will be improved—but only because we cannot endure to be deprived of our national and individual rights, and subjected to a process of intolerable oppression.

We wish to remain on the land of our fathers. We have a perfect and original right to claim this, without interruption or molestation. The treaties with us, and laws of the United States made in pursuance of treaties, guaranty our residence, and our privileges, and secure us against intruders. Our only request is, that these treaties may be fulfilled, and these laws executed.

But if we are compelled to leave our country, we see nothing but ruin before us. The country west of the Arkansas territory is unknown to us. From what we can learn of it, we have no prepossessions in its favor. All the inviting parts of it, as we believe, are preoccupied by various Indian nations, to which it has been assigned. They would regard us as intruders, and look upon us with an evil eye. The far greater part of that region is, beyond all controversy, badly supplied with wood and water; and no Indian tribe can live as agriculturists without these articles. All our neighbors, in case of our removal, though crowded into our near vicinity, would speak a language totally different from ours, and practice different customs. The original possessors of that region are now wandering savages, lurking for prey in the neighborhood. They have always been at war, and would be easily tempted to turn their arms against peaceful emigrants. Were the country to which we are urged much better than it is represented to be, and were it free from the objections which we have made to it, still it is not the land of our birth, nor of our affections. It contains neither the scenes of our childhood, nor the graves of our fathers.

9

Capital versus Labor

Western growth did not devitalize New England and the middle Atlantic states as many people from these sections feared it would. Instead, in the decades before the Civil War, the Northeast experienced a burst of economic growth and change that soon made it the most dynamic and prosperous part of the country, the pioneer of an industrial regime that would eventually penetrate every corner of the nation.

The most significant economic advance of these years was the replacement of the small handicraft shop by the system of factories employing masses of wage workers tending power-driven machines under one roof. The first American factories in the modern sense were spinning mills in southern New England that produced cotton thread and yarn. The machines were run by water power and were based on British models brought to America by immigrants who carried the plans in their heads. These mills usually employed whole families, including children, much as did the contemporary farm.

In 1815 the Boston Manufacturing Company, headed by Francis Cabot Lowell, began to operate at Waltham, Massachusetts, using the power generated by the Charles River. Employing mostly young, unmarried women, the Waltham mills produced finished cloth and sold it at good prices to a receptive market. So profitable was the enterprise that the promoters soon established factories at other power sites. The most elaborate development was the multimill factory complex and residential town located on the Merrimack River and named after Francis Lowell. The Lowell community soon became the emblem of the new industrial revolution, and visitors in droves came to the neat, bustling little city to observe and to marvel at its enterprise and its social harmony.

The New England textile industry was only one sector of a broad front of economic change. The half-century following 1810 ushered in a transportation revolution based on turnpikes, canals, steamboats, and railroads that broke down isolation and knit the nation into a single economic entity. It witnessed the beginnings of mechanization in grain-growing on the prairies and the arrival of the telegraph, presaging a communications revolution. Before long the nation was transformed from a collection of self-sufficient communities to a market economy where goods moved freely and cheaply hundreds of miles between consumers and producers. Presiding over the process was a new class of entrepreneurs who, through their wealth and vigor, expanded the influence of capitalist institutions and values in a nation already committed to the pursuit of riches and material abundance.

The new economic surge clearly increased overall wealth. It also magnified inequality and created social strains. The documents below focus on the great economic changes taking place in the North as the nation advanced through the half-century preceding the Civil War. The observers include both defenders of the new business system and those who opposed it. Their views open anew the issue of business values versus human values that is still alive today.

9.1:   The Lowell System (1842, 1845, 1846)

The directors of the Boston Manufacturing Company tapped an under-used pool of labor for their new mills: unmarried rural Yankee women. These young women came to Lowell, Chicopee, Lawrence, Holyoke, and the other textile mill towns to work for a few years while accumulating savings to help their families or to provide themselves with a marriage dowry. To reassure parents and entice "operatives," the mill owners housed the young women in clean, chaperoned boarding houses, and provided them with schools, lecture halls, libraries, churches, and even, in the case of Lowell, a subsidy to publish a newspaper (The Lowell Offering).

The selections below highlight two opposing views of the labor system in the Lowell-type mills. The first, by Charles Dickens, is highly favorable. Dickens was already a famous writer when he visited America in 1842, and wherever he went he was treated as a celebrity. Americans sought to show him their best, but the English novelist was not to be deceived. When he returned home, he wrote a highly critical account of America and a scathing novel set in the contemporary United States.

What audience is Dickens writing for in this piece from his American Notes? *His tone suggests that his readers may be skeptical of what he reports about the "Lowell girls." Why might he think that? What frame of reference regarding textile mills would his audience already have? Was Dickens apt to be an objective observer of the Lowell mill workers? Do his views of America make his conclusions more or less believable? Do you know whether in his writings generally Dickens was sympathetic to the poor and exploited? How might his views of his own country's working class affect your evaluation of his conclusions?*

The second, more negative view comes from a group of brief pieces written by "mill girls" themselves. They date from 1845–46, a few years after Dickens's visit to America. The first four items are by young women who worked in the mills in Exeter, New Hampshire; the last two are from Lowell operatives.

What are the complaints of the young women? Are they entirely economic? What other criticisms of their treatment do they make? To what does the mention of the Lowell girls' rebellion refer? How do you square Dickens's views with those in these documents? Note the difference in dates between Dickens's account and the attacks of the young women. Could the passage of time have accounted for the change?

A Positive View of the Lowell Girls

CHARLES DICKENS

These girls, as I have said, were all well dressed: and that phrase necessarily includes extreme cleanliness. They had serviceable bonnets, good warm cloaks, and shawls; and were not above clogs and pattens. Moreover, there were places in the mill in which they could deposit these things without injury; and there were conveniences for washing. They were healthy in appearance, many of them remarkably so, and had the manners and deportment of young women: not of degraded brutes of burden. If I had seen in one of those mills (but I did not, though I looked for something of this kind with a sharp eye), the most lisping, mincing, affected, and ridiculous young creature that my imagination could suggest. I should have thought of the careless, moping, slatternly, degraded, dull reverse (I *have* seen that), and should have been still well pleased to look upon her.

The rooms in which they worked, were as well ordered as themselves. In the windows of some, there were green plants, which were trained to shade the glass; in all, there was as much fresh air, cleanliness, and comfort, as the nature of the occupation would possibly admit of. Out of so large a number of females, many of whom were only then just verging upon womanhood, it may be reasonably supposed that some were delicate and fragile in appearance: no doubt there were. But I solemnly declare, that from all the crowd I saw in the different factories that day, I cannot recall or separate one young face that gave me a painful impression; nor one young girl whom, assuming

Charles Dickens, *American Notes and Pic–Nic Papers* (Philadelphia: T. B. Paterson and Brothers, 1842), pp. 40–41.

it to be matter of necessity that she should gain her daily bread by the labour of her hands, I would have removed from those works if I had had the power.

 . . . .

I am now going to state three facts, which will startle a large class of readers on this side of the Atlantic, very much.

Firstly, there is a joint-stock piano in a great many of the boarding-houses. Secondly, nearly all these young ladies subscribe to circulating libraries. Thirdly, they have got up among themselves a periodical called THE LOWELL OFFERING, "A repository of original articles, written exclusively by females actively employed in the mills,"—which is duly printed, published, and sold; and whereof I brought away from Lowell four hundred good solid pages, which I have read from beginning to end.

The large class of readers, startled by these facts, will exclaim, with one voice, "How very preposterous!" On my deferentially inquiring why, they will answer, "These things are above their station." In reply to that objection, I would beg to ask what their station is.

It is their station to work. And they *do* work. They labour in these mills, upon an average, twelve hours a day, which is unquestionably work, and pretty tight work too. Perhaps it is above their station to indulge in such amusements, on any terms. Are we quite sure that we in England have not formed our ideas of the "station" of working people, from accustoming ourselves to the contemplation of that class as they are, and not as they might be? I think that if we examine our own feelings, we shall find that the pianos, and the circulating libraries, and even the Lowell Offering, startle us by their novelty, and not by their bearing upon any abstract question of right or wrong.

The "Factory Girls" Tell Their Own Story[1]

The Operatives' Life

The numerous class of females who are operatives in mills, are required to devote *fifteen twenty-fourths* of every working day to the laborious task incumbent upon them, being thirteen hours of incessant toil, and two hours devoted to meals &c. Is not this fact a painful one? Is it not degrading to the age in which we live? It indicates that barbarism still exists among us, and it would be well for some people to take moral and humane lessons from savage life even. It is not a matter of marvel, that the Lowell girls should rebel against such treatment and petition the legislature of Massachusetts to establish a ten hour system: neither is it surprising that the federal *wise-acres*, who

Philip Foner, ed., *The Factory Girls* (Urbana: The University of Illinois Press, 1977), pp. 79–85.
[1]Footnotes deleted.

constituted that body, considered it inexpedient to legislate upon the sub-ject—*they* do not legislate for the protection of the *poor*, but for the protec-tion of the *rich*; the *gold* that lies within their grasp benumbs their sensibili-ties; and prevents the administration of that *justice* which humanity demands. We begin to doubt the utility or justice of any legislation for the protection of capital; indeed, if *barbarism* is to be the result of *protection*, we trust that the enlightened and philanthropic inhabitants of this country will cheerfully dispense with such *aid*, and, (as experience teaches it,) consider that legislation for the benefit of the *few*, is inimical to the best interests of the *whole*.

Think of girls being obliged to labor *thirteen* hours each working day, for a net compensation of *two cents per hour*, which is above the average net wages, being $1.56 per week. Two cents per hour for severe labor! Is not such a les-son enough to make an American curse the hour, when in an evil mood our lawmakers first granted a charter to enable the *few* to wield the wealth and power of *hundreds?* Is it not necessary to the maintenance of our rights, that some change be speedily effected in those laws by which our corporations are governed. We trust the friends of *equal rights,* will petition our legislature to make such a revision of these laws, as will cause the more general distribu-tion of those benefits which were designed for all. If such a course is taken, let the tyrants tremble.

A Factory Girl's Album

Exeter, N.H., June 20, 1846

Independence

Dialogue of a Lowell girl with the overseer of a factory:—"Well, Mr. Buck, I am informed that you wish to cut down my wages?" "Yes, such is my determi-nation." "Do you suppose that I would go into that room to work again, at lower price than I received before?" "Why, it's no more than fair and reason-able, considering the hard times." "Well, all I have to say is, that before I'll do it, I'll see you in Tophet, pumping thunder at three cents a clap!" It is needless to say that she was invited to resume her duties.

A Factory Girl's Album

Exeter, N.H., September 19, 1846

Beauties of Factory Life

Hundreds of operatives who work in our mills, are scarcely paid sufficient to board themselves, and are obliged to dress poorly, or, run in debt for their clothing. The consequence is, they become discouraged—lose confidence in themselves, and then, regardless of consequences, abandon their virtue to obtain favors. A goodly proportion of those in large cities, who inhabit "dens of shame," are first initiated into this awful vice in manufacturing places.

Soon after, most of them commence the downward road to destruction—they become known, and are compelled to leave their work in the mills and emigrate to large cities. We repeat what we have often done—girls leave not your homes in the country. It will be better for you to stay at home on your fathers farms than to run the risk of being ruined in a manufacturing village—Man. Pal.

How painfully true is the above. Many young, amiable and virtuous girls are yearly initiated into a life of vice and shame, through the baneful influences of the present corrupt factory system in New England. And when we hear of the depraved condition of those whom we had formerly known as the fairest of their sex, but who have since gone astray through dire necessity, or been duped by the arts of the wily men who frequent manufacturing villages, we are led to exclaim in the language of [William] Cowper,

> *My ear is pained,*
> *My soul is sick with every day's report*
> *Of wrong and outrage with which earth is filled.*
> *There is no flesh for man; the natural bond*
> *of brotherhood is severed as the flax,*
> *That falls asunder at the touch of fire.*

Factory Girl's Album

Exeter, N.H., October 31, 1846

Letter from a Local Factory Girl

I write to let the public know the cruel story of a sister operative of mine in Lowell. She is a young woman who had been employed in one of the factories of that city and left it, for the purpose of removing to another of the mills in which she thought she could labor with much better satisfaction to herself. But on application for work at that mill, she was denied employment, because the overseer (*driver* in the Southern term) of the mill she had left, had denounced her to the overseers (or drivers) of every mill in the place, as a girl not worthy to be employed. She applied to each mill in the city for employment, but was repulsed at all in succession for the same reason that employment was refused her at the first one. She sued the driver in a civil suit for slander, but was defeated in her suit for damages because the mill owners had established amongst themselves a rule, which custom had made law, making the ill-report of the overseer of one mill imperative cause of rejection by all the mills of the place;—for which ill-report as reason is asked of the overseer, and it stands by itself unexplained, final and imperative.

The issue of this case proves the existence of a rule and combination among the Lowell corporation that prevents any person upon leaving a corporation from obtaining work in any other corporation, if, *in the opinion of the overseer* of the corporation where the person formerly worked, he or she is not a suitable person to be employed. And it is of no consequence what induces that opinion—bad temper, immoral conduct, or nothing, on the part of the girl, or private pique, the gratification of an envious favorite, revenge for disappointed lechery, or any other cause, no matter how trivial or how wicked, on the part of the overseer—it may and does result in hunting and driving a girl out of the city if the overseer chooses to exercise his power over her destiny and her reputation.

Now I defy the most vehement ranters against Southern slavery to produce a section of the "black code" of any State, which makes more of a slave in the Southern plantation driver the female negro who has a master and an owner to protect her, than under the rule above established by the mill owners of Lowell, and as "priviledged communications" *made supreme over the common law of the State,* are the thousands of unprotected white females of Lowell slaves to the overseers of a dozen or two of cotton mills, who hold not only the bread, but the characters of those girls, in the palms of their hands, and can do with them as any passion may dictate or any caprice suggest, with perfect impunity of the law, and safety from all consequences to themselves.

When chartered and specially protected monopolies obtain such power and exercise such outrageous tyranny over the *women* of the U. States, making their laws of *custom* and *"privilege"* paramount to the common law of the land, placing thousands of virtuous and noble females under worse than Turkish subjection to the male tyrants of the cotton mills, who associated millions pension United States Senators and buy up legislators "like cattle in the market," it is indeed high time for the men of the United States, if there are any left this side of the Rio Grande, to seriously inquire whether these things are tending, and whether there is no remedy for such a slavish condition of *American white women?*

A Factory Girl in the Nashua Corporation

Nashua (N.H.) Gazette, October 1, 1846

Are the Operatives Well Off?

Mr. Editor:

We are told by gentlemen both in this country and abroad that the Lowell factory operatives are exceedingly well off. Good wages, sure pay, not very hard work, comfortable food and lodgings, and such unparalleled opportunities for intellectual cultivation, (why, they even publish a Magazine there!!) what more can one desire? Really gentlemen! would you not reckon your wives and sisters fortunate if they could by any possibility be elevated into the situation of operatives? When in the tender transports of first love, you paint for the fairest and fondest of mortal maidens a whole life of uninterrupted joy, do you hope for her as the supremest felicity, the lot of a factory girl? The operatives are well enough off!—Indeed! Do you receive them in your parlors, are they admitted to visit your families, do you raise your hats to them in the street, in a word, are they your *equals?*

Oliva

Lowell, Sept. 16, 1845

The Voice of the Sufferers

It is a subject of comment and general complaint, among the operatives, that while they tend three or four looms, where they used to tend but two, making nearly twice the number of yards of cloth, the pay is not increased to them, while the increase, to the owners is very great. Is this just? Twenty-five cents per week for each week, additional pay, would not increase the cost of the cloth, one mill a yard; no, not the half of a mill.

Now while I am penning this paragraph, a young lady enters my room with "Oh dear! Jane, I am sick and what shall I do? I have worked for three years, and never gave out, before. I stuck to my work, until I fainted at my loom. The Doctor says I must quit work and run about and amuse myself; but I have nowhere to go, and do not know what to do with myself." I have given the language, as it struck my ear; the conversation going on behind me. It is but the feelings of a thousand homeless, suffering females, this moment chanting "the Voice of Industry in this wilderness of sin."

One of the Vast Army of Sufferers

Voice of Industry, March 13, 1846

The "Beauties of Factory Life"

Mr. Editor:

Those who write so effusively about the "Beauties of Factory Life," tell us that we are indeed happy creatures, and how truly grateful and humbly submissive we should be. Can it be that any of us are so stupified as not to realize the exalted station and truly delightful influences which we enjoy? If so, let them take a glance at pages 195 and 196 of Rev. H. Miles' book, and they will surely awake to gratitude and be content. Pianos, teachers of music, evening schools, lectures, libraries and all these sorts of advantages are, says he, enjoyed by the operatives. (Query—when do they find time for all or any of these? When exhausted nature demands repose?) Very pretty picture that to write about; but we who work in the factory know the sober reality to be quite another thing altogether.

After all, it is easier to write a book than it is to *do* right. It is easier to smooth over and plaster up a deep festering rotten system, which is sapping the life-blood of our nation, widening and deepening the yawning gulf which will ere long swallow up the laboring classes in dependent servitude and serfdom, like that of Europe, than it is to probe to the very bottom of this death-spreading monster.

Juliana

Voice of Industry, June 12, 1846

9.2: An Economist Defends Capitalism (1835)

From Alexander Hamilton's day until our own, many Americans have believed economic growth to be the only valid formula for national affluence. Economic progress, it is argued, benefits not only the capitalists but also their employees. To hinder it in any way is to assure poverty for all.

The following selection is from a book by Philadelphian Henry C. Carey, a respected writer on economic subjects of the pre–Civil War era. Carey later became a supporter of the protective tariff, but at this point he still believed in unqualified free trade and laissez-faire.

What is the gist of Carey's argument? Is it convincing? Has it been widely applied in the United States? During what periods in particular has the formula enjoyed wide support?

Worker Benefit from High Profits

HENRY C. CAREY

Wages and profits have been represented by many political economists as natural antagonists, the Ormuzd and Ahriman[1] of political economy, one of which could rise only at the expense of the other. Such has been the belief of the great mass of the people who receive wages, which belief has given rise to trades' unions, so numerous in England, and obtaining in the United States; as well as to the cry of *the poor against the rich*. A large portion of those who pay, as well as those who receive wages, believe that the rate is altogether arbitrary, and that changes may be made at will. To this belief we are indebted for the numerous "strikes," or "turns out" we have seen, the only effect of which has been loss to both employers and workmen. Had the journeymen tailors of London understood the laws by which the distribution of the proceeds between the workman and the capitalist is regulated, they would have saved themselves and their employers the enormous loss that has

Henry C. Carey, *Essay on the Rate of Wages with an Examination of the Causes of the Differences in the Condition of the Labouring Population throughout the World* (Philadelphia: Carey, Lea, and Blanchard, 1835), pp. 15–18.
[1]That is, the A to Z of political economy—ED.

arisen out of their recent combination, and would have retained their situations instead of seeing themselves pushed from their stools by the influx of
Germans, who seized gladly upon the places vacated by their English fellow
workmen. Believing, as they do, that their wages are depressed for the benefit of their employers, they believe also that those employers are bound to
give them a portion of their profits in the advance of wages, when, in fact,
the employers are also sufferers by the same causes which produce the
depression, and are unable to advance them, however willing they may be. If
the real causes of the depression were understood, instead of combining
against their employers, they would unite with them to free their country
from those restrictions and interferences which produce the effect of which
they complain, and would thus secure permanent advantage, instead of a
temporary advance of wages, which is all that can be hoped for from combination, even if successful, which is rarely the case. Fortunately, in the United
States there have been fewer interferences, and there is therefore less to
alter, than in any other country; and if the workmen and labourers could be
made to understand the subject, they would see that the division between
themselves and the capitalist, or the rate of wages, is regulated by a law
immutable as are those which govern the motion of the Heavenly bodies;
that attempts at legislative interference can produce only disadvantageous
effects; and, that the only mode of increasing wages is by rendering labour
more productive, which can only be accomplished by allowing every man to
employ his capital and talent in the way which he deems most advantageous
to himself. They would see that all attempts on the part of the capitalist, to
reduce wages below the natural rate, as well as all on their part to raise it
above that rate, must fail, as any such reduction must be attended with an
unusual rate of profit to the employer, which must, in its turn, beget competition among the possessors of capital, and raise the rate of wages; while such
elevation in any employment must reduce the rate of profit so far as to drive
capital therefrom, and reduce wages again to the proper standard.

They should see in the fact that the great majority of the master workmen
have risen by their own exertions to the situations they at present occupy,
abundant evidence that nothing is wanting to them but industry and economy. They should desire nothing but freedom of action for themselves, and
that security both of person and property which prompts the capitalist to
investment; and so far should they be from entertaining feelings of jealousy
towards those who, by industry and economy, succeed in making themselves
independent, that they should see with pleasure the increase of capital, certain that such increase must produce new demands for their labour, accompanied by increased comfort and enjoyment for them. With such a system
the population of this country might increase still more rapidly than it has
done; the influx of people from abroad might be triple or quadruple what it
has been, and each successive year find the comforts of the labouring population in a regular course of increase, as the same causes which drive the
labourers of Europe here, to seek that employment and support denied

them at home, impel the capitalist to seek here a market for his capital, at the higher rate of interest which our system enables us to pay him with profit to ourselves.

9.3:   The Workingmen's Party Indicts Capitalism (1840)

It is an open question among scholars whether a majority of wage earners accepted the entrepreneurial spirit of the pre–Civil War age. We do know that many voted for the Whigs, clearly the party that best exemplified that spirit. But it is also clear that there was a strong insurgent voice among the men and women who toiled in the shops and factories of the era.

Below is an eloquent dissent from the position that Henry C. Carey represents. It is from an 1841 address of the Workingmen's Party of Charlestown, Massachusetts to "their brethren" throughout the state and nation.

The "Workies" (as they were called) claim special consideration from the community at large. On what bases? It is often said that American working people did not feel class resentment very strongly. Does this document support that view? The authors of this statement suggest that the condition of the laboring classes in America was deteriorating at this time. Was it? Were times good in 1840? How representative of labor attitudes is this document do you suppose? How would you estimate how prevalent such views were among wage workers?

Workers Are Exploited and Oppressed

THE WORKINGMEN'S PARTY OF CHARLESTOWN, MASSACHUSETTS

"Brethren:—The time seems to have arrived, when we, the real workingmen of the country, should pause, and survey our condition; ascertain our actual state, what are our rights, and the means of securing their full enjoyment.

"We are in this country, as in all others, the great majority of the population. We are the real producers. By our toil and sweat, our skill and industry, is produced all the wealth of the community. We have felled the primeval forests of this western world, converted them into fruitful fields, and planted the rose in the wilderness. We have erected these cities and villages which smile where lately was the Indian's wigwam, or the lair of the wild beast. We

"Address of the Workingmen's Party of Charlestown, Massachusetts to Their Brethren throughout the Commonwealth and the Union, 1840," *Boston Quarterly Review*, vol. 4 (January 1841), pp. 119–23.

have called into existence American manufactures, and been the instruments by which Commerce has amassed her treasures; our labor has digged the canals, and constructed the railways, which are intersecting the country in all directions, and opening its resources. We have built and manned the ships which navigate every ocean, and furnished the houses of the rich with all their comforts and luxuries. Our labor has done it all. And yet what is our condition? We toil on from morning to night, from one year's end to another, increasing our exertions with each year, and with each day, and still we are the poor and dependent. Here, as everywhere else, they, who pocket the proceeds of our labor, look upon us as the lower class, and term us the mob. We are but laborers, operatives, *vulgar* workingmen. We are poor. Our wages barely suffice to supply us the necessaries of life. We rarely have either leisure or opportunity to cultivate our minds, or to acquire that general knowledge of men and things, which no human being should grow up without. We are doomed by our position to grow up ignorant, and often in total neglect of all our nobler endowments. Our rights and interests attract no general attention. Legislators have no leisure to attend to our wants. And politicians have no further concern with us, than to wheedle us out of our votes by fair speeches and vague promises. The great concern is to take care of the rich and prosperous, the educated and powerful—of those who fill the high places of society, ride in carriages, sit on cushioned seats, and feast their dainty palates on luxuries culled from every clime. The wants of these are urgent. *Their* rights, privileges, and interests will brook no delay. But we, we, who bear all the burdens of society, pay all the revenues of Government, and the incomes of the rich, why we may go our way till a more convenient season.

"Now, Brethren, against this state of things, we enter a loud, an indignant protest. Our pockets may be empty, our faces may be sunburnt, and our hands may be hard; but we are men, with the souls of men, and the rights of men. There is a spirit within us, that assures us we were not born to be slaves; that we were not made merely to toil and sweat, to endure hunger, and cold, and nakedness, and death, that the few might grow fat on our labors and sufferings, and then turn round and kick us. We feel that we were made for something better, and that we have a right to aspire to something higher. An apostle has said, "If any man will not work, neither shall he eat." And this we believe should apply to one man as well as to another. Why, if we must bear all the burthens of society, shall we not in common justice enjoy all its blessings?

"Brethren, we have reflected on our condition, and we have come to the conclusion, that it is not the true condition of men. We are made of the same blood with those who work us as they do their horses and oxen, and who value us only for the profit they can derive from our labors. As pure blood courses in our veins as in theirs; as generous, as noble emotions swell our bosoms, and we have by nature capacities, to say the least, every way equal to theirs. Why then are they regarded as the better sort? Why then do they fatten on our labors? Why then are they rich and we poor? Why shall not our condition be as good as theirs? Why shall they call themselves our masters, and work us for their profit?. . .

"How stands the case with us? We labor more hours and with more intensity than we did formerly. We are aided by the discoveries of science and the introduction of machinery which gives to our labor a thousand fold additional power of production; and yet our condition relatively to the capitalist does by no means become better. There is scarcely a country in Europe where, in proportion to the labor they perform, the laboring classes are worse off than they are here. If we worked no more hours in a day, no more days in a week, and with no more intensity, than do the Italian peasants, we should find ourselves in a condition scarcely superior to theirs. We receive only about the same proportion of the proceeds of our labor.

"Moreover everything is tending to reduce the workingmen of this country to the condition they are sunk to in the old world. And what is that condition? In England, Scotland, and Wales, fourteen millions of the population, it is said, are obliged to subsist on an annual income of about ninety dollars a year and under. Five millions of these subsist on an annual income of less than twenty-five dollars each. In some counties in England, prior to the new poor laws, the paupers amounted to 63 per cent on the whole population, and in Liverpool every third individual was in indigence. Of Ireland, we need say nothing more than that one third of the whole population experience a deficiency of even third rate potatoes for thirty weeks out of fifty-two. In France, out of a population of about thirty-two millions, nearly thirty-one millions receive an annual income of under seventy-five dollars each; seven millions five hundred thousand, under twenty-five dollars; seven millions five hundred thousand, about eighteen dollars each. The expense of living is higher in England than in this country, and probably about one fourth less in France. But what must be the condition of the laboring classes even in France, where it is better than in England, and perhaps as good as in any country in Europe with the exception of Belgium?

"Now, what saves us from a similar condition? We are saved from a similar condition mainly by the paucity of our numbers, and the superior freedom of our industry, which creates a greater competition among capitalists, and therefore a greater demand for laborers. But this competition is less among manufacturers than it was. The principal manufacturers having adopted in regard to labor nearly uniform prices, rarely bid upon one another. The multiplication of large corporations is rapidly changing the whole character of our laboring population, by bringing them under the control of corporate bodies. These corporations check individual enterprise, lessen competition between individual capitalists, bind the capitalists together in close affinity of interest, and enable them to exert a sovereign control over the prices of labor. Let these corporations continue to increase for a few years longer, and they will be able to reduce our wages to the minimum of human subsistence. There will grow up around them a population bearing but little resemblance to that which won our political independence. It will be enfeebled in mind and body, and without either the mental or physical energy to shift its employment, or to make a firm stand for the amelioration of its condition.

"Hitherto the great mass of our laboring population has been bred in the agricultural districts, and consequently could easily shift from the city or the factory village to the farm. But this will not continue to be the case for another generation. Nor is this all. Lands are monopolized; the whole earth is foreclosed. However well disposed the laborer might be to cultivate the soil, he has not the means of becoming its owner. He has no spot on which to erect him a cabin, or on which he may raise a few potatoes to feed his wife and little ones; for the broad hands of the few cover it all over.

"Nor can we stop here. It would seem that the more we produced the better should be our condition. But this is not the fact except for short seasons. We suffer from over-production. To-day the supply is small, and the demand is brisk, we find employment and receive tolerable wages. But a hundred capitalists have rushed simultaneously into the work of producing; all hands are employed; forthwith the demand is supplied; the market is glutted; sales are diminished; and the diminished sales return upon us in the shape of a reduction of wages. To make up for this reduction of wages, we must labor more hours, or with greater intensity, and increase the amount of our production; and this increased amount of production, returns upon us again in the shape of a still farther reduction of our wages; and thus on, till they are reduced to the lowest point compatible with our existence.

"Brethren, put these things together, and tell us, if the natural tendency in this country is not to reduce us, and that at no distant day, to the miserable condition of the laboring classes in the old world? We stand on the declivity; we have already begun to descend! What is to save us?

"Brethren, this is a question of fearful import to us and our children. It is a question we must put to ourselves in sober earnest. It is a question we must put *now*, for a little more delay and it will be TOO LATE. Is it not already too late? God forbid! We will not believe it too late; but we feel that not a moment is to be lost. Now or never, must our salvation be secured. How shall it be done?

"Brethren, our salvation must, through the blessing of God, come from ourselves. It is useless to expect it from those whom our labors enrich. It is for their interest to augment our numbers and our poverty. It is their interest to purchase our labor at the lowest rate possible; it is ours to sell it at the highest rate possible. Their interest and ours, then, stand in direct opposition to each other. The greater our numbers, the more necessitous our condition, the greater is the facility with which they can obtain laborers, and the lower the price they are obliged to pay for labor. The fewer our numbers, the more independent our condition, the higher is the price we can demand and obtain for our labor. This refutes the pretensions of the aristocracy, that their interests and ours are one and the same. As men, as human beings, no doubt their interest and ours are the same; but their interests as capitalists, and ours as laborers, are directly opposite, and mutually destructive. In fact there is less identity of interest between the capitalists and us, than there is between the master and the slave. The slave is the master's property, and it is for the master's interest to take care of his property; it is for his interest to give his slave a sufficiency of food, and to be careful not to overwork him; for the sickness or death of his slave would be a loss of property. The same principle, which leads a man to take good care of his horses, sheep, and oxen, would lead him to take good care of his slaves. But the capitalist has no other interest in us, than to get as much labor out of us as possible. We are hired men, and hired men, like hired horses, have no souls. If a man owns the horse he drives, he will take care not to injure him; but if the horse be a hired one, what he will do, is told in a common saying, "Hired horses have no souls; drive on." "Hired men have no souls; drive on." If we sicken and die, the loss is ours, not the employer's. *There are enough more ready to take our places.*

"Brethren, we conjure you, therefore, not to believe a word of what is said about your interest and that of your employers being the same. Your interests and theirs are in the nature of things, hostile and irreconcilable. Then do not look to them for relief. Be not so mad as to suppose that they will voluntarily work out your salvation for you. You must expect them to be governed mainly by their own interests, and must never rely on their doing, as a body, what it is not for their interest to do. If then you have ever expected the capitalist, the accumulator, contractor, and employer, to conspire to elevate your condition, expect it no longer. As well might the poor and depressed have expected the Gospel, which is good news to the poor, from the scribes and pharisees, the chief priests and elders, who crucified Jesus for proclaiming it."

10

Jacksonian Democracy

The inauguration of Andrew Jackson as president in 1829 marked the appearance of a new political force in America. Following the War of 1812 the Federalists had virtually disappeared as a party, leaving the Jeffersonian Republicans without organized opposition for a decade or more. However much they gave lip service to the "people's" sovereignty, the Jeffersonian leaders were well-educated gentlemen who governed in the name of the people without being men of the people. In this era, elections were often weakly contested, and voter turnouts were usually low. The public trusted its patrician leaders and saw little reason to become embroiled in political campaigns that promised little change.

Jackson's advent transformed the nation's political culture. Andy Jackson, the victor of the Battle of New Orleans, the famous Indian fighter, was a hero to the masses. Unlike his predecessors, he was a self-made man from a humble background. He was also the first president from the new West, and carried to Washington its rough vigor, egalitarianism, and suspicion of eastern business enterprise.

Jackson polarized American politics by his deeds and personality. Hotheaded and contentious, vengeful toward his enemies and fiercely loyal to his friends, he was a high-handed and overbearing man. His political opponents called him "King Andrew" and likened themselves to the Whig opponents of King George III during the Revolution. But his enemies were not moved solely by personal dislike. They also deplored his attacks on the Second Bank of the United States and his opposition to federal aid to "internal improvements." Most of all, they decried what they considered his pandering to the ignorant and unruly masses. In the eyes of the Whig opposition, the Democrats, as the Jackson party came to be called, represented the nation's "leveling" forces, hostile to wealth, order, and good breeding. The Jacksonians, they said, stood for the triumph of numbers over merit.

Jackson's friends naturally saw "Old Hickory" in a different light. He was a man of the people, an opponent of the rich and powerful. The Democrats reversed the Whig estimate of the emerging new parties. The Whigs were the "silk-stocking" party of the social elite, who used government favors to advance their narrow and privileged economic interests.

Modern scholars are often skeptical of these party characterizations. Some see the Jacksonian leaders as recruits from the same class of rich lawyers, landowners, and merchants as their Whig counterparts. Others detect an important entrepreneurial component in the Jackson party. In this view the Jacksonians represent a class of newer business promoters who opposed the efforts of better established groups to retain their advantages and privileges. If anything, they better represented the spirit of free market capitalism than their adversaries.

Whatever the sources of Jackson's support, by the time "Old Hickory" left office in 1837 a "second party system" of Whigs and Democrats had taken shape that would last until the mid-1850s. Both new parties were coalitions, and their ideology and socio-cultural composition overlapped. Yet contemporaries would feel that it made a difference whether the Whigs or Democrats won, and they would show this at the polls. The two new political organizations would each win the passionate loyalty of large blocks of citizens. Election turnouts would soar; political campaigns would become exciting contests marked by pageantry and florid oratory.

10.1: Andrew Jackson Vetoes the Bank Bill (1832)

No political act did so much to define the party conflicts of the Jackson era as King Andrew's veto of the bill to recharter the Second Bank of the United States. Established in 1816 in the flush of nationalist fervor that followed the War of 1812, the bank, under its third president, Nicholas Biddle, had become stern regulator of the nation's monetary system and a force for stability and economic growth. In 1831 Biddle and his supporters sought to get Congress to renew the bank's charter due to expire in 1836. Congress obliged in July 1832, but Jackson vetoed the bill, setting off a major national debate.

The bank issue deeply divided the nation. On one side were the "agrarians," who detested all banks in general as sources of chicanery and corruption, and the Bank of the United States in particular as a "monster," controlled by the rich and possessing powers to manipulate the politicians and negate the popular will. Allied with these agrarians were various business groups, especially in the South and West, that resented Biddle's restrictive financial policies for curtailing their profits. On the other side of the bank issue were those like Henry Clay and Daniel Webster, who favored Hamiltonian policies of federal aid and guidance to economic growth and considered the bank a bulwark of sound money and orderly expansion. Eastern bankers and merchants usually favored the national bank as well.

The following document is a condensed version of Jackson's 1832 veto message. It was actually ghosted by Amos Kendall, a member of Jackson's "kitchen cabinet," his group of informal advisers, and by Roger Taney, the Democratic attorney general, but it accurately expressed the president's views.

Some of Jackson's attack on the bank centers on fears of foreign control of the American economy. Were these charges valid? Other arguments concern the dubious constitutionality of a federal charter for a bank and the extent to which the bill violated states' rights. But the central theme, emphasized in this excerpt, is that the bank is a source of privilege for some at the expense of "the humble members of society." Was this charge demagoguery, or was it a valid view of the bank's role in contemporary America? Do large private corporations pose a hazard to a democratic society, or are they indispensable for prosperity?

Why I Vetoed the BUS Recharter

ANDREW JACKSON

The present corporate body, denominated the president, directors, and company of the Bank of the United States, will have existed at the time this act is intended to take effect twenty years. It enjoys an exclusive privilege of banking under the authority of the General Government, a monopoly of its favor and support, and, as a necessary consequence, almost a monopoly of the foreign and domestic exchange. The powers, privileges, and favors bestowed upon it in the original charter, by increasing the value of the stock far above its par value, operated as a gratuity of many millions to the stockholders. . . .

The act before me proposes another gratuity to the holders of the same stock, and in many cases to the same men, of at least seven millions more. . . . It is not our own citizens only who are to receive the bounty of our Government. More than eight millions of the stock of this bank are held by foreigners. By this act the American Republic proposes virtually to make them a present of some millions of dollars. For these gratuities to foreigners and to some of our own opulent citizens the act secures no equivalent whatever. They are the certain gains of the present stockholders under the operation of this act, after making full allowance for the payment of the bonus.

James D. Richardson, *A Compilation of the Messages and Papers of the Presidents* (New York: Bureau of National Literature, 1897), vol. 3, pp. 1139–54.

Every monopoly and all exclusive privileges are granted at the expense of the public, which ought to receive a fair equivalent. The many millions which this act proposes to bestow on the stockholders of the existing bank must come directly or indirectly out of the earnings of the American people. . . .

It is not conceivable how the present stockholders can have any claim to the special favor of the Government. The present corporation has enjoyed its monopoly during the period stipulated in the original contract. If we must have such a corporation, why should not the Government sell out the whole stock and thus secure to the people the full market value of the privileges granted? Why should not Congress create and sell twenty-eight millions of stock, incorporating the purchasers with all the powers and privileges secured in this act and putting the premium upon the sales into the Treasury?

But this act does not permit competition in the purchase of this monopoly. It seems to be predicated on the erroneous idea that the present stockholders have a prescriptive right not only to the favor but to the bounty of Government. It appears that more than a fourth part of the stock is held by foreigners and the residue is held by a few hundred of our own citizens, chiefly of the richest class. For their benefit does this act exclude the whole American people from competition in the purchase of this monopoly and dispose of it for many millions less than it is worth. This seems the less excusable because some of our citizens not now stockholders petitioned that the door of competition might be opened, and offered to take a charter on terms much more favorable to the Government and country.

But this proposition, although made by men whose aggregate wealth is believed to be equal to all the private stock in the existing bank, has been set aside, and the bounty of our Government is proposed to be again bestowed on the few who have been fortunate enough to secure the stock and at this moment wield the power of the existing institution. I can not perceive the justice or policy of this course. If our Government must sell monopolies, it would seem to be its duty to take nothing less than their full value, and if gratuities must be made once in fifteen or twenty years let them not be bestowed on the subjects of a foreign government nor upon a designated and favored class of men in our own country. It is but justice and good policy, as far as the nature of the case will admit, to confine our favors to our own fellow-citizens, and let each in his turn enjoy an opportunity to profit by our bounty. In the bearings of the act before me upon these points I find ample reasons why it should not become a law. . . .

Is there no danger to our liberty and independence in a bank that in its nature has so little to bind it to our country? The president of the bank has told us that most of the State banks exist by its forbearance. Should its influence become concentered, as it may under the operation of such an act as this, in the hands of a self-elected directory whose interests are identified with those of the foreign stockholders, will there not be cause to tremble for the purity of our elections in peace and for the independence of our country in war? Their power would be great whenever they might choose to exert it; but if this monopoly were regularly renewed every fifteen or twenty years on terms proposed by themselves, they might seldom in peace put forth their strength to influence elections or control the affairs of the nation. But if any private citizen or public functionary should interpose to curtail its powers or prevent a renewal of its privileges, it can not be doubted that he would be made to feel its influence.

Should the stock of the bank principally pass into the hands of the subjects of a foreign country, and we should unfortunately become involved in a war with that country, what would be our condition? Of the course which would be pursued by a bank almost wholly owned by the subjects of a foreign power, and managed by those whose interests, if not affections, would run in the same direction there can be no doubt. All its operations within would be in aid of the hostile fleets and armies without. Controlling our currency, receiving our public moneys, and holding thousands of our citizens in dependence, it would be more formidable and dangerous than the naval and military power of the enemy.

If we must have a bank with private stockholders, every consideration of sound policy and every impulse of American feeling admonishes that it should be *purely American*. Its stockholders should be composed exclusively of our own citizens, who at least ought to be friendly to our Government and willing to support it in times of difficulty and danger. . . .

The bank is professedly established as an agent of the executive branch of the Government, and its constitutionality is maintained on that ground. Neither upon the propriety of present action nor upon the provisions of this act was the Executive consulted. It has had no opportunity to say that it neither needs nor wants a agent clothed with such powers and favored by such exemptions. There is nothing in its legitimate functions which makes it necessary or proper. Whatever interest or influence, whether public or private, has given birth to this act, it can not be found either in the wishes or necessities of the executive department, by which present action is deemed premature, and the powers conferred upon its agent not only unnecessary, but dangerous to the Government and country.

It is to be regretted that the rich and powerful too often bend the acts of government to their selfish purposes. Distinctions in society will always exist under every just government. Equality of talents, of education, or of wealth can not be produced by human institutions. In the full enjoyment of the gifts of Heaven and the fruits of superior industry, economy, and virtue, every man is equally entitled to protection by law; but when the laws undertake to add to these natural and just advantages artificial distinctions, to grant titles, gratuities, and exclusive privileges, to make the rich richer and the potent more powerful, the humble members of society—the farmers, mechanics, and laborers—who have neither the time nor the means of securing like favors to themselves, have a right to complain of the injustice of their Government. There are no necessary evils in government. Its evils exist only in its abuses. If it would confine itself to equal protection, and, as Heaven does its rains, shower its favors alike on the high and the low, the rich and the poor, it would be an unqualified blessing. In the act before me there seems to be a wide and unnecessary departure from these just principles.

Nor is our Government to be maintained or our Union preserved by invasions of the rights and powers of the several States. In thus attempting to make our General Government strong we make it weak. Its true strength consists in leaving individuals and States as much as possible to themselves— in making itself felt, not in its power, but in its beneficence; not in its control, but in its protection; not in binding the States more closely to the center, but leaving each to move unobstructed in its proper orbit.

Experience should teach us wisdom. Most of the difficulties our Government now encounters and most of the dangers which impend over our Union have sprung from an abandonment of the legitimate objects of Government by our national legislation, and the adoption of such principles as are embodied in this act. Many of our rich men have not been content with equal protection and equal benefits, but have besought us to make them richer by act of Congress. By attempting to gratify their desires we have in the results of our legislation arrayed section against section, interest against interest, and man against man, in a fearful commotion which threatens to shake the foundations of our Union. It is time to pause in our career to review our principles, and if possible revive that devoted patriotism and spirit of compromise which distinguished the sages of the Revolution and the fathers of our Union. If we can not at once, in justice to interests vested under improvident legislation, make our Government what it ought to be, we can at least take a stand against all new grants of monopolies and exclusive privileges, against any prostitution of our Government to the advancement of the few at the expense of the many, and in favor of compromise and gradual reform in our code of laws and system of political economy.

10.2:   Daniel Webster Replies to the Veto (1832)

Within hours of Andrew Jackson's veto of the bill to renew the charter of the Second Bank, Daniel Webster, Whig senator from Massachusetts, rose to defend the bank. Webster had a personal interest in its fate: he was an attorney for the bank, one of its frequent borrowers, and a close friend of Nicholas Biddle, the bank's president. As we read the selection below, we must take these facts into consideration, yet we should judge Webster's arguments on their merits. Does he deal effectively with Jackson's criticisms? What, in Webster's view, were the bank's advantages to the country at large?

Daniel Webster Defends the BUS

DANIEL WEBSTER

Mr. President I will not conceal my opinion that the affairs of the country are approaching an important and dangerous crisis. At the very moment of almost unparalleled general prosperity, there appears an unaccountable disposition to destroy the most useful and most approved institutions of the government. Indeed, it seems to be in the midst of all this national happiness that some are found openly to question the advantages of the Constitution itself; and many more ready to embarrass the exercise of its just power, weaken its authority, and undermine its foundations. How far these notions may be carried it is impossible yet to say. We have before us the practical result of one of them. The bank has fallen, or is to fall. . . .

Before proceeding to the constitutional question, there are some other topics, treated in the [veto] message, which ought to be noticed. It commences by an inflamed statement of what it calls the "favor" bestowed upon the original bank by the government, or, indeed, as it is phrased, the "monopoly of its favor and support"; and through the whole message all possible changes are rung on the "gratuity," the "exclusive privileges," and "monopoly," of the bank charter. Now, Sir, the truth is, that the powers conferred on the bank are such, and no others, as are usually conferred on similar institutions. They constitute no monopoly, although some of them are of necessity, and with propriety, exclusive privileges. "The original act," says the message, "operated as a gratuity of many millions to the stockholders." What fair foundation is there for this remark? The stockholders received their charter, not gratuitously, but for a valuable consideration in money, prescribed by Congress, and actually paid. At some times the stock has been above *par*, at other times below *par*, according to prudence in management, or according to commercial occurrences. But if, by a judicious administration of its affairs, it had kept its stock always above *par*, what pretence would there be, nevertheless, for saying that such augmentation of its value was a "gratuity" from government? The message proceeds to declare, that the present act proposes another donation, another gratuity, to the same men, of at least seven millions more. It seems to me that this is an extraordinary statement, and an extraordinary style of argument, for such a subject and on such an occasion. In the first place, the facts are all assumed; they are taken for true without evidence. There are no proofs that any benefit to that amount will accrue to the stockholders, nor any experience to justify the expectation of it. It rests on random estimates, or mere conjecture. But suppose the continuance of the charter should prove beneficial to the stockholders; do they not pay for it? They give twice as much for a charter of fifteen years, as was given before for one of twenty. And if the proposed *bonus*,

Daniel Webster, *Works of Daniel Webster*, ed. (Boston: Charles C. Little and James Brown, 1851), vol. 3, pp. 423–47.

or premium, be not, in the President's judgment, large enough, would he, nevertheless, on such a mere matter of opinion as that, negative the whole bill? May not Congress be trusted to decide even on such a subject as the amount of the money premium to be received by government for a charter of this kind?

But, Sir, there is a larger and a much more just view of this subject. The bill was not passed for the purpose of benefiting the present stockholders. Their benefit, if any, is incidental and collateral. Nor was it passed on any idea that they had a right to a renewed charter, although the message argues against such right, as if it had been somewhere set up and asserted. No such right has been asserted by any body. Congress passed the bill, not as a bounty or a favor to the present stockholders, nor to comply with any demand of right on their part; but to promote great public interests, for great public objects. Every bank must have some stockholders, unless it be such a bank as the President has recommended, and in regard to which he seems not likely to find much concurrence of other men's opinions; and if the stockholders, whoever they may be, conduct the affairs of the bank prudently, the expectation is always, of course, that they will make it profitable to themselves, as well as useful to the public. If a bank charter is not to be granted, because, to some extent, it may be profitable to the stockholders, no charter can be granted. The objection lies against all banks.

Sir, the object aimed at by such institutions is to connect the public safety and convenience with private interests. It has been found by experience, that banks are safest under private management, and that government banks are among the most dangerous of all inventions. Now, Sir, the whole drift of the message is to reverse the settled judgment of all the civilized world, and to set up government banks, independent of private interest or private control. For this purpose the message labors, even beyond the measure of all its other labors, to create jealousies and prejudices, on the ground of the alleged benefit which individuals will derive from the renewal of this charter. Much less effort is made to show that government, or the public, will be injured by the bill, than that individuals will profit by it. Following up the impulses of the same spirit, the message goes on gravely to allege, that the act, as passed by Congress, proposes to make a *present* of some millions of dollars to foreigners, because a portion of the stock is held by foreigners. Sir, how would this sort of argument apply to other cases? The President has shown himself not only willing, but anxious, to pay off the three per cent stock of the United States at *par,* notwithstanding that it is notorious that foreigners are owners of the greater part of it. Why should he not call that a donation to foreigners of many millions? . . .

From the commencement of the government, it has been thought desirable to invite, rather than to repel, the introduction of foreign capital. Our stocks have all been open to foreign subscriptions; and the State banks, in like manner, are free to foreign ownership. Whatever State has created a debt has been willing that foreigners should become purchasers, and desirous of it. How long is it, Sir, since Congress itself passed a law vesting new powers in the President of the United States over the cities in this District, for the very purpose of increasing their credit abroad, the better to enable them to borrow money to pay their subscriptions to the Chesapeake and Ohio Canal? It is easy to say that there is danger to liberty, danger to independence, in a bank open to foreign stockholders, because it is easy to say any thing. But neither reason nor experience proves any such danger. The foreign stockholder cannot be a director. He has no voice even in the choice of directors. His money is placed entirely in the management of the directors appointed by the President and Senate and by the American stockholders. So far as there is dependence or influence either way, it is to the disadvantage of the foreign stockholder. He has parted with the control over his own property, instead of exercising control over the property or over the actions of others. . . .

In order to justify its alarm for the security of our independence, the message supposes a case. It supposes that the bank should pass principally into the hands of the subjects of a foreign country, and that we should be involved in war with that country, and then it exclaims, "What would be our condition?" Why, Sir, it is plain that all the advantages would be on our side. The bank would still be our institution, subject to our own laws, and all its directors elected by ourselves; and our means would be enhanced, not by the confiscation and plunder, but by the proper use, of the foreign capital in our hands. And, Sir, it is singular enough, that this very state of war, from which this argument against a bank is drawn, is the very thing which, more than all others, convinced the country and the government of the necessity of a national bank. So much was the want of such an institution felt in the late war, that the subject engaged the attention of Congress, constantly, from the declaration of that war down to the time when the existing bank was actually established; so that in this respect, as well as in others, the argument of the message is directly opposed to the whole experience of the government, and to the general and long-settled convictions of the country. . . .

Mr. President, we have arrived at a new epoch. We are entering on experiments, with the government and the Constitution of the country, hitherto untried, and of fearful and appalling aspect. This message calls us to the contemplation of a future which little resembles the past. Its principles are at war with all that public opinion has sustained, and all which the experience of the government has sanctioned. It denies first principles; it contradicts truths, heretofore received as indisputable. It denies to the judiciary the interpretation of law, and claims to divide with Congress the power of originating statutes. It extends the grasp of executive pretension over every power of the government. But this is not all. It presents the chief magistrate of the Union in the attitude of arguing away the powers of that government over which he has been chosen to preside; and adopting for this purpose modes of reasoning which, even under the influence of all proper feeling towards high official station, it is difficult to regard as respectable. It appeals to every prejudice which may betray men into a mistaken view of their own interests, and to every passion which may lead them to disobey the impulses of their understanding. It urges all the specious topics of State rights and national encroachment against that which a great majority of the States have affirmed to be rightful, and in which all of them have acquiesced. It sows, in an unsparing manner, the seeds of jealousy and ill-will against that government of which its author is the official head. It raises a cry, that liberty is in danger, at the very moment when it puts forth claims to powers heretofore unknown and unheard of. It effects alarm for the public freedom, when nothing endangers that freedom so much as its own unparalleled pretenses. This, even, is not all. It manifestly seeks to inflame the poor against the rich; it wantonly attacks whole classes of the people, for the purpose of turning against them the prejudices and the resentments of other classes. It is a state paper which finds no topic too exciting for its use, no passion too inflammable for it address and its solicitation.

Such is this message. It remains now for the people of the United States to choose between the principles here avowed and their government. These cannot subsist together. The one or the other must be rejected. If the sentiments of the message shall receive general approbation, the Constitution will have perished even earlier than the moment which its enemies originally allowed for the termination of its existence. It will not have survived to its fiftieth year.

10.3:   Jacksonian Enterprise (1837)

Not all Jacksonians accepted the antibusiness bias displayed in the 1832 veto message. Clearly many of Old Hickory's staunchest supporters hated the bank, not as a symbol of business as such, but as a monopoly that stifled other enterprises, both other banks and other business ventures generally.

One Jacksonian of this temper was Roger Taney, Jackson's close friend and a member of his cabinet. It was Secretary of Treasury Taney who, on Jackson's orders, removed the government deposits in the Second Bank in 1833 and placed them in the "pet banks" (state banks favored by the Jacksonians), thereby administering the final blow to the bank. In 1836 Jackson appointed Taney as chief justice of the Supreme Court, where he served until his death in 1864.

As chief justice, Taney used the Supreme Court to overturn legal monopolies and assert freedom of enterprise. One blow for the doctrine of laissez faire was his decision in Charles River Bridge v. Warren Bridge in 1837. The case decided a suit brought by the stockholders of a toll bridge, the Charles River Bridge in Boston, to stop construction of an adjacent and competing bridge, the Warren Bridge. The plaintiffs in-

sisted that their charter from the state conferred on them an exclusive privilege and that the charter for the new bridge violated that privilege. In the decision excerpted here Taney decided against the Charles River Bridge company.

On what grounds did Taney base his decision? In what way did his decision reflect the spirit of enterprise of the age? What might have been the course of economic development in the United States if the Supreme Court had upheld the exclusive charter of the Charles River Bridge?

The Chief Justice Defends Economic Progress

ROGER TANEY

Borrowing, as we have done, our system of jurisprudence from the English law . . . it would present a singular spectacle, if, while the courts in England are restraining, within the strictest limits, the spirit of monopoly, and exclusive privileges in nature of monopolies, and confining corporations to the privileges plainly given to them in their charter, the courts of this country should be found enlarging these privileges by implication; and construing a statute more unfavorably to the public, and to the rights of the community, than would be done in a like case in an English court of justice.

But we are not now left to determine for the first time the rules by which public grants are to be construed in this country. The subject has already been considered in this court, and the rules of construction above stated fully established. In the case of the *United States* v. *Arredondo,* 8 Pet. 738, the leading cases upon this subject are collected together by the learned judge who delivered the opinion of the court, and the principle recognized that, in grants by the public nothing passes by implication. . . .

But the case most analogous to this, and in which the question came more directly before the court, is the case of *Providence Bank* v. *Billings,* 4 Pet. 514, which was decided in 1830. In that case it appeared that the legislature of Rhode Island had chartered the bank, in the usual form of such acts of incorporation. The charter contained no stipulation on the part of the State that it would not impose a tax on the bank, nor any reservation of the right to do so. It was silent on this point. Afterwards a law was passed imposing a tax on all banks in the State, and the right to impose this tax was resisted by the Providence Bank upon the ground that if the State could impose a tax, it might tax so heavily as to render the franchise of no value, and destroy the institution; that the charter was a contract, and that a power which may in effect destroy the charter is inconsistent with it, and is impliedly renounced in granting it. But the court said that the taxing power is of vital importance and essential to the existence of government, and that the relinquishment of such a power is never to be assumed. . . . The case now before the court is, in

The Lawyers' Co-Operative Publishing Company, *Cases Argued and Decided in the Supreme Court of the United States,* Book 9 (Rochester, NY, 1926), p. 551–53.

principle, precisely the same. It is a charter from a state; the act of incorporation is silent in relation to the contested power. The argument in favor of the proprietors of the Charles River bridge, is the same, almost in words, with that used by the Providence Bank; that is, that the power claimed by the state, if it exists, may be so used as to destroy the value of the franchise they have granted to the corporation. The argument must receive the same answer; and the fact that the power has been already exercised, so as to destroy the value of the franchise, cannot in any degree affect the principle. The existence of the power does not, and cannot, depend upon the circumstance of its having been exercised or not.

It may, perhaps, be said, that in the case of the Providence Bank, this court were speaking of the taxing power; which is of vital importance to the very existence of every government. But the object and end of all government is to promote the happiness and prosperity of the community by which it is established; and it can never be assumed, that the government intended to diminish its power of accomplishing the end for which it was created. And in a country like ours, free, active and enterprising, continually advancing in numbers and wealth, new channels of communication are daily found necessary, both for travel and trade, and are essential to the comfort, convenience and prosperity of the people. A state ought never to be presumed to surrender this power, because, like the taxing power, the whole community have an interest in preserving it undiminished. And when a corporation alleges, that a state has surrendered, for seventy years, its power of improvement and public accommodation, in a great and important line of travel, along which a vast number of its citizens must daily pass, the community have a right to insist, in the language of this court, above quoted, "that its abandonment ought not to be presumed, in a case, in which the deliberate purpose of the state to abandon it does not appear." The continued existence of a government would be of no great value, if, by implications and presumptions, it was disarmed of the powers necessary to accomplish the ends of its creation, and the functions it was designed to perform, transferred to the hands of privileged corporations. The rule of construction announced by the court, was not confined to the taxing power, nor is it so limited, in the opinion delivered. On the contrary, it was distinctly placed on the ground, that the interests of the community were concerned in preserving, undiminished, the power then in question; and whenever any power of the state is said to be surrendered or diminished, whether it be the taxing power, or any other affecting the public interest, the same principle applies, and the rule of construction must be the same. No one will question, that the interests of the great body of the people of the state, would, in this instance, be affected by the surrender of this great line of travel to a single corporation, with the right to exact toll, and exclude competition, for seventy years. While the rights of private property are sacredly guarded, we must not forget, that the community also have rights, and that the happiness and well-being of every citizen depends on their faithful preservation.

Adopting the rule of construction above stated as the settled one, we proceed to apply it to the charter of 1785 to the proprietors of the Charles River bridge. This act of incorporation is in the usual form, and the privileges such as are commonly given to corporations of that kind. It confers on them the ordinary faculties of a corporation, for the purpose of building the bridge; and establishes certain rates of toll, which the company are authorized to take. This is the whole grant. There is no exclusive privilege given to them over the waters of Charles river, above or below their bridge; no right to erect another bridge themselves, nor to prevent other persons from erecting one, no engagement from the State, that another shall not be erected; and no undertaking not to sanction competition, nor to make improvements that may diminish the amount of its income. Upon all these subjects the charter is silent; and nothing is said in it about a line of travel, so much insisted on in the argument, in which they are to have exclusive privileges. No words are used from which an intention to grant any of these rights can be inferred. If the plaintiff is entitled to them, it must be implied, simply from the nature of the grant, and cannot be inferred from the words by which the grant is made. . . .

The inquiry then is, does the charter contain such a contract on the part of the State? Is there any such stipulation to be found in that instrument? It must be admitted on all hands, that there is none—no words that even relate to another bridge, or to the diminution of their tolls, or to the line of travel. If a contract on that subject can be gathered from the charter, it must be by implication, and cannot be found in the words used. Can such an agreement be implied? The rule of construction before stated is an answer to the question. In charters of this description, no rights are taken from the public, or given to the corporation, beyond those which the words of the charter, by their natural and proper construction, purport to convey. There are no words which import such a contract as the plaintiffs in error contend for, and none can be implied; and the same answer must be given to them that was given by this court to the Providence Bank. The whole community are interested in this inquiry, and they have a right to require that the power of promoting their comfort and convenience, and of advancing the public prosperity, by providing safe, convenient, and cheap ways for the transportation of produce and the purposes of travel, shall not be construed to have been surrendered or diminished by the State, unless it shall appear by plain words that it was intended to be done. . . .

Indeed, the practice and usage of almost every State in the Union old enough to have commenced the work of internal improvement, is opposed to the doctrine contended for on the part of the plaintiffs in error. Turnpike roads have been made in succession, on the same line of travel; the later ones interfering materially with the profits of the first. These corporations have, in some instances, been utterly ruined by the introduction of newer and better modes of transportation and travelling. In some cases, railroads have rendered the turnpike roads on the same line of travel so entirely use-less, that the franchise of the turnpike corporation is not worth preserving. Yet in none of these cases have the corporations supposed that their privi-leges were invaded, or any contract violated on the part of the State. . . .

And what would be the fruits of this doctrine of implied contracts on the part of the States, and of property in a line of travel by a corporation, if it should now be sanctioned by this court? To what results would it lead us? If it is to be found in the charter to this bridge, the same process of reasoning must discover it, in the various acts which have been passed, within the last forty years, for turnpike companies. . . . If this court should establish the principles now contended for, what is to become of the numerous railroads established on the same line of travel with turnpike companies, and which have rendered the franchises of the turnpike corporations of no value? Let it once be understood that such charters carry with them these implied con-tracts, and give this unknown and undefined property in a line of travelling, and you will soon find the old turnpike corporations awakening from their sleep and calling upon this court to put down the improvements which have taken their place. The millions of property which have been invested in rail-roads and canals upon lines of travel which had been before occupied by turnpike corporations will be put in jeopardy. We shall be thrown back to the improvements of the last century, and obliged to stand still until the claims of the old turnpike corporations shall be satisfied, and they shall con-sent to permit these States to avail themselves of the lights of modern sci-ence, and to partake of the benefit of those improvements which are now adding to the wealth and prosperity, and the convenience and comfort, of every other part of the civilized world. . . .

Judgment affirmed.

STORY, J., delivered a dissenting opinion in which THOMPSON, J., con-curred.

10.4: Democratic Egalitarianism (1836)

Just as there was an entrepreneurial wing of the Democratic Party, there was also a radical wing. In New York it took form as the "Loco Focos,"[1] a group that went beyond the regular Democrats in demanding equality. For a time the Loco Focos remained loyal Democrats, although fighting the Tammany Hall conservatives who represented the conservative "regu-lars," for supremacy within the New York Democratic Party. In 1836

---

[1] The term comes from the name for a new form of self-lighting matches. These were used by the radical Democrats to light candles at a Tammany Hall meeting in 1835, when the New York regulars turned out the gas lights to force their equal rights opponents to adjourn a gathering called to reject the regulars' candidates and party platform.

they held a separate state convention at Utica, established the Equal Rights Party, and nominated a separate ticket for state offices.

The following letter was written by Isaac S. Smith of Buffalo on the occasion of his nomination for governor by the Utica convention. What political principles does Smith support? What are his economic principles? From what ideas or sources does he derive these principles? Why does he emphasize paper money so strongly? Why does he also emphasize education? In what sense might Smith be considered a radical? Do the views of the Loco Focos have any resonance today? (Note the resemblance between Smith's views and those of the Charlestown "Workies" in Chapter 9.)

The Positions of the Loco Focos

ISAAC S. SMITH

Buffalo, September 29th, 1836.

Gentlemen:—

Your letter of the 26th instant, in behalf of the convention of Mechanics, Farmers, and Workingmen, accompanied by a Declaration of rights adopted by them at Utica, and presented for my consideration, is before me.

Fully approving the resolution which requires of candidates for elective offices, avowals of their political principles, I cheerfully state the following as mine.

The first great political truth to be impressed on the minds of our youth is, that they are born free, and that no acts of legislation should deprive them of perfect equality in rights. This principle will constantly stimulate those of humble birth to compete with the favorites of fortune, and teach them that without personal merit, no one can have just claims to honorable distinction.

Although the first declaration, that "all men are created free and equal," is subscribed to by a vast majority, yet our legislatures have not framed their acts in conformity to it: I allude to their acts of incorporation, generally granted to active and intriguing partisans, who make a trade of electioneering, and find their zeal and fidelity rewarded by valuable monopolies and lucrative offices.

Our legislatures can have no more right to take from the people and confer upon individuals, special and exclusive privileges, than they have to confer titles of nobility.

Indirect taxes on articles of necessity, or which by habit have become so, as well as all demands for personal services without equivalents, which oper-

Francis Byrdsall, *The History of the Loco Foco or Equal Rights Party* (New York: Clement & Packard, 1842), pp. 75–76.

ate oppresively on the poor, and are not felt by the rich, are unjust, and should not exist.

All wealth is an accumulation of surplus labor, from which alone the expenses and burthens of government should be borne. No person possessing mental or physical ability, can have a *moral* right to consume that which he does not in some manner contribute to produce.

None of our institutions have so strong a tendency to create and perpetuate the odious distinctions betwixt the rich and the poor, as the paper money banks. Those incorporations, and others not more meritorious, and yet equally monopolizing, have been the greatest cause of truckling and corruption in legislatures.

The worst feature in the proceedings of the past legislatures, has been the wasteful appropriation of large sums, ostensibly for public improvements, but in reality for party purposes; and the granting of charters for banks, with which to strengthen the hands of party leaders. The great majority of the people have but little interest individually in these plunderings of the many for the benefit of the few.

The genius of our institutions requires that the majority shall govern, therefore no legislature can in all cases bind their successors.

The doctrine of vested rights, as heretofore promulgated, is dangerous, and cannot be sustained. ·

I conceive the term, *paper money,* an absurdity; therefore, I would sanction nothing but silver and gold as a circulating medium. Bankers' notes of large denominations, and bills of exchange, which must exist, cannot come within my definition of circulating medium. My creed is to leave commercial men to manage their own affairs.

As the difference in education is one great cause of the distinctions in society, and as our own and the experience of other countries show that a well educated community is the least liable to anarchy; that nothing approaching equality can exist between ignorance and intelligence, I deem it essential to the perpetuation of the best of our institutions, and to promote the happiness of generations to come, that our common schools be established upon a basis that will insure to every child the advantages of equal education. At this time, it is not possible in most parts of our country to obtain any more than the rudiments of the plainest education, unless the children be sent from home, and provided for at a great expense in the towns; this expense being beyond the means of most men, their children neglected, and being comparatively in ignorance, must eventually become the proper subjects for demagogues.

Those who produce all the wealth should not submit to have their families kept in ignorance and degradation, and the common schools held in disrepute, while the public bounty is showered upon those for the education of the aristocratical few. Too much cannot be done for common schools.

As a citizen, having their interests warmly at heart, I approve the Declaration of Rights made by the Mechanics, Farmers and Workingmen, transmitted by you to me; and as they have thought the use of my name would benefit the cause, I do not feel at liberty to decline the nomination with which they have honored me.

I am very respectfully yours,

Isaac S. Smith.

To Messrs. E. G. Barney, John Commerford, Daniel Gorham, F. Byrdsall, W. F. Piatt.

10.5:   A "Knickerbocker" Gentleman Flays the "Rabble" (1836, 1837)

Philip Hone was a rich merchant of New York during the Jackson era. He was a self-made man, but his wealth gained him entrée into the social circle of the city's Knickerbocker elite, the descendants of the old New York families, many of Dutch extraction. Hone was a devout Whig. He despised Jackson and closely associated with the Whig leaders Henry Clay, Daniel Webster, and William Henry Seward. His social views were those of the "silk-stocking" element in the Whig party: aristocratic and antiegalitarian.

Hone kept a diary from the late 1820s until his death in the 1850s. It is a remarkable view of a rich, conservative New Yorker—his ideas, his politics, his amusements, his business activities, his relations with his family and friends. In his journal Hone chronicled the growing assertiveness of the "common" folk as expressed in their attitudes toward their elected representatives and their employers. In the following diary entries for 1836 and 1837, he describes a New York judge's response to a strike of tailors to raise their wages and Mayor William Beach Lawrence's New Year's reception in 1837. Is Hone's attitude toward the tailor's strike more than snobbery? What stronger term might be more accurate? What is his tone concerning the mayor's reception? What do you suppose those whom Hone disparages would say about the reception?

A Whig Gentleman's View of the Working Class

PHILIP HONE

Monday, June 6 [1836].—

Journeymen Tailors. In corroboration of the remarks which I have occasionally made of late, on the spirit of faction and contempt of the laws which per-

Philip Hone, *The Diary of Philip Hone, 1828–1857,* ed. Allan Nevins (New York: Dodd, Mead and Company, 1927), vol. 1, pp. 211–12, 235–36.

vades the community at this time, is the conduct of the journeymen tailors instigated by a set of vile foreigners (principally English), who, unable to endure the restraint of wholesome laws, well administered in their own country, take refuge here, establish trade unions, and villify Yankee judges and juries. Twenty odd of these "knights of the thimble" were convicted at the oyer and terminer [i.e., a criminal court] of a conspiracy to raise their wages and to prevent any of the craft from working at prices less than those for which they "struck." Judge Edwards gave notice that he would proceed to sentence them this day, but in consequence of the continuance of Robinson's trial the court postponed the sentence until Friday.

This, however, being the day on which it was expected, crowds of people have been collected in the park, ready for any mischief to which they may have been instigated, and a most diabolical and inflammatory handbill was circulated yesterday, headed by a coffin. The board of Aldermen held an informal meeting this evening, at which a resolution was adopted authorizing the mayor to offer a reward for the discovery of the author, printer, publisher, or distributor of this incendiary publication. The following was the handbill:—

"The *Rich* Against the *Poor!*

"Judge Edwards, the tool of the aristocracy, against the people! Mechanics and Workingmen! A deadly blow has been struck at your *Liberty!* The prize for which your fathers fought has been robbed from you! The freemen of the North are now on a level with the slaves of the South! With no other privilege than laboring, that drones may fatten on your life-blood! Twenty of your brethren have been found guilty for presuming to resist a reduction of their wages! And Judge Edwards has charged an American jury, and agreeably to that charge, they have established the precedent that workingmen have no right to regulate the price of labor, or, in other words, the rich are the only judges of the wants of the poor man. On Monday, June 6, 1836, at ten o'clock, these freemen are to receive their sentence, to gratify the hellish appeties of the aristocrats!

"On Monday, the liberty of the workingmen will be interred! Judge Edwards is to chant the requiem! Go! Go! Every freeman and workingman and hear the hollow and the melancholy sound of the earth on the coffin of equality! Let the courtroom, the City Hall, yea! the whole park be filled with *mourners.* But remember, offer no violence to Judge Edwards. Bend meekly, and receive the chain wherewith you are to be bound! Keep the peace! Above all things, keep the peace!"

Tuesday, Jan. 3 [1837].—

Mr. [William Beach] Lawrence, the Mayor, kept open house yesterday, according to custom from time immemorable, but the manners as well as the times have sadly changed. Formerly gentlemen visited the mayor, saluted him by an honest shake of the hand, paid him the compliment of the day, and took their leave; one out of twenty perhaps taking a single glass of wine or cherry bounce and a morsel of pound cake or New Year's cookies. But that respectable functionary is now considered the mayor of a party, and the rabble considering him "hail fellow well met," use his house as a Five Points[1] tavern. Mr. Lawrence has been much annoyed on former occasions, but the scene yesterday defies description. At ten o'clock the doors were beset by a crowd of importunate *sovereigns,* some of whom had already laid the foundations of *regal* glory and expected to become *royally* drunk at the hospitable house of His Honor. The rush was tremendous; the tables were taken by storm, the bottles emptied in a moment. Confusion, noise, and quarreling ensued, until the mayor with the assistance of his police cleared the house and locked the doors, which were not reopened until every eatable and drinkable were removed, and a little decency and order restored.

I called soon after this change had taken place. The mayor related the circumstances to me with strong indignation, and I hope the evil will be remedied hereafter. All this comes of Mr. Lawrence being the mayor of a party and not of the city. Every scamp who has bawled out "Huzza for Lawrence" and "Down With the Whigs" considered himself authorized to use him and his house and furniture at his pleasure; to wear his hat in his presence, to smoke and spit upon his carpet, to devour his beef and turkey, and wipe his greasy fingers upon the curtains, to get drunk with his liquor, and discharge the reckoning with riotous shouts of "Huzza for our mayor." *We* put him in and *we* are entitled to the use of him. Mr. Lawrence (party man as he is) is too much of a gentleman to submit to this, and sometimes wishes his constituents and his office all to the devil, if I am not greatly mistaken, and if he rejects (as he has now done) their kind tokens of brotherly affection, they will be for sending him there ere long, and will look out for somebody of their own class less troubled than him with aristocratical notions of decency, order, and sobriety.

---

[1] A crime-ridden area of New York City—ED.

11

The Ferment of Reform

The generation preceding the Civil War was one of extraordinarily rapid change. These were years when thousands of immigrants, primarily from Ireland and Germany, descended on American shores. In 1854 alone 460,000 aliens arrived in the United States at a time when the nation's total population was only 26.5 million. It was an era of economic transformation, especially in the North. In the 1790s the first spinning mills for cotton yarn were established in New England. Twenty years later the first integrated textile factories began pouring out acres of cotton cloth. Canals and steamboats meanwhile made the movement of freight and people in the nation's interior relatively swift and efficient. The railroads arrived in the late 1830s, and by 1860 the country was covered by a network of track on which freight and passenger cars moved as fast as fifty miles an hour. An information revolution was also underway. In May 1844 Samuel F. B. Morse transmitted the proceedings of the Democratic Party's national convention from Baltimore to Washington over the lines of the brand new electric telegraph. Two years later Richard Hoe invented the rotary printing press, thus making possible vast runs of daily newspapers selling at a penny a copy.

The slave-holding South was largely impervious to these improvements, but they converted the North into a social caldron where new ideas and movements bubbled constantly to the surface of daily life. Many of these movements emphasized improving the world through legislation. Others sought personal regeneration through augmented personal resolve. Still others urged withdrawal from the corrupting world into miniature experimental societies of the virtuous. Thousands of people were swept up in the wave of zeal to remake the world. "We are all a little wild here with numberless projects of social reform," Ralph Waldo Emerson, the Concord philosopher, wrote the English essayist Thomas Carlyle in 1840. "Not a reading man but has a draft of a new community in his waistcoat pocket."

Not every American welcomed the enthusiasm for social change. Many deplored the "isms" breaking out all over, especially those like abolitionism and feminism, which threatened to subvert institutions deeply intrenched in the social system. The documents below deal with various aspects of the pre–Civil War reform surge. Inevitably they leave out large areas of the many-sided reform wave of the era, but they do concern several of the most important. The selections also include several critiques of the reformers and their causes.

11.1:   Abolitionism (1831)

Few of the pre–Civil War reform movements had such a powerful impact on the nation as abolitionism. Attacks on slavery go back as far as the early eighteenth century. The assault grew more intense during the era of the American Revolution and expanded into a movement that effectively terminated the "peculiar institution" north of the Mason-Dixon line by the 1820s. Although it survived in the South, uneasiness with slavery led to a wave of personal emancipations by slave owners and a liberalization of southern slave codes. During this period antislavery advocates supported the gradual emancipation of the country's remaining slaves and sought to press their program by appealing to the consciences of southerners and slaveholders.

This moderate movement changed abruptly on January 1, 1831, with the appearance of a new antislavery publication, The Liberator, *published in Boston. Its editor was William Lloyd Garrison, a Massachusetts-born printer and editor, whose antislavery convictions derived from those of Benjamin Lundy, a Quaker abolitionist. Garrison rejected Lundy's mild tone and gentle tactics, however. He demanded "immediate" abolition, by which he meant that the process of freeing the slaves must begin at once, not be phased-in as had been done earlier in the northern states. He harshly condemned both slavery and slaveholders, and rejected a view then common among antislavery advocates that freed blacks should be sent back to Africa ("colonized"). In 1833 Garrison founded the American Antislavery Society, which soon had scores of local affiliates all over the North that helped spread the antislavery message widely. By the end of the decade the antislavery societies had several thousand members, including a contingent of free blacks, men and women, who were among the most committed and effective members. By this time the antislavery movement had fissured into feuding groups, several of which deplored Garrison and his followers.*

The document that follows is the opening editorial of The Liberator, *in effect Garrison's prospectus. Do you think his tone helped or hurt the antislavery cause? What would you expect the reaction to the Garrisonian challenge to be in the North? In the South? Among other antislavery advocates? In fighting a malevolent institution like slavery, is it better to be militant or compassionate?*

Manifesto of a New Antislavery Movement[1]

WILLIAM LLOYD GARRISON

To The Public.

In the month of August, I issued proposals for publishing "THE LIBERATOR" in Washington City; but the enterprise, though hailed in different sections of the country, was palsied by public indifference. Since that time, the removal of the *Genius of Universal Emancipation*[2] to the Seat of Government has rendered less imperious the establishment of a similar periodical in that quarter.

During my recent tour for the purpose of exciting the minds of the people by a series of discourses on the subject of slavery, every place that I visited gave fresh evidence of the fact, that a greater revolution in public sentiment was to be effected in the free States—*and particularly in New-England*—than at the South. I found contempt more bitter, opposition more active, detraction more relentless, prejudice more stubborn, and apathy more frozen, than among slave-owners themselves. Of course, there were individual exceptions to the contrary. This state of things afflicted, but did not dishearten me. I determined, at every hazard, to lift up the standard of emancipation in the eyes of the nation, *within sight of Bunker Hill and in the birthplace of liberty*. That standard is now unfurled; and long may it float, unhurt by the spoliations of time or the missiles of a desperate foe—yea, till every chain be broken, and every bondman set free! Let Southern oppressors tremble—let their secret abettors tremble—let their Northern apologists tremble—let all the enemies of the persecuted blacks tremble.

I deem the publication of my original Prospectus unnecessary, as it has obtained a wide circulation. The principles therein inculcated will be steadily pursued in this paper, excepting that I shall not array myself as the political partisan of any man. In defending the great cause of human rights, I wish to derive the assistance of all religions and of all parties.

Assenting to the "self-evident truth" maintained in the American Declaration of Independence, "that all men are created equal, and endowed by their Creator with certain inalienable rights—among which are life, liberty,

William Lloyd Garrison, 1805–1879: The Story of His Life Told by His Children (New York: The Century Company, 1885), vol. 1, pp. 224–26.
[1]Original footnotes deleted.
[2]The antislavery publication of Garrison's mentor, Benjamin Lundy—ED.

and the pursuit of happiness," I shall strenuously contend for the immediate enfranchisement of our slave population. In Park-Street Church [in Boston], on the Fourth of July, 1829, in an address on slavery, I unreflectingly assented to the popular but pernicious doctrine of *gradual* abolition. I seize this opportunity to make a full and unequivocal recantation, and thus publicly to ask pardon of my God, of my country, and of my brethren the poor slaves, for having uttered a sentiment so full of timidity, injustice, and absurdity. A similar recantation, from my pen, was published in the *Genius of Universal Emancipation* at Baltimore, in September, 1829. My conscience is now satisfied.

I am aware that many object to the severity of my language; but is there not cause for severity? I *will be* as harsh as truth, and as uncompromising as justice. On this subject, I do not wish to think, or speak, or write, with moderation. No! No! Tell a man whose house is on fire to give a moderate alarm; tell him to moderately rescue his wife from the hands of the ravisher; tell the mother to gradually extricate her babe from the fire into which it has fallen;—but urge me not to use moderation in a cause like the present. I am in earnest—I will not equivocate—I will not excuse—I will not retreat a single inch—AND I WILL BE HEARD. The apathy of the people is enough to make every statue leap from its pedestal, and to hasten the resurrection of the dead.

It is pretended, that I am retarding the cause of emancipation by the coarseness of my invective and the precipitancy of my measures. *The charge is not true.* On this question my influence,—humble as it is,—is felt at this moment to a considerable extent, and shall be felt in coming years—not perniciously, but beneficially—not as a curse, but as a blessing; and posterity will bear testimony that I was right. I desire to thank God, that he enables me to disregard "the fear of man which bringeth a snare," and to speak his truth in its simplicity and power. And here I close with this fresh dedication:

> "*Oppression! I have seen thee, face to face,*
> *And met thy cruel eye and cloudy brow;*
> *But thy soul-withering glance I fear not now—*
> *For dread to prouder feelings doth give place*
> *Of deep abhorrence! Scorning the disgrace*
> *Of slavish knees that at thy footstool bow,*
> *I also kneel—but with far other vow*
> *Do hail thee and thy herd of hirelings base:—*
> *I swear, while life-blood warms my throbbing veins,*
> *Still to oppose and thwart, with heart and hand,*
> *Thy brutalising sway—till Afric's chains*
> *Are burst, and Freedom rules the rescued land,—*
> *Trampling Oppression and his iron rod:*
> Such is the vow I take—SO HELP ME GOD!*"

WILLIAM LLOYD GARRISON.

BOSTON, January 1, 1831.

11.2:   Women's Rights (1848)

American women were prominent in many of the pre–Civil War reform organizations and movements. During the earliest years of the nineteenth century, they had been active in Christian missionary and tract publishing societies dedicated to uplifting the "heathen" at home or on the remote shores of Oregon, Africa, or Asia. When the reform wave broadened during the 1830s, women established parallel all-female reform societies and auxiliaries to help with fund-raising and housekeeping services for the male-run organizations.

However devoted to social change, many of the male reformers refused to accept women as full equals. When dedicated female antislavery advocates like Angelina Grimké[1] sought to address mixed male-female audiences, they were renounced by all but the followers of William Lloyd Garrison, the most radical of the abolitionist leaders. At the 1840 World Anti-Slavery Convention in London, American women abolitionists were denied seats and were relegated to the gallery. It was at this London convention that Elizabeth Cady Stanton and Lucretia Mott met and began the association that would alter the fundamental relations between men and women.

In 1848 Stanton, backed by Mott, issued a call for a meeting to consider women's rights at Seneca Falls, New York. The Seneca Falls convention assembled in a year when much of the Euro-American world was in great social and political ferment. Moreover, the small community near Rochester was in the heart of the "Burned Over" district of western New York where waves of evangelical revivals had shaken people out of accustomed beliefs and modes of behavior. It was the right time and right setting for a call to revolutionary change.

The document below is excerpted from Elizabeth Cady Stanton's opening remarks to the delegates at Seneca Falls. It is less famous than the convention's Declaration of Sentiments, which was modeled after the Declaration of Independence, but it is also a more complete statement of feminist grievances and a more eloquent indictment of "woman's" oppressors.

In what ways, according to Stanton, were American women oppressed in 1848? What objections to women's rights is she seeking to refute? What male fears is she trying to quiet? She mentions the fact that many

---

[1] Angelina and Sarah Grimké were two South Carolina sisters who despised the slavery of their home state and fled to Philadelphia in the 1820s. There they became Quakers and activists in the antislavery movement. Angelina later married the eloquent abolitionist Theodore Dwight Weld, one of Garrison's more moderate colleagues.

women themselves rejected the women's rights movement. Does she explain why?

Almost a century and a half has elapsed since the Seneca Falls convention. Has the feminist description of a male-dominated American society changed drastically? Since women have long since acquired the vote, how do you explain the sense of oppression some women still feel? Did Stanton and her colleagues exaggerate the importance of the franchise in liberating women?

Women's Rights

ELIZABETH CADY STANTON

I should feel exceedingly diffident to appear before you at this time, having never before spoken in public, were I not nerved by a sense of right and duty, did I not feel the time had fully come for the question of woman's wrongs to be laid before the public, did I not believe that woman herself must do this work; for woman alone can understand the height, the depth, the length, and the breadth of her own degradation. Man cannot speak for her, because he has been educated to believe that she differs from him so materially, that he cannot judge of her thoughts, feelings, and opinions by his own. . . .

Among the many important questions which have been brought before the public, there is none that more vitally affects the whole human family than that which is technically called Woman's Rights. Every allusion to the degraded and inferior position occupied by women all over the world has been met with scorn and abuse. From the men of highest mental cultivation to the most degraded wretch who staggers in the streets do we meet ridicule, and coarse jests, freely bestowed upon those who dare assert that woman stands by the side of man, his equal, placed there by her God, to enjoy with him the beautiful earth, which is her home as it is his, having the same sense of right and wrong, and looking to the same Being for guidance and support. So long has man exercised tyranny over her, injurious to himself and benumbing to her faculties, that few can nerve themselves to meet the storm; and so long has the chain been about her that she knows not there is a remedy. . . .

As the nations of the earth emerge from a state of barbarism, the sphere of woman gradually becomes wider, but not even under what is thought to be the full blaze of the sun of civilization is it what God designed it to be. In every country and clime does man assume the responsibility of marking out the path for her to tread. In every country does he regard her as a being inferior to himself, and one whom he is to guide and control. . . .

Elizabeth Cady Stanton, *Address of Elizabeth Cady Stanton Delivered at Seneca Falls and Rochester, N.Y., July 19 and August 2nd, 1848* (New York: Robert J. Johnston Printer, 1870), pp. 3–19.

In all eastern countries she is a mere slave, bought and sold at pleasure. There are many differences in habits, manners, and customs among the heathen nations of the Old World, but there is little change for the better in woman's lot. She is either the drudge of man to perform all the hard labor of the field, and all the menial duties of the hut, tent, or house, or she is the idol of his lust, the mere creature of his varying whims and will. . . .

There is a class of men who believe in their natural, inborn, inbred superiority, and their heaven-descended right to dominion over the fish of the sea, the fowl of the air, and last, though not least, the immortal being called woman. I would recommend this class to the attentive perusal of their Bibles, . . . to historical research, to foreign travel, to a closer observation of the manifestations of mind about them, and to a humble comparison of themselves with such women as Catherine of Russia and Elizabeth of England, distinguished for their statesmanlike qualities; Harriet Martineau and Madame De Stael, for their literary attainments; or Catherine Herschel and Mary Somerville for their scientific researches. . . .

Man's intellectual superiority cannot be a question until woman has had a fair trial. When we shall have had our freedom to find out our own sphere, when we shall have had our colleges, our professions, our trades, for a century, a comparison then may be justly instituted. When woman, instead of being taxed to endow colleges where she is forbidden to enter . . . shall first educate herself . . . we shall not then hear so much about this boasted superiority. How often, now, we see young men carelessly throwing away the intellectual food their sisters crave. A little music, that she may while away an hour pleasantly, a little French, a smattering of the sciences, and in rare instances, some slight classical knowledge, a woman is considered highly educated. She leaves her books and studies just as a young man is entering thoroughly into his. Then comes the gay routine of fashionable life, courtship and marriage, the perplexities of house and children, and she knows nothing besides. Her sphere is home. And whatever yearning her spirit may have felt for a higher existence, whatever may have been the capacity she well knew she possessed for more elevated enjoyments, . . . all is buried beneath the weight of undivided cares.

Men, bless their innocence, are fond of representing themselves as beings of reason, of intellect, while women are creatures of the affections. This is a self-conceit that makes the possessor infinitely happy. . . . But so far as we can observe, it is pretty much now-a-days as it was with Adam of old. . . . [Stanton demonstrates that it was Adam, not Eve, who was moved by passion to eat of the apple in the Garden of Eden.]

In consideration of man's claim to moral superiority, glance now at our theological seminaries, our divinity students, . . . the immaculate priesthood, and what do we find here? . . . Every sect has its God, every sect its Bible, and there is much bitterness, envy, hatred, and malice between those contending sects. . . . And the leaders of these sects . . . are they distinguished among men for their holy aspirations, their virtue, purity and chastity? . . . By no

means. Not a year passes but we hear of some sad, soul-sickening deed perpetrated by some of this class. . . .The lamentable want of principle among
our lawyers, generally, is too well known to need comment. The everlasting
backbiting and bickering of our physicians is [*sic*] proverbial. The disgraceful riots at our polls, where man, in performing the highest duty of citizenship, and ought surely to be sober-minded, the perfect rowdyism that now
characterizes the debates in our national Congress,—all these are great facts
which rise up against man's claim for moral superiority. In my opinion, he is
infinitely woman's inferior in every moral quality, not by nature, but made
so by a false education. . . .

Let us now consider man's claim to physical superiority. Methinks I hear
some say, surely, you do not contend for equality here. Yes, we must not give
an inch, lest you take an ell. . . . If you claim the advantage of size, merely,
why it may be that under any course of training, . . . man might still be the
larger of the two, though we do not grant even this. But the perfection of
the physique is great power combined with great endurance. Now your
strongest men are not always the tallest men, . . . but very often the small
elastic man, who is well built, tightly put together, and possessed of an
indomitable will. . . . We cannot say what the woman might be physically, if
the girl were allowed all the freedom of the boy in romping, climbing, swimming, playing whoop and ball. . . . Physically, as well as intellectually, it is use
that produces growth and development.

But there is a class of objectors, who say they do not claim superiority,
they merely assert a difference. But you will find by following them up closely, that they soon run this difference into the old groove of superiority. . . .

We have met here today to discuss our rights and wrongs, civil and political, and not, as some have supposed, to go into the detail of social life alone.
We do not propose to petition the legislature to make our husbands just,
generous, and courteous, to seat every man at the head of a cradle, and to
clothe every woman in male attire. None of these points, however important
they may be considered by leading men, will be touched in this Convention.
As to their costume, the gentlemen need feel no fear of our imitating that,
for we think it a violation of every principle of taste, beauty and dignity. . . .
But we are assembled to protest against a form of government, existing without the consent of the governed—to declare our right to be free as man is
free, to be represented in the government which we are taxed to support, to
have such disgraceful laws as give man the power to chastise and imprison
his wife, to take the wages she earns, the property which she inherits, and, in
case of separation, the children of her love; laws which make her the mere
dependent on his bounty. It is to protest against such unjust laws as these
that we are assembled today, and to have them, if possible, forever erased
from our statute-books, deeming them a shame and a disgrace in a Christian
republic in the nineteenth century. . . .

And, strange as it may seem to many, we now demand our right to vote
according to the declaration of the government under which we live. This

right no one pretends to deny. We need not prove ourselves equal to Daniel Webster to enjoy this privilege, for the ignorant Irishman in the ditch has all the civil rights he has. We need not prove our muscular power equal to this same Irishman to enjoy this privilege, for the most tiny, weak, ill-shaped stripling of twenty-one, has all the civil rights of the Irishman. . . . [A]ll white men in this country have the same rights, however they may differ in mind, body, or estate. The right is ours. . . . Have it, we must. Use it, we will. The pens, the tongues, the fortunes, the indomitable wills of many women are already pledged to secure this right. The great truth, that no just government can be formed without the consent of the governed, we shall echo and re-echo in the ears of the unjust judge, until by continual coming we shall weary him.

But, say some, would you have women vote? What, refined, delicate women at the polls, mingling with such scenes as violence and vulgarity? Most certainly. . . . Much is said of woman's influence, might not her presence do much good toward softening down this violence, refining this vulgarity? Depend upon it, the places that by their impure atmosphere, are unfit for women, cannot but be dangerous to her sires and sons. . . .

But what would woman gain by voting? Men must know the advantages of voting for they all seem very tenacious about the right. Think you, if woman had the vote in this government, that all those laws affecting her interests would so entirely violate every principle of right and justice? Had woman a vote to give, might not the office-holders and seekers propose some change in her condition?

"But are you not already represented by your fathers, husbands, brothers, sons?" Let your statute-books answer the question. We have had enough of such representation. In nothing is woman's true happiness consulted. Men like to call her an angel—to feed her what they think sweet food—nourishing her vanity; to make her believe her organization is much finer than theirs, that she is not fitted to struggle with the tempests of public life, but needs their care and protection! Care and protection—such as the wolf gives the lamb—such as the eagle the hare that he carries to his eyrie!!

The most discouraging, the most lamentable aspect our cause wears is the indifference, indeed, the contempt with which women themselves regard the movement. Where the subject is introduced, among those even who claim to be intelligent and educated, it is met by the scornful curl of the lip and by expression of ridicule and disgust. But we shall hope better things of them when they are enlightened in regard to their present position. When women know the laws and constitutions under which they live, they will not publish their degradation by declaring themselves satisfied, nor their ignorance, by declaring they have all the rights they want. . . .

One common objection to this movement is, that if the principles of freedom and equality which we advocate were put into practice, it would destroy all harmony in the domestic circle. Here let me ask, how many truly harmonious households have we now? Look around your circle of friends: on the one hand you will find the meek, sad-looking, thoroughly subdued wife, with no freedom of thought or action, her days passed in the dull routine of household cares, and her nights half perchance in making tattered garments whole, and the other half in slumbers oft disturbed by sick and restless children. She knows nothing of the great world without; she has not time to read. . . .

On the other hand, in these "harmonious households," you sometimes find the so-called "hen-pecked husband" ofttimes a kind, generous, noble-minded man, who hates contention and is willing to do anything for peace. He having unwarily caught a Tartar, tries to make the best of her. . . . He can absent himself from home, as much as possible, but he does not feel like a free man. . . .

The only happy households we now see are those in which husband and wife share equally in counsel and government. There can be no true dignity or independence where there is subordination to the absolute will of another, no happiness without freedom. Let us then have no fears that this movement will disturb what is seldom found, a truly united and happy family. . . .

The world has never yet seen a truly great and virtuous nation, because in the degradation of woman the very fountains of life are poisoned at their source. It is vain to look for silver and gold from mines of copper and lead. It is the wise wife that has the wise son. So long as your women are slaves you may throw your colleges and churches to the winds. You can't have scholars and saints so long as your mothers are ground to powder between the upper and nether millstone of tyranny and lust. . . .

In every generation God calls some men and women for the utterance of truth, a heroic action. . . .We do not expect our path will be strewn with the flowers of popular applause, but over the thorns of bigotry and prejudice will be our way, and on our banners will beat the dark storm-clouds of opposition from those who have entrenched themselves behind the . . . bulwarks of custom and authority, and who have fortified their position by every means, holy and unholy. But we will steadfastly abide the result. Unmoved we will bear it aloft. Undauntedly we will unfurl it to the gale since we know that the storm cannot rend from it a shred, that the electric flash will but more clearly show to us the glorious words inscribed upon it, "Equality of Rights."

11.3: Dorothea L. Dix and the Plight of the Mentally Ill (1843)

Among the most vigorous and determined reformers of the pre–Civil War era was Dorothea L. Dix, a Maine-born school teacher who abandoned her profession in 1835 when her health failed. In 1841 Dix discovered her true vocation when, in the course of teaching a Sunday school class in the House of Correction in East Cambridge, Massachusetts, she dis-

covered that the authorities had packed a group of mentally ill people into filthy, unheated cells where they had been neglected and mistreated.

Dix spent the next two years investigating the condition of the mentally ill poor in Massachusetts, and her revulsion and horror grew. In 1843 she addressed a memorial to the state legislature, which is excerpted below, describing her findings and requesting an appropriation to provide more humane and medically useful treatment facilities for these unfortunate people. The state responded by expanding the existing Worcester Insane Asylum.

Dix soon extended her horizons beyond her own state and became the standard-bearer of a new movement to provide clean, well equipped, well administered "asylums" where the mentally ill could find havens and receive treatment. During the next decade she helped induce eleven state legislatures to appropriate funds to build asylums and even convinced Congress to approve a federal land grant to support care of the mentally ill. This measure was vetoed by President Franklin Pierce, however. Dix was also interested in the emerging nursing profession, and during the Civil War she served the Union as Superintendent of Women Nurses.

Why does Dix appear so humble in her petition? The horrendous conditions she describes may seem ample explanation for her activities, but were they new conditions? How had Americans provided for the mentally impaired in earlier periods? Had the conditions Dix recounts existed for many years? Why might a person like Dix have been particularly empathetic toward those she describes? Did the state-supported asylum system she helped create achieve the results she desired? What has happened to that system in recent years?

Memorial to the Legislature of Massachusetts

DOROTHEA L. DIX

GENTLEMEN,

I respectfully ask to present this Memorial, believing that the *cause*, which actuates to and sanctions so unusual a movement, presents no equivocal claim to public consideration and sympathy. Surrendering to calm and deep convictions of duty my habitual views of what is womanly and becoming, I proceed briefly to explain what has conducted me before you unsolicited and unsustained, trusting, while I do so, that the memorialist will be speedily forgotten in the memorial.

About two years since leisure afforded opportunity, and duty prompted me to visit several prisons and alms-houses in the vicinity of this metropolis. I

Dorothea L. Dix, Memorial to the Legislature of Massachusetts, 1843. In *On Behalf Of the Insane Poor: Selected Reports* (New York: Arno Press, 1971), pp. 3–9.

found, near Boston, in the Jails and Asylums for the poor, a numerous class brought into unsuitable connexion with criminals and the general mass of Paupers. I refer to Idiots and Insane persons, dwelling in circumstances not only adverse to their own physical and moral improvement, but productive of extreme disadvantages to all other persons brought into association with them. I applied myself diligently to trace the causes of these evils, and sought to supply remedies. As one obstacle was surmounted, fresh difficulties appeared. Every new investigation has given depth to the conviction that it is only by decided, prompt, and vigorous legislation the evils to which I refer, and which I shall proceed more fully to illustrate, can be remedied. I shall be obliged to speak with great plainness, and to reveal many things revolting to the taste, and from which my woman's nature shrinks with peculiar sensitiveness. But truth is the highest consideration. *I tell what I have seen*—painful and shocking as the details often are—that from them you may feel more deeply the imperative obligation which lies upon you to prevent the possibility of a repetition or continuance of such outrages upon humanity. If I inflict pain upon you, and move you to horror, it is to acquaint you with sufferings which you have the power to alleviate, and make you hasten to the relief of the victims of legalized barbarity.

I come to present the strong claims of suffering humanity. I come to place before the Legislature of Massachusetts the condition of the miserable, the desolate, the outcast: I come as the advocate of helpless, forgotten, insane and idiotic men and women; of beings, sunk to a condition from which the most unconcerned would start with real horror; of beings wretched in our Prisons, and more wretched in our Alms-Houses. And I cannot suppose it needful to employ earnest persuasion, or stubborn argument, in order to arrest and fix attention upon a subject, only the more strongly pressing in its claims, because it is revolting and disgusting in its details.

I must confine myself to few examples, but am ready to furnish other and more complete details, if required. If my pictures are displeasing, coarse, and severe, my subjects, it must be recollected, offer no tranquil, refined, or composing features. The condition of human beings, reduced to the extremest states of degradation and misery, cannot be exhibited in softened language, or adorn a polished page.

I proceed, Gentlemen, briefly to call your attention to the *present* state of Insane Persons confined within this Commonwealth, in *cages, closets, cellars, stalls, pens! Chained, naked, beaten with rods,* and *lashed* into obedience!

As I state cold, severe *facts,* I feel obliged to refer to persons, and definitely to indicate localities. But it is upon my subject, not upon localities or individuals, I desire to fix attention; and I would speak as kindly as possible of all Wardens, Keepers, and other responsible officers, believing that *most* of these have erred not through hardness of heart and wilful cruelty, so much as want of skill and knowledge, and want of consideration. Familiarity with suffering, it is said, blunts the sensibilities, and where neglect once finds a footing other injuries are multiplied. This is not all, for it may justly and strongly be added that, from the deficiency of adequate means to meet the wants of these cases, it has been an absolute impossibility to do justice in this matter. Prisons are not constructed in view of being converted into County Hospitals, and Alms-Houses are not founded as receptacles for the Insane. And yet, in the face of justice and common sense, Wardens are by law compelled to receive, and the Masters of Alms-Houses not to refuse, Insane and Idiotic subjects in all stages of mental disease and privation.

It is the Commonwealth, not its integral parts, that is accountable for most of the abuses which have lately, and do still exist. I repeat it, it is defective legislation which perpetuates and multiplies these abuses.

In illustration of my subject, I offer the following extracts from my Note-Book and Journal:—

Springfield

In the jail, one lunatic woman, furiously mad, a state pauper, improperly situated, both in regard to the prisoners, the keepers, and herself. It is a case of extreme self-forgetfulness and oblivion to all the decencies of life; to describe which, would be to repeat only the grossest scenes. She is much worse since leaving Worcester. In the almshouse of the same town is a woman apparently only needing judicious care, and some well-chosen employment, to make it unnecessary to confine her in solitude, in a dreary unfurnished room. Her appeals for employment and companionship are most touching, but the mistress replied, 'she had no time to attend to her.' . . .

Plympton

One insane, three idiots; condition wretched.

Besides the above, I have seen many who, part of the year, are chained or caged. The use of cages all but universal; hardly a town but can refer to some not distant period of using them: chains are less common: negligences frequent: wilful abuse less frequent than sufferings proceeding from ignorance, or want of consideration. I encountered during the last three months many poor creatures wandering reckless and unprotected through the country. Innumerable accounts have been sent me of persons who had roved away unwatched and unsearched after; and I have heard that responsible persons, controlling the almshouses, have not thought themselves culpable in sending away from their shelter, to cast upon the chances of remote relief, insane men and women. These, left on the highways, unfriended and incompetent to control or direct their own movements, sometimes have found refuge in the hospital, and others have not been traced. But I cannot particularize; in traversing the state I have found hundreds of insane persons in every variety of circumstance and condition; many whose situation could not and need not be improved; a less number, but that very large, whose lives are the saddest pictures of human suffering and degradation. I give a few illustrations; but description fades before reality.

Danvers

November; visited the almshouse; a large building, much out of repair; understand a new one is in contemplation. Here are from fifty-six to sixty inmates; one idiotic; three insane; one of the latter in close confinement at all times.

Long before reaching the house, wild shouts, snatches of rude songs, imprecations, and obscene language, fell upon the ear, proceeding from the occupant of a low building, rather remote from the principal building to which my course was directed. Found the mistress, and was conducted to the place, which was called '*the home*' of the *forlorn* maniac, a young woman, exhibiting a condition of neglect and misery blotting out the faintest idea of comfort, and outraging every sentiment of decency. She had been, I learnt, "a respectable person; industrious and worthy; disappointments and trials shook her mind, and finally laid prostrate reason and self-control; she became a maniac for life! She had been at Worcester Hospital for a considerable time, and had been returned as incurable." The mistress told me she understood that, while there, she was "comfortable and decent." Alas! what a change was here exhibited! She had passed from one degree of violence and degradation to another, in swift progress; there she stood, clinging to, or beating upon, the bars of her caged apartment, the contracted size of which afforded space only for increasing accumulations of filth, a *foul* spectacle; there she stood with naked arms and dishevelled hair; the unwashed frame invested with fragments of unclean garments, the air so extremely offensive, though ventilation was afforded on all sides save one, that it was not possible to remain beyond a few moments without retreating for recovery to the outward air. Irritation of body, produced by utter filth and exposure, incited her to the horrid process of tearing off her skin by inches; her face, neck, and person, were thus disfigured to hideousness; she held up a fragment just rent off; to my exclamation of horror, the mistress replied, "oh, we can't help it; half the skin is off sometimes; we can do nothing with her; and it makes no difference what she eats, for she consumes her own filth as readily as the food which is brought her."

It is now January; a fortnight since, two visitors reported that most wretched outcast as "wallowing in dirty straw, in a place yet more dirty, and without clothing, without fire. Worse cared for than the brutes, and wholly lost to consciousness of decency!" Is the whole story told? What was seen, is; what is reported is not. These gross exposures are not for the pained sight of one alone; all, all, coarse, brutal men, wondering, neglected children, old and young, each and all, witness this lowest, foulest state of miserable humanity. And who protects her, that worse than Paria outcast, from other wrongs and blacker outrages? I do not *know* that such *have been*. I do know that they are to be dreaded, and that they are not guarded against.

Some may say these things cannot be remedied; these furious maniacs are not to be raised from these base conditions. I *know* they are; could give *many* examples; let *one* suffice. A young woman, a pauper, in a distant town, *Sandisfield*, was for years a raging maniac. A cage, chains, and *the whip*, were the agents for controlling her, united with harsh tones and profane language. Annually, with others (the town's poor) she was put up at auction, and bid off at the lowest price which was declared for her. One year, not long past, an old man came forward in the number of applicants for the poor wretch; he was taunted and ridiculed; "what would he and his old wife do with such a mere beast?" "My wife says yes," replied he, "and I shall take her." She was given to his charge; he conveyed her home; she was washed, neatly dressed, and placed in a decent bed-room, furnished for comfort and opening into the kitchen. How altered her condition! As yet *the chains* were not off. The first week she was somewhat restless, at times violent, but the quiet kind ways of the old people wrought a change; she received her food decently; forsook acts of violence, and no longer uttered blasphemous or indecent language; after a week, the chain was lengthened, and she was received as a companion into the kitchen. Soon she engaged in trivial employments. "After a fortnight," said the old man, "I knocked off the chains and made her a free woman." She is at times excited, but not violently; they are careful of her diet; they keep her very clean; she calls them "father" and "mother." Go there now and you will find her "clothed," and though not perfectly in her "right mind," so far restored as to be a safe and comfortable inmate.

Newburyport

Visited the almshouse in June last; eighty inmates; seven insane, one idiotic. Commodious and neat house; several of the partially insane apparently very comfortable; two very improperly situated, namely, an insane man, not considered incurable, in an out-building, whose room opened up on what was called 'the dead room, affording in lieu of companionship with the living, a contemplation of corpses! The other subject was a woman in a *cellar.* I desired to see her; much reluctance was shown. I pressed the request; the Master of the House stated that she was *in the cellar,* that she was *dangerous to be approached*; that 'she had lately attacked his wife;' and *was often naked.* I persisted; 'if you will not go with me, give me the keys and I will go alone.' Thus importuned, the outer doors were opened. I descended the stairs from within; a strange, unnatural noise seemed to proceed from beneath our feet; at the moment I did not much regard it. My conductor proceeded to remove a padlock, while my eye explored the wide space in quest of the poor woman. All for a moment was still. But judge my horror and amazement, when a door to a closet *beneath* the *staircase* was opened, revealing in the imperfect light a female apparently wasted to a skeleton, partially wrapped in blankets, furnished for the narrow bed on which she was sitting; her countenance furrowed, not by age, but suffering, was the image of distress; in that contracted space, unlighted, unventilated, she poured forth the wailings of despair: mournfully she extended her arms and appealed to me, "why am I consigned to hell? dark—dark—I used to pray, I used to read the Bible—I have done no crime in my heart; I had friends, why have all forsaken me!—my God! my God! why hast *thou* forsaken me!" Those groans, those wailings come up daily, mingling, with how many others, a perpetual and sad memorial. When the good Lord shall require an account of our stewardship, what shall all and each answer!

Perhaps it will be inquired how long, how many days or hours was she imprisoned in these confined limits? *For years!* In another part of the cellar were other small closets, only better, because higher through the entire length, into one of which she by turns was transferred, so as to afford opportunity for fresh whitewashing, &c.

11.4:   Sarah Josepha Hale on Women and Peace Societies (1840)

Although educated, middle-class women were disproportionately represented in virtually all the reform societies, they were undoubtedly a minority of their group. Most women, as most people generally, were probably indifferent to all public causes. And others actively opposed the female reformers as unappealing social disrupters and betrayers of their sex.

One conservative female voice of this era was Sarah Josepha Hale, literary editor of the popular and successful magazine for women, the Lady's Book. *Hale fought for better education for women and deplored restrictions on married women, but she also opposed the women's suffrage activists and the militant female reformers, who to her seemed "unwomanly." In the selection below she advises her readers against joining peace societies and against adopting the ways of the more extreme "non-resisters," who were opposed to all war regardless of cause. ("Peace societies" were part of a movement begun during the late 1820s to abolish war. It eventually attracted the attention of William Lloyd Garrison as well as Elizabeth Cady Stanton and the Grimké sisters, who joined its extreme pacifist, "non-resister" wing opposed to all war, defensive as well as offensive.)*

Why is Hale's editorial focused on George Washington? What does she believe the proper stand on peace for women to take? Why does she believe that peace may have its problems too? How might Hale's position at the magazine have influenced her views of reform?

Ought Ladies to Form Peace Societies?

SARAH JOSEPHA HALE

We had the honour of a letter, some time since, from a distinguished advocate of the peace cause, on the above subject. The writer blamed the ladies

Sarah Josepha Hale, "Ought Ladies to Form Peace Societies?" *Lady's Book,* vol. 21 (July–December 1840), pp. 88–89.

of America, particularly the literary ladies, severely, for the encouragement they give to the warlike spirit among men. Mrs. Hemans[1] poetry was denounced in round terms, mothers were accused of kindling the martial enthusiasm of their sons by allowing them drums as playthings, and the opportunity of seeing military parades, and worse than these, it was affirmed, was the character and example of our Washington, to which these young aspirants for fame were always referred, as to a pattern of perfection.

Now it appears to us that the name of Washington is a surer check to the fierce and fiend-like passions enkindled by war, and to the lust of conquest, than all the prudential arguments which were ever urged by the advocates of peace. His example has thrown shame on the selfish ambition of warriors who, for their own glory, poured out the blood of their soldiers, and freed their country from foreign oppressors only to fix a more galling yoke of servitude to themselves. Public opinion has a *new and moral model for a hero*. It is a model that will accelerate the reign of peace. It has made justice, self-denial, and humanity necessary to the soldier. The example of Washington withered the laurels of Bonaparte; it prevented Bolivar from placing a crown on his head. The war, therefore, in which Washington triumphed, should be kept in remembrance by every one who wishes the advancement of the world in knowledge, peace and happiness. From the history of that period, all may learn their duties as men, citizens, Christians. But the picture must be exhibited, if we wish to have it examined. Mothers must tell their sons of the virtues of Washington, of the trials he endured, the wars in which he was engaged, if they wish them to profit by the example of prudence, justice, fortitude, moderation and *piety* which he has left as a most precious legacy to his countrymen.

And if the history of our Revolution must be withheld from our sons, lest they should acquire an admiration for war, we must also prohibit the Bible from being read, for we are there assured that God has taught "hands to war," and given "strength for the battle." And we as fully believe that God blessed the labours of our patriots, and directed the movements of our armies, as he did those of Israel of old, and that we are bound to remember his goodness and give him grateful thanks for inspiring the colonists with courage to resist their oppressors, thus exhibiting an example to the world of the holy patriotism of a people called to be free, and the pattern of a perfect hero.

We fully agree with our respected correspondent that this subject of "peculiar worth" is one which ought deeply to interest our own sex. Though the sins of war are chiefly perpetrated by men, the sufferings fall most heavily on the women. Devoutly do we wish the reign of universal peace; but we do not think that the cause will be materially advanced by the formation of "Ladies Peace Societies;" nor, indeed, by urging on men to become profes-

[1]Felicia Hemans, a minor pre-Civil War poet—ED.

sors of the "non-resistance principle." In all humility, we would suggest that *peace* has its dangers and temptations as well as war. It is far more likely that the virtues and liberties of our country will be destroyed by the luxuries of the former than the wasting of the latter. The tree which grew stronger for the tempest will in the hot sunshine droop and wither; the canker-worm may destroy what the lion could not have overturned.

Our peace societies must exert their influence in suppressing the peculiar vices which prosperity engenders, those which spring from idleness, security, and abundance, before they will deserve to be esteemed as of much benefit to public morals. What advantage is it to stay the thunderbolt, if the impure vapours are permitted to accumulate? The lightning might destroy a few lives, the pestilence will sweep away multitudes. All history attests the fact, that luxury, such as grows rank among the people of a Republic, only in times of peace, is more baneful than the ambition of renown. Greece, Rome, Venice, all perished by the corruptions of wealth, not the crimes of war. Carthage only, of all the ancient Republics, was destroyed in battle; that would not have occurred had not the soldiers of Hannibal been enervated by the luxuries of peace at Capus.

It appears to us, therefore, that our American ladies will act the wiser part to teach their children to be temperate in all things, to do, in all cases as they would wish to be done by, to practise self-denial and the noble spirit of forgiveness towards their enemies, and of ready kindness to every one, than to spend their time in discussions on the propriety of a "Congress of nations in settling the peace of the world," or even devising how they shall prevent their little sons from looking on a military review. We deem it better that woman should study the things which make for peace at home, rather than devote her thoughts to the dissemination of peace principles abroad. Is she careful to promote peace in her own family and neighbourhood, is she gentle, kind, and charitable in her opinion of others? She may be sure that she is fulfilling the duties assigned by her divine *Teacher,* and that these humble duties, when performed in a right spirit, will be blessed to the promotion of his kingdom of peace on earth.

11.5: A Southerner Denounces Northern Reform and Social Experimentation (1857)

Many northerners were critical of the reformers and their efforts. To some they seemed ridiculous and naïve zealots, while to others they seemed dangerous fanatics who were certain to do more harm than good.

Few Americans, however, were as skeptical of the impulse to improve and purify society as were southern intellectuals. One of the most ardent antagonists of the reform movements was George Fitzhugh, a Virginia lawyer and occasional newspaper editor, who had rejected entirely the Jeffersonian liberalism that had imbued his home state a half-century before. Fitzhugh believed that all creative societies in the past had relied on slaves and that no society could achieve a high level of civilization without men and women to do its degrading, but essential, dirty work. The North's vaunted freedom, he argued, simply papered over a system of wage slavery that reduced white people to the same status as southern black slaves. That freedom also unleashed licentiousness, infidelity, and greed.

As the selection that follows shows, Fitzhugh despised the northern reformers and blamed them for undermining the foundations of society and destroying traditional Christian values. Fitzhugh links the various "isms" to abolitionism. Is he correct? Did the other reform movements and social experiments derive from abolitionism? Or were they merely parallel impulses? Does Fitzhugh's warning against the dangers of freedom have any validity? Or was he merely defending a benighted and besieged system of human oppression? Have voices similar to his in recent years emphasized the dangers of institutional reform and social experimentation?

In What Slavery Ends

GEORGE FITZHUGH

Mr. [Thomas] Carlyle[1] very properly contends that abolition and the other social movements of the day propose little or no government as the moral panacea that is to heal and save a suffering world. [Pierre Joseph] Proudhon[2] expressly advocates anarchy; and Stephen Pearl Andrews, the ablest of American socialistic and abolition philosophers, elaborately attacks all existing social relations, and all legal and governmental restraints, and proposes No-Government as their substitute. He is the author of the Free Love experiment in New York, and a co-laborer and eulogist of similar experiments in villages or settlements in Ohio, Long Island and other places in the North and Northwest. He is a follower of Josiah Warren[3] who was associated with [Robert] Owen[4] of Lanark at New Harmony. We do not know that there is any essential difference between his system and that which has been for many years past practically carried out in Oneida County, New York, by the Perfectionists, who construe the Bible into authority for the unrestrained indulgence of every sensual appetite. The doctrines of [Charles] Fourier,[5] of Owen and Fanny Wright,[6] and the other early

Reprinted by permission of the publishers from *Cannibals All! Or, Slaves Without Masters* by George Fitzhugh, edited by C. Vann Woodward, Cambridge, MA: The Belknap Press of Harvard University Press. Copyright © 1960 by the President and Fellows of Harvard College, © 1988 by Comer Vann Woodward.

[1]A conservative nineteenth-century British essayist—ED.

[2]A radical nineteenth-century French social theorist—ED.

[3]An early nineteenth-century American labor reformer—ED.

[4]A British industrialist and philanthropist who came to America in 1824 and founded a utopian socialist community, New Harmony, in Indiana—ED.

Socialists, all lead to No-Government and Free Love. 'Tis probable they foresaw and intended this result, but did not suggest or propose it to a world then too wicked and unenlightened to appreciate its beatific purity and loveliness. The materials as well as the proceedings of the infidel, woman's rights, negro rights, free-everything and anti-every school, headed and conducted in Boston by [William Lloyd] Garrison, [Theodore] Parker,[7] [Wendell] Phillips,[8] and their associated women and negroes, show that they too are busy with "assiduous wedges" in loosening the whole frame of society, and preparing for the glorious advent of Free Love and No-Government. All the Infidel and Abolition papers in the North betray a similar tendency. The Abolitionists of New York, headed by Gerrit Smith and Wm. Goodell, are engaged in precisely the same projects, but being Christians, would dignify Free Love and No-Government with the appellation of a Millennium. Probably half the Abolitionists at the North expect a great social revolution soon to occur by the advent of the Millennium. If they would patiently await that event, instead of attempting to get it up themselves, their delusions, however ridiculous, might at least be innocuous. But these progressive Christian Socialists differ not at all from the Infidel Socialists of Boston. They are equally intent and busy in pulling down the priesthood, and abolishing or dividing all property—seeing that whether the denouement be Free Love or a Millennium, the destruction of all existing human relations and human institutions is prerequisite to their full fruition.

Many thousand as have been of late years the social experiments attempting to practice community of property, of wives, children, &c., and numerous as the books inculcating and approving such practices, yet the existence and growth of Mormonism[9] is of itself stronger evidence than all other of the tendency of modern free society towards No-Government and Free Love. In the name of polygamy, it has practically removed all restraints to the intercourse of sexes, and broken up the Family. It promises, too, a qualified community of property and a fraternal association of labor. It beats up monthly thousands of recruits from free society in Europe and America, but makes not one convert in the slaveholding South. Slavery is satisfied and conservative. Abolition, finding that all existing legal, religious, social and governmental institutions restrict liberty and occasion a quasi-slavery, is resolved not to stop short of the subversion of all those institutions, and the inauguration of Free Love and No-Government. The only cure for all this is for free

[5]A nineteenth-century French social thinker who inspired numerous socialist communities in America—ED.

[6]Frances Wright was an English reformer and "free thinker" who collaborated with Robert Owen in the New Harmony experiment—ED.

[7]A Unitarian minister of Boston active in the abolitionist movement—ED.

[8]A Massachusetts abolitionist and disciple of Garrison—ED.

[9]Followers of the prophet Joseph Smith who, in the 1820s, discovered a "lost" Book of Mormon, which inspired him to establish a new religion. The Mormons, for a time, believed in "plural marriage" or polygamy—ED.

society sternly to recognize slavery as right in principle, and necessary in practice, with more or less of modification, to the very existence of government, of property, of religion, and of social existence.

We shall not attempt to reconcile the doctrines of the Socialists, which propose to remove all legal restraints, with their denunciations of Political Economy. Let Alone [i.e., laissez faire] is the essence of Political Economy and the whole creed of most of the Socialists. The Political Economists, Let Alone, for a fair fight, for universal rivalry, antagonism, competition, and cannibalism. They say the eating up the weaker members of society, the killing them out by capital and competition, will improve the breed of men and benefit society. They foresee the consequences of their doctrine, and are consistent. [Thomas] Hobbes[10] saw men devouring one another, under their system, two hundred years ago, and we all see them similarly engaged now. The Socialists promise that when society is wholly disintegrated and dissolved, by inculcating good principles and "singing fraternity over it," all men will cooperate, love, and help one another.

They place men in positions of equality, rivalry, and antagonism, which must result in extreme selfishness of conduct, and yet propose this system as a cure for selfishness. To us their reasonings seem absurd.

Yet the doctrines so prevalent with Abolitionists and Socialists, of Free Love and Free Lands, Free Churches, Free Women and Free Negroes—of No-Marriage, No-Religion, No-Private Property, No-Law and No-Government, are legitimate deductions, if not obvious corollaries from the leading and distinctive axiom of political economy—Laissez Faire, or Let Alone.

All the leading Socialists and Abolitionists of the North, we think, agree with Fanny Wright, that the gradual changes which have taken place in social organization from domestic slavery to prædial serfdom and thence to the present system of free and competitive society, have been mere transitive states, each placing the laborer in a worse condition than that of absolute slavery, yet valuable as preparing the way for a new and more perfect social state. They value the present state of society the more highly because it is intolerable, and must the sooner usher in a Millennium or Utopia.

[10]Hobbes was a seventeenth-century English philosopher who believed people to be driven by personal interest and kept from mutual destruction only by strong government—ED.

12

The Mexican War

The generation preceding the Civil War was a time of explosive physical growth for the United States. During the 1840s and 1850s, the country added 1.2 million square miles to its geographical limits. The largest block of new territory by far was wrenched from our southern neighbor, Mexico—through annexation of Texas in 1845 and by the Mexican Cession following victory in war in 1848.

Our relations with Mexico during these years were at best morally dubious. Long after wresting its independence from Spain in the 1820s, Mexico remained a poor, weak, and chaotic nation. The government in Mexico City was in constant flux as conflicting elites fought for control. The rapid shifts disturbed relations with the United States. Mexico's internal turmoil led to the loss of American lives and the destruction of American property.

The most serious Mexican-American difficulties, however, concerned the borderlands. The Mexican government's hold on its sparsely populated, distant northern borders—the region adjoining the United States—was at best feeble. Mexico's weakness seemed America's opportunity. Encouraged by development-minded officials in Mexico City (*federalistas*), Americans began to drift into the borderlands soon after Mexican independence. In 1835 one group of Texas settlers, initially welcomed by Mexican authorities, rose in revolt against the central government when new, unfriendly officials (*centralistas*) came to power. After defeating the Mexican army, the secessionists established the Texas Republic. In 1845 the United States, to Mexico's dismay, annexed Texas as a state of the Union.

The remaining borderlands—California and New Mexico—remained tempting prizes to Americans. In 1846, for reasons explored below, the United States went to war with Mexico. For the Americans, victory followed victory, and in 1848 the defeated Mexicans ceded the two vast border provinces to the United States for the sum of $15 million.

Contemporaries differed over the causes of the Mexican War. Not surprisingly there were fundamental disgreements between citizens of the two republics. But Americans also disagreed among themselves. The following documents express a variety of attitudes concerning the origins of the Mexican War and the justice of the American cause.

12.1:   Manifest Destiny (1845)

Clearly many Americans in the period 1830–60 believed that some irresistible moral, economic, demographic, or geographic imperative sanctioned the extension of their country's borders to include much of the North American continent. This view was given a name in 1845 by John L. O'Sullivan, a New York Democratic newspaper editor. It was America's "manifest destiny," O'Sullivan proclaimed, to extend its territory from coast to coast and from the arctic to the tropics.

O'Sullivan published the following editorial in the summer of 1845, soon after Congress had voted to annex Texas to the United States. Although the decision had been made, criticism continued, and O'Sullivan sought to defend it. But his remarks go beyond the matter of Texas annexation to embrace the issue of United States expansion generally. O'Sullivan is sensitive to several charges against the expansionists. What are these charges? Does he answer them convincingly in the case of Texas? What is his explanation for American expansionism? How does a transcontinental railroad fit into O'Sullivan's view of American destiny? It has often been said that arguments such as O'Sullivan's are merely crude rationalizations for greed and other self-serving drives. Do they in fact merely disguise more selfish motives? Or were they sincere beliefs that by themselves served to spur action?

Manifest Destiny

JOHN L. O'SULLIVAN

It is time now for opposition to the Annexation of Texas to cease, all further agitation of the waters of bitterness and strife, at least in connexion with this question,—even though it may perhaps be required of us as a necessary condition of the freedom of our institutions, that we must live on for ever in a state of unpausing struggle and excitement upon some subject of party division or other. But, in regard to Texas, enough has now been given to Party.

John L. O'Sullivan, "Annexation," *The United States Magazine and Domestic Review*, vol. 17 (July and August 1845) pp. 5–10.

It is time for the common duty of Patriotism to the Country to succeed;—or if this claim will not be recognized, it is at least time for common sense to acquiesce with decent grace in the inevitable and the irrevocable.

Texas is now ours. Already, before these words are written, her Convention has undoubtedly ratified the acceptance, by her Congress, of our proffered invitation into the Union; and made the requisite changes in her already republican form of constitution to adopt it to its future federal relations. Her star and her stripe may already be said to have taken their place in the glorious blazon of our common nationality; and the sweep of our eagle's wing already includes within its circuit the wide extent of her fair and fertile land. She is no longer to us a mere geographical space—a certain combination of coast, plain, mountain, valley, forest and stream. She is no longer to us a mere country on the map. She comes within the dear and sacred designation of Our Country; no longer a *"pays,"* she is a part of *"la patrie,"* and that which is at once a sentiment and a virtue,[1] Patriotism, already begins to thrill for her too within the national heart. . . .

Why, were other reasoning wanting, in favor of now elevating this question of the reception of Texas into the Union, out of the lower region of our past party dissensions, up to its proper level of a high and broad nationality, it surely is to be found, found abundantly, in the manner in which other nations have undertaken to intrude themselves into it, between us and the proper parties to the case, in a spirit of hostile interference against us, for the avowed object of thwarting our policy and hampering our power, limiting our greatness and checking the fulfilment of our manifest destiny to overspread the continent allotted by Providence for the free development of our yearly multiplying millions. . . .

It is wholly untrue, and unjust to ourselves, the pretence that the Annexation has been a measure of spoliation, unrightful and unrighteous— of military conquest under forms of peace and law—of territorial aggrandizement at the expense of justice, and justice due by a double sanctity to the weak. This view of the question is wholly unfounded, and has been before so amply refuted in these pages, as well as in a thousand other modes, that we shall not again dwell upon it. The independence of Texas was complete and absolute. It was an independence, not only in fact but of right. No obligation of duty towards Mexico tended in the least degree to restrain our right to effect the desired recovery of the fair province once our own—whatever motives of policy might have prompted a more deferential consideration of her feelings and her pride, as involved in the question. If Texas became peopled with an American population, it was by no contrivance of our government, but on the express invitation of that of Mexico herself; accompanied with such guaranties of State independence, and the maintenance of a federal system analogous to our own, as constituted a compact

---

[1] O'Sullivan is here distinguishing essentially between a slice of geography and a nation—ED.

fully justifying the strongest measures of redress on the part of those after-wards deceived in this guaranty, and sought to be enslaved under the yoke imposed by its violation. She was released, rightfully and absolutely released, from all Mexican allegiance, or duty of cohesion to the Mexican political body, by the acts and fault of Mexico herself, and Mexico alone. There never was a clearer case. It was not revolution; it was resistance to revolution; and resistance under such circumstances as left independence the necessary resulting state, caused by the abandonment of those with whom her former federal association had existed. What then can be more preposterous than all this clamor by Mexico and the Mexican interest, against Annexation, as a violation of any rights of hers, any duties of ours? . . .

Nor is there any just foundation of the charge that Annexation is a great pro-slavery measure—calculated to increase and perpetuate that institution. Slavery had nothing to do with it. . . . The country which was the subject of Annexation in this case, from its geographical position and relations, hap-pens to be—or rather the portion of it now actually settled, happens to be—a slave country. But a similar process might have taken place in proximity to a different section of our Union; and indeed there is a great deal of Annexation yet to take place, within the life of the present generation, along the whole line of our northern border. Texas has been absorbed into the Union in the inevitable fulfilment of the general law which is rolling our population westward; the connexion of which with that ratio of growth in population which is destined within a hundred years to swell our numbers to the enormous population of *two hundred and fifty millions* (if not more), is too evident to leave us in doubt of the manifest design of Providence in regard to the occupation of this continent. It was disintegrated from Mexico in the natural course of events, by a process perfectly legitimate on its own part, blameless on ours; and in which all the censures due to wrong, perfidy and folly, rest on Mexico alone. And possessed as it was by a population which was in truth but a colonial detachment from our own, and which was still bound by myriad ties of the very heartstrings to its old relations, domestic and political, their incorporation into the Union was not only inevitable, but the most natural, right and proper thing in the world—and it is only aston-ishing that there should be any among ourselves to say it nay. . . .

California will, probably, next fall away from the loose adhesion which, in such a country as Mexico, holds a remote province in a slight equivocal kind of dependence on the metropolis. Imbecile and distracted, Mexico never can exert any real governmental authority over such a country. The impo-tence of the one and the distance of the other, must make the relation one of virtual independence; unless, by stunting the province of all natural growth, and forbidding that immigration which can alone develop its capa-bilities and fulfil the purposes of its creation, tyranny may retain a military dominion which is no government in the legitimate sense of the term. In the case of California this is now impossible. The Anglo-Saxon foot is already on its borders. Already the advance guard of the irresistible army of Anglo-

Saxon emigration has begun to pour down upon it, armed with the plough and the rifle, and marking its trail with schools and colleges, courts and representative halls, mills and meeting-houses. A population will soon be in actual occupation of California, over which it will be idle for Mexico to dream of dominion. They will necessarily become independent. All this without agency of our government, without responsibility of our people—in the natural flow of events, the spontaneous working of principles, and the adaptation of the tendencies and wants of the human race to the elemental circumstances in the midst of which they find themselves placed. And they will have a right to independence—to self-government—to the possession of the homes conquered from the wilderness by their own labors and dangers, sufferings and sacrifices—a better and a truer right than the artificial title of sovereignty in Mexico a thousand miles distant, inheriting from Spain a title good only against those who have none better. Their right to independence will be the natural right of self-government belonging to any community strong enough to maintain it—distinct in position, origin and character, and free from any mutual obligations of membership of a common political body, binding it to others by the duty of loyalty and compact of public faith. This will be their title to independence; and by this title, there can be no doubt that the population now fast streaming down upon California will both assert and maintain that independence. Whether they will then attach themselves to our Union or not, is not to be predicted with any certainty. Unless the projected rail-road across the continent to the Pacific be carried into effect, perhaps they may not; though even in that case, the day is not distant when the Empires of the Atlantic and Pacific would again flow together into one, as soon as their inland border should approach each other. But that great work, colossal as appears the plan on its first suggestion, cannot remain long unbuilt. Its necessity for this very purpose of binding and holding together in its iron clasp our fast settling Pacific region with that of the Mississippi valley—the natural facility of the route—the ease with which any amount of labor for the construction can be drawn in from the overcrowded populations of Europe, to be paid in the lands made valuable by the progress of the work itself—and its immense utility to the commerce of the world with the whole eastern coast of Asia, alone almost sufficient for the support of such a road—these considerations give assurance that the day cannot be distant which shall witness the conveyance of the representatives from Oregon and California to Washington within less time than a few years ago was devoted to a similar journey by those from Ohio; while the magnetic telegraph will enable the editors of the "San Francisco Union," the "Astoria Evening Post," or the "Nootka Morning News" to set up in type the first half of the President's Inaugural, before the echoes of the latter half shall have died away beneath the lofty porch of the Capitol, as spoken from his lips.

Away, then, with all idle French talk of *balances of power* on the American

Continent. There is no growth in Spanish America! Whatever progress of population there may be in the British Canadas, is only for their own early severance of their present colonial relation to the little island three thousand miles across the Atlantic; soon to be followed by Annexation, and destined to swell the still accumulating momentum of our progress. And whatsoever may hold the balance, though they should cast into the opposite scale all the bayonets and cannon, not only of France and England, but of Europe entire, how would it kick the beam against the simple solid weight of the two hundred and fifty or three hundred millions—and American millions—destined to gather beneath the flutter of the stripes and stars, in the fast hastening year of the Lord 1945?

12.2: James K. Polk Calls for War against Mexico (1846)

President James K. Polk, a Tennessee Democrat, was one of the most ardent expansionists of this period. Determined to fulfill America's territorial destiny in the Southwest, he preferred buying land to fighting for it. In late 1845 Polk sent John Slidell to Mexico to settle outstanding U.S. claims against Mexico for loss of American lives and property and to negotiate the purchase of California. But when the Mexicans refused to receive Slidell, Polk felt free to consider other ways of satisfying his territorial ambitions.

At the time of the Texas annexation, the United States claimed that the new state's valid southwestern boundary was the Rio Grande del Norte rather than the Nueces River, as the Mexicans insisted. Most historians now conclude that the American view was incorrect, but to back up the American assertion, in 1846 Polk ordered U.S. troops to occupy the disputed region between the rivers. The Mexicans, already angry over the Texas annexation and convinced that they stood a good chance to humble the Americans in a military encounter, determined to attack. On April 25, 1846, the Mexican commander at Matamoros crossed the Rio Grande and assaulted an American army patrol, inflicting sixteen casualties.

Polk was ready to go to war before he heard of the attack. But as he prepared his war message to Congress, news of the clash arrived in Washington and provided far better ammunition than any he previously had, and he used it. The document below is an excerpt from Polk's request for a declaration of war by Congress.

Is the statement of grievances against Mexico sincere, or does it seem contrived or hypocritical? Was Polk being honest when he declared that he desired "to establish peace with Mexico on liberal and honourable terms"? Or was this merely a cloak for American ambition?

Polk's War Message

JAMES K. POLK

The strong desire to establish peace with Mexico on liberal and honourable terms, and the readiness of this Government to regulate and adjust our boundary and other causes of difference with that power on such fair and equitable principles as would lead to permanent relations of the most friendly nature, induced me in September last [1845] to seek the reopening of diplomatic relations between the two countries. Every measure adopted on our part had for its object the furtherance of these desired results. In communicating to Congress a succinct statement of the injuries we had suffered from Mexico, and which have been accumulating during a period of more than twenty years, every expression that could tend to inflame the people of Mexico or defeat or delay a pacific result was carefully avoided. An envoy of the United States [John Slidell] repaired to Mexico with full powers to adjust every existing difference. But though present on Mexican soil by agreement between the two Governments, invested with full powers, and bearing evidence of the most friendly dispositions, his mission has been unavailing. The Mexican Government not only refused to see him or listen to his propositions, but after a long-continued series of menaces have at last invaded our territory and shed the blood of our fellow-citizens on our own soil. . . .

Thus the Government of Mexico, though solemnly pledged by official acts in October last to receive and accredit an American envoy, violated their plighted faith and refused the offer of a peaceful adjustment of our difficulties. Not only was the offer rejected, but the indignity of its rejection was enhanced by the manifest breach of faith in refusing to admit the envoy who came because they had bound themselves to receive him. . . .

In my message at the commencement of the present session [of Congress] I informed you that upon the earnest appeal of the Congress and the convention of Texas I had ordered an efficient military force to take a position between "the Nueces and the [Rio Grande] Del Norte." This had become necessary to meet a threatened invasion of Texas by the Mexican forces, for which extensive military preparations had been made. The invasion was threatened solely because Texas had determined, in accordance with a solemn resolution of the Congress of the United States, to annex herself to our Union, and under these circumstances it was plainly our duty to extend our protection over her citizens and soil. . . .

James D. Richardson ed., *A Compilation of the Messages and Papers of the Presidents* (New York: Bureau of National Literature 1896), vol. 5, pp. 2287–93.

Meanwhile Texas, by the final action of our Congress, had become an integral part of our Union. The Congress of Texas, by its act of December 19, 1836, had declared the Rio del Norte to be the boundary of that Republic. Its jurisdiction had been extended and exercised beyond the Nueces. The country between that river and the Del Norte had been represented in the Congress and in the convention of Texas, had thus taken part in the act of annexation itself, and is now included within one of our Congressional districts. Our own Congress had, moreover, with great unanimity, by the act approved December 31, 1845, recognized the country beyond the Nueces as a part of our territory by including it within our own revenue system, and a revenue officer to reside within that district has been appointed by and with the advice and consent of the Senate. It became, therefore, of urgent necessity to provide for the defense of that portion of our country. Accordingly, on the 13th of January last instructions were issued to the general in command of these troops to occupy the left bank of the Del Norte. This river, which is the southwestern boundary of the State of Texas, is an exposed frontier. From this quarter invasion was threatened; upon it and in its immediate vicinity, in the judgment of high military experience, are the proper stations for the protecting forces of the Government. . . .

The movement of the troops to the Del Norte was made by the commanding general under positive instructions to abstain from all aggressive acts toward Mexico or Mexican citizens and to regard the relations between that Republic and the United States as peaceful unless she should declare war or commit acts of hostility indicative of a state of war. He was specially directed to protect private property and respect personal rights.

The Army moved from Corpus Christi on the 11th of March, and on the 28th of that month arrived on the left bank of the Del Norte opposite to Matamoras, where it encamped on a commanding position, which has since been strengthened by the erection of fieldworks. A depot has also been established at Point Isabel, near the Brazos Santiago, 30 miles in rear of the encampment. The selection of his position was necessarily confided to the judgment of the general in command.

The Mexican forces at Matamoras assumed a belligerent attitude, and on the 12th of April General Ampudia, then in command, notified General [Zachary] Taylor to break up his camp within twenty-four hours and to retire beyond the Nueces River, and in the event of his failure to comply with these demands announced that arms, and arms alone, must decide the question. But no open act of hostility was committed until the 24th of April. On that day General Arista, who had succeeded to the command of the Mexican forces, communicated to General Taylor that "he considered hostilities commenced and should prosecute them." A party of dragoons of 63 men and officers were on the same day dispatched from the American camp up the Rio del Norte, on its left bank, to ascertain whether the Mexican troops had crossed or were preparing to cross the river, "became engaged with a large body of these troops, and after a short affair, in which some 16 were killed and wounded, appear to have been surrounded and compelled to surrender."

The grievous wrongs perpetrated by Mexico upon our citizens throughout a long period of years remain unredressed, and solemn treaties pledging her public faith for this redress have been disregarded. A government either unable or unwilling to enforce the execution of such treaties fails to perform one of its plainest duties.

Our commerce with Mexico has been almost annihilated. It was formerly highly beneficial to both nations, but our merchants have been deterred from prosecuting it by the system of outrage and extortion which the Mexican authorities have pursued against them, whilst their appeals through their own Government for indemnity have been made in vain. Our forbearance has gone to such an extreme as to be mistaken in its character. Had we acted with vigor in repelling the insults and redressing the injuries inflicted by Mexico at the commencement, we should doubtless have escaped all the difficulties in which we are now involved.

Instead of this, however, we have been exerting our best efforts to propitiate her good will. Upon the pretext that Texas, a nation as independent as herself, thought proper to unite its destinies with our own, she has affected to believe that we have severed her rightful territory, and in official proclamations and manifestoes has repeatedly threatened to make war upon us for the purpose of reconquering Texas. In the meantime we have tried every effort at reconciliation. The cup of forbearance had been exhausted even before the recent information from the frontier of the Del Norte. But now, after reiterated menaces, Mexico has passed the boundary of the United States, has invaded our territory and shed American blood upon the American soil. She has proclaimed that hostilities have commenced, and that the two nations are now at war.

As war exists, and, notwithstanding all our efforts to avoid it, exists by the act of Mexico herself, we are called upon by every consideration of duty and patriotism to vindicate with decision the honor, the rights, and the interests of our country.

12.3:   The Mexican View (1850)

Needless to say, Mexicans did not share the American view of the 1846–48 war—as the selection below, by a group of patriotic Mexican scholars and journalists, shows. What factors do the Mexican commentators focus on in making their case against U.S. actions toward their country? Is their case convincing? Does it leave out some of the relevant background to the Mexican-American dispute? Do you detect any begrudging admiration of the United States in their remarks?

The Mexican View of the War

RAMON ALCARAZ

To explain then in a few words the true origin of the war, it is sufficient to say that the insatiable ambition of the United States, favored by our weakness, caused it. But this assertion, however veracious and well founded, requires the confirmation which we will present, along with some former transactions, to the whole world. This evidence will leave no doubt of the correctness of our impressions.

In throwing off the yoke of the mother country, the United States of the North appeared at once as a powerful nation. This was the result of their excellent elementary principles of government established while in colonial subjection. The Republic announced at its birth, that it was called upon to represent an important part in the world of Columbus. Its rapid advancement, its progressive increase, its wonderful territory, the uninterrupted augmentation of its inhabitants, and the formidable power it had gradually acquired, were many proofs of its becoming a colossus, not only for the feeble nations of Spanish America, but even for the old populations of the ancient continent.

The United States did not hope for the assistance of time in their schemes of aggrandizement. From the days of their independence they adopted the project of extending their dominions, and since then, that line of policy has not deviated in the slightest degree. This conduct, nevertheless, was not perceptible to the most enlightened: but reflecting men, who examined events, were not slow in recognising it. Conde de Aranda,[1] from whose perception the ends which the United States had resolved upon were not concealed, made use of some celebrated words. These we shall now produce as a prophecy verified by events. "This nation has been born a pigmy: in the time to come, it will be a giant, and even a colossus, very formidable in these vast regions. Its first step will be an appropriation of the Floridas to be master of the Gulf of Mexico."

The ambition of the North Americans has not been in conformity with this. They desired from the beginning to extend their dominion in such manner as to become the absolute owners of almost all this continent. In two ways they could accomplish their ruling passion: in one by bringing under their laws and authority all America to the Isthmus of Panama; in another, in opening an overland passage to the Pacific Ocean, and making good harbors to facilitate its navigation. By this plan, establishing in some way an easy communication of a few days between both oceans, no nation could compete with them. England herself might show her strength before

Ramon Alcaraz et al., eds., *The Other Side, or Notes for the History of the War between Mexico and the United States,* trans. by Albert C. Ramsey (New York, n.p., 1850), pp. 2–3, 30–32.
[1] Pedro de Aranda, a Mexican patriot of the early nineteenth century who participated in the revolt against Spain that brought Mexico its independence—ED.

yielding the field to her fortunate rival, and the mistress of the commercial world might for a while be delayed in touching the point of greatness to which she aspires.

In the short space of some three quarters of a century events have verified the existence of these schemes and their rapid development. The North American Republic has already absorbed territories pertaining to Great Britain, France, Spain, and Mexico. It has employed every means to accomplish this—purchase as well as usurpation, skill as well as force, and nothing has restrained it when treating of territorial acquisition. Louisiana, the Floridas, Oregon, and Texas, have successively fallen into its power. . . .

While the United States seemed to be animated by a sincere desire not to break the peace, their acts of hostility manifested very evidently what were their true intentions. Their ships infested our coasts; their troops continued advancing upon our territory, situated at places which under no aspect could be disputed. Thus violence and insult were united: thus at the very time they usurped part of our territory, they offered to us the hand of treachery, to have soon the audacity to say that our obstinacy and arrogance were the real causes of the war.

To explain the occupation of the Mexican territory by the troops of General [Zachary] Taylor, the strange idea occurred to the United States that the limits of Texas extended to the Rio Grande del Norte. This opinion was predicated upon two distinct principles: one, that the Congress of Texas had so declared it in December, in 1836; and another, that the river mentioned had been the natural line of Louisiana. To state these reasons is equivalent at once to deciding the matter; for no one could defend such palpable absurdities. The first, which this government prizing its intelligence and civilization, supported with refined malice, would have been ridiculous in the mouth of a child. Whom could it convince that the declaration of the Texas Congress bore a legal title for the acquisition of the lands which it appropriated to itself with so little hesitation? If such a principle were recognised, we ought to be very grateful to these gentlemen senators who had the kindness to be satisfied with so little. Why not declare the limits of the rebel state extended to San Luis, to the capital, to our frontier with Guatemala?

The question is so clear in itself that it would only obscure by delaying to examine it further. We pass then to the other less nonsensical than the former. In the first place to pretend that the limits of Louisiana came to the Rio Grande, it was essential to confound this province with Texas, which never can be tolerated. In the beginning of this article we have already shown the ancient and peaceable possession of Spain over the lands of the latter. Again, this same province, and afterwards State of Texas, never had extended its territory to the Rio Grande, being only to the Nueces, in which always had been established the boundary. Lastly, a large part of the territory situated on the other side of the Grande, belonged, without dispute or doubt, to other states of the Republic—to New Mexico, Tamaulipas, Coahuila, and Chihuahua.

Then, after so many and such plain proceedings, is there one impartial man who would not consider the forcible occupation of our territory by the North American arms a shameful usurpation? Then further, this power desired to carry to the extreme the sneer and the jest. When the question had resolved itself into one of force which is the *ultima ratio* of nations as well as of kings, when it had spread desolation and despair in our populations, when many of our citizens had perished in the contest, the bloody hand of our treacherous neighbors was turned to present the olive of peace. The Secretary of State, Mr. Buchanan, on the 27th of July, 1846, proposed anew, the admission of an Envoy to open negotiations which might lead to the concluding of an honorable peace. The national government answered that it could not decide, and left it to Congress to express its opinion of the subject. Soon to follow up closely the same system of policy, they ordered a commissioner with the army, which invaded us from the east, to cause it to be understood that peace would be made when our opposition ceased. Whom did they hope to deceive with such false appearances? Does not the series of acts which we have mentioned speak louder than this hypocritical language? By that test then, as a question of justice, no one who examines it in good faith can deny our indisputable rights. Among the citizens themselves, of the nation which has made war on us, there have been many who defended the cause of the Mexican Republic. These impartial defenders have not been obscure men, but men of the highest distinction. Mexico has counted on the assistance, ineffectual, unfortunately, but generous and illustrious, of a [Henry] Clay, [John Quincy] Adams, a [Daniel] Webster, a[n Albert] Gallatin; that is to say, on the noblest men, the most appreciated for their virtues, for their talents, and for their services. Their conduct deserves our thanks, and the authors of this work have a true pleasure in paying, in this place, the sincere homage of their gratitude.

Such are the events that abandoned us to a calamitous war; and, in the relation of which, we have endeavored not to distort even a line of the private data consulted, to prove, on every occasion, all and each of our assertions.

From the acts referred to, it has been demonstrated to the very senses, that the real and effective cause of this war that afflicted us was the spirit of aggrandizement of the United States of the North, availing itself of its power to conquer us. Impartial history will some day illustrate for ever the conduct observed by this Republic against all laws, divine and human, in an age that is called one of light, and which is, notwithstanding, the same as the former—one of *force and violence.*

12.4:   Dissent at Home (1846, 1847)

Opposition to the war against Mexico in the United States itself came from two chief sources: Whigs and northern antislavery adherents.

The first selection below is by the Massachusetts poet James Russell Lowell. His antiwar poem, written in rural Yankee dialect, expresses the views of Hosea Biglow, a fictional character Lowell uses as his spokesman. In fact, farmer Biglow spoke for many in New England and other parts of the Northeast. What is the theory of the Mexican War advanced by Biglow? Was it correct? What factors might explain the sectional split implied here? What do the last two lines suggest about why some northerners objected to new slave territory? (You must make allowances for Lowell's use of the term "nigger." Unfortunately, the expression was widely employed in American speech in this period.)

The second selection comes from a speech by Ohio Whig leader Thomas Corwin to the United States Senate in 1847, on the occasion of a bill to appropriate additional money to finance the war. Politics clearly influenced Corwin's attitude; other Whig politicians, including Congressman Abraham Lincoln of Illinois, were equally skeptical of the war, which they saw as a Democratic venture. But do partisan politics alone explain Corwin's harsh tone? Opponents called the Ohio senator unpatriotic, but is there something authentically American about his response? Does Corwin dispose effectively of the argument that Americans needed more room for living space?

The Mexican War Is on Behalf of Slavery

JAMES RUSSELL LOWELL

'T would n't suit them Southun fellers,
　They're a dreffle[1] graspin' set,
We must ollers[2] blow the bellers[3]
　Wen they want their irons het[4];
May be it's all right ez preachin',
　But my narves it kind o' grates,
Wen I see the overreachin'
　O' them nigger-driven' States. . . .

Ez fer war, I call it murder,—
　There you hev it plain an' flat;
I don't want to go no furder
　Than my Testyment fer that;
God hez sed so plump an' fairly,
　It's ez long ez it is broad,
　An' you've gut to git up airly
Ef you want to take in God. . . .

James Russell Lowell, *The Biglow Papers* (Boston: Houghton Mifflin Company, 1891), pp. 64–70.
[1] Dreadful—ED.
[2] Always—ED.
[3] Bellows—ED.
[4] Heated—ED.

Wut's the use o' meetin'-goin'
    Every Sabbath, wet or dry,
Ef it's right to go amowin'
    Feller-men like oats an' rye?
I dunno but wut it's pooty
    Trainin' round in botail coats,—
But it's curus Christian dooty
    This 'ere cuttin' folks's throats.

They may talk o' Freedom's airy[5]
    Tell they're pupple in the face,—
It's a grand gret cemetary
    For the barthrights of our race;
They jest want this Californy
    So's to lug new slave-states in
To abuse ye, an' to scorn ye,
    An' to plunder ye like sin.

Aint it cute[6] to see a Yankee
    Take sech everlastin' pains,
All to get the Devil's thankee
    Helpin' on 'em weld their chains!
Wy, it's jest ez clear ez figgers,
    Clear ez one an' one make two,
Chaps thet make black slaves o' niggers
    Want to make wite slaves o' you.

The War with Mexico Is Morally Wrong

THOMAS CORWIN

Mr. President, I . . . beg the indulgence of the Senate to some reflections on the particular bill now under consideration. I voted for a bill somewhat like the present at the last session—our army was then in the neighborhood of our line. I then hoped that the President did sincerely desire a peace. Our army had not then penetrated far into Mexico, and I did hope, that with the two millions then proposed, we might get peace, and avoid the slaughter, the shame, the crime, of an aggressive, unprovoked war. But now you have overrun half of Mexico—you have exasperated and irritated her people— you claim indemnity for all expenses incurred in doing this mischief, and boldly ask her to give up New Mexico and California; and, as a bribe to her patriotism, seizing on her property, you offer three millions to pay the soldiers she has called out to repel your invasion, on condition that she will give up to you at least one-third of her whole territory. . . .

But, sir, let us see what, as the chairman of the Committee on Foreign Relations explains it, we are to get by the combined processes of conquest and treaty.

---

[5] Freedom's nest, which is the United States, the home of freedom—ED.
[6] Here the word means clever, in a facetious way—ED.
Congressional Globe, 29th Cong., 2d sess., 1847, Appendix, pp. 216–17.

What is the territory, Mr. President, which you propose to wrest from Mexico? It is consecrated to the heart of the Mexican by many a well-fought battle with his old Castilian master. His Bunker Hills, and Saratogas, and Yorktowns, are there! The Mexican can say, "There I bled for liberty! and shall I surrender that consecrated home of my affections to the Anglo-Saxon invaders? What do they want with it? They have Texas already. They have possessed themselves of the territory between the Nueces and the Rio Grande. What else do they want? To what shall I point my children as memorials of that independence which I bequeath to them when those battlefields shall have passed from my possession?"

Sir, had one come and demanded Bunker Hill of the people of Massachusetts, had England's Lion ever showed himself there, is there a man over thirteen and under ninety who would not have been ready to meet him? Is there a river on this continent that would not have run red with blood? Is there a field but would have been piled high with the unburied bones of slaughtered Americans before these consecrated battlefields of liberty should have been wrested from us? But this same American goes into a sister republic and says to poor, weak Mexico, "Give up your territory, you are unworthy to possess it; I have got one-half already, and all I ask of you is to give up the other!" England might as well, in the circumstances I have described, have come and demanded of us, "Give up the Atlantic slope— give up this trifling territory from the Alleghany [sic] Mountains to the sea; it is only from Maine to St. Mary's—only about one-third of your republic, and the least interesting portion of it." What would be the response? They would say, we must give this up to John Bull. Why? "He wants room." The Senator from Michigan says he must have this. Why, my worthy Christian brother, on what principle of justice? "I want room!"

Sir, look at this pretence of want of room. With twenty millions of people, you have about one thousand millions of acres of land, inviting settlement by every conceivable argument, bringing them down to a quarter of a dollar an acre, and allowing every man to squat where he pleases. But the Senator from Michigan says we will be two hundred millions in a few years, and we want room. If I were a Mexican I would tell you, "Have you not room in your own country to bury your dead men? If you come into mine, we will greet you with bloody hands, and welcome you to hospitable graves."

Why, says the chairman of this Committee on Foreign Relations, it is the most reasonable thing in the world! We ought to have the Bay of San Francisco. Why? Because it is the best harbor on the Pacific! It has been my fortune, Mr. President, to have practised a good deal in criminal courts in the course of my life, but I never yet heard a thief, arraigned for stealing a horse, plead that it was the best horse that he could find in the country! We want California. What for? Why, says the Senator from Michigan, we will have it; and the Senator from South Carolina, with a very mistaken view, I think, of policy, says you can't keep our people from going there. I don't desire to prevent them. Let them go and seek their happiness in whatever country or clime it pleases them.

All I ask of them is, not to require this Government to protect them with that banner consecrated to war waged for principles—eternal, enduring truth. Sir, it is not meet that our old flag should throw its protecting folds over expeditions for lucre or for land. But you still say you want room for your people. This has been the plea of every robber chief from Nimrod to the present hour.

13

Slavery and the "Old South"

The "Old South"—the slave states before 1860—was diverse in economy, geography, class, race, religion, and culture. Yet the institution of slavery gave it both a cohesion and a uniqueness that set it apart from the rest of the United States.

No segment of the American past has been the focus of so much misunderstanding and myth as the Old South. To the average American today the name summons up images of vast cotton plantations with their slaves and masters. This picture may seem benign or malignant, depending on the race or ideology of the viewer, but it is, in any case, a simplistic view of a complex reality.

There were, of course, masters and slaves in the Old South, and the relations of the two formed a fundamental fact of the region's social and economic life. It is important to know how each viewed the other and how each perceived the circumstances under which they lived. But there were other significant members of Old South society besides slaveholders and slaves. We know that most southern whites were not slaveowners. Did they support the "peculiar institution," the South's distinctive system of chattel slavery? And what opinions did nonsoutherners have about Dixie? The Old South was defined to some degree by those on the outside who observed and criticized its institutions. What did the people of the free North have to say about the institutions and values of the region?

The selections below provide a sampling of contemporary opinion regarding the Old South. Judging from these documents, how should we perceive the society that developed in the slave states before the Civil War?

13.1:   Slavery from the Victim's Viewpoint (1848)

Among our best sources for evidence on how slavery affected slaves are the descriptions of slave refugees. Hundreds of slaves escaped the South each year, especially from the border states of Virginia, Maryland, Kentucky, and Missouri. A small proportion of these fugitives were literate men and women who wrote about their lives under the "peculiar institution." These poignant firsthand accounts found a sympathetic audience and were popular with the growing number of antislavery advocates in the North.

One of the best of these slave autobiographies is the Narrative of William Brown, A Fugitive Slave, *published in 1848, some thirteen years after Brown escaped from slavery. Like most slaves, Brown received no formal education, but he became a talented writer who published a number of books including a novel, the first by an African American.*

The following excerpt is the first two chapters of Brown's Narrative. *It contains descriptions of physical cruelty. But it also reveals the psychological costs of slavery. What are these, as depicted by Brown? Brown describes several brutal slaveowners. Does he suggest that some slave masters were better than these cruel men?*

My Life as a Slave

WILLIAM BROWN

I was born in Lexington, Ky. The man who stole me as soon as I was born, recorded the births of all the infants which he claimed to be born [on] his property, in a book which he kept for that purpose. My mother's name was Elizabeth. She had seven children, viz.: Solomon, Leander, Benjamin, Joseph, Millford, Elizabeth, and myself. No two of us were children of the same father. My father's name, as I learned from my mother, was George Higgins. He was a white man, a relative of my master, and connected with some of the first families in Kentucky.

My master owned about forty slaves, twenty-five of whom were field hands. He removed from Kentucky to Missouri when I was quite young, and settled thirty or forty miles above St. Charles, on the Missouri, where, in addition to his practice as a physician, he carried on milling, merchandizing and farming. He had a large farm, the principal productions of which were tobacco and hemp. The slave cabins were situated on the back part of the farm, with the house of the overseer, whose name was Grove Cook, in their midst. He had the entire charge of the farm, and having no family, was allowed a

William Brown, *Narrative of William Brown, A Fugitive Slave* (Boston: Published at the Anti-Slavery Office, 1848), pp. 1–7.

woman to keep house for him, whose business it was to deal out the provisions for the hands.

A woman was also kept at the quarters to do the cooking for the field hands, who were summoned to their unrequited toil every morning at four o'clock, by the ringing of a bell, hung on a post near the house of the overseer. They were allowed half an hour to eat their breakfast, and get to the field. At half past four a horn was blown by the overseer, which was his signal to commence work; and every one that was not on the spot at the time, had to receive ten lashes from the negro-whip, with which the overseer always went armed. The handle was about three feet long, with the butt-end filled with lead, and the lash, six or seven feet in length, made of cow-hide, with platted wire on the end of it. This whip was put in requisition very frequently and freely, and a small offence on the part of a slave furnished an occasion for its use. During the time that Mr. Cook was overseer, I was a house servant—a situation preferable to that of a field hand, as I was better fed, better clothed, and not obliged to rise at the ringing of the bell, but about half an hour after. I have often laid and heard the crack of the whip, and the screams of the slave. My mother was a field hand, and one morning was ten or fifteen minutes behind the others in getting into the field. As soon as she reached the spot where they were at work, the overseer commenced whipping her. She cried, "Oh! pray—Oh! pray—Oh! pray"— these are generally the words of slaves, when imploring mercy at the hands of their oppressors. I heard her voice, and knew it, and jumped out of my bunk, and went to the door. Though the field was some distance from the house, I could hear every crack of the whip, and every groan and cry of my poor mother. I remained at the door, not daring to venture any further. The cold chills ran over me, and I wept aloud. After giving her ten lashes, the sound of the whip ceased, and I returned to my bed, and found no consolation but in my tears. Experience has taught me that nothing can be more heart-rending than for one to see a dear and beloved mother or sister tortured, and to hear their cries, and not be able to render them assistance. But such is the position which an American slave occupies.

My master, being a politician, soon found those who were ready to put him into office, for the favors he could render them; and a few years after his arrival in Missouri he was elected to a seat in the legislature. In his absence from home everything was left in charge of Mr. Cook, the overseer, and he soon became more tyrannical and cruel. Among the slaves on the plantation was one by the name of Randall. He was a man about six feet high, and well-proportioned, and known as a man of great strength and power. He was considered the most valuable and able-bodied slave on the plantation; but no matter how good or useful a slave may be, he seldom escapes the lash. But it was not so with Randall. He had been on the plantation since my earliest recollection, and I had never known of his being flogged. No thanks were due to the master or overseer for this. I have often heard him declare that no white man should ever whip him—that he would die first.

Cook, from the time that he came upon the plantation, had frequently declared that he could and would flog any nigger that was put into the field to work under him. My master had repeatedly told him not to attempt to whip Randall, but he was determined to try it. As soon as he was left sole dictator, he thought the time had come to put his threats into execution. He soon began to find fault with Randall, and threatened to whip him if he did not do better. One day he gave him a very hard task—more than he could possibly do; and at night, the task not being performed, he told Randall that he should remember him the next morning. On the following morning, after the hands had taken breakfast, Cook called out to Randall, and told him that he intended to whip him, and ordered him to cross his hands and be tied. Randall asked why he wished to whip him. He answered, because he had not finished his task the day before. Randall said that the task was too great, or he should have done it. Cook said it made no difference—he should whip him. Randall stood silent for a moment, and then said, "Mr. Cook, I have always tried to please you since you have been on the plantation, and I find you are determined not to be satisfied with my work, let me do as well as I may. No man has laid hands on me, to whip me, for the last ten years, and I have long since come to the conclusion not to be whipped by any man living." Cook, finding by Randall's determined look and gestures, that he would resist, called three of the hands from their work, and commanded them to seize Randall, and tie him. The hands stood still;—they knew Randall—and they also knew him to be a powerful man, and were afraid to grapple with him. As soon as Cook had ordered the men to seize him, Randall turned to them, and said—"Boys, you all know me; you know that I can handle any three of you, and the man that lays hands on me shall die. This white man can't whip me himself, and therefore he has called you to help him." The overseer was unable to prevail upon them to seize and secure Randall, and finally ordered them all to go to their work together.

Nothing was said to Randall by the overseer for more than a week. One morning, however, while the hands were at work in the field, he came into it, accompanied by three friends of his, Thompson, Woodbridge and Jones. They came up to where Randall was at work, and Cook ordered him to leave his work, and go with them to the barn. He refused to go; whereupon he was attacked by the overseer and his companions, when he turned upon them, and laid them, one after another, prostrate on the ground. Woodbridge drew out his pistol, and fired at him, and brought him to the ground by a pistol ball. The others rushed upon him with their clubs, and beat him over the head and face, until they succeeded in tying him. He was then taken to the barn, and tied to a beam. Cook gave him over one hundred lashes with a heavy cowhide, had him washed with salt and water, and left him tied during the day. The next day he was untied, and taken to a blacksmith's shop, and had a ball and chain attached to his leg. He was compelled to labor in the field, and perform the same amount of work that the other hands did. When his master returned home, he was much pleased to find that Randall had been subdued in his absence.

Soon afterwards, my master removed to the city of St. Louis, and pur-chased a farm four miles from there, which he placed under the charge of an overseer by the name of Friend Haskell. He was a regular Yankee from New England. The Yankees are noted for making the most cruel overseers.

My mother was hired out in the city, and I was also hired out there to Major Freeland, who kept a public house. He was formerly from Virginia, and was a horse-racer, cock-fighter, gambler, and withal an inveterate drunk-ard. There were ten or twelve servants in the house, and when he was pre-sent, it was cut and slash—knock down and drag out. In his fits of anger, he would take up a chair, and throw it at a servant; and in his more rational moments, when he wished to chastise one, he would tie them up in the smoke-house, and whip them; after which, he would cause a fire to be made of tobacco stems, and smoke them. This he called "*Virginia play.*"

I complained to my master of the treatment which I received from Major Freeland; but it made no difference. He cared nothing about it, so long as he received the money for my labor. After living with Major Freeland five or six months, I ran away, and went into the woods back of the city; and when night came on, I made my way to my master's farm, but was afraid to be seen, knowing that if Mr. Haskell, the overseer, should discover me, I should be again carried back to Major Freeland; so I kept in the woods. One day, while in the woods, I heard the barking and howling of dogs, and in a short time they came so near that I knew them to be the bloodhounds of Major Benjamin O'Fallon. He kept five or six, to hunt runaway slaves with.

As soon as I was convinced that it was them, I knew there was no chance of escape. I took refuge in the top of a tree, and the hounds were soon at its base, and there remained until the hunters came up in a half or three quar-ters of an hour afterwards. There were two men with the dogs, who, as soon as they came up, ordered me to descend. I came down, was tied, and taken to St. Louis jail. Major Freeland soon made his appearance, and took me out, and ordered me to follow him, which I did. After we returned home, I was tied up in the smoke-house, and was very severely whipped. After the major had flogged me to his satisfaction, he sent out his son Robert, a young man eighteen or twenty years of age, to see that I was well smoked. He made a fire of tobacco stems, which soon set me to coughing and sneezing. This, Robert told me, was the way his father used to do to his slaves in Virginia. After giving me what they conceived to be a decent smoking, I was untied and again set to work.

Robert Freeland was a "chip of the old block." Though quite young, it was not unfrequently that he came home in a state of intoxication. He is now, I believe, a popular commander of a steamboat on the Mississippi river. Major Freeland soon after failed in business, and I was put on board the steamboat Missouri, which plied between St. Louis and Galena. The commander of the boat was William B. Culver. I remained on her during the sailing season, which was the most pleasant time for me that I had ever experienced. At the close of navigation I was hired to Mr. John Colburn, keeper of the Missouri Hotel. He was from one of the free states; but a more inveterate hater of the negro I do not believe ever walked God's green earth. This hotel was at that time one of the largest in the city, and there were employed in it twenty or thirty servants, mostly slaves.

Mr. Colburn was very abusive, not only to the servants, but to his wife also, who was an excellent woman, and one from whom I never knew a servant to receive a harsh word; but never did I know a kind one to a servant from her husband. Among the slaves employed in the hotel was one by the name of Aaron, who belonged to Mr. John F. Darby, a lawyer. Aaron was the knife-cleaner. One day, one of the knives was put on the table, not as clean as it might have been. Mr. Colburn, for this offence, tied Aaron up in the wood-house, and gave him over fifty lashes on the bare back with a cow-hide, after which, he made me wash him down with rum. This seemed to put him into more agony than the whipping. After being untied he went home to his master, and complained of the treatment which he had received. Mr. Darby would give no heed to anything he had to say, but sent him directly back. Colburn, learning that he had been to his master with complaints, tied him up again, and gave him a more severe whipping than before. The poor fellow's back was literally cut to pieces; so much so, that he was not able to work for ten or twelve days.

There was, also, among the servants, a girl whose master resided in the country. Her name was Patsey. Mr. Colburn tied her up one evening, and whipped her until several of the boarders came out and begged him to desist. The reason for whipping her was this. She was engaged to be married to a man belonging to Major William Christy, who resided four or five miles north of the city. Mr. Colburn had forbid her to see John Christy. The reason of this was said to be the regard which he himself had for Patsey. She went to meeting that evening, and John returned home with her. Mr. Colburn had intended to flog John, if he came within the inclosure; but John knew too well the temper of his rival, and kept at a safe distance:—so he took vengeance on the poor girl. If all the slave-drivers had been called together, I do not think a more cruel man than John Colburn—and he too a northern man—could have been found among them.

While living at the Missouri hotel, a circumstance occurred which caused me great unhappiness. My master sold my mother, and all her children, except myself. They were sold to different persons in the city of St. Louis.

13.2: A Southern Apologist Views Slavery (1859)

For a generation following the Revolution, many southern whites harbored serious moral reservations about slavery. By the 1830s these reservations began to erode, however, and by the 1850s slavery had gone from being regarded as a necessary evil to a positive good by most white southerners. By the Civil War the South had forged a complex proslavery defense that obliterated almost all former doubts.

One of the most effective defenders of slavery was Edward A. Pollard, a Virginia journalist. In the following selection from a volume of letters to a fictional northern friend, Pollard depicts slaves and slavery as most Southern whites preferred to see them. How would you characterize the slave types that Pollard sketches? Were his descriptions invalid on their face? Compare Pollard's Aunt Debby with William Brown's Randall in the previous selection. How did they differ in their response to the white master class? Is Aunt Debby a believable character?

Happy "Darkies"

EDWARD A. POLLARD

But it is not my purpose to trouble you with a dissertation on "the vexed question," or the social system of the South, or any of the political aspects of Slavery. I merely design to employ a few leisure hours in a series of unpretending sketches of the condition, habits, and peculiarities of the negro-slave. The field, you know, has furnished a number of books; and I am sure, my dear C., that you are too sensible of the large share of public attention *niggers* occupy in this country to slight them. Besides, I am thoroughly convinced that the negro portraits of the fiction writers are, most of them, mere caricatures, taking them all, from [Harriet Beecher Stowe's] "Uncle Tom's Cabin," down to the latest reply thereto—"a book" from a Virginia authoress, in which the language put in the mouth of her leading character is a mixture of Irish idioms with the dialect of the Bowery. Who ever heard a Southern negro say, as the Virginia lady's sable hero does, "The tip-top of the morning to you, young ladies!" or "What's to pay now?" Nor will we find any of Mrs. Stowe's *Uncle Toms* in the South, at least so far as the religious portraiture goes. The negro, in his religion, is not a solemn old gentleman, reading his Bible in corners and praying in his closet: his piety is one of fits and starts, and lives on prayer-meetings, with its rounds of 'zortations, shoutings, and stolen sweets of baked pig.

You already know my opinion of the peculiarities of the negro's condition in the South, in the provision made for his comfort, and in the attachment between him and his master. The fact is, that, in wandering from my native soil to other parts of the world, I have seen slavery in many forms and aspects. We have all heard enough of the colliers and factory operatives of England, and the thirty thousand costermongers [peddlars] starving in the streets of London; as also of the serfs and crown-peasants of Russia, who are considered not even as chattels, but as part of the land, and who have their wives selected for them by their masters. I have seen the hideous slavery of Asia. I have seen the coolies of China "housed on the wild sea with wilder

Edward A. Pollard, *Black Diamonds Gathered in the Darkey Homes of the South* (New York: Pudney and Russell, 1859), pp. 20–25.

usages," or creeping with dejected faces into the suicide houses of Canton. I have seen the Siamese slave creeping in the presence of his master on all-fours—a human quadruped. It was indeed refreshing, after such sights, to get back to the Southern institution, which strikes one after so many years of absence, with a novelty that makes him appreciate more than ever the evidences of comfort and happiness on the plantations of the South.

The first unadulterated negro I had seen for a number of years (having been absent for the most of that time on a foreign soil), was on the railroad cars in Virginia. He looked like *home*. I could have embraced the old uncle, but was afraid the passengers, from such a demonstration, might mistake me for an abolitionist. I looked at him with my face aglow, and my eyelids touched with tears. How he reminded me of my home—of days gone by—that poetry of youth, "when I was a boy," and wandered with my sable playmates over the warm, wide hills of my sweet home, and along the branches, fishing in the shallow waters with a crooked pin! But no romancing with the past! So we continue our journey onward to "the State of railways and revolvers."

Arrived in Georgia, I find plenty of the real genuine *woolly-heads*, such as don't part their hair in the middle, like Mass'r [Charles] Fremont. My first acquaintance is with Aunt Debby. I insist upon giving her a shake of the hand, which she prepares for by deprecatingly wiping her hand on her apron. Aunt Debby is an aged colored female of the very highest respectability, and, with her white apron, and her head mysteriously enveloped in the brightest of bandannas, she looks (to use one of her own rather obscure similes) "like a new pin." She is very fond of usurping the authority of her mistress below stairs, and has the habit of designating every one of her own color, not admitted to equality, as "*de nigger*." Aunt Debby is rather spoiled, if having things her own way means it. If at times her mistress is roused to dispute her authority, Aunt Debby is sure to resume the reins when quiet ensues. "Debby," cries her mistress, "what's all this noise in the kitchen—what are you whipping Lucy for?" "La, missis, I'se jest makin' her 'have herself. She too busy *walling* her eyes at me, and spilt the water on the steps." Among the children, Aunt Debby is a great character. She is, however, very partial; and her favorite is little Nina, whom she calls (from what remote analogy we are at a loss to conjecture) "her *jelly-pot*." I flatter myself that I am in her good graces. Her attention to me has been shown by a present of ground-peas, and accessions of fat lightwood to my fire in the morning.

The religious element is very strong in Aunt Debby's character, and her *repertoire* of pious minstrelsy is quite extensive. Her favorite hymn is in the following words, which are repeated over and over again:

"Oh run, brother, run! Judgement day is comin'!
Oh run, brother, run! Why don't you come along?
The road so rugged, and the hill so high—
And my Lord call me home,
To walk the golden streets of my New Jerusalem."

Aunt Debby's religion is of that sort—always begging the Lord to take her up to glory, and professing the greatest anxiety to go *right now!* This religious enthusiasm, however, is not to be taken at its word.

You have doubtless heard the anecdote of Caesar, which is too good not to have been told more than once; though even if you have heard the story before, it will bear repetition for its moral. Now, Caesar one day had caught it, not from Brutus, but from Betty—an allegorical coquette in the shape of a red cowhide. On retiring to the silence of his cabin at night, Caesar commenced to soliloquize, rubbing the part of his body where the castigation had been chiefly administered, and bewailing his fate with tragic desperation, in the third person. "Caesar," said he, "most done gone—don't want to live no longer! Jist come, good Lord, swing low de chariot, and take dis chile away! Caesar ready to go—he *wants* to go!" An irreverent darkey outside, hearing these protestations, tapped at the door. "Who dar?" replied Caesar, in a low voice of suppressed alarm. "De angel of de Lord come for Caesar, 'cordin to request." The dread summons had indeed come, thought Caesar; but blowing out the light with a sudden whiff, he replied, in an unconcerned tone, "*De nigger don't live here.*"

There is one other trait wanting to complete Aunt Debby's character. Though at an advanced age, she is very coquettish; and keeps a regular assault on a big lout of the name of Sam, whom she affects to despise as "jist 'de meanest nigger de Lord ever put breath in." I overheard some words between them last holiday. "I'se a white man to-day," says Sam, "and I'se not gwine to take any of your imperence, old ooman;" at the same time, taking the familiar liberty of poking his finger into her side like a brad-awl. "Get 'long, Sa-ten!" replied Aunt Debby, with a shove, but a smile at the same time, to his infernal majesty. And then they both fell to laughing for the space of half a minute, although I must confess, that I could not understand what they were laughing at.

Aunt Debby may serve you, my dear C., as a picture of the happy, contented, Southern slave. Some of your Northern politicians would represent the slaves of the South as sullen, gloomy, isolated from life—in fact, pictures of a living death. Believe me, nothing could be further from the truth. Like Aunt Debby, they have their little prides and passions, their amusements, their pleasantries, which constitute the same sum of happiness as in the lives of their masters.

13.3:   The Southern Plantation Idyll (1832)

Most white southerners not only defended slavery as such; they also defended the white society it carried on its back. The following selection is from a novel by John Pendleton Kennedy, a native of Baltimore related through his mother to several aristocratic families of Virginia. Kennedy was not a typical defender of the southern plantation idyll, but his book,

Swallow Barn, *a novel in the form of letters, helped construct the myth of the gracious, happy plantation where everyone, masters and slaves alike, lived a genial and civilized, if deferential, existence.*

Kennedy's hero, Frank Meriwether, is an idealized type. What are his chief characteristics? Do you think there were actually people like Meriwether in the antebellum South? Were there plantations like Swallow Barn? Or were they—the Meriwethers and the Swallow Barns—all creations of southern propaganda?

(It is worth noting that after the Civil War Kennedy became a Republican!)

The Southern Plantation Idyll

JOHN PENDLETON KENNEDY

Swallow Barn is an aristocratical old edifice which sits, like a brooding hen, on the southern bank of the James River. It looks down upon a shady pocket or nook, formed by an indentation of the shore, from a gentle acclivity thinly sprinkled with oaks whose magnificent branches afford habitation to sundry friendly colonies of squirrels and woodpeckers.

This time-honored mansion was the residence of the family of Hazards. But in the present generation, the spells of love and mortgage have translated the possession to Frank Meriwether, who having married Lucretia, the eldest daughter of my late Uncle Walter Hazard, and lifted some gentleman-like incumbrances which had been sleeping for years upon the domain, was thus inducted into the proprietary rights. The adjacency of his own estate gave a territorial feature to this alliance, of which the fruits were no less discernible in the multiplication of negroes, cattle, and poultry, than in a flourishing clan of Meriwethers.

The main building is more than a century old. It is built with thick brick walls, but one story in height, and surmounted by a double-faced or hipped roof, which gives the idea of a ship bottom upwards. Later buildings have been added to this, as the wants or ambition of the family have expanded. These are all constructed of wood, and seem to have been built in defiance of all laws of congruity, just as convenience required. But they form altogether an agreeable picture of habitation, suggesting the idea of comfort in the ample space they fill, and in their conspicuous adaptation to domestic uses.

The hall door is an ancient piece of walnut, which has grown too heavy for its hinges, and by its daily travel has furrowed the floor in a quadrant, over which it has an uneasy journey. It is shaded by a narrow porch, with a carved pediment upheld by massive columns of wood, somewhat split by the sun. An ample court-yard, inclosed by a semi-circular paling, extends in

John Pendleton Kennedy, *Swallow Barn, Or, A Sojourn in the Old Dominion* (Philadelphia: J. B. Lippincott, 1861), pp. 22–35.

front of the whole pile, and is traversed by a gravel road leading from a rather ostentatious iron gate, which is swung between two pillars of brick surmounted by globes of cut stone. Between the gate and the house a large willow spreads its arched and pendent drapery over the grass. A bridle rack stands within the inclosure, and near it a ragged horse-nibbled plum-tree—the current belief being that a plum-tree thrives on ill usage—casts its skeleton shadow on the dust. . . .

Appendant to this homestead is an extensive tract of land which stretches some three or four miles along the river, presenting alternately abrupt promontories mantled with pine and dwarf oak, and small inlets terminating in swamps. Some sparse portions of forest vary the landscape, which, for the most part, exhibits a succession of fields clothed with Indian corn, some small patches of cotton or tobacco plants, with the usual varieties of stubble and fallow grounds. These are inclosed by worm fences of shrunken chestnut, where lizards and ground-squirrels are perpetually running races along the rails.

A few hundred steps from the mansion, a brook glides at a snail's pace towards the river, holding its course through a wilderness of laurel and alder, and creeping around islets covered with green mosses. Across the stream is thrown a rough bridge, which it would delight a painter to see; and not far below it an aged sycamore twists its roots into a grotesque framework to the pure mirror of a spring, which wells up its cool waters from a bed of gravel and runs gurgling to the brook. There it aids in furnishing a cruising ground to a squadron of ducks who, in defiance of all nautical propriety, are incessantly turning up their sterns to the skies. On the grass which skirts the margin of the spring, I observe the family linen is usually spread out by some three or four negro women, who chant shrill music over their wash-tubs, and seem to live in ceaseless warfare with sundry little besmirched and bow-legged blacks, who are never tired of making somersets, and mischievously pushing each other on the clothes laid down to dry. . . .

The master of this lordly domain is Frank Meriwether. He is now in the meridian of life—somewhere about forty-five. Good cheer and an easy temper tell well upon him. The first has given him a comfortable, portly figure, and the latter a contemplative turn of mind, which inclines him to be lazy and philosophical.

He has some right to pride himself on his personal appearance, for he has a handsome face, with a dark blue eye and a fine intellectual brow. His head is growing scant of hair on the crown, which induces him to be somewhat particular in the management of his locks in that locality, and these are assuming a decided silvery hue.

It is pleasant to see him when he is going to ride to the Court House on business occasions. He is then apt to make his appearance in a coat of blue broadcloth, astonishingly glossy, and with an unusual amount of plaited ruffle strutting through the folds of a Marseilles waistcoat. A worshipful finish is given to this costume by a large straw hat, lined with green silk. There is a magisterial fulness in his garments which betokens condition in the world, and a heavy bunch of seals, suspended by a chain of gold, jingles as he moves, pronouncing him a man of superfluities.

It is considered rather extraordinary that he has never set up for Congress: but the truth is, he is an unambitious man, and has a great dislike to currying favor—as he calls it. And, besides, he is thoroughly convinced that there will always be men enough in Virginia willing to serve the people, and therefore does not see why he should trouble his head about it. Some years ago, however, there was really an impression that he meant to come out. By some sudden whim, he took it into his head to visit Washington during the session of Congress, and returned, after a fortnight, very seriously distempered with politics. He told curious anecdotes of certain secret intrigues which had been discovered in the affairs of the capital, gave a clear insight into the views of some deep-laid combinations, and became, all at once, painfully florid in his discourse, and dogmatical to a degree that made his wife stare. Fortunately, this orgasm soon subsided, and Frank relapsed into an indolent gentleman of the opposition; but it had the effect to give a much more decided cast to his studies, for he forthwith discarded the "Richmond Whig" from his newspaper subscription, and took to "The Enquirer,"[1] like a man who was not to be disturbed by doubts. And as it was morally impossible to believe all that was written on both sides, to prevent his mind from being abused, he from this time forward took a stand against the re-election of Mr. [John Quincy] Adams to the Presidency, and resolved to give an implicit faith to all alleged facts which set against his administration. The consequence of this straight-forward and confiding deportment was an unexpected complimentary notice of him by the Executive of the State. He was put into the commission of the peace, and having thus become a public man against his will, his opinions were observed to undergo some essential changes. He now thinks that a good citizen ought neither to solicit nor decline office; that the magistracy of Virginia is the sturdiest pillar which supports the fabric of the Constitution; and that the people, "though in their opinions they may be mistaken, in their sentiments they are never wrong;"—with some such other dogmas as, a few years ago, he did not hold in very good repute. In this temper, he has of late embarked on the millpond of county affairs, and nothwithstanding his amiable character and his doctrinary republicanism, I am told he keeps the peace as if he commanded a garrison, and administers justice like a Cadi. . . .

A landed proprietor, with a good house and a host of servants, is naturally a hospitable man. A guest is one of his daily wants. A friendly face is a necessary of life, without which the heart is apt to starve, or a luxury without which it grows parsimonious. Men who are isolated from society by distance, feel these wants by an instinct, and are grateful for the opportunity to relieve

---

[1]The *Whig* was a partisan of the nationalist and moderate Whig party; The *Enquirer* was the more pro-South Democratic paper—ED.

them. In Meriwether, the sentiment goes beyond this. It has, besides, something dialectic in it. His house is open to every body, as freely almost as an inn. But to see him when he has had the good fortune to pick up an intelligent, educated gentleman,—and particularly one who listens well!—a respectable, assentatious stranger!—All the better if he has been in the Legislature, or better still, if in Congress. Such a person caught within the purlieus of Swallow Barn, may set down one week's entertainment as certain—inevitable, and as many more as he likes—the more the merrier. He will know something of the quality of Meriwether's rhetoric before he is gone.

Then again, it is very pleasant to see Frank's kind and considerate bearing towards his servants and dependents. His slaves appreciate this, and hold him in most affectionate reverence, and, therefore, are not only contented, but happy under his dominion. . . .

He thinks lightly of the mercantile interest, and, in fact, undervalues the manners of the large cities generally. He believes that those who live in them are hollow-hearted and insincere, and wanting in that substantial intelligence and virtue, which he affirms to be characteristic of the country. He is an ardent admirer of the genius of Virginia, and is frequent in his commendation of a toast in which the state is compared to the mother of the Gracchi[2]:—indeed, it is a familiar thing with him to speak of the aristocracy of talent as only inferior to that of the landed interest,—the idea of a freeholder inferring to his mind a certain constitutional pre-eminence in all the virtues of citizenship, as a matter of course.

13.4:   A Nonslaveholding Southerner Attacks the "Peculiar Institution" (1857)

Not all white southerners supported slavery. A minority deplored the institution, and a very few even publicly denounced it. Among the most vocal white southern opponents of the "peculiar institution" was Hinton Rowan Helper, a North Carolinian from the mountainous western part of the state, where there were few slaves and almost no plantations. Helper spoke in the name of the southern white small farmer, who, in his view, suffered severely from the domination of the planter "oligarchy." He was, however, no friend to blacks and indeed advocated their expulsion from the United States!

In 1857 Helper blasted the slaveowners in a volume that no one in the South would publish. The Impending Crisis of the South *finally came out under antislavery auspices and was adopted as a Republican campaign document in the 1860 presidential election. As if that were*

[2]Agrarian reformers of the late Roman Republic—ED.

not bad enough in the eyes of white Southerners, the volume seemed to condone a bloody uprising of slaves against their masters. Overnight Helper became a pariah in his home section.

What are the charges Helper levels against slavery? Do they overlap those expressed by William Brown above? Does Helper add other items to the indictment of slavery besides cruelty? Was his view that slavery hurt the South's nonslaveholding whites correct? Do you know if slavery made the pre–Civil War South overall poorer than the North?

Slavery Hurts Non-Slaveholding Whites

HINTON ROWAN HELPER

As a striking illustration of the selfish and debasing influences which slavery exercises over the hearts and minds of slaveholders themselves, we will here state the fact that, when we, the non-slaveholders, remonstrate against the continuance of such a manifest wrong and inhumanity—a system of usurpation and outrage so obviously detrimental to *our* interests—they fly into a terrible passion, exclaiming, among all sorts of horrible threats, which are not unfrequently executed, "It's none of your business!"—meaning to say thereby that their slaves do not annoy us, that slavery affects no one except the masters and their chattels personal and that *we* should give ourselves no concern about it, whatever! To every man of common sense and honesty of purpose the preposterousness of this assumption is so evident, that any studied attempt to refute it would be a positive insult. Would it be none of our business, if they were to bring the small-pox into the neighborhood, and, with premeditated design, let "foul contagion spread?" Or, if they were to throw a pound of strychnine into a public spring, would that be none of our business? Were they to turn a pack of mad dogs loose on the community, would we be performing the part of good citizens by closing ourselves within doors for the space of nine days, saying nothing to anybody? Small-pox is a nuisance; strychnine is a nuisance; mad dogs are a nuisance; slavery is a nuisance; slaveholders are a nuisance, and so are slave-breeders; it is our business, nay, it is our imperative duty, to abate nuisances; we propose, therefore, with the exception of strychnine, which is the least of all these nuisances, to exterminate this catalogue from beginning to end.

We mean precisely what our words express, when we say we believe thieves are, as a general rule, less amenable to the moral law than slaveholders; and here is the basis of our opinion: Ordinarily, thieves wait until we acquire a considerable amount of property, and then they steal a dispensable part of it; but they deprive no one of physical liberty, nor do they fetter the mind; slaveholders, on the contrary, by clinging to the most barbarous

Hinton Rowan Helper, *The Impending Crisis of the South: How to Meet It* (New York: Burdick Brothers, 1857), pp. 139–41, 380–82.

relic of the most barbarous age, bring disgrace on themselves, their neighbors, and their country, depreciate the value of their own and others' lands,
degrade labor, discourage energy and progress, prevent non-slaveholders
from accumulating wealth, curtail their natural rights and privileges, doom
their children to ignorance, and all its attendant evils, rob the negroes of
their freedom, throw a damper on every species of manual and intellectual
enterprise, that is not projected under their own roofs and for their own
advantage, and, by other means equally at variance with the principles of justice, though but an insignificant fractional part of the population, they constitute themselves the sole arbiters and legislators for the entire South. Not
merely so; the thief rarely steals from more than one man out of an hundred; the slaveholder defrauds ninety and nine, and the hundredth does not
escape him. Again, thieves steal trifles from rich men; slaveholders oppress
poor men, and enact laws for the perpetuation of their poverty. Thieves
practice deceit on the wise; slaveholders take advantage of the ignorant.

We contend, moreover, that slaveholders are more criminal than common murderers. We know all slaveholders would not wilfully imbue their
hands in the blood of their fellow-men; but it is a fact, nevertheless, that all
slaveholders are under the shield of a perpetual license to murder. This
license they have issued to themselves. According to their own infamous
statutes, if the slave raises his hand to ward off an unmerited blow, they are
permitted to take his life with impunity. We are personally acquainted with
three ruffians who have become actual murderers under circumstances of
this nature. One of them killed two negroes on one occasion; the other two
have murdered but one each. Neither of them has ever been subjected to
even the preliminaries of a trial; not one of them has ever been arrested;
their own private explanations of the homicides exculpated them from all
manner of blame in the premises. They had done nothing wrong in the eyes
of the community. The negroes made an effort to shield themselves from
the tortures of a merciless flagellation, and were shot dead on the spot.
Their murderers still live, and are treated as honorable members of society!
No matter how many slaves or free negroes may witness the perpetration of
these atrocious homicides, not one of them is ever allowed to lift up his
voice in behalf of his murdered brother. In the South, negroes, whether
bond or free, are never, under any circumstances, permitted to utter a sylla-
ble under oath, except for or against persons of their own color; their testimony against white persons is of no more consequence than the idle zephyr
of the summer. . . .

Black slave labor, though far less valuable, is almost invariably better paid
than free white labor. The reason is this: The fiat of the oligarchy has made
it *fashionable* to "have negroes around," and there are, we are grieved to say,
many non-slaveholding whites, (lickspittles), who, in order to retain on their
premises a hired slave whom they falsely imagine secures to them not only
the appearance of wealth, but also a position of high social standing in the
community, keep themselves in a perpetual strait.

Last Spring, we made it our special business to ascertain the ruling rates of wages paid for labor, free and slave, in North Carolina. We found sober, energetic white men, between twenty and forty years of age, engaged in agricultural pursuits at a salary of $84 per annum—including board only; negro men, slaves, who performed little more than half the amount of labor, and who were exceedingly sluggish, awkward, and careless in all their movements, were hired out on adjoining farms at an average of about $115 per annum, including board, clothing, and medical attendance. Free white men and slaves were in the employ of the North Carolina Railroad Company; the former, whose services, in our opinion, were at least twice as valuable as the services of the latter, received only $12 per month each; the masters of the latter received $16 per month for every slave so employed. Industrious, tidy white girls, from sixteen to twenty years of age, had much difficulty in hiring themselves out as domestics in private families for $40 per annum—board only included; negro wenches, slaves, of corresponding ages, so ungraceful, stupid and filthy that no decent man would ever permit one of them to cross the threshold of his dwelling, were in brisk demand at from $65 to $70 per annum, including victuals, clothes, and medical attendance. These are facts, and in considering them, the students of political and social economy will not fail to arrive at conclusions of their own.

Notwithstanding the greater density of population in the free States, labor of every kind is, on an average, about one hundred per cent higher there than it is in the slave States. This is another important fact, and one that every non-slaveholding white should keep registered in his mind.

Poverty, ignorance, and superstition, are the three leading characteristics of the non-slaveholding whites of the South. Many of them grow up to the age of maturity, and pass through life without ever owning as much as five dollars at any one time. Thousands of them die at an advanced age, as ignorant of the common alphabet as if it had never been invented. All are more or less impressed with a belief in witches, ghosts, and supernatural signs. Few are exempt from habits of sensuality and intemperance. None have anything like adequate ideas of the duties which they owe either to their God, to themselves, or to their fellow-men. Pitiable, indeed, in the fullest sense of the term, is their condition.

It is the almost utter lack of an education that has reduced them to their present unenviable situation. In the whole South there is scarcely a publication of any kind devoted to their interests. They are now completely under the domination of the oligarchy, and it is madness to suppose that they will ever be able to rise to a position of true manhood, until after the slave power shall have been utterly overthrown.

13.5:   A Northerner Describes the Old South
(1854)

Many northerner visitors were charmed by the Old South and were happy to confirm its own self-evaluation. One observer who demurred was the New York gentleman farmer and landscape architect Frederick Law Olmstead.

Olmstead disliked slavery, but was unwilling to condemn the system or its beneficiaries outright. This attitude led to frequent arguments with his good friend Charles Loring Brace, a dedicated abolitionist, and in 1850 Olmstead decided to see the South for himself. Before Olmstead left, Brace contacted Henry J. Raymond, editor of the New York Times, *who agreed to appoint Olmstead as special correspondent and publish his letters as dispatches in the* Times.

In all, from late 1852 to the summer of 1854, Olmstead spent fourteen months traveling through eleven slave states on three separate expeditions. He traveled by horseback along the dirt roads and back country trails that made up the rough communication system of the rural South. He spoke to everyone he could—planters, slaves, townspeople, yeoman, and poor whites—and relied on private hospitality rather than hotels for his meals and shelter. It was often tedious and grueling work, but he managed to send back a stream of descriptive letters that Raymond eagerly published. Collected in three books between 1856 and 1860, these were praised by most critics and widely read in the North and in England. The three volumes were condensed into a single two-volume work, The Cotton Kingdom, *to meet the surge of demand after the Civil War broke out in 1861.*

Below are two excerpts from The Cotton Kingdom. *The first, written in 1854, tells of Olmstead's overnight stay at a white yeoman's farm in central Mississippi. The second is Olmstead's overview of the living arrangements of the planter class as he found them, and a contrast with their northern counterparts.*

Is either description complimentary? In the case of the yeoman family, what seems to have been the general level of physical comfort and education? What are Olmstead's conclusions about the comforts and "civilization" of the southern planters? As a northerner, can Olmstead's views be considered reliable? Remember, although he was not an abolitionist and in fact at times defended slavery against its angrier detractors, one cannot dismiss the influence of his free state origins—and those of his readers. There is another factor to keep in mind in evaluating Olmstead's observations: they are anecdotal, based on a relatively few experiences rather than a scientific sampling. Can this spotty quality have affected the overall picture? There is an obvious contrast between the descriptions in The Cotton Kingdom *and in John Pendleton Kennedy's* Swallow Barn. *Aside from sectional bias, can the fact that Kennedy focuses on Virginia and Olmstead on the newer areas of the South help explain the differences in their depictions?*

(It might be interesting to contrast Olmstead's criticism of the Old South with George Fitzhugh's criticism, in Chapter 11, of the contemporary North.)

A Northern Traveler Views Southern Slavery

FREDERICK LAW OLMSTEAD

The next house at which I arrived was one of the commonest sort of cabins. I had passed twenty like it during the day, and I thought I would take the opportunity to get an interior knowledge of them. The fact that a horse and waggon were kept, and that a considerable area of land in the rear of the cabin was planted with cotton, showed that the family were by no means of the lowest class, yet, as they were not able even to hire a slave, they may be considered to represent very favourably, I believe, the condition of the poor whites of the plantation districts. The whites of the county, I observe, by the census, are three to one of the slaves; in the nearest adjoining county, the proportion is reversed; and within a few miles the soil was richer, and large plantations occurred.

It was raining, and nearly nine o'clock. The door of the cabin was open, and I rode up and conversed with the occupant as he stood within. He said that he was not in the habit of taking in travellers, [sic] and his wife was about sick, but if I was a mind to put up with common fare, he didn't care. Grateful, I dismounted and took the seat he had vacated by the fire, while he led away my horse to an open shed in the rear—his own horse ranging at large, when not in use, during the summer.

The house was all comprised in a single room, twenty-eight by twenty-five feet in area, and open to the roof above. There was a large fireplace at one end and a door on each side—no windows at all. Two bedsteads, a spinning-wheel, a packing-case, which served as a bureau, a cupboard, made of rough hewn slabs, two or three deer-skin seated chairs, a Connecticut clock, and a large poster of Jayne's patent medicines, constituted all the visible furniture, either useful or ornamental in purpose. A little girl, immediately, without having had any directions to do so, got a frying-pan and a chunk of bacon from the cupboard, and cutting slices from the latter, set it frying for my supper. The woman of the house sat sulkily in a chair tilted back and leaning against the logs, spitting occasionally at the fire, but took no notice of me, barely nodding when I saluted her. A baby lay crying on the floor. I quieted it and amused it with my watch till the little girl, having made "coffee" and put a piece of corn-bread on the table with the bacon, took charge of it.

I hoped the woman was not very ill.

"Got the headache right bad," she answered. "Have the headache a heap, I do. Knew I should have it to-night. Been cuttin' brush in the cotton this

Frederick Law Olmstead, *The Cotton Kingdom: A Traveller's Observations on Cotton and Slavery in the American Slave States* (New York: Mason Brothers, 1861), vol. 2, pp. 78–82, 285–89.

afternoon. Knew't would bring on my headache. Told him so when I begun."

As soon as I had finished my supper and fed [my horse] Jude, the little girl put the fragments and the dishes in the cupboard, shoved the table into a corner, and dragged a quantity of quilts from one of the bedsteads, which she spread upon the floor, and presently crawled among them out of sight for the night. The woman picked up the child—which, though still a suckling, she said was twenty-two months old—and nursed it, retaking her old position. The man sat with me by the fire, his back towards her. The baby having fallen asleep was laid away somewhere, and the woman dragged off another lot of quilts from the beds, spreading them upon the floor. Then taking a deep tin pan, she filled it with alternate layers of corn-cobs and hot embers from the fire. This she placed upon a large block, which was evidently used habitually for the purpose, in the centre of the cabin. A furious smoke arose from it, and we soon began to cough. "Most *too* much smoke," observed the man. "Hope 'twill drive out all the gnats, then," replied the woman. (There is a very minute flying insect here, the bite of which is excessively sharp.)

The woman suddenly dropped off her outer garment and stepped from the midst of its folds, in her petticoat; then, taking the baby from the place where she had deposited it, lay down and covered herself with the quilts upon the floor. The man told me that I could take the bed which remained on one of the bedsteads, and kicking off his shoes only, rolled himself into a blanket by the side of his wife. I ventured to take off my cravat and stockings, as well as my boots, but almost immediately put my stockings on again, drawing their tops over my pantaloons. The advantage of this arrangement was that, although my face, eyes, ears, neck, and hands, were immediately attacked, the vermin did not reach my legs for two or three hours. Just after the clock struck two, I distinctly heard the man and the woman, and the girl and the dog scratching, and the horse out in the shed stamping and gnawing himself. Soon afterward the man exclaimed, "Good God Almighty— mighty! mighty! mighty!" and jumping up pulled off one of his stockings, shook it, scratched his foot vehemently, put on the stocking, and lay down again with a groan. The two doors were open, and through the logs and the openings in the roof, I saw the clouds divide and the moon and stars reveal themselves. The woman, after having been nearly smothered by the smoke from the pan which she had originally placed close to her own pillow, rose and placed it on the sill of the windward door, where it burned feebly and smoked lustily, like an altar to the Lares, all night. Fortunately the cabin was so open that it gave us little annoyance, while it seemed to answer the purpose of keeping all flying insects at a distance.

When, on rising in the morning, I said that I would like to wash my face, water was given me for the purpose in an earthen pie-dish. Just as breakfast, which was of exactly the same materials as my supper, was ready, rain began to fall, presently in such a smart shower as to put the fire out and compel us to move the table under the least leaky part of the roof. . . .

I think that the error which prevails in the South, with regard to the general condition of our working people, is much strengthened by the fact, that a different standard of comfort is used by most persons at the South from that known at the North, and that used by Northern writers. People at the South are content and happy with a condition which few accept at the North unless with great complaint, or with expressions of resignation such as are the peculiar property of slaves at the South. If, reader, you had been travelling all day through a country of the highest agricultural capability, settled more than twenty years ago, and toward nightfall should be advised by a considerate stranger to ride five miles further, in order to reach the residence of Mr. Brown, because Mr. Brown, being a well-to-do man, and a right good fellow, had built an uncommonly good house, and got it well furnished, had a score of servants, and being at a distance from neighbours, was always glad to entertain a respectable stranger—after hearing this, as you continued your ride somewhat impatiently in the evening chill, what consolations would your imagination find in the prospect before you? My New England and New York experience would not forbid the hope of a private room, where I could, in the first place, wash off the dust of the road, and make some change of clothing before being admitted to a family apartment. This family room would be curtained and carpeted, and glowing softly with the light of sperm candles or a shaded lamp. When I entered it, I could expect that a couch or an arm-chair, and a fragrant cup of tea, with refined sugar, and wholesome bread of wheaten flour, leavened, would be offered me. I should think it likely that I could then have the snatch of "Tannhäuser" or "Trovatore," which had been running faintly in my head all day, fingered clearly out to my entire satisfaction upon a pianoforte. I should then look with perfect confidence to being able to refer to Shakespeare, or Longfellow, or Dickens, if anything I had seen or thought during the day had haply led me to wish to do so. I should expect, as a matter of course, a clean, sweet bed, where I could sleep alone and undisturbed, until possibly in the morning a jug of hot water should be placed at my door, to aid the removal of a traveller's rigid beard. I should expect to draw a curtain from before a window, to lift the sash without effort, to look into a garden and fill my lungs with fragrant air; and I should be certain when I came down of a royal breakfast. A man of these circumstances in this rich country, he will be asking my opinion of his fruits. A man of his disposition cannot exist in the country without ladies, and ladies cannot exist in the country without flowers; and might I not hope for the refinement which decks even the table with them? and that the breakfast would be a meal as well as a feed—an institution of mental and moral sustenance as well as of palatable nourishment to the body? My horse I need hardly look after, if he be a sound brute;—good stables, litter, oats, hay, and water, grooming, and discretion in their use, will never be wanting in such a man's house in the country.

In what civilized region, after such advice, would such thoughts be preposterous, unless in the Slave States? Not but that such men and such houses, such family and home comforts may be found in the South. I have found them—a dozen of them, delightful homes. But then in a hundred cases where I received such advice, and heard houses and men so described, I did not find one of the things imagined above, nor anything ranging with them. In my last journey of nearly three months between the Mississippi and the Upper James River, I saw not only none of those things, received none of those attentions, but I saw and met nothing of the kind. Nine times out of ten, at least, after such a promise, I slept in a room with others, in a bed which stank, supplied with but one sheet, if with any; I washed with utensils common to the whole household; I found no garden, no flowers, no fruit, no tea, no cream, no sugar, no bread (for corn pone—let me assert, in parenthesis, though possibly as tastes differ, a very good thing of its kind for ostriches—is not bread: neither does even flour, salt, fat, and water, stirred together and warmed, constitute bread); no curtains, no lifting windows (three times out of four absolutely no windows), no couch—if one reclined in the family room it was on the bare floor—for there were no carpets or mats. For all that, the house swarmed with vermin. There was no hay, no straw, no oats (but mouldy corn and leaves of maize), no discretion, no care, no honesty, at the————there was no stable, but a log-pen; and besides this, no other outhouse but a smoke-house, a corn-house, and a range of nigger houses.

In nine-tenths of the houses south of Virginia, in which I was obliged, making all reasonable endeavour to find the best, to spend the night, there were none of these things. And most of these had been recommended to me by disinterested persons on the road as being better than ordinary—houses where they "sot up for travellers and had things." From the banks of the Mississippi to the banks of James, I did not (that I remember) see, except perhaps in one or two towns, a thermometer, nor a book of Shakespeare, nor a pianoforte or sheet of music; nor the light of a carcel or other good centretable or reading-lamp, nor an engraving or copy of any kind, of a work of art of the slightest merit. I am not speaking of what are commonly called "poor whites"; a large majority of all these houses were the residences of shareholders, a considerable proportion cotton-planters.

14

The Clash of Sections

So long as the contention over slavery was primarily between abolitionists and militant slavery defenders, it did not seriously threaten national
unity. Neither group had enough followers to tear the political fabric
apart. But then, in the late 1840s, the issue of slavery *expansion* into the
western territories brought North-South antagonisms to a boil. A much
larger public in both sections was soon locked in an angry debate that
jeopardized the nation's very survival.

Whether Congress had the right to determine if slavery should be
excluded from the territories had stirred discord between North and
South as far back as 1820, when Missouri, part of the Louisiana
Purchase, had applied for admission to the Union as a slave state. The
issue affected sectional balance, especially in the Senate, where each
state was equally represented. It had been settled by the Missouri
Compromise, which admitted one free and one slave state and divided
the remainder of the Louisiana Purchase along the line 39° 30′ into free
and slave territory. The Mexican War, which added an enormous slab
of new territory to the United States, raised the slavery extension issue
between the sections anew.

The first act of the new North-South showdown was the battle over
the Wilmot Proviso, a motion introduced into Congress in August 1846
to exclude slavery from any region acquired as a result of the war with
Mexico then underway. The Proviso set off a North-South confrontation
that moved through successively belligerent stages that led to the
South's secession in 1860–61.

The documents below mark the progression of the sectional debate
from the Proviso to the final crisis point. What are the essential principles of each side? Was the South right to feel besieged and oppressed?
Were the North and "free society" victims of a southern conspiracy?
Was there a moral dimension to the sectional dispute?

14.1:   A Southern Champion Demands Equal Rights for the South (1850)

In 1850 the readiness of California for admission to the Union forced Congress to confront longstanding North-South grievances and consider how to balance competing sectional views and interests. The discussion that year coalesced around a set of proposals introduced by Henry Clay, which included the admission of California as a free state, a stronger federal fugitive slave law, the settlement of the boundary and debts of Texas, the prohibition of the slave trade in the District of Columbia, and the organization of the New Mexico and Utah territories without mention of slavery.[1] The debate in the Senate particularly became a clash of sectional champions, many of them aging titans of an earlier political era, others representing the new leadership that would govern the nation through the Civil War period.

The first selection below is an excerpt from the speech delivered by John C. Calhoun of South Carolina, the venerable defender of southern rights, in response to the Clay compromise proposals. Sixty-eight years old in 1850, Calhoun was deathly ill and too feeble to deliver his address himself. Wrapped in blankets to warm his wasted frame, he listened intently from his Senate seat as James Mason of Virginia read the speech to the members.

Calhoun does not speak specifically to the Clay proposals. Rather, he lays out the whole array of southern grievances as they had evolved since the days of Thomas Jefferson. Is Calhoun correct when he blames northern policies for the South's numerical inferiority? How could the North have imposed its policies if the two sections had been equal in power at the outset? Why, for example, did most immigrants go to the free rather than the slave states? How does Calhoun account, if at all, for the fact that slavery was excluded from most new territory added to the United States after 1800? How valid are his charges that the antislavery agitation was destroying the bonds that held the Union together? Even if Calhoun was right about the divisive nature of the antislavery movement, what could have been done, given Bill of Rights' protection for freedom of speech and the press, to stop the agitation? Calhoun depicts himself as a unionist. Was he?

---

[1] These items actually represent a revised set of proposals introduced by Stephen Douglas after the somewhat different original scheme, proposed by Clay, had been defeated.

The South Defended

JOHN C. CALHOUN

I have, Senators, believed from the first that the agitation of the subject of slavery would . . . end in disunion. Entertaining this opinion, I have . . . endeavored to call the attention of both the two great parties which divide the country to adopt some measure to prevent so great a disaster, but without success. The agitation has been permitted to proceed, with almost no attempt to resist it, until it has reached a point when it can no longer be disguised or denied that the Union is in danger. You have thus had forced upon you the greatest and the gravest question that can ever come under your consideration—How can the Union be preserved?

To give a satisfactory answer to this mighty question, it is indispensable to have an accurate and thorough knowledge of the nature and the character of the cause by which the Union is endangered. . . . The first question, then, presented for our consideration, in the investigation I propose to make, . . . is—What is it that has endangered the Union?

To this question there can be but one answer,—that the immediate cause is the almost universal discontent which pervades all the States composing the Southern section of the Union. This widely-extended discontent is not of recent origin. It commenced with the agitation of the slavery question, and has been increasing ever since. The next question, going one step further back, is—What has caused this widely diffused and almost universal discontent?

It is a great mistake to suppose . . . that it originated with demagogues, who excited the discontent with the intention of aiding their personal advancement, or with the disappointed ambition of certain politicians, who resorted to it as a means of retrieving their fortunes. On the contrary, all the great political influences of the [Southern] section were arrayed against excitement, and exerted to the utmost to keep the people quiet. . . . The leaders and the presses of both parties [i.e., Whigs and Democrats] were very solicitous to prevent excitement and preserve quiet; because it was seen that the effects of the former would necessarily tend to weaken, if not destroy, the political ties which united them with their respective parties in other sections. . . . No; some cause, far deeper and more powerful than the one supposed, must exist, to account for the discontent so wide and deep. . . . What is the cause of this discontent? It will be found in the belief of the people of the Southern States . . . that they cannot remain, as things now are, consistently with honor and safety, in the Union. The next question to be considered is—What has caused this belief?

Congressional Globe, 31st Cong., 1st sess., 21, pt. 1, 1850, pp. 451–55.

One of the causes is, undoubtedly, to be traced to the long-continued agitation of the slave question on the part of the North, and the many aggressions which they have made on the rights of the South. . . .

There is another lying back of it . . . that may be regarded as the great and primary cause. This is to be found in the fact that the equilibrium between the two sections . . . has been destroyed. At that time [i.e., at the beginning of the republic] there was nearly a perfect equilibrium between the two, which afforded ample means to each to protect itself against the aggression of the other; but, as it now stands, one section has the exclusive power of controlling the Government, which leaves the other without any adequate means of protecting itself against its encroachment and oppression. To place this subject distinctly before you, I have, Senators, prepared a brief statistical statement, to show the relative weight of the two sections in the Government under the first census of 1790 and the last census of 1840.

.   .   .   .

[Here follows an analysis demonstrating the more rapid growth of population in the North than in the South and the consequent gap in favor of the North in representation in the electoral college and the House of Representatives. Calhoun also assumes that the census of 1850 will show a further increase in the power of the North over the federal government.]

The prospect is . . . that a great increase will be added to its [i.e., the North's] preponderance in the Senate, during the period of the decade, by the addition of two new States. Two territories, Oregon and Minnesota, are already in progress, and strenuous efforts are making to bring in three additional States from the territory recently acquired from Mexico; which, if successful, will add three other States in a short time to the Northern section, making five States; and increasing the present number of its States from fifteen to twenty, and of its Senators from thirty to forty. On the contrary, there is not a single territory in progress in the Southern section, and no certainty that any additional State will be added to it during the decade. The prospect then is, that the two sections in the Senate, should the efforts now made to exclude the South from the newly acquired territories succeed, will stand, before the end of the decade, twenty Northern States to fourteen Southern, . . . and forty Northern Senators to twenty-eight Southern. This great increase of Senators, added to the great increase of members of the House of Representatives and the electoral college on the part of the North, which must take place under the next decade, will effectually and irretrievably destroy the equilibrium which existed when the Government commenced.

Had this destruction been the operation of time, without the interference of Government, the South would have had no reason to complain; but such was not the fact. It was caused by the legislation of this Government, which was appointed, as the common agent of all, and charged with the protection of the interests and security of all. The legislation by which it has been effected, may be classed under three heads. The first is, that series of acts by which the South has been excluded from the common territory belonging to all the States as members of the Federal Union—which have had the effect of extending vastly the portion allotted to the Northern section, and restricting within narrow limits the portion left to the South. The next consists of adopting a system of revenue and disbursements, by which an undue proportion of the burden of taxation has been imposed upon the South, and an undue proportion of its proceeds appropriated to the North; and the last is the system of political measures, by which the original character of the Government has been radically changed. . . .

The first of the series of acts by which the South was deprived of its due share of the territories originated with the confederacy which preceded the existence of this Government. It is to be found in the provision of the ordinance of 1787. Its effect was to exclude the South entirely from the vast and fertile region which lies between the Ohio and the Mississippi rivers, now embracing five states and one territory. The next of the series is the Missouri compromise, which excluded the South from that portion of Louisiana which lies north of 36° 30', excepting what is included in the State of Missouri. The last of the series excluded the South from the whole of the Oregon Territory. . . . By these several acts, the South was excluded from 1,238,025 square miles. . . . To the South was left the portion of the Territory of Louisiana lying south of 36° 30' and . . . the Indian country [Oklahoma]. . . .

I have not included the territory recently acquired by the treaty with Mexico. The North is making the most strenuous efforts to appropriate the whole to itself by excluding the South from every foot of it. If she should succeed, it will add to that from which the South has already been excluded, 526,078 square miles, and would increase the whole which the North has appropriated to herself, to 1,764,023. . . . To sum up the whole, the United States, since they declared their independence, have acquired 2,373,046 square miles of territory, from which the North will have excluded the South, if she should succeed in monopolizing the newly acquired territories, about three-fourths of the whole, leaving to the South but about one-fourth.

Such is the first and great cause that has destroyed the equilibrium between the two sections in the Government.

The next is the system of revenue and disbursements which has been adopted by the Government. It is well known that the Government has derived its revenue mainly from duties on imports. I shall not undertake to show that such duties must necessarily fall mainly on the exporting States, and that the South, as the great exporting portion of the Union, has in reality paid vastly more than her due proportion of the revenue. . . . Nor shall I . . . undertake to show that a far greater portion of the revenue has been disbursed at the North, than its due share; and that the joint effect of these causes has been to transfer a vast amount from South to North. . . . If to this be added, that many of the duties were imposed, not for revenue, but for protection,—that is, intended to put money, not in the treasury, but directly into the pocket of the manufacturers,—some conception may be formed of the immense amount which . . . has been transferred from South to North. . . . Under the most moderate estimate, it would be sufficient to add greatly to the wealth of the North, and thus greatly increase her population by attracting emigration from all quarters to that section. . . .

But while these measures were destroying the equilibrium between the two sections, the action of the Government was leading to a radical change in its character, by concentrating all the power of the system in itself. . . .

That the Government claims . . . the right to decide in the last resort, as to the extent of its powers, will scarcely be denied by any one conversant with the political history of the country. That it also claims the right to resort to force to maintain whatever power it claims, against all opposition, is equally certain. . . . [H]ow can the separate governments of the States maintain and protect the powers reserved to them by the constitution . . . ? [I]t . . . follows that the character of the Government has been changed . . . from a federal republic, as it originally came from the hands of its framers, into a great national consolidated democracy. . . .

The result of the whole of these causes combined is—that the North has acquired a decided ascendancy over the whole department of this Government, and through it a control over all the powers of the system. A single section governed by the will of the numerical majority, has now, in fact, the control of the Government and the entire powers of the system. What was once a constitutional federal republic is now converted, in reality, into one as absolute as that of the Autocrat of Russia [i.e., the Russian czar], and as despotic in its tendency as any absolute government.

[I]f there was no question of vital importance to the South, in reference to which there was a diversity of views between the sections, this state of things might be endured. . . . But . . . there is a question of vital importance to the Southern section, in reference to which the views and feelings of the two sections are as opposite and hostile as they can possibly be.

I refer to the relation between the two races in the Southern section, which constitutes a vital portion of her social organization. Every portion of the North entertains views and feelings more or less hostile to it. Those most opposed and hostile, regard it as a sin, and consider themselves under the most sacred obligation to use every effort to destroy it. . . . Those less opposed and hostile, regard it as a crime—an offence against humanity, as they call it; and, although not so fanatical, feel themselves bound to use all efforts to effect the same object; while those who are least opposed and hostile, regard it as a blot and a stain on the character of what they call the Nation, and feel themselves accordingly bound to give it no countenance or support. On the contrary, the Southern section regards the relation as one which cannot be destroyed without subjecting the two races to the greatest calamity, and the section to poverty, desolation, and wretchedness; and accordingly they feel bound, by every consideration of interest and safety, to defend it.

.   .   .   .

[Calhoun recounts the history of the antislavery movement since the 1830s, including the dispersal of "incendiary" publications and the antislavery petition campaign against the internal slave trade and against slavery in the District of Columbia. He shows how the antislavery campaign grew increasingly loud and zealous.]

Such is a brief history of the agitation, as far as it has yet advanced. Now I ask, Senators, what is there to prevent its further progress, until it fulfills the ultimate end proposed; unless some decisive measure should be adopted to prevent it? . . . Is it . . . not certain, that if something is not done to arrest it, the South will be forced to choose between abolition and secession? Indeed, as events are now moving, it will not require the South to secede, in order to dissolve the Union. Agitation will of itself effect it. . . .

It is a great mistake to suppose that disunion can be effected by a single blow. The cords which bound these States together in one common Union, are far too numerous and powerful for that. Disunion must be the work of time. . . . It is only through a long process . . . that the cords can be snapped, until the whole fabric falls asunder. Already the agitation of the slavery question has snapped some of the most important and has greatly weakened all the others, as I shall proceed to show.

.   .   .   .

[Calhoun describes how the Protestant denominations, including the Baptists and Methodists, had broken apart over the slavery issue.]

The strongest cord, of a political character, consists of the many and powerful ties that have held together the two great parties which have, with some modifications, existed from the beginning of the Government. They both extended to every portion of the Union, and strongly contributed to hold all its parts together. But this powerful cord has fared no better than the spiritual. It resisted, for a long time, the explosive tendency of the [antislavery] agitation, but it has finally snapped under its force—if not entirely, in great measure. . . .

If the agitation goes on, the same force, acting with increased intensity, . . . will finally snap every cord, when nothing will be left to hold the States together except force. But, surely, that can, with no propriety of language, be called a Union, when the only means by which the weaker is held connected with the stronger portion, is *force*. It may, indeed, keep them connected; but the connection will partake more of the character of subjugation, on the part of the weaker to the stronger, than the union of free, independent, and sovereign States, in one confederation, as they stood in the early stages of the Government, and which only is worthy of the sacred name of Union.

Having now, Senators, explained what it is that endangers the Union, and traced it to its cause, and explained its nature and character, the question again recurs—How can the Union be saved? To this I answer, there is but one way it can be—and that is—by adopting such measures as will satisfy the States belonging to the Southern section, that they can remain in the Union consistently with their honor and safety. There is, again, only one way by which this can be effected, and that is—by removing the causes by which this belief had been produced. Do *this*, and discontent will cease—harmony and kind feelings between the sections be restored—and every apprehension of danger to the Union removed.

14.2:   A Northern Unionist Supports the Compromise of 1850 (1850)

The other giant of the past who spoke on the Clay proposals was Daniel Webster, the senator from Massachusetts. The "God-like Daniel" represented a state whose citizens were at the forefront of the movement to limit slavery expansion. He himself had voted for the slavery-restricting Wilmot Proviso. Many of his constituents were opposed to compromise with the South if it meant extending the area where the "peculiar institution" was legal. But Webster was a passionate unionist who had long denounced secession, a threat often used by the South to force concessions from the North. Here, in his famous speech of March 7, 1850, he once more deplores secession and yet seeks to satisfy southern grievances. Webster's address would help the passage of the measures called the Compromise of 1850, but he would be widely condemned in his home state as a betrayer of freedom, a man from whom "the soul has fled."

Webster clearly was responding in part to the charges leveled by John C. Calhoun. What are Webster's specific arguments against Calhoun's claims? To what "law of nature" is Webster referring? Is his argument convincing? Have later events confirmed or refuted that law of nature?

Webster's Seventh of March Speech Favoring the Compromise Measures

DANIEL WEBSTER

Mr. President, I wish to speak to-day, not as a Massachusetts man, nor as a northern man, but as an American, and a member of the Senate of the United States. . . .

Congressional Globe, 31st Cong., 1st sess., 21, pt. 1, 1850, pp. 476–83.

It is not to be denied that we live in the midst of strong agitations, and surrounded by very considerable dangers to our institutions of government. . . . The East, the West, the North, and the stormy South, all combine to throw the whole ocean into commotion, to toss its billows to the skies, and to disclose its profoundest depths. I do not expect, Mr. President, to hold . . . the helm in this combat of the political elements; but I have a duty to perform, and I mean to perform it with fidelity. . . . I have a part to act, not for my own security or safety, for I am looking out for no fragment upon which to float away from the wreck, if wreck there must be, but for the good of the whole, and the preservation of the whole. . . . I speak to-day for the preservation of the Union. . . . I speak to-day, out of a solicitous and anxious heart, for the restoration to the country of that quiet and harmony which make the blessings of this Union so rich and so dear to us all. . . .

And now let us consider, sir, for a moment what was the state of sentiment, North and South, in regard to slavery at the time this Constitution was adopted. A remarkable change has taken place since, but what did the wise and great men of all parts of the country think of slavery? In what estimation did they hold it in 1787, when the Constitution was adopted? No, it will be found, sir, that there was no great diversity of opinion between the North and the South upon the subject of slavery; and it will be found that both parts of the country held it equally an evil—a moral and political evil. It will not be found, that either at the North or at the South, there was much, though there was some, invective against slavery as inhuman and cruel. The great ground of objection to it was political; that it weakened the social fabric; that, taking the place of free labor, society was less strong, and labor was less productive; and, therefore, . . . that slavery was an evil. . . . The eminent men, the most eminent men, and nearly all the conspicuous men of the South, held the same sentiments, that slavery was an evil, a blight, a blast, a mildew, a scourge, and a curse. . . .

This was the state of things, sir, and this the state of opinion, under which those two very important matters were arranged, and those two important things done; that is, the establishment of the Constitution, with a recognition of slavery as it existed in the States, and the establishment of the ordinance [the Northwest Ordinance of 1787] prohibiting, to the full extent of all territory owned by the United States, the introduction of slavery into those territories. . . . But opinions, sir, have changed—greatly changed—changed North and changed South. . . .

The North [since that time has been] growing much more warm and strong against slavery, and the South [has been] growing much more warm and strong in its support. . . . What . . . have been the causes which have created so new a feeling in favor of slavery in the South . . . and from being thought of as described in the terms that I mentioned, . . . it has now become an institution, a cherished institution there; no evil, no scourge, but a great religious, social, and moral blessing, as I think I have heard it latterly described? I suppose this, sir, is owing to the sudden uprising and rapid growth of the cotton plantations of the South. So far as any motive of honor, justice, and general judgement could act, it was the cotton interest that gave a new desire to promote slavery, to spread it and to use its labor. . . .

Well, sir, we know what follows. The age of cotton became a golden age for our southern brethren. It gratified their desire for improvement and accumulation, at the same time that it excited it. The desire grew by what it fed upon, and there soon came to be an eagerness for other territory—a new area or areas for the cultivation of the cotton crop; and measures were brought about, somewhat rapidly, one after another, under the head of southern men at the head of Government—they having a majority in both branches of the Government—to accomplish their ends. The honorable member from Carolina [i.e., Calhoun] observed, that there has been a majority all along in favor of the North. If that be true, sir, the North acted either very liberally and kindly, or very weakly; for they never exercised that majority five times in the history of the Government. . . . [N]o man acquainted with the history of the country, can deny, that the general lead in the politics of the country, for three-fourths of the period that has lapsed since the adoption of the Constitution, has been a southern lead. . . .

Now, as to California and New Mexico, I hold slavery to be excluded from those territories by a law even superior to that which admits and sanctions it in Texas—I mean the law of nature—of physical geography—the law of the formation of the earth. That law settles forever, with a strength beyond all terms of human enactment, that slavery cannot exist in California or New Mexico. Understand me, sir—I mean slavery as we regard it; slaves in the gross, of the colored race, transferable by sale and delivery like other property. . . . California and New Mexico are Asiatic in their formation and scenery. They are composed of vast ridges of mountains, of enormous height, with sometimes broken ridges and deep valleys. The sides of these mountains are barren—entirely barren—their tops capped by perennial snow. There may be in California, now made free by its constitution, . . . some tracts of valuable land. But it is not so in New Mexico. . . . What is there in New Mexico that could by any possibility induce any body to go there with slaves? There are some narrow strips of tillable land on the borders of the rivers; but the rivers themselves dry up before midsummer is gone. All that the people can do is raise some little articles . . . by irrigation. And who expects to see a hundred black men cultivating tobacco, corn, rice or anything else, on lands in New Mexico made fertile only by irrigation? I look upon it, therefore, as a fixed fact, . . . that both California and New Mexico are destined to be free, so far as they are settled at all, which I believe, especially in regard to New Mexico, will be very little for a great length of time. . . . I have therefore to say . . . that this country is fixed for freedom . . . by as irrepealable . . . a . . . law [as] . . . the law that attaches to the right of holding slaves in Texas. . . . I would not take pains to reaffirm an ordinance of nature, nor to reenact the will of God. And I would put in no Wilmot Proviso for the purpose of a taunt or a reproach. I would put into it no evidence of the votes of superior power, to wound the pride, even whether a just pride, a rational pride, or an irrational pride—to wound the pride of the gentlemen who belong to the southern States. . . . I propose to inflict no such wound upon any body, unless something essentially important to the country, and efficient to the preservation of liberty and freedom, is to be effected. . . .

Sir, wherever there is a particular good to be done—wherever there is a foot of land to be staid back from becoming slave territory—I am ready to assert the principle of the exclusion of slavery. . . . [B]ut I will not do a thing unnecessary, that wounds the feelings of others, or does disgrace to my own understanding.

Mr. President, in the excited times in which we live, there is found to exist a state of crimination and recrimination between the North and the South. There are lists of grievances produced by each; and those grievances, real or supposed, alienate the minds of one portion of the country from the other, exasperate the feelings, subdue the sense of fraternal connection, and patriotic love, and mutual regard. I shall bestow a little attention, sir, upon these various grievances, produced on the one side or the other. I begin with the complaints of the South: I will now answer, farther than I have, the general statements of the Senator from South Carolina, that the North has grown upon the South in consequence of the manner of administrating this Government, in the collection of its revenues, and so forth. . . . I will state these complaints, especially one complaint of the South, which has in my opinion just foundation; and that is, that there has been found in the North, among individuals and among the Legislatures of the North, a disinclination to perform, fully, their constitutional duties in regard to the return of persons bound to service [i.e., slaves], who have escaped into the free States. In that respect, it is my judgement that the South is right, and the North is wrong. Every member of every northern Legislature is bound, by oath, like every other officer in the country, to support the Constitution of the United States; and this article of the Constitution, which says to these States, they shall deliver up fugitives from service, is binding in honor and conscience as any other article. . . .

Therefore, I repeat, sir, that there is ground of complaint against the North, well founded, which ought to be removed—which is now in the power of the different departments of this Government to remove—which calls for the enactment of proper laws, authorizing the judicature of this Government, in the several States, to do all that is necessary for the recapture of fugitive slaves, and for the restoration of them to those who claim them. Wherever I go, and whenever I speak on the subject . . . I say that the South has been injured in this respect and has a right to complain; and the North has been careless of what I think the Constitution peremptorily and emphatically enjoins upon it as a duty. . . .

There can be no such thing as peaceable secession. Peaceable secession is an utter impossibility. Is the great Constitution under which we live here . . . to be thawed and melted away by secession? . . . No sir! no sir! I will not say what might produce the disruption of the States; but, sir, I see it as plainly as I see the sun in heaven—I see that disruption must produce such a war as I will not describe. . . .

Peaceable secession! peaceable secession! . . . A voluntary separation, with alimony on one side and on the other. Why, what would be the result? Where is the line to be drawn? What States are to secede? What is to remain American? What am I to be?—an American no longer? Where is the flag of the republic to remain? Where is the eagle still to tower? Or is he to cower, and shrink, and fall to the ground? Why, sir, our ancestors—our fathers, and our grandfathers . . . —would rebuke and reproach us; and our children, and our grandchildren, would cry out, Shame upon us! if we, of this genera-tion, should dishonor these ensigns of the power of the Government, and the harmony of the Union. . . . What is to become of the army? What is to become of the navy? What is to become of the public lands? How is each of the thirty States to defend itself? . . . We could not separate the States by [a] . . . line, if we were to draw it. We could not sit here to-day, and draw a line of separation, that would satisfy any five men in the country. There are nat-ural causes that would keep and tie us together, and there are domestic and social relations, which we could not break, if we would, and which we should not, if we could.

Sir, nobody can look over the face of this country at the present moment . . . without being ready to admit . . . that ere long, America will be in the val-ley of the Mississippi. Well, now sir, I beg to inquire what the wildest enthusi-ast has to say, on the possibility of cutting off that river, and leaving the free States at its source and its branches, and slave States down near its mouth? . . . Here, sir, are five millions of freemen in the free States north of the river Ohio: can anybody suppose that this population can be severed by a line that divides them from the territory of a foreign and alien government, down somewhere, the Lord knows where, upon the lower banks of the Mississippi? . . . To break up! to break up this great Government! to dismember this great country! to astonish Europe with an act of folly, such as Europe for two centuries has never beheld in any government! No, sir! no, sir! There will be no secession. Gentlemen are not serious when they talk of secession. . . .

And now, Mr. President, instead of speaking of the possibility or utility of secession, . . . let us come out into the light of day; let us enjoy the fresh air of liberty and union; let us cherish those hopes which belong to us; let us devote ourselves to those great objects that are fit for our consideration and action; let us raise our conceptions to the magnitude and the importance of the duties that devolve upon us; let our comprehension be as broad as the country for which we act, our aspirations as high as its certain destiny; let us not be pygmies in a case that calls for men. Never did there devolve, on any generation of men, higher trusts than now devolve upon us for the preserva-tion of this Constitution, and the harmony and peace of all who are destined to live under it. Let us make our generation one of the strongest, and the brightest link in that golden chain which is destined, I fully believe, to grap-ple the people of all the States to this Constitution, for ages to come.

14.3:   Antislavery Leaders Respond to the Kansas-Nebraska Act (1854)

The Compromise of 1850, based on the Clay proposals as revised and managed by Stephen Douglas, the Democratic senator from Illinois, ended talk of secession for a time. The Fugitive Slave Law, which made up part of the compromise package, would deeply offend the sensibilities of many northerners and lead to defiant resistance in several northern communities. Still, for a time the sectional agreement quieted North-South agitation.

Then, in 1854 Douglas reopened the issue of slavery expansion, this time as applied to the remaining unsettled portions of the Louisiana Purchase territory. His Kansas-Nebraska bill repealed the Missouri Compromise of 1820 and opened up the region from which Congress had excluded slavery to possible settlement by slaveholders and their property. Douglas was moved initially by a desire primarily to encourage settlement of the Nebraska country. His original bill had said nothing of slavery in the region. But the "Little Giant," who agreed with Webster that slavery could not take root in the plains, was pushed to support an explicit repeal of the Missouri Compromise by a group of southern senators who felt deeply that any act of Congress excluding them and their property from any part of the federal public domain was a heinous sectional affront. Strongly supported by the Democratic administration under President Franklin Pierce, Douglas's bill, including the explicit Missouri Compromise repeal, passed.

The result was a political explosion in the North. Even moderate northerners saw the new law as a deplorable concession to the slave South. Among the strong antislavery voters and politicians, the Kansas-Nebraska Act seemed to confirm the existence of a behind-the-scenes deal uniting the "slavocracy" and "northern men with southern principles." The following document is one expression of this view. Signed by group of antislavery leaders in Congress even before the Kansas-Nebraska Act had passed, it became a manifesto of an emerging political force focused on slavery limitation that would soon crystallize as the Republican Party.

Have you encountered in any previous document in this section another charge of the illegitimate use of power for sectional ends? How do you distinguish a wide-ranging political plot from the usual behind-the-scenes maneuvering by politicians in the course of passing routine legislation? Do the "Independent Democrats" who composed and signed this appeal betray any compassion for slaves? Or do they seem concerned only for the rights of white nonslaveholders?

The Kansas-Nebraska Act: A Plot Against the North

"INDEPENDENT DEMOCRATS"

As Senators and Representatives in the Congress of the United States it is our duty to warn our constituents, whenever imminent danger menaces the freedom of our institutions or the permanency of the Union.

Such danger, as we firmly believe, now impends, and we earnestly solicit your prompt attention to it.

At the last session of Congress a bill for the organization of the Territory of Nebraska passed the House of Representatives by an overwhelming majority. That bill was based on the principle of excluding slavery from the new Territory. It was not taken up for consideration in the Senate and consequently failed to become a law.

At the present session a new Nebraska bill has been reported by the Senate Committee on Territories, which, should it unhappily receive the sanction of Congress, will open all the unorganized Territories of the Union to the ingress of slavery.

We arraign this bill as a gross violation of a sacred pledge; as a criminal betrayal of precious rights; as part and parcel of an atrocious plot to exclude from a vast unoccupied region immigrants from the Old World and free laborers from our own States, and convert it into a dreary region of despotism, inhabited by masters and slaves.

Take your maps, fellow citizens, we entreat you, and see what country it is which this bill gratuitously and recklessly proposes to open to slavery. . . .

This immense region, occupying the very heart of the North American Continent, and larger, by thirty-three thousand square miles, than all the existing free States—including California . . . this immense region the bill now before the Senate, without reason and without excuse, but in flagrant disregard of sound policy and sacred faith, purposes to open to slavery.

We beg your attention, fellow-citizens, to a few historical facts:

The original settled policy of the United States, clearly indicated by the Jefferson proviso of 1784 and the Ordinance of 1787, was non-extension of slavery.

In 1803 Louisiana was acquired by purchase from France. . . .

In 1818, six years later, the inhabitants of the Territory of Missouri applied to Congress for authority to form a State constitution, and for admission into the Union. There were, at that time, in the whole territory acquired from France, outside of the State of Louisiana, not three thousand slaves.

J. W. Schuckers, Appeal of the Independent Democrats, *Life and Public Services of Salmon P. Chase* (New York: D. Appleton and Company, 1874), pp. 140–44.

There was no apology, in the circumstances of the country, for the continuance of slavery. The original national policy was against it, and not less the plain language of the treaty under which the territory had been acquired from France.

It was proposed, therefore, to incorporate in the bill authorizing the formation of a State government, a provision requiring that the constitution of the new State should contain an article providing for the abolition of existing slavery, and prohibiting the further introduction of slaves.

This provision was vehemently and pertinaciously opposed, but finally prevailed in the House of Representatives by a decided vote. In the Senate it was rejected, and—in consequence of the disagreement between the two Houses—the bill was lost.

At the next session of Congress, the controversy was renewed with increased violence. It was terminated at length by a compromise. Missouri was allowed to come into the Union with slavery; but a section was inserted in the act authorizing her admission, excluding slavery forever from all the territory acquired from France, not included in the new State, lying north of 36° 30'. . . .

Nothing is more certain in history than the fact that Missouri could not have been admitted as a slave State had not certain members from the free States been reconciled to the measure by the incorporation of this prohibition into the act of admission. Nothing is more certain than that this prohibition has been regarded and accepted by the whole country as a solemn compact against the extension of slavery into any part of the territory acquired from France lying north of 36° 30', and not included in the new State of Missouri. The same act—let it be ever remembered—which authorized the formation of a constitution by the State, without a clause forbidding slavery, consecrated, beyond question and beyond honest recall, the whole remainder of the Territory to freedom and free institutions forever. For more than thirty years—during more than half our national existence under our present Constitution—this compact has been universally regarded and acted upon as inviolable American law. In conformity with it, Iowa was admitted as a free State and Minnesota has been organized as a free Territory.

It is a strange and ominous fact, well calculated to awaken the worst apprehensions and the most fearful forebodings of future calamities, that it is now deliberately proposed to repeal this prohibition, by implication or directly—the latter certainly the manlier way—and thus to subvert the compact, and allow slavery in all the yet unorganized territory.

We cannot, in this address, review the various pretenses under which it is attempted to cloak this monstrous wrong, but we must not altogether omit to notice one.

It is said that Nebraska sustains the same relations to slavery as did the territory acquired from Mexico prior to 1850, and that the pro-slavery clauses of the bill are necessary to carry into effect the compromise of that year.

No assertion could be more groundless. . . .

The statesmen whose powerful support carried the Utah and New Mexico acts never dreamed that their provisions would be ever applied to Nebraska. . . .

Here is proof beyond controversy that the principle of the Missouri act prohibiting slavery north of 36° 30', far from being abrogated by the Compromise Acts, is expressly affirmed; and that the proposed repeal of this prohibition, instead of being an affirmation of the Compromise Acts, is a repeal of a very prominent provision of the most important act of the series. It is solemnly declared in the very Compromise Acts *"that nothing herein contained shall be construed to impair or qualify"* the prohibition of slavery north of 36° 30'; and yet in the face of this declaration, that sacred prohibition is said to be overthrown. Can presumption further go? To all who, in any way, lean upon these compromises, we commend this exposition.

The pretenses, therefore, that the territory covered by the positive prohibition of 1820, sustains a similar relation to slavery with that acquired from Mexico, covered by no prohibition except that of disputed constitutional or Mexican law, and that the Compromises of 1850 require the incorporation of the pro-slavery clauses of the Utah and New Mexico Bill in the Nebraska act, are mere inventions, designed to cover up from public reprehension meditated bad faith. Were he living now, no one would be more forward, more eloquent, or more indignant in his denunciation of that bad faith, than Henry Clay, the foremost champion of both compromises. . . .

We appeal to the people. We warn you that the dearest interests of freedom and the Union are in imminent peril. Demagogues may tell you that the Union can be maintained only by submitting to the demands of slavery. We tell you that the Union can only be maintained by the full recognition of the just claims of freedom and man. The Union was formed to establish justice and secure the blessings of liberty. When it fails to accomplish these ends it will be worthless, and when it becomes worthless it cannot long endure.

We entreat you to be mindful of that fundamental maxim of Democracy—EQUAL RIGHTS AND EXACT JUSTICE FOR ALL MEN. Do not submit to become agents in extending legalized oppression and systematized injustice over a vast territory yet exempt from these terrible evils.

We implore Christians and Christian ministers to interpose. Their divine religion requires them to behold in every man a brother, and to labor for the advancement and regeneration of the human race.

Whatever apologies may be offered for the toleration of slavery in the States, none can be offered for its extension into Territories where it does not exist, and where that extension involves the repeal of ancient law and the violation of solemn compact. Let all protest, earnestly and emphatically, by correspondence, through the press, by memorials, by resolutions of public meetings and legislative bodies, and in whatever other mode may seem expedient, against this enormous crime.

For ourselves, we shall resist it by speech and vote, and with all the abilities which God has given us. Even if overcome in the impending struggle, we shall not submit. We shall go home to our constituents, erect anew the standard of freedom, and call on the people to come to the rescue of the country from the domination of slavery. We will not despair; for the cause of human freedom is the cause of God.

S. P. Chase
Charles Sumner
J. R. Giddings
Edward Wade
Gerritt Smith
Alexander De Witt.

14.4:   John Brown and the Remission of Sins by Blood (1859)

The Kansas-Nebraska Act let loose a wave of violence in Kansas. Some of this derived from disputed land claims among settlers who poured into the region after its passage, but the primary cause was a contest to impose either free labor or slavery on the territory.

One participant in the struggle to decide the future of Kansas was John Brown, an antislavery zealot who believed that "without the shedding of blood there is no remission of sins." In May 1856, in retaliation for the sack of the free staters' settlement at Lawrence by proslavery guerrillas, Brown and his sons massacred several prosouthern farmers at Pottawatamie Creek.

Unpunished for this crime, Brown went east and hatched a scheme to stir up a slave insurrection in the upper South as the first step in dismantling the institution of slavery. Encouraged and supported by several prominent eastern abolitionists, he and his small band, including several of his sons, captured the federal arsenal at Harpers Ferry, Virginia, on the evening of October 16, 1859. The rebels hoped to arouse the local slaves and, apparently, expected to escape into the mountains with a small army equipped with their captured arms. The plan was bungled. The group's efforts to arouse the slaves were feeble and they failed to consider adequate plans for escape. State militia and U.S. marines besieged the arsenal and quickly killed or captured the rebels.

Brown and four others were captured alive, tried by a Virginia court for treason, and sentenced to be hanged. To many Americans Brown's scheme seemed an act of a murderous madman. To many southerners it confirmed their belief in the willingness of abolitionist fanatics to resort to any extreme to express hatred of Dixie. Even partisan Republican

*politicians condemned the resort to violence. But for a segment of the
northern public, Brown seemed a righteous Old Testament prophet smit-
ing sin and injustice regardless of consequences. During his incarcera-
tion before execution, his prison cell became a mecca for many fervent
antislavery advocates. At his death he became a martyr to the cause of
freedom for the slave.*

*In the selection below Brown explains his motives, just before the court
pronounced sentence, in simple, moving language that reinforced his
martyr image. Was Brown being entirely candid about his motives? Do
you think his brief speech was an attempt to avoid the death penalty? Or
was it intended more for posterity than for the judge and his immediate
audience?*

John Brown Explains His Actions[1]

Senator Mason: Can you tell us who furnished money for your expedition?

John Brown: I furnished most of it myself; I cannot implicate others. It is by
my own folly that I have been taken. I could easily have saved myself from it,
had I exercised my own better judgment rather than yielded to my feelings.

Mason: You mean if you had escaped immediately?

Brown: No. I had the means to make myself secure without any escape; but
I allowed myself to be surrounded by a force by being too tardy. I should
have gone away; but I had thirty odd prisoners, whose wives and daughters
were in tears for their safety, and I felt for them. Besides, I wanted to allay
the fears of those who believed we came here to burn and kill. For this
reason I allowed the train to cross the bridge, and gave them full liberty to
pass on. I did it only to spare the feelings of those passengers and their families, and to allay the apprehensions that you had got here in your vicinity a
band of men who had no regard for life and property, nor any feelings of humanity.

Mason: But you killed some people passing along the streets quietly.

Brown: Well, sir, if there was anything of that kind done, it was without my
knowledge. Your own citizens who were my prisoners will tell you that every
possible means was taken to prevent it. I did not allow my men to fire when
there was danger of killing those we regarded as innocent persons, if I could
help it. They will tell you that we allowed ourselves to be fired at repeatedly,
and did not return it.

Franklin B. Sanborn, *The Life and Letters of John Brown, Liberator of Kansas and Martyr of Virginia*
(Boston: Roberts Brothers, 1885), pp. 562–69.
[1] Original footnotes deleted.

A Bystander: That is not so. You killed an unarmed man at the corner of the house over there at the water-tank, and another besides.

Brown: See here, my friend; it is useless to dispute or contradict the report of your own neighbors who were my prisoners.

Mason: If you would tell us who sent you here,—who provided the means,—that would be information of some value.

Brown: I will answer freely and faithfully about what concerns myself,—I will answer anything I can with honor,—but not about others.

Mr. Vallandigham (who had just entered):   Mr. Brown, who sent you here?

Brown: No man sent me here; it was my own prompting and that of my Maker, or that of the Devil,—whichever you please to ascribe it to. I acknowledge no master in human form.

Vallandigham: Did you get up the expedition yourself?

Brown: I did.

Vallandigham: Did you get up this document that is called a Constitution[2]?

Brown: I did. They are a constitution and ordinances of my own contriving and getting up.

Vallandigham: How long have you been engaged in this business?

Brown: From the breaking out of the difficulties in Kansas. Four of my sons had gone there to settle, and they induced me to go. I did not go there to settle, but because of the difficulties.

Mason: How many are there engaged with you in this movement?

Brown: Any questions that I can honorably answer I will,—not otherwise. So far as I am myself concerned, I have told everything truthfully. I value my word, sir.

Mason: What was your object in coming?

Brown: We came to free the slaves, and only that.

A Volunteer: How many men, in all, had you?

Brown: I came to Virginia with eighteen men only, besides myself.

Volunteer: What in the world did you suppose you could do here in Virginia with that amount of men?

Brown: Young man, I do not wish to discuss that question here.

Volunteer: You could not do anything.

Brown: Well, perhaps your ideas and mine on military subjects would differ materially.

---

[2] The Harpers Ferry rebels drew up a Constitution for the community of insurgents they hoped to create—ED.

Mason: How do you justify your acts?

Brown: I think, my friend, you are guilty of a great wrong against God and humanity,—I say it without wishing to be offensive,—and it would be perfectly right for any one to interfere with you so far as to free those you wilfully and wickedly hold in bondage. I do not say this insultingly.

Mason: I understand that.

Brown: I think I did right, and that others will do right who interfere with you at any time and at all times. I hold that the Golden Rule, "Do unto others as ye would that others should do unto you," applies to all who would help others to gain their liberty.

Lieutenant Stuart:[3]   But don't you believe in the Bible?

Brown: Certainly I do.

. . . .

Mason: Did you consider this a military organization in this Constitution? I have not yet read it.

Brown: I did, in some sense. I wish you would give that paper close attention.

Mason: You consider yourself the commander-in-chief of these "provisional" military forces?

Brown: I was chosen, agreeably to the ordinance of a certain document, commander-in-chief of that force.

Mason: What wages did you offer?

Brown: None.

Stuart: "The wages of sin is death."

Brown: I would not have made such a remark to you if you had been a prisoner, and wounded, in my hands.

A Bystander: Did you not promise a negro in Gettysburg twenty dollars a month?

Brown: I did not.

Mason: Does this talking annoy you?

Brown: Not in the least.

Vallandigham: Have you lived long in Ohio?

Brown: I went there in 1805. I lived in Summit County, which was then Portage County. My native place is Connecticut; my father lived there till 1805.

Vallandigham: Have you been in Portage County lately?

---

[3] This was Jeb Stuart, later famous as a dashing Confederate Cavalry officer—ED.

Brown: I was there in June last.

Vallandigham: When in Cleveland, did you attend the Fugitive Slave Law Convention there?

Brown: No. I was there about the time of the sitting of the court to try the Oberlin rescuers.[4] I spoke there publicly on that subject; on the Fugitive Slave Law and my own rescue. Of course, so far as I had any influence at all, I was supposed to justify the Oberlin people for rescuing the slave, because I have myself forcibly taken slaves from bondage. I was concerned in taking eleven slaves from Missouri to Canada last winter. I think I spoke in Cleveland before the Convention. I do not know that I had conversation with any of the Oberlin rescuers. I was sick part of the time I was in Ohio with the ague, in Ashtabula County.

Vallandigham: Did you see anything of Joshua R. Giddings[5] there?

Brown: I did meet him.

Vallandigham: Did you converse with him?

Brown: I did. I would not tell you, of course, anything that would implicate Mr. Giddings;   but I certainly met with him and had conversations with him.

Vallandigham: About that rescue case?

Brown: Yes; I heard him express his opinions upon it very freely and frankly.

Vallandigham: Justifying it?

Brown: Yes, sir; I do not compromise him, certainly, in saying that.

Vallandigham: Will you answer this: Did you talk with Giddings about your expedition here?

Brown: No, I won't answer that; because a denial of it I would not make, and to make any affirmation of it I should be a great dunce.

Vallandigham: Have you had any correspondence with parties at the North on the subject of this movement?

Brown: I have had correspondence.

A Bystander: Do you consider this a religious movement?

Brown: It is, in my opinion, the greatest service man can render to God.

Bystander: Do you consider yourself an instrument in the hands of Providence?

Brown: I do.

---

[4] Oberlin, Ohio, was the site of an attempt to rescue fugitive slaves—ED.

[5] An antislavery Republican congressman from Ohio—ED.

Bystander: Upon what principle do you justify your acts?

Brown: Upon the Golden Rule. I pity the poor in bondage that have none to help them: that is why I am here; not to gratify any personal animosity, revenge, or vindictive spirit. It is my sympathy with the oppressed and the wronged, that are as good as you and as precious in the sight of God.

Bystander: Certainly. But why take the slaves against their will?

Brown: I never did.

Bystander: You did in one instance, at least.

Stephens, the other wounded prisoner, here said, "You are right. In one case I know the negro wanted to go back."

Bystander: Where did you come from?

Stephens: I lived in Ashtabula County, Ohio.

Vallandigham: How recently did you leave Ashtabula County?

Stephens: Some months ago. I never resided there any length of time; have been through there.

Vallandigham: How far did you live from Jefferson?

Brown: Be cautious, Stephens, about any answers that would commit any friend. I would not answer that.

[Stephens turned partially over with a groan of pain, and was silent.]

Vallandigham: Who are your advisers in this movement?

Brown: I cannot answer that. I have numerous sympathizers throughout the entire North.

Vallandigham: In northern Ohio?

Brown: No more there than anywhere else; in all the free States.

Vallandigham: But you are not personally acquainted in southern Ohio?

Brown: Not very much.

A Bystander: Did you ever live in Washington City?

Brown: I did not. I want you to understand, gentlemen, and [to the reporter of the "New York Herald"] you may report that,—I want you to understand that I respect the rights of the poorest and weakest of colored people, oppressed by the slave system, just as much as I do those of the most wealthy and powerful. That is the idea that has moved me, and that alone. We expected no reward except the satisfaction of endeavoring to do for those in distress and greatly oppressed as we would be done by. The cry of distress of the oppressed is my reason, and the only thing that prompted me to come here.

Bystander: Why did you do it secretly?

Brown: Because I thought that necessary to success; no other reason.

Bystander: Have you read Gerrit Smith's[6] last letter?

Brown: What letter do you mean?

Bystander: The "New York Herald" of yesterday, in speaking of this affair, mentions a letter in this way:—

> "Apropos of this exciting news, we recollect a very significant passage in one of Gerrit Smith's letters, published a month or two ago, in which he speaks of the folly of attempting to strike the shackles off the slaves by the force of moral suasion or legal agitation, and predicts that the next movement made in the direction of negro emancipation would be an insurrection in the South."

Brown: I have not seen the "New York Herald" for some days past; but I presume, from your remark about the gist of the letter, that I should concur with it. I agree with Mr. Smith that moral suasion is hopeless. I don't think the people of the slave States will ever consider the subject of slavery in its true light till some other argument is resorted to than moral suasion.

Vallandigham: Did you expect a general rising of the slaves in case of your success?

Brown: No, sir; nor did I wish it. I expected to gather them up from time to time, and set them free.

Vallandigham: Did you expect to hold possession here till then?

Brown: Well, probably I had quite a different idea. I do not know that I ought to reveal my plans. I am here a prisoner and wounded, because I foolishly allowed myself to be so. You overrate your strength in supposing I could have been taken if I had not allowed it. I was too tardy after commencing the open attack—in delaying my movements through Monday night, and up to the time I was attacked by the Government troops. It was all occasioned by my desire to spare the feelings of my prisoners and their families and the community at large. I had no knowledge of the shooting of the negro Heywood.[7]

Vallandigham: What time did you commence your organization in Canada?

Brown: That occurred about two years ago; in 1858.

Vallandigham: Who was the secretary?

Brown: That I would not tell if I recollected; but I do not recollect. I think the officers were elected in May, 1858. I may answer incorrectly, but not

---

[6] A prominent abolitionist of upstate New York who encouraged and helped finance Brown—ED.

[7] Probably Dangerfield Newby, one of Brown's black followers.—ED.

intentionally. My head is a little confused by wounds, and my memory obscure on dates, etc.

Dr. Biggs: Were you in the party at Dr. Kennedy's house?[8]

Brown: I was the head of that party. I occupied the house to mature my plans. I have not been in Baltimore to purchase caps.

Dr. Biggs: What was the number of men at Kennedy's?

Brown: I decline to answer that.

Dr. Biggs: Who lanced that woman's neck on the hill?

Brown: I did. I have sometimes practised in surgery when I thought it a matter of humanity and necessity, and there was no one else to do it; but I have not studied surgery.

Dr. Biggs: It was done very well and scientifically. They have been very clever to the neighbors, I have been told, and we had no reason to suspect them, except that we could not understand their movements. They were represented as eight or nine persons; on Friday there were thirteen.

Brown: There were more than that.

Q: Where did you get arms?   *A:*   I bought them.

Q: In what State?   *A:*   That I will not state.

Q: How many guns?   *A:*   Two hundred Sharpe's rifles and two hundred revolvers,—what is called the Massachusetts Arms Company's revolvers, a little under navy size.

Q: Why did you not take that swivel you left in the house?   *A:*   I had no occasion for it. It was given to me a year or two ago.

Q: In Kansas?   *A:*   No. I had nothing given to me in Kansas.

Q: By whom, and in what State?   *A:*   I decline to answer. It is not properly a swivel; it is a very large rifle with a pivot. The ball is larger than a musket ball; it is intended for a slug.

Reporter: I do not wish to annoy you; but if you have anything further you would like to say, I will report it.

Brown: I have nothing to say, only that I claim to be here in carrying out a measure I believe perfectly justifiable, and not to act the part of an incendiary or ruffian, but to aid those suffering great wrong. I wish to say, furthermore, that you had better—all you people at the South—prepare yourselves for a settlement of this question, that must come up for settlement sooner than you are prepared for it. The sooner you are prepared the better. You may dispose of me very easily,—I am nearly disposed of now; but this question is still to be settled,—this negro question I mean; the end of that is not

---

[8] A house rented by Brown and his accomplices as their house of operations as they planned the Harpers Ferry raid—ED.

yet. These wounds were inflicted upon me—both sabre cuts on my head and bayonet stabs in different parts of my body—some minutes after I had ceased fighting and had consented to surrender, for the benefit of others, not for my own. I believe the Major would not have been alive; I could have killed him just as easy as a mosquito when he came in, but I supposed he only came in to receive our surrender. There had been loud and long calls of "surrender" from us,—as loud as men could yell; but in the confusion and excitement I suppose we were not heard. I do not think the Major, or any one, meant to butcher us after we had surrendered.

An Officer: Why did you not surrender before the attack?

Brown: I did not think it was my duty or interest to do so. We assured the prisoners that we did not wish to harm them, and they should be set at liberty. I exercised my best judgment, not believing the people would wantonly sacrifice their own fellow-citizens, when we offered to let them go on condition of being allowed to change our position about a quarter of a mile. The prisoners agreed by a vote among themselves to pass across the bridge with us. We wanted them only as a sort of guarantee of our own safety,—that we should not be fired into. We took them, in the first place, as hostages and to keep them from doing any harm. We did kill some men in defending ourselves, but I saw no one fire except directly in self-defence. Our orders were strict not to harm any one not in arms against us.

Q: Brown, suppose you had every nigger in the United States, what would you do with them? *A:*   Set them free.

Q: Your intention was to carry them off and free them? *A:*   Not at all.

A Bystander: To set them free would sacrifice the life of every man in this community.

Brown: I do not think so.

Bystander: I know it. I think you are fanatical.

Brown: And I think you are fanatical. "Whom the gods would destroy they first make mad," and you are mad.

Q: Was it your only object to free the negroes? *A:*   Absolutely our only object.

Q: But you demanded and took Colonel Washington's[9] silver and watch? *A:*   Yes; we intended freely to appropriate the property of slaveholders to carry out our object. It was for that, and only that, and with no design to enrich ourselves with any plunder whatever.

Bystander: Did you know Sherrod in Kansas? I understand you killed him.

Brown: I killed no man except in fair fight. I fought at Black Jack Point and at Osawatomie; and if I killed anybody, it was at one of these places.

---

[9] Lewis Washington, great grandson of George Washington's brother.—ED.

14.5:   The South Secedes (1860)

The Harpers Ferry attack, continued violence in Kansas, and a host of real or imagined sectional slights and offenses encouraged the further sectionalizing of national politics. By the late 1850s the Whigs had collapsed as a party, with many of its northern members joining the new Republican organization. Dedicated to stopping the spread of slavery so as to "place it . . . in the course of ultimate extinction," the new party was almost purely northern in its support.

In 1860 the Republican candidate for president, Abraham Lincoln, won election in a field of four. Lincoln was not an abolitionist, but to the South his victory seemed an indescribable affront that could only be answered by the secession of the slave states from the Union. Within weeks of the election, the deep South states of South Carolina, Mississippi, Florida, Alabama, Georgia, Louisiana, and Texas all had passed ordinances of secession repudiating the compact known as the Constitution. In February 1861 representatives from these states met at Montgomery, Alabama, and established a provisional government for the Confederate States of America.

The following document is part of the "Declaration of Causes" that accompanied South Carolina's Ordinance of Secession of December 1860. What are the chief grievances of the secession convention delegates? How seriously do they take the constitutional arguments they advance, do you suppose? Why was the resistance by the free states to returning fugitive slaves so offensive to the South Carolinians? Why was Lincoln's election such an incitement to them?

Why South Carolina Is Leaving the Union

SOUTH CAROLINA SECESSION CONVENTION

DECLARATION OF CAUSES WHICH INDUCED THE SECESSION OF SOUTH CAROLINA.

The people of the State of South Carolina in Convention assembled, on the 2d day of April, A. D. 1832, declared that the frequent violations of the Constitution of the United States by the Federal Government, and its encroachments upon the reserved rights of the States, fully justified this State in their withdrawal from the Federal Union; but in deference to the opinions and wishes of the other Slaveholding States, she forbore at that

"Declaration of Causes," ed. Frank Moore, *The Rebellion Record: A Diary of American Events with Documents, Narratives, Illustrative Incidents. . . .* , (New York: G. P. Putnam, 1862), vol. 1, pp. 3–4.

time to exercise this right. Since that time these encroachments have continued to increase, and further forbearance ceases to be a virtue.

And now the State of South Carolina having resumed her separate and equal place among nations, deems it due to herself, to the remaining United States of America, and to the nations of the world, that she should declare the immediate causes which have led to this act. . . .

[Here follows a review of the history of the formation of the American union from the late colonial period, through the Revolution, and then to the adoption of the Constitution.]

By this Constitution, certain duties were imposed upon the several States, and the exercise of certain of their powers was restrained, which necessarily impelled their continued existence as sovereign states. But, to remove all doubt, an amendment was added, which declared that the powers not delegated to the United States by the Constitution, nor prohibited by it to the States, are reserved to the States respectively, or to the people. On the 23d May, 1788, South Carolina, by a Convention of her people, passed an ordinance assenting to this Constitution, and afterwards altered her own Constitution to conform herself to the obligations she had undertaken.

Thus was established, by compact between the States, a Government with defined objects and powers, limited to the express words of the grant. This limitation left the whole remaining mass of power subject to the clause reserving it to the States or the people, and rendered unnecessary any specification of reserved rights. We hold that the Government thus established is subject to the two great principles asserted in the Declaration of Independence; and we hold further, that the mode of its formation subjects it to a third fundamental principle, namely, the law of compact. We maintain that in every compact between two or more parties, the obligation is mutual; that the failure of one of the contracting parties to perform a material part of the agreement, entirely releases the obligation of the other; and that, where no arbiter is provided, each party is remitted to his own judgment to determine the fact of failure, with all its consequences.

In the present case, that fact is established with certainty. We assert that fourteen of the States have deliberately refused for years past to fulfil their constitutional obligations, and we refer to their own statutes for the proof.

The Constitution of the United States, in its fourth Article, provides as follows:

> "No person held to service or labor in one State under the laws thereof, escaping into another, shall, in consequence of any law or regulation therein, be discharged from such service or labor, but shall be delivered up, on claim of the party to whom such service or labor may be due."

This stipulation was so material to the compact that without it that compact would not have been made. The greater number of the contracting parties held slaves, and they had previously evinced their estimate of the value of such a stipulation by making it a condition in the Ordinance for the government of the territory ceded by Virginia, which obligations, and the laws of the General Government, have ceased to effect the objects of the Constitution. The States of Maine, New Hampshire, Vermont, Massachusetts, Connecticut, Rhode Island, New York, Pennsylvania, Illinois, Indiana, Michigan, Wisconsin, and Iowa, have enacted laws which either nullify the acts of Congress, or render useless any attempt to execute them. In many of these States the fugitive is discharged from the service of labor claimed, and in none of them has the State Government complied with the stipulation made in the Constitution. The State of New Jersey, at an early day, passed a law in conformity with her constitutional obligation; but the current of Anti-Slavery feeling has led her more recently to enact laws which render inoperative the remedies provided by her own laws and by the laws of Congress. In the State of New York even the right of transit for a slave has been denied by her tribunals; and the States of Ohio and Iowa have refused to surrender to justice fugitives charged with murder, and with inciting servile insurrection in the State of Virginia. Thus the constitutional compact has been deliberately broken and disregarded by the non-slaveholding States; and the consequence follows that South Carolina is released from her obligation.

The ends for which this Constitution was framed are declared by itself to be "to form a more perfect union, to establish justice, insure domestic tranquillity, provide for the common defence, promote the general welfare, and secure the blessings of liberty to ourselves and our posterity."

These ends it endeavored to accomplish by a Federal Government, in which each State was recognized as an equal, and had separate control over its own institutions. The right of property in slaves was recognized by giving to free persons distinct political rights; by giving them the right to represent, and burdening them with direct taxes for, three-fifths of their slaves; by authorizing the importation of slaves for twenty years; and by stipulating for the rendition of fugitives from labor.

We affirm that these ends for which this Government was instituted have been defeated, and the Government itself has been destructive of them by the action of the non-slaveholding States. Those States have assumed the right of deciding upon the propriety of our domestic institutions; and have denied the rights of property established in fifteen of the States and recognized by the Constitution; they have denounced as sinful the institution of Slavery; they have permitted the open establishment among them of societies, whose avowed object is to disturb the peace of and eloin[1] the property of the citizens of other States. They have encouraged and assisted thousands of our slaves to leave their homes; and those who remain, have been incited by emissaries, books, and pictures, to servile insurrection.

For twenty-five years this agitation has been steadily increasing, until it has now secured to its aid the power of the common Government. Observing

---

[1] That is, to alienate, or remove—ED.

the *forms* of the Constitution, a sectional party has found within that article establishing the Executive Department, the means of subverting the Constitution itself. A geographical line has been drawn across the Union, and all the States north of that line have united in the election of a man to the high office of President of the United States whose opinions and purposes are hostile to Slavery. He is to be intrusted with the administration of the common Government, because he has declared that that "Government cannot endure permanently half slave, half free," and that the public mind must rest in the belief that Slavery is in the course of ultimate extinction.

This sectional combination for the subversion of the Constitution has been aided, in some of the States, by elevating to citizenship persons who, by the supreme law of the land, are incapable of becoming citizens,[2] and their votes have been used to inaugurate a new policy, hostile to the South, and destructive of its peace and safety.

On the 4th of March next this party will take possession of the Government. It has announced that the South shall be excluded from the common territory, that the Judicial tribunal shall be made sectional, and that a war must be waged against Slavery until it shall cease throughout the United States.

The guarantees of the Constitution will then no longer exist; the equal rights of the States will be lost. The Slaveholding States will no longer have the power of self-government, or self-protection, and the Federal Government will have become their enemy.

Sectional interest and animosity will deepen the irritation; and all hope of remedy is rendered vain, by the fact that the public opinion at the North has invested a great political error with the sanctions of a more erroneous religious belief.

We, therefore, the people of South Carolina, by our delegates in Convention assembled, appealing to the Supreme Judge of the world for the rectitude of our intentions, have solemnly declared that the Union heretofore existing between this State and the other States of North America is dissolved, and that the State of South Carolina has resumed her position among the nations of the world, as separate and independent state, with full power to levy war, conclude peace, contract alliances, establish commerce, and to do all other acts and things which independent States may of right do.

---

[2] Refers to the grant of voting rights to free blacks by several northern states—ED.

15

The Civil War

From the very outset of the tragic sectional encounter we call the Civil War, Americans sought to discern its ultimate causes. We might assume that Unionists and Confederates inevitably reached different conclusions. But this would be an oversimplification. Americans as a whole differed over the causes of the North-South clash, but the divisions did not necessarily follow sectional lines. Rather, northerners and southerners often agreed on the war's causes but extracted different lessons and meanings from their conclusions. Contemporaries did differ on the origins and inner meaning of the war, but the arguments were as often *within as between* the sections.

In the selections below you will encounter a range of interpretations by contemporaries of the war's ultimate sources. From your general knowledge of the period, see if you can evaluate the respective views expressed. What do *you* think was the core issue over which Americans fought the Civil War, based on the evidence presented here?

15.1: The War Is about Slavery (1861)

It is difficult to deny the role of slavery as the key to southern secession and the Civil War. And the claim of slavery's importance came from both sides, North and South. The first selection below is from an 1861 speech by Alexander H. Stephens, vice president of the Confederate States of America. Stephens here is describing the new Confederate constitution and comparing it with the one of 1787 under which the two sections had lived together for three-quarters of a century. In the excerpt he tells his cheering audience that the Confederate constitution, unlike its predecessor, makes a total and unequivocal affirmation of slavery.

Nowhere in his speech does Stephens declare slavery the cause of the Civil War, yet clearly that is the implication. In what way does he imply that slavery lay behind southern secession? Was Stephens right?

Many northerners would have agreed with Stephens that slavery was the key issue of the war. The second piece, an excerpt from a Republican newspaper in Indiana, the Evansville Daily Journal, *provides a counterpoint to Stephens's emphasis on slavery. Although both statements make slavery a central issue, they obviously express different attitudes toward its role in the expanding sectional conflict. How are the two views different?*

Slavery Is the Cornerstone of the Confederacy

ALEXANDER H. STEPHENS

But not to be tedious in enumerating the numerous changes for the better, allow me to allude to one other—though last, not least. The new constitution has put at rest, *forever,* all the agitating questions relating to our peculiar institution—African slavery as it exists amongst us—the proper *status* of the negro in our form of civilization. This was the immediate cause of the late rupture and present revolution. Jefferson in his forecast, had anticipated this, as the "rock upon which the old Union would split." He was right. What was conjecture with him, is now a realized fact. But whether he fully comprehended the great truth upon which that rock *stood* and *stands,* may be doubted. The prevailing ideas entertained by him and most of the leading statesmen at the time of the formation of the old constitution, were that the enslavement of the African was in violation of the laws of nature; that it was wrong in *principle,* socially, morally, and politically. It was an evil they knew not well how to deal with, but the general opinion of the men of that day was that, somehow or other in the order of Providence, the institution would be evanescent and pass away. This idea, though not incorporated in the constitution, was the prevailing idea at that time. The constitution, it is true, secured every essential guarantee to the institution while it should last, and hence no argument can be justly urged against the constitutional guarantees thus secured, because of the common sentiment of the day. Those ideas, however, were fundamentally wrong. They rested upon the assumption of the equality of races. This was an error. It was a sandy foundation, and the government built upon it fell, when the "storm came and the wind blew."

Our new government is founded upon exactly the opposite idea; its foundations are laid, its corner-stone rests upon the great truth, that the negro is not equal to the white man; that slavery—subordination to the superior race—is his natural and normal condition.

Henry Cleveland, *Alexander H. Stephens in Public and Private* (Philadelphia: National Publishing Company, 1866), pp. 721–23.

This, our new government, is the first, in the history of the world, based upon this great physical, philosophical, and moral truth. This truth has been slow in the process of its development, like all other truths in the various departments of science. It has been so even amongst us. Many who hear me, perhaps, can recollect well, that this truth was not generally admitted, even within their day. The errors of the past generation still clung to many as late as twenty years ago. Those at the North, who still cling to these errors, with a zeal above knowledge, we justly denominate fanatics. All fanaticism springs from an aberration of the mind—from a defect in reasoning. It is a species of insanity. One of the most striking characteristics of insanity, in many instances, is forming correct conclusions from fancied or erroneous premises; so with the anti-slavery fanatics; their conclusions are right if their premises were. They assume that the negro is equal, and hence conclude that he is entitled to equal privileges and rights with the white man. If their premises were correct, their conclusions would be logical and just—but their premise being wrong, their whole argument fails. I recollect once of having heard a gentleman from one of the northern States, of great power and ability, announce in the House of Representatives, with imposing effect, that we of the South would be compelled, ultimately, to yield upon this subject of slavery, that it was as impossible to war successfully against a principle in politics, as it was in physics or mechanics. That the principle would ultimately prevail. That we, in maintaining slavery as it exists with us, were warring against a principle, a principle founded in nature, the principle of the equality of men. The reply I made to him was, that upon his own grounds, we should, ultimately, succeed, and that he and his associates, in this crusade against our institutions, would ultimately fail. The truth announced, that it was as impossible to war successfully against a principle in politics as it was in physics and mechanics, I admitted; but told him that it was he, and those acting with him, who were warring against a principle. They were attempting to make things equal which the Creator had made unequal.

In the conflict thus far, success has been on our side, complete throughout the length and breadth of the Confederate States. It is upon this, as I have stated, our social fabric is firmly planted; and I cannot permit myself to doubt the ultimate success of a full recognition of this principle throughout the civilized and enlightened world.

As I have stated, the truth of this principle may be slow in development, as all truths are and ever have been, in the various branches of science. It was so with the principles announced by Galileo—it was so with Adam Smith and his principles of political economy. It was so with [William] Harvey, and his theory of the circulation of the blood. It is stated that not a single one of the medical profession, living at the time of the announcement of the truths made by him, admitted them. Now, they are universally acknowledged. May we not, therefore, look with confidence to the ultimate universal acknowledgment of the truths upon which our system rests? It is the first government ever instituted upon the principles in strict conformity to nature, and the ordination of Providence, in furnishing the materials of human society. Many governments have been founded upon the principle of the subordination and serfdom of certain classes of the same race; such were and are in violation of the laws of nature. Our system commits no such violation of nature's laws. With us, all of the white race, however high or low, rich or poor, are equal in the eye of the law. Not so with the negro. Subordination is his place. He, by nature, or by the curse against Canaan, is fitted for that condition which he occupies in our system. The architect, in the construction of buildings, lays the foundation with the proper material—the granite; then comes the brick or the marble. The substratum of our society is made of the material fitted by nature for it, and by experience we know that it is best, not only for the superior, but for the inferior race, that it should be so. It is, indeed, in conformity with the ordinance of the Creator. It is not for us to inquire into the wisdom of his ordinances, or to question them. For his own purposes, he has made one race to differ from another, as he has made "one star to differ from another star in glory."

The great objects of humanity are best attained when there is conformity to his laws and decrees, in the formation of governments as well as in all things else. Our confederacy is founded upon principles in strict conformity with these laws. This stone which was rejected by the first builders "is become the chief of the corner"—the real "corner-stone"—in our new edifice.

I have been asked, what of the future? It has been apprehended by some that we would have arrayed against us the civilized world. I care not who or how many they may be against us, when we stand upon the eternal principles of truth, *if we are true to ourselves and the principles for which we contend*, we are obliged to, and must triumph.

Thousands of people who begin to understand these truths are not yet completely out of the shell; they do not see them in their length and breadth. We hear much of the civilization and christianization of the barbarous tribes of Africa. In my judgment, those ends will never be attained, but by first teaching them the lesson taught to Adam, that "in the sweat of his brow he should eat his bread," and teaching them to work, and feed, and clothe themselves.

The War Will Destroy Slavery

The fearful commotion that is now shaking the country to its foundation, is incomprehensible to human understanding, except as interpreted in the light of Divine Providence. God uses man to carry out his mysterious purposes. In this instance, the believer in an overruling Providence can readily comprehend that God has some great end to accomplish, and makes use of the differences of this people, on the slavery question, to bring it about. Men on either side are carried in one direction or the other against their will, and forced to take sides, however much they may resist. A couple of weeks ago, or less, the people were divided into parties. Each man had his place, and each side opposed violently the opposing parties. Now, looking at the North, we find men almost unanimous for the Government. Party lines are obliterated, and whatever a man may have formerly been, almost all now are determined to stand by the lawful authorities and establish the fact that we have a government competent to perpetuate its own unequaled privileges and to punish traitors. This is the common feeling which actuates the people of the North, and, to their honor be it said, a host of gallant Union men in the South. We have in mind scores and scores of Democrats and Bell men[1] in this State and elsewhere who have opposed the Republican party violently, but who now lose sight of party considerations and stand by the constituted authorities for the preservation of law, order, and liberty. . . .

Surely when we see such a great change in the public mind in so short a time, we can but think that the hand of Providence has specially brought it about for a great purpose. What that purpose is, we can only imagine. Perhaps Providence wishes to punish the people of this country for their pride, arrogance, and corruption. Perhaps we do not appreciate the unnumbered blessings that he has literally showered down on us. Perhaps we do not sufficiently prize the glorious boon of freedom and good government that he has vouchsafed us. And—not to multiply the surmises that crowd on us— perhaps God has instituted the present troubles to rid the country of the predominance of slavery in its public affairs. The whole country, North as well as South, has been instrumental in the endeavor to spread it over the continent, and to force it on unwilling people. While the South has been actively propagating and perpetuating the institution, the North has winked at the wrongful business and encouraged it.—Therefore, in the coming troubles, the North must not expect to escape the penalty of her lack of principle. She must suffer, like the South.

It may even be possible that Providence designs by means of these troubles to put a summary end to slavery. The institution has gone on to spread until it interferes materially with the progress of the Nation. Our country can never reach its full stature and importance so long as this baleful influence extends over it. It is a paradoxical state of things to see a country, which boasts of its freedom, nursing and sustaining the most odious system of slavery known on earth. This is against nature, and our country cannot long endure it, as a permanent arrangement. There is truly an "irrepressible conflict" between free and slave labor, and eventually the country must be all slave or all free, or the two parts must separate; which, we shall soon know.

[1]John Bell was a Whig Senator from Tennessee who ran in 1860 for President on the Constitutional Union Party ticket. The Bell candidacy represented an effort to avoid the divisive sectional issues of the day—ED.

The only question is, when this will come to pass, and whether the time has now come for the final issue. A few weeks will decide this point. The events transpiring throughout the country indicate that the end is not far off.

This quarrel has been brought about against the earnest efforts of the North, and forced on her after the most surprising forbearance. "Whom the gods would destroy they first make mad" is an old adage. So it seems in the case of the Southern madcaps who have forced the country into this deplorable war for their own villainous purposes. If slavery is crushed out between the "upper and nether mill-stones" of the opposing forces, those who brought this difficulty on the country can console themselves with the reflection that they themselves were the cause of its death.

The people of the North as a body have been willing to let slavery alone—to have nothing to do with it one way or the other. They have no other desire now. But if the war goes on, God only knows what will come to pass. This much is certain—the institution of slavery must be affected for better or worse. The principle of eternal right forbids that it should in this Nineteenth century be benefited by such a movement. We must conclude, then—and we have asserted the same thing before—that the contest sound[s] the death-knell of slavery. Thomas Jefferson said, that, in such a contest as the present, God has no attribute that could cause him to take sides with the slave-own-ers.—No person can doubt the issue of the conflict between Freedom and Slavery—Order and Disorder—Law and Anarchy, which has commenced. It must result in favor of the *right*. To believe otherwise, we must believe history to be a lie, and that Satan rules on earth, instead of a benignant and just Providence. And, if the peculiar institution is doomed to come to an end by the acts of its friends, who will mourn its loss? It has kept the country in a ferment since its organization and hindered its progress and it would be truly a God's blessing to be rid of it. So every patriot feels in his heart of hearts.

15.2:   The War Is for Free Government (1861)

If for many northerners and southerners the Civil War was a confronta-tion over slavery, to others it seemed a struggle for political freedom. Northerners who held this view saw secession as a fundamental chal-lenge to the American experiment in free, democratic government, and Lincoln himself, in his immortal Gettysburg Address, drew this conclu-sion explicitly. Paradoxically Southerners, although living in a slave society, also saw the Confederacy as fighting for liberty. The South, they said—the white South—was asserting its rights against northern oppres-sion.

The first selection below is the inaugural address of Jefferson Davis, the Confederacy's first and only president. In what way does Davis's speech illustrate the shared political values of both sections. Does the phrase "consent of the governed," as used by Davis, have the same meaning as it would have for us today? Who among the South's population might Davis exclude from the category of the "governed"?

The second selection is from an editorial in the Philadelphia Public Ledger *in June 1861, early in the war. Is the writer's position that southern secession was a critical challenge to free government valid? Note the talk of "aristocratic assumption." What does the author mean by this phrase? Had the South won, would republican government have been seriously undermined in the world? On what basis could you argue this position?*

Inaugural Address

JEFFERSON DAVIS

Gentlemen of the Congress of the Confederate States of America:

Called to the difficult and responsible station of Executive Chief of the Provisional Government which you have instituted, I approach the discharge of the duties assigned me with an humble distrust of my abilities, but with a sustaining confidence in the wisdom of those who are to aid and guide me in the administration of public affairs, and an abiding faith in the patriotism and virtue of the people. Looking forward to the speedy establishment of a provisional government to take the place of the present one, and which, by its great moral and physical powers, will be better able to contend with the difficulties which arise from the conflicting incidents of separate nations, I enter upon the duties of the office for which I have been chosen with the hope that the beginning of our career as a Confederacy may not be obstructed by hostile opposition to the enjoyment of that separate and independent existence which we have asserted, and which, with the blessing of Providence, we intend to maintain.

Our present position has been achieved in a manner unprecedented in the history of nations. It illustrates the American idea that government rests upon the consent of the governed, and that it is the right of the people to alter or abolish a government whenever it becomes destructive of the ends for which it was established. The declared purposes of the compact of Union from which we have withdrawn were to establish justice, insure domestic tranquility, to provide for the common defence, to promote the general welfare, and to secure the blessings of liberty for ourselves and our posterity; and when in the judgment of the sovereign States now comprising this Confederacy it had been perverted from the purposes for which it was

Southern Historical Papers, vol. 1 (January–June 1876), pp. 19–23.

ordained, and had ceased to answer the ends for which it was established, an appeal to the ballot-box declared that so far as they were concerned the government created by that compact should cease to exist. In this they merely asserted a right which the Declaration of Independence of 1776 defined to be inalienable. Of the time and occasion for its exercise, they, as sovereign, were the final judges each for itself. The impartial and enlightened verdict of mankind will vindicate the rectitude of our conduct, and He who knows the hearts of men will judge the sincerity with which we have labored to preserve the government of our fathers, in its spirit and in those rights inherent in it, which were solemnly proclaimed at the birth of the States, and which have been affirmed and re-affirmed in the Bills of Rights of the several States. When they entered into the Union of 1789, it was with the undeniable recognition of the power of the people to resume the authority delegated for the purposes of that government, whenever, in their opinion, its functions were perverted and its ends defeated. By virtue of this authority, the time and occasion requiring them to exercise it having arrived, the sovereign States here represented have seceded from that Union, and it is a gross abuse of language to denominate the act rebellion or revolution. They have formed a new alliance, but in each State its government has remained as before. The rights of person and property have not been disturbed. The agency through which they have communicated with foreign powers has been changed, but this does not necessarily interrupt their international relations.

Sustained by a consciousness that our transition from the former Union to the present Confederacy has not proceeded from any disregard on our part of our just obligations, or any failure to perform every constitutional duty—moved by no intention or design to invade the rights of others—anxious to cultivate peace and commerce with all nations—if we may not hope to avoid war, we may at least expect that posterity will acquit us of having needlessly engaged in it. We are doubly justified by the absence of wrong on our part, and by wanton aggression on the part of others. There can be no cause to doubt that the courage and patriotism of the people of the Confederate States will be found equal to any measure of defence which may be required for their security. Devoted to agricultural pursuits, their chief interest is the export of a commodity required in every manufacturing country. Our policy is peace, and the freest trade our necessities will permit. It is alike our interest, and that of all those to whom we would sell and from whom we would buy, that there should be the fewest practicable restrictions upon interchange of commodities. There can be but little rivalry between us and any manufacturing or navigating community, such as the Northwestern States of the American Union.

It must follow, therefore, that mutual interest would invite good will and kindness between them and us. If, however, passion or lust of dominion should cloud the judgment and inflame the ambition of these States, we must prepare to meet the emergency, and maintain, by the final arbitrament of the sword, the position we have assumed among the nations of the earth. We have now entered upon our career of independence, and it must be inflexibly pursued.

Through many years of controversy with our late associates, the Northern States, we have vainly endeavored to secure tranquility and obtain respect for the rights to which we were entitled. As a necessity, not a choice, we have resorted to separation, and henceforth our energies must be devoted to the conducting of our own affairs, and perpetuating the Confederacy we have formed. If a just perception of mutual interest shall permit us peaceably to pursue our separate political career, my most earnest desire will have been fulfilled. But if this be denied us, and the integrity and jurisdiction of our territory be assailed, it will but remain for us with a firm resolve to appeal to arms and invoke the blessings of Providence upon a just cause.

As a consequence of our new constitution, and with a view to meet our anticipated wants, it will be necessary to provide a speedy and efficient organization of the several branches of the executive departments having special charge of our foreign intercourse, financial and military affairs, and postal service. For purposes of defence, the Confederate States may, under ordinary circumstances, rely mainly upon their militia; but it is deemed advisable, in the present condition of affairs, that there should be a well instructed, disciplined army, more numerous than would be usually required for a peace establishment.

I also suggest that for the protection of our harbors and commerce on the high seas, a navy adapted to those objects be built up. These necessities have doubtless engaged the attention of Congress.

With a constitution differing only in form from that of our forefathers, in so far as it is explanatory of their well known intents, freed from sectional conflicts which have so much interfered with the pursuits of the general welfare, it is not unreasonable to expect that the States from which we have parted may seek to unite their fortunes with ours under the government we have instituted. For this your constitution has made adequate provision, but beyond this, if I mistake not the judgment and will of the people, our reunion with the States from which we have separated is neither practicable nor desirable. To increase power, develop the resources, and promote the happiness of this Confederacy, it is necessary that there should be so much homogeneity as that the welfare of every portion be the aim of the whole. When this homogeneity does not exist, antagonisms are engendered which must and should result in separation.

Actuated solely by a desire to protect and preserve our own rights and promote our own welfare, the secession of the Confederate States has been marked by no aggression upon others, and followed by no domestic convulsion. Our industrial pursuits have received no check; the cultivation of our fields has progressed as heretofore; and even should we be involved in war, there would be no considerable diminution in the production of the great staple which constitutes our exports, and in which the commercial world has an interest scarcely less than our own. This common interest of producer and consumer can only be interrupted by external force, which would obstruct shipments to foreign markets—a course of conduct which would be detrimental to manufacturing and commercial interests abroad. Should reason guide the action of the government from which we have separated, a policy so injurious to the civilized world, the Northern States included, could not be dictated even by the strongest desire to inflict injury upon us; but if otherwise, a terrible responsibility will rest upon it, and the suffering of millions will bear testimony to the folly and wickedness of our aggressors. In the meantime there will remain to us, besides the ordinary remedies before suggested, the well known resources for retaliation upon the commerce of our enemy.

Experience in public stations of subordinate grade to this which your kindness has conferred on me, has taught me that care and toil and disappointments are the price of official elevation. You will have many errors to forgive, many deficiencies to tolerate, but you will not find in me either a want of zeal or fidelity to a cause that has my highest hopes and most enduring affection. Your generosity has bestowed upon me an undeserved distinction—one which I neither sought nor desired. Upon the continuance of that sentiment, and upon your wisdom and patriotism, I rely to direct and support me in the performance of the duties required at my hands. We have changed the constituent parts, not the system of our government. The constitution formed by our fathers is the constitution of the "Confederate States." In *their* exposition of it, and in the judicial constructions it has received, it has a light that reveals its true meaning. Thus instructed as to the just interpretations of that instrument, and ever remembering that all public offices are but trusts, held for the benefit of the people, and that delegated powers are to be strictly construed, I will hope that by due diligence in the discharge of my duties, though I may disappoint your expectations, yet to retain, when retiring, something of the good will and confidence which welcome my entrance into office. It is joyous in perilous times to look around upon a people united in heart, who are animated and actuated by one and the same purpose and high resolve, with whom the sacrifices to be made are not weighed in the balance against honor, right, liberty and equality. Obstacles may retard, but cannot prevent their progressive movements. Sanctified by justice and sustained by a virtuous people, let me reverently invoke the God of our fathers to guide and protect us in our efforts to perpetuate the principles which by HIS blessing they were able to vindicate, establish and transmit to their posterity, and with the continuance of HIS favor, ever to be gratefully acknowledged, let us look hopefully forward to success, to peace, and to prosperity.

The North Is Fighting for Free Government

Setting aside the moral aspects of the case as involved in such a contest, it will be seen, by a little consideration, that there are important political and social principles at stake also, in this issue. When our Constitution was framed, it was adopted as the fundamental law, for the protection of the natural and political rights of each individual citizen residing in the republic. All distinctions of classes were set aside; all titles resting upon supposed honor or acquired wealth were abolished; each individual citizen was clothed with the same political rights, and stood the equal of his fellow-citizen under the laws, no matter what his wealth or the social consideration in which he was held. With no artificial barriers interposed between him and his welfare, there was no bar to his enterprise and his ambition; and the immense development of the physical resources of this country, and the prosperity which everywhere is exhibited, are the practical benefits arising from this political equality. But under this theory of equality which has benefited so much the enterprising white race in America, there was also, unfortunately, a system of labor existing which was directly antagonistic, and which asserted the right of property in man if his skin was black. That system, socially encouraged for so many years, and protected under our constitution for three-fourths of a century, could not exist without producing essential changes in the social bearing and political instincts of the people among whom it existed. Labor, from being the employment of menials only, was looked upon as the badge of servitude, and from holding property in laborers of one color, it was very natural that the property owners should regard all labor as the just object of ownership, and with this barbarous dogma, should seek to establish such changes in the political government of the country as would take from labor the power of controlling its own destiny. Under the constitution of the United States this could not be done. Hence we have a revolution to establish a "Southern Confederacy on a military basis, with suffrage largely restricted." This is the leading idea of the revolutionists—the avowed object of South Carolina, the moving spirit in this rebellion—though, for prudential reasons, the Montgomery [Alabama] Congress has seen proper to ignore it temporarily.

"*What* are we fighting for?" We are fighting for everything for which this Government was established. We are fighting to preserve our republican institutions in their purity; to maintain our Union in its integrity; to establish the authority of the Constitution and laws over violence and anarchy; to secure popular rights against aristocratic assumption; and to prove to the other nations of the earth whether we have a Government or not. The fundamental principle which is assailed in the present rebellion is the principle

Philadelphia Public Ledger, June 7, 1861, in Howard C. Perkins, ed., *Northern Editorials on Secession* (New York: Appleton-Century-Crofts, 1942), vol. 2, pp. 845–47.

of equal rights as recognized under our Constitution. It is the underlying principle of our republic, and when that is destroyed, the principle which gives vitality to our democratic representative government is gone also, and with it the faith of mankind in popular government. We are fighting, therefore, to preserve the Government as it was established, on pure republican principles, in which artificial distinctions merely, shall not impair political rights.

But if the principle of republican government is assailed by the aristocratic pretensions now put forth by the leaders who inaugurated this rebellion, the Government established upon it is fatally endangered by the attempt to break up the Union, and the changes of policy and interests which will be created by its rupture. Contemporaneous with the establishment of the Government was the avowed policy that no European Government should be permitted to meddle with the political institutions of this country, or to establish the principle of aristocratic or monarchical rule upon the soil which has been devoted to democratic representative government. To maintain this policy, union is indispensable. To keep this Northern division of the continent as the field for millions of the white race to claim their natural birthright in, and exercise their energies and their talents for their own advantage and the general prosperity, it is essential that but one Government shall exercise authority from the Gulf of Mexico to Canada, and from the Atlantic to the Pacific. What would this country be, broken up into pieces, and divided into different confederacies, with rival interests, and rival institutions? How could the enterprise and industry of the free North develope itself with another and rival government, based on principles so entirely opposite to free labor, limiting its expansion southwardly, and holding three-fourths of the line of sea coast of the country in its own possession? If there is anything which distinguishes the labor of the free white men of the North, it is its enterprise and its energy, and these flourish alike on land and on the ocean. The whole commercial activity of the nation equaling that of England, arises from the entire freedom with which the labor of the North is allowed to extend its operations. To be cut off at one blow from this privilege, and to be deprived of the freedom of the coasting trade, would be ruinous to our commercial interests, and crippling to every other pursuit on which our prosperity is founded. It would be dwarfing energies which require a whole continent as the field of their operations, and driving the people back again into poverty and misery.

But independently of these conditions, we are fighting for another great fundamental principle of republican Government—the right of the majority to rule. When the ballot-box was substituted for revolution, it was thought that all violent changes in established governments, all sudden overthrowing of political structures, would be obviated, for the will of the people could be peacefully known through the ballot, and their legally established rule be patiently submitted to. So long as it answered the purpose of maintaining power in the hands of the would-be-oligarchs, its decrees were acknowledged as binding; but so soon as it threatened to put power really in the hands of the majority, those who labor for their living, then the discovery is made that our institutions rest on a wrong basis, and that political equality is neither desirable for social prosperity, nor practicable for political permanency. We are fighting to expunge this great political error, and to prove to the world, that the free Democratic spirit which established the government, is equal to its protection and its maintenance. If this is not worth fighting for, then our revolt against England was a crime, and our republican Government a fraud.

15.3:   The War Is a Clash of Economic Interests (1860, 1861)

Contemporaries, as well as later historians, argued that the Civil War was at heart a confrontation of two societies defined by distinctive and antagonistic economic interests. The South's slave system, directly or obliquely, committed it to plantation agriculture; the North's free labor system and capitalist values committed it to commerce and industry. The two sections, this view notes, had fought major battles in Congress over tariffs, a Pacific railroad, a federally chartered bank, and the use of the national government generally to advance business enterprise. These struggles, then, must be considered in any analysis of the escalating sectional contention that ended in secession.

The selections below consider the Civil War as a contest of rival economic interests and the triumph in the end of northern commercial-industrial policies and values over southern agrarian ones.

The first piece is an editorial from the Vicksburg Daily Whig *of January 18, 1860, a year before actual secession. The* Whig, *as its name implies, was a Mississippi paper affiliated with the more traditionally conservative and unionist of the two southern parties. Southern Whigs were also more commercially oriented than southern Democrats. How are these characteristics revealed by the editorial below? There was less disagreement between southern Whigs and northern Republicans than between southern Democrats and Republicans, but this editorial nonetheless catches the flavor of southern economic resentment of the North. What are these resentments? How does the author express them?*

The next selection is from a speech delivered by Edward Everett of Massachusetts in July 1861, after actual fighting between the two sections had broken out. A Unitarian clergyman, Everett had served as Whig congressman and governor of his state. In 1860 he ran for vice president on the Constitutional Union Party ticket, a moderate group representing conservative unionists unwilling to support either

Democrats or Republicans, both of whom they considered sectionally divisive.

In this document Everett defends the Union cause by seeking to refute the southern charge that the tariff, supported by northern business leaders and politicians, had oppressed Dixie. What are Everett's essential arguments? Are they convincing? Do you know which policy—northern protectionism (protariff) or southern free-trade (antitariff)—had prevailed in the years immediately preceding 1860? Was the tariff a major issue during the 1860 presidential campaign?

The North Opposed the South Economically

VICKSBURG DAILY WHIG

Whilst this journal would by no means advocate the commercial independence of the South, as a distinctive measure, intended as an initiatory step for dissolving the Union; still, we are free to declare that, in our opinion, the South ought, without further delay, to commence a system of measures for her own protection. The Southern Conventions, as they are called, which have from time to time assembled, were not only abortive, but positively injurious. Those assemblages, indeed, were conceived in a spirit of Disunion, and were hot beds for the speedy propagation of *fire-eating* sentiments. Such being their character, this journal, of course, had no sympathies with them; nor did we ever expect any substantial good to spring from their deliberations. However, it is manifest to even a casual observer of ordinary intelligence, that the policy in trade and commerce uniformly pursued by the South is not only blind and simple, but absolutely suicidal to our pecuniary prosperity.

By mere supineness, the people of the South have permitted the Yankees to monopolize the carrying trade, with its immense profits. We have yielded to them the manufacturing business, in all its departments, without an effort, until recently, to become manufacturers ourselves. We have acquiesced in the claims of the North to do all the importing, and most of the exporting business, for the whole Union. Thus, the North has been aggrandised, in a most astonishing degree, at the expense of the South. It is no wonder that their villages have grown into magnificent cities. It is not strange that they have "merchant princes," dwelling in gorgeous palaces and reveling in luxuries transcending the luxurious appliances of the East! How could it be otherwise? New York city, like a mighty queen of commerce, sits proudly upon her island throne, sparkling in jewels and waving an undisputed commercial scepter over the South. By means of her railways and navigable streams, she sends out her *long arms* to the extreme South; and, with an

Vicksburg Daily Whig, January 18, 1860, in Dwight L. Dumond, ed., *Southern Editorials on Secession* (New York: Appleton-Century-Crofts, 1931), pp. 13–16.

avidity rarely equaled, grasps our gains and transfers them to herself—taxing us at every step—and depleting us as extensively as possible without actually destroying us. Meantime, the South remains passive—in a state of torpidity—making cotton bales for the North to manufacture, and constantly exerting ourselves to increase the production as much as possible. We have no ships in the foreign carrying trade, or very few indeed. No vessels enter Southern harbors (comparatively speaking) laden with the rich "merchandise" of foreign climes directly imported from those distant countries. We extend but little encouragement to the various mechanical arts, but buy most of our farming implements from the Northern people. Although Mississippi has within her limits an extensive seaboard, affording capacious and secure harbors, capable almost of sheltering the shipping of the world, still the blue waters of our harbors are unbroken by a single keel, save the diminutive fishing smacks which frequent those waters. Although nature hath prepared for us most beautiful positions for commercial cities, and pointed, with her unerring finger, to the advantages spread before our *blind eyes;* still, we have no seaboard cities, except so far as they exist in imagination, or are delineated *on paper*, or are shadowed forth in pompous resolutions emanating from disunion conventions! Why is this? Why are we so far behind in the great march of improvement? Simply because we have *failed to act* in obedience to the dictates of sound policy. Simply because we have been almost criminally neglectful of our own pecuniary interests. What should we do? What remedy have we?

Why, in the first place, let us withdraw one-third, or even one-half of our capital from agricultural operations, and invest it in the establishment of manufactures of cotton. Thus, we will greatly reduce the production of the raw material; and, as a necessary consequence, greatly enhance the market price of our great staple. The business of manufacturing the common cotton fabrics can be as profitably conducted here in Mississippi as it can be in Massachusetts. This fact has been demonstrated by the humble history of the few manufacturies already operating in our State. It has been proven that the business of making cotton goods in Mississippi pays from 10 to 12 per cent profit per annum on the investment. Now, suppose we had extensive establishments for producing common fabrics of cotton in every county of Mississippi, created by Southern capital, and owned and worked by our own people; we could clothe ourselves at a small expense, comparatively, and sell the Yankees our surplus cloth, and thus realize a profit, instead of buying for ourselves. Consider the enhanced price of cotton, consequent upon the reduced supply; calculate the profits of manufacturing at home; refer to the opportunity we would thus have of becoming stock raisers, and producers of the small grains and fruits which our climate and soil are capable of maturing; and who does not see, at a glance, how eminently advantageous and profitable such a system would be. Connected with this policy, let us encourage the mechanical arts. Let us fabricate here all of our carriages and wagons; all of our farming implements; every article of furniture required by our people; and thus secure to ourselves an accession of valuable citizens, those multiplied thousands of industrious, honorable, moral artisans, who are producers, instead of consumers, and who are valuable, indeed, to any community that can secure their presence. Let us sedulously cultivate the sentiment, so true in itself, that *labor is honorable and dignified.* Lastly, let us at once begin the business of direct importation and direct exportation, and thus keep at home the millions of dollars which we annually pay to the North. The business of direct importation and direct exportation would, of course, build up, as if by the wand of a magician, splendid Southern cities of commercial grandeur and opulence; and thus we might become the most happy, prosperous, wealthy and intelligent people upon whom the sun has ever smiled. All this we should do—not in spitefulness—not in a spirit of envy—not with a view of breaking the ties of national Union—not with a design of engendering sectional animosity, but in obedience merely to the dictates of enlightened sectional policy, and in obedience to that universal principle, so well understood and acted upon by our Yankee friends, of consulting our own pecuniary interests, and adding to our general and individual pecuniary emoluments.

This is a fruitful topic. It might be spoken of in *volumes.* We have but glanced at it in the foregoing observations. After all, what we have penned, so far from being original suggestions, is but the recapitulation of self-evident propositions, suggesting themselves to every intelligent mind. It remains to be seen whether the South will awake from her ignoble slumber, and act for herself, or whether she will indolently remain inactive, and continue to be mere "hewers of wood and drawers of water," for the merchant princes of the North.

The North's Economic Grievances Against the South

EDWARD EVERETT

But the tariff is, with one exception, the alleged monster wrong—for which South Carolina in 1832[1] drove the Union to the verge of a civil war, and which, next to the slavery question, the South has been taught to regard as the most grievous of the oppressions which she suffers at the hands of the North, and that by which she seeks to win the sympathy of the manufacturing States of Europe. It was so treated in the debate referred to. I am certainly not going so far to abuse your patience, as to enter into a discussion of the constitutionality or expediency of the protective policy, on which I am aware that opinions at the North differ, nor do I deem it necessary to expose the

---

Frank Moore, ed., *The Rebellion Record: A Diary of American Events* (New York: G. P. Putnam, 1862), vol. 1, pp. 27–30.
[1]The Tariff of 1832, passed by Northern votes, so offended South Carolina leaders that they sought to nullify the measure, thereby precipitating a Constitutional crisis—ED.

utter fallacy of the monstrous paradox, that duties, enhancing the price of imported articles, are paid, not by the consumer of the merchandise imported, but by the producer of the last article of export given in exchange. It is sufficient to say that for this maxim, (the forty-bale theory so called,) which has grown into an article of faith at the South, not the slightest authority ever has been, to my knowledge, adduced from any political economist of any school. Indeed, it can be shown to be a shallow sophism, inasmuch as the *consumer* must be, directly or indirectly, the *producer* of the equivalents given in exchange for the article he consumes. But without entering into this discussion, I shall make a few remarks to show the great injustice of representing the protective system as being in its origin an oppression, of which the South has to complain on the part of the North.

Every such suggestion is a complete inversion of the truth of history. Some attempts at manufactures by machinery were made at the North before the Revolution, but to an inconsiderable extent. The manufacturing system as a great Northern interest is the child of the restrictive policy of 1807–1812, and of the war [of 1812]. That policy was pursued against the earnest opposition of the North, and to the temporary prostration of their commerce, navigation, and fisheries. Their capital was driven in this way into manufactures, and on the return of peace, the foundations of the protective system were laid in the square yard duty on cotton fabrics, in the support of which Mr. [John C.] Calhoun, advised that the growth of the manufacture would open a new market for the staple of the South, took the lead. As late as 1821 the Legislature of South Carolina unanimously affirmed the constitutionality of protective duties, though denying their expediency,—and of all the States of the Union Louisiana has derived the greatest benefit from this policy; in fact, she owes the sugar culture to it, and has for that reason given it her steady support. In all the tariff battles while I was a member of Congress, few votes were surer for the policy than that of Louisiana. If the duty on an article imported is considered as added to its price in our market, (which, however, is far from being invariably the case,) the sugar duty, of late, has amounted to a tax of five millions of dollars annually paid by the consumer, for the benefit of the Louisiana planter.

As to its being an unconstitutional policy, it is perfectly well known that the protection of manufactures was a leading and avowed object for the formation of the Constitution. The second law, passed by Congress after its formation, was a revenue law. Its preamble is as follows: "Whereas it is necessary for the support of Government, for the discharge of the debts of the United States, and the encouragement and protection of manufactures, that duties be laid on goods, wares, and merchandise imported." That act was reported to the House of Representatives by Mr. [James] Madison, who is entitled as much as any one to be called the father of the Constitution. While it was pending before the House, and in the first week of the first session of the first Congress, two memorials were presented praying for protective duties; and it is a matter of some curiosity to inquire, from what part of the country this first call came for that policy, now put forward as one of the acts of Northern oppression, which justify the South in flying to arms. The first of these petitions was from Baltimore. It implored the new Government to lay a protecting duty on all articles imported from abroad, which can be manufactured at home. The second was from the shipwrights, not of New York, not of Boston, not of Portland, but of Charleston, South Carolina, praying for "such a general regulation of trade and the establishment of such A NAVIGATION ACT, as will relieve the particular distresses of the petitioners, in common with those of their fellow-shipwrights throughout the Union"! and if South Carolina had always been willing to make common cause with their fellow-citizens throughout the Union, it would not now be rent by civil war.

The Cotton Culture Introduced Under Protection

But the history of the great Southern staple is most curious and instructive. His Majesty "King Cotton," on his throne, does not seem to be aware of the influences which surrounded his cradle. The culture of cotton, on any considerable scale, is well known to be of recent date in America. The household manufacture of cotton was coeval with the settlement of the country. A century before the piano-forte or the harp was seen on this continent, the music of the spinning-wheel was heard at every fire-side in town and country. The raw materials were wool, flax, and cotton, the last imported from the West Indies. The colonial system of Great Britain before the Revolution forbade the establishment of any other than household manufactures. Soon after the Revolution, cotton mills were erected in Rhode Island and Massachusetts, and the infant manufacture was encouraged by State duties on the imported fabric. The raw material was still derived exclusively from the West Indies. Its culture in this country was so extremely limited and so little known, that a small parcel sent from the United States to Liverpool in 1784 was seized at the custom-house there, as an illicit importation of British colonial produce. Even as late as 1794, and by persons so intelligent as the negotiators of [John] Jay's treaty, it was not known that cotton was an article of growth and export from the United States. In the twelfth article of that treaty, as laid before the Senate, Cotton was included with Molasses, Sugar, Coffee, and Cocoa, as articles which American vessels should not be permitted to carry from the islands *or from the United States* to any foreign country.

In the Revenue law of 1789, as it passed through the House of Representatives, cotton, with other raw materials, was placed on the free list. When the bill reached the Senate a duty of 3 cents per pound was laid upon cotton, not to encourage, not to protect, but to *create* the domestic culture. On the discussion of this amendment in the House, a member from South Carolina declared that "Cotton was in contemplation" in South Carolina and Georgia, "and *if good seed could be procured he hoped it might succeed.*" On this hope the amendment of the Senate was concurred in, and the duty of three cents per pound was laid on cotton. In 1791, [Alexander] Hamilton, in his report on the manufactures, recommended the repeal of this duty, on the ground that it was "a very serious impediment to the manufacture of cotton," but his recommendation was disregarded.

Thus, in the infancy of the cotton manufacture of the North, at the moment when they were deprived of the protection extended to them before the Constitution by State laws, and while they were struggling against English competition under the rapidly improving machinery of [Richard] Arkwright,[2] which it was highly penal to export to foreign countries, a heavy burden was laid upon them by this protecting duty, to enable the planters of South Carolina and Georgia to explore the tropics for a variety of cotton seed adapted to their climate. For seven years at least, and probably more, this duty was in every sense of the word a protecting duty. There was not a pound of cotton spun, no not for candle-wicks to light the humble industry of the cottages of the North, which did not pay this tribute to the Southern planter. The growth of the native article, as we have seen, had not in 1794 reached a point to be known to Chief Justice Jay as one of actual or probable export. As late as 1796, the manufacturers of Brandywine in Delaware petitioned Congress for the repeal of this duty on imported cotton, and the petition was rejected on the Report of a Committee, consisting of a majority from the Southern States, on the ground, that "to repeal the duty on raw cotton imported would be to damp the growth of cotton in our own country." Radicle and plumule, root and stalk, blossom and boll, the culture of the cotton plant in the United States was in its infancy the foster-child of the Protective System.

When therefore the pedigree of King Cotton is traced, he is found to be the lineal child of the tariff; called into being by a specific duty; reared by a tax laid upon the manufacturing industry of the North, to create the culture of the raw material in the South. The Northern manufacturers of America were slightly protected in 1789 because they were too feeble to stand alone. Reared into magnitude under the restrictive system and the war of 1812, they were upheld in 1816 because they were too important to be sacrificed, and because the great staple of the South had a joint interest in their prosperity. King Cotton alone, not in his manhood, not in his adolescence, not in his infancy, but in his very embryo state, was pensioned upon the Treasury,—before the seed from which he sprung was cast "in the lowest parts of the earth." In the book of the tariff "his members were written, which in continuance were fashioned, when as yet there were none of them."

But it was not enough to create the culture of cotton at the South, by taxing the manufactures of the North with a duty on the raw material; the extension of that culture and the prosperity which it has conferred upon the South are due to the mechanical genius of the North. What says Mr. Justice

---

[2]Inventor of the spinning jenny—ED.

Johnson of the Supreme Court of the United States, and a citizen of South Carolina? "With regard to the utility of this discovery" (the cotton gin of [Eli] Whitney) "the court would deem it a waste of time to dwell long upon this topic. Is there a man who hears us that has not experienced its utility? The whole interior of the Southern States was languishing, and its inhabitants emigrating, for want of some object to engage their attention and employ their industry, when the invention of this machine at once opened views to them which set the whole country in active motion. From childhood to age it has presented us a lucrative employment. Individuals who were depressed in poverty and sunk in idleness, have suddenly risen to wealth and respectability. Our debts have been paid off, our capitals increased, and our lands trebled in value. We cannot express the weight of obligation which the country owes to this invention; the extent of it cannot now be seen."—Yes, and when happier days shall return, and the South, awakening from her suicidal delusion, shall remember who it was that sowed her sunny fields with the seeds of those golden crops with which she thinks to rule the world, she will cast a veil of oblivion over the memory of the ambitious men who have goaded her to her present madness, and will rear a monument of her gratitude in the beautiful City of Elms, over the ashes of her greatest benefactor—ELI WHITNEY.

16

Reconstruction

In April 1865 the nation faced colossal problems of readjustment and repair. The South was a devastated region, its railroads, its banking system, and many of its towns and cities reduced to ruins. The human cost in the former Confederacy had been enormous. Thousands of young southern men had died or been maimed. Most difficult of all, in some ways, 4 million former slaves had been wrenched from their accustomed place within the South's social and labor systems and left without clear roles and firm moorings.

The new circumstances also raised urgent constitutional problems for the nation as a whole. Having fought to leave the Union, the South was now out of constitutional alignment with the rest of the states. Should the North accept the logic of its own position—that secession was illegal—and simply allow the former Confederate states to return to full constitutional status without conditions? That response would go easy on the ex-rebels and at the same time allow the southern states a free hand in dealing with the newly freed men and women. Could white southerners be trusted to be fair to the former slaves? Should erstwhile Confederates be allowed to resume their place in the Union without punishment for committing atrocities against Union prisoners, for violating federal oaths of office, for creating the mountain of dead and wounded the American people had suffered?

For over a decade following Confederate defeat, the nation's politics would be roiled by the debate over how to manage the Reconstruction process. Americans would be deeply divided. Congress would battle the president, southerners would battle northerners, whites would battle blacks, Democrats would battle Republicans. On each issue there would often be a bewildering array of positions not easily categorized as pro or con.

The documents below express a range of views on important

Reconstruction problems. They do not exhaust the full spectrum of either opinions or issues on this complex event in our history; they are only a sample of how Americans thought. As you read the selections that follow, try to determine the gist of each argument and try to understand why particular individuals felt the way they did.

16.1: Harsh versus Lenient Victors (1865)

Besides being influenced by differing ideologies or philosophies, northern leaders were swayed in their approaches to Reconstruction by differences of temperament and personality. Abraham Lincoln, a pragmatist and a compassionate man, was inclined to make the return of the southern states to full constitutional equality a relatively easy process. In several states that had been occupied by Union forces before the final Confederate surrender, he was able to put his lenient policies in effect.

The first selection below is an excerpt from Lincoln's last recorded address, remarks he made from the White House balcony to a group of citizens who had come to "serenade" him just four days before his death by an assassin's bullet. Lincoln discusses the issue of the constitutional status of the seceded states, a legalistic issue that had important implications for policy. If it was held that the southern states had never actually left the Union, then they remained sovereign entities like the other states, and Washington had only limited powers over them. But if it was decided that they had left the Union and reverted to territorial status, as some believed, then Congress could constitutionally impose a wide range of conditions on them.

What does Lincoln say about this issue? What is his overall tone? Was his estimate of the best thing for the nation to do valid in light of all that followed? How would you characterize Lincoln's views of the rights of the former slaves?

The second selection is a May 1865 proclamation by President Andrew Johnson establishing a provisional government for South Carolina. In the next two months Johnson issued six other proclamations establishing governments for other former Confederate states.

Johnson was himself a southerner (from Tennessee), but a strong unionist who had refused to disavow his government when his state seceded. Like Lincoln, he believed the southern states should be readmitted to the Union with as few preconditions as possible. What preconditions are imposed by the president's proclamation? Are they severe? What obvious conditions that might have been imposed are omitted? Is there any mention of a role for Congress in the Reconstruction process? Should

Johnson have assumed sole leadership in this all-important matter?

The third selection is from a speech by Representative Thaddeus Stevens of Pennsylvania. Stevens was a "Radical Republican." During the war he had, as other Radicals, pushed for the early emancipation of the slaves and aggressive policies against the Confederacy and its leaders. After the war he and his fellow Radicals would demand that the South be compelled to repudiate its prewar planter leadership and guarantee equal social and political rights for the freedmen.[1] Southerners and conservative northerners, mostly Democrats, would call Stevens and his colleagues mean-spirited "vindictives," who lacked Christian compassion toward their former enemies and were moved primarily by partisan political ends.

After Lincoln's assassination, Stevens rallied the congressional opposition to President Johnson's lenient Reconstruction policy. He and his supporters would seize from the president the management of the Reconstruction process. Ultimately they would break completely with Johnson, and in 1868 the Radical-controlled Congress would impeach the president—although not convict him—for defying the will and the laws of Congress.

From the excerpt below, would you say that Stevens deserves to be considered vindictive? Do his sympathies for the freed slaves seem sincere? Does his reference to "perpetual ascendency to the party of the Union" seem like a blatant grab for power by Republicans? Putting yourself in Stevens's shoes, how can such a partisan position be justified?

Reconstruction Must Be Gradual and Careful

ABRAHAM LINCOLN

I have been shown a letter . . . in which the writer expresses regret that my mind has not seemed to be definitely fixed upon the question whether the seceded States, so called, are in the Union or out of it. I would perhaps add astonishment to his regret were he to learn that since I have found professed Union men endeavoring to answer that question, I have purposely forborne any public expression upon it. As appears to me, that question has not been nor yet is a practically material one, and that any discussion of it, while it thus remains practically immaterial, could have no effect other than the mischievous one of dividing our friends. As yet, whatever it may become, that question is bad as the basis of a controversy, and good for nothing at

[1] Though the term might seem sexist today it was used to refer to *all* the freed slaves after 1865, and it is still so used—ED.

Arthur B. Lapsley, *Writings of Abraham Lincoln*, (New York: G. P. Putnam's Sons, 1906), vol. 7, pp. 362–68.

all—a merely pernicious abstraction. We all agree that the seceded States, so called, are out of their proper practical relation with the Union, and that the sole object of the Government, civil and military, in regard to these States, is to again get them into their proper practical relation. I believe that is not only possible, but in fact [it is] easier to do this without deciding or even considering whether these States have ever been out of the Union, than with it. Finding themselves safely at home, it would be utterly immaterial whether they have been abroad. Let us all join in doing the act necessary to restore the proper practical relations between these States and the Union, and each forever after innocently indulge his own opinion whether, in doing the acts, he brought the States from without the Union, or only gave them proper assistance, they never having been out of it. The amount of constituency, so to speak, on which the Louisiana government rests, would be more satisfactory to all if it contained fifty thousand, or thirty thousand, or even twenty thousand, instead of twelve thousand, as it does. It is also unsatisfactory to some that the elective franchise is not given to the colored man. I would myself prefer that it were now conferred on the very intelligent, and on those who serve our cause as soldiers. Still, the question is not whether the Louisiana government, as it stands, is quite all that is desirable. The question is, Will it be wiser to take it as it is and help to improve it, or to reject and disperse[sic]? Can Louisiana be brought into proper practical relation with the Union sooner by sustaining or by discarding her new State government? Some twelve thousand voters in the heretofore Slave State of Louisiana have sworn allegiance to the Union, assumed to be the rightful political power of the State, held elections, organized a State government, adopted a Free State constitution, giving the benefit of public schools equally to black and white, and empowering the Legislature to confer the elective franchise upon the colored man. This Legislature has already voted to ratify the Constitutional Amendment recently passed by Congress, abolishing slavery throughout the nation. These twelve thousand persons are thus fully committed to the Union, and to perpetuate freedom in the State—committed to the very things, and nearly all things, the nation wants—and they ask the nation's recognition and its assistance to make good this committal. Now, if we reject and spurn them, we do our utmost to disorganize and disperse them. We, in fact, say to the white man: You are worthless or worse; we will neither help you nor be helped by you. To the blacks we say: This cup of liberty which these, your old masters, held to your lips, we will dash from you, and leave you to the chances of gathering the spilled and scattered contents in some vague and undefined when, where, and how. If this course, discouraging and paralyzing both white and black, has any tendency to bring Louisiana into proper practical relations with the Union, I have so far been unable to perceive it. If, on the contrary, we recognize and sustain the new government of Louisiana, the converse of all this is made true. We encourage the hearts and nerve the arms of twelve thousand to adhere to their work, and argue for it, and proselyte for it, and fight for it, and feed it, and grow it, and ripen it to a complete success. The colored man, too, in seeing all united for him, is inspired with vigilance, and energy, and daring to the same end. Grant that he desires the elective franchise, will he not attain it sooner by saving the already advanced steps towards it, than by running backward over them? Concede that the new government of Louisiana is only to what it should be as the egg is to the fowl, we shall sooner have the fowl by hatching the egg than by smashing it. Again, if we reject Louisiana, we also reject one vote in favor of the proposed amendment to the National Constitution. To meet this proposition, it has been argued that no more than three fourths of those States which have not attempted secession are necessary to validly ratify the amendment. I do not commit myself against this, further than to say that such a ratification would be questionable, and sure to be persistently questioned, while a ratification by three fourths of all the States would be unquestioned and unquestionable. I repeat the question, Can Louisiana be brought into proper practical relation with the Union sooner by sustaining or by discarding her new State government? What has been said of Louisiana will apply to other States. And yet so great peculiarities pertain to each State, and such important and sudden changes occur in the same State, and withal so new and unprecedented is the whole case, that no exclusive and inflexible plan can safely be prescribed as to details and collaterals. Such exclusive and inflexible plan would surely become a new entanglement. Important principles may and must be inflexible. In the present situation as the phrase goes, it may be my duty to make some new announcement to the people of the South. I am considering, and shall not fail to act, when satisfied that action will be proper.

Amnesty Proclamation

ANDREW JOHNSON

By the President of the United States of America. A Proclamation.

Whereas the fourth section of the fourth article of the Constitution of the United States declares that the United States shall guarantee to every State in the Union a republican form of government and shall protect each of them against invasion and domestic violence; and

Whereas the President of the United States is by the Constitution made Commander in Chief of the Army and Navy, as well as chief civil executive officer of the United States, and is bound by solemn oath faithfully to execute the office of President of the United States and to take care that the laws be faithfully executed; and

Whereas the rebellion which has been waged by a portion of the people of the United States against the properly constituted authorities of the

James D. Richardson, ed., *A Compilation of the Messages and Papers of the Presidents* (New York: Bureau of National Literature, 1897), vol. 8, pp. 3508–10.

Government thereof in the most violent and revolting form, but whose organized and armed forces have now been almost entirely overcome, has in its revolutionary progress deprived the people of the State of South Carolina of all civil government; and

Whereas it becomes necessary and proper to carry out and enforce the obligations of the United States to the people of South Carolina in securing them in the enjoyment of a republican form of government:

Now, therefore, in obedience to the high and solemn duties imposed upon me by the Constitution of the United States and for the purpose of enabling the loyal people of said State to organize a State government whereby justice may be established, domestic tranquillity insured, and loyal citizens protected in all their rights of life, liberty, and property, I, Andrew Johnson, President of the United States and Commander in Chief of the Army and Navy of the United States, do hereby appoint Benjamin F. Perry, of South Carolina, provisional governor of the State of South Carolina, whose duty it shall be, at the earliest practicable period, to prescribe such rules and regulations as may be necessary and proper for convening a convention composed of delegates to be chosen by that portion of the people of said State who are loyal to the United States, and no others, for the purpose of altering or amending the constitution thereof, and with authority to exercise within the limits of said State all the powers necessary and proper to enable such loyal people of the State of South Carolina to restore said State to its constitutional relations to the Federal Government and to present such a republican form of State government as will entitle the State to the guaranty of the United States therefor and its people to protection by the United States against invasion, insurrection, and domestic violence: *Provided,* That in any election that may be hereafter held for choosing delegates to any State convention as aforesaid no person shall be qualified as an elector or shall be eligible as a member of such convention unless he shall have previously taken and subscribed the oath of amnesty as set forth in the President's proclamation of May 29, A.D. 1865, and is a voter qualified as prescribed by the constitution and laws of the State of South Carolina in force immediately before the 17th day of November, A.D. 1860, the date of the so-called ordinance of secession; and the said convention, when convened, or the legislature that may be thereafter assembled, will prescribe the qualification of electors and the eligibility of persons to hold office under the constitution and laws of the State—a power the people of the several States composing the Federal Union have rightfully exercised from the origin of the Government to the present time.

And I do hereby direct—

First. That the military commander of the department and all officers and persons in the military and naval service aid and assist the said provisional governor in carrying into effect this proclamation; and they are enjoined to abstain from in any way hindering, impeding, or discouraging the loyal people from the organization of a State government as herein authorized.

Second. That the Secretary of State proceed to put in force all laws of the United States the administration whereof belongs to the State Department applicable to the geographical limits aforesaid.

Third. That the Secretary of the Treasury proceed to nominate for appointment assessors of taxes and collectors of customs and internal revenue and such other officers of the Treasury Department as are authorized by law and put in execution the revenue laws of the United States within the geographical limits aforesaid. In making appointments the preference shall be given to qualified loyal persons residing within the districts where their respective duties are to be performed; but if suitable residents of the districts shall not be found, then persons residing in other States or districts shall be appointed.

Fourth. That the Postmaster-General proceed to establish post-offices and post routes and put into execution the postal laws of the United States within the said State, giving to loyal residents the preference of appointment; but if suitable residents are not found, then to appoint agents, etc., from other States.

Fifth. That the district judge for the judicial district in which South Carolina is included proceed to hold courts within said State in accordance with the provisions of the act of Congress. The Attorney-General will instruct the proper officers to libel and bring to judgment, confiscation, and sale property subject to confiscation and enforce the administration of justice within said State in all matters within the cognizance and jurisdiction of the Federal courts.

Sixth. That the Secretary of the Navy take possession of all public property belonging to the Navy Department within said geographical limits and put in operation all acts of Congress in relation to naval affairs having application to the said State.

Seventh. That the Secretary of the Interior put in force the laws relating to the Interior Department applicable to the geographical limits aforesaid.

Why We Must Have a Radical Reconstruction

THADDEUS STEVENS

It is obvious . . . that the first duty of Congress is to pass a law declaring the condition of these outside or defunct States, and providing proper civil governments for them. Since the conquest they have been governed by martial law. Military rule is necessarily despotic, and ought not to exist longer than is absolutely necessary. As there are no symptoms that the people of these provinces will be prepared to participate in constitutional government for some years, I know of no arrangement so proper for them as territorial governments. There they can learn the principles of freedom and eat the fruit

Congressional Globe, 39th Cong., 1st sess., December 18, 1865, pp. 72–75.

of foul rebellion. Under such governments, while electing members to the Territorial Legislatures, they will necessarily mingle with those to whom Congress shall extend the right of suffrage. In Territories Congress fixes the qualifications of electors; and I know of no better place nor better occasion for the conquered rebels and the conqueror to practice justice to all men, and accustom themselves to make and to obey equal laws.

As these fallen rebels cannot at their option reënter the heaven which they have disturbed, the garden of Eden which they have deserted, and flaming swords are set at the gates to secure their exclusion, it becomes important to the welfare of the nation to inquire when the doors shall be reopened for their admission.

According to my judgment they ought never to be recognized as capable of acting in the Union, or of being counted as valid States, until the Constitution shall have been so amended as to make it what its framers intended; and so as to secure perpetual ascendency to the party of the Union; and so as to render our republican Government firm and stable forever. The first of those amendments is to change the basis of representation among the States from Federal numbers to actual voters. Now all the colored freemen in the slave States, and three fifths of the slaves, are represented, though none of them have votes. The States have nineteen representatives of colored slaves. If the slaves are now free then they can add, for the other two fifths, thirteen more, making the slave representation thirty-two. I suppose the free blacks in those States will give at least five more, making the representation of non-voting people of color about thirty-seven. The whole number of representatives now from the slave States is seventy. Add the other two fifths and it will be eighty-three.

If the amendment prevails, and those States withhold the right of suffrage from persons of color, it will deduct about thirty-seven, leaving them but forty-six. With the basis unchanged, the eighty-three southern members, with the Democrats that will in the best times be elected from the North, will always give them a majority in Congress and in the Electoral College. They will at the very first election take possession of the White House and the halls of Congress. I need not depict the ruin that would follow. Assumption of the rebel debt or repudiation of the Federal debt would be sure to follow. The oppression of the freedmen; the reamendment of their State constitutions, and the reëstablishment of slavery would be the inevitable result. That they would scorn and disregard their present constitutions, forced upon them in the midst of martial law, would be both natural and just. No one who has any regard for freedom of elections can look upon those governments, forced upon them in duress, with any favor. If they should grant the right of suffrage to persons of color, I think there would always be Union white men enough in the South, aided by the blacks, to divide the representation, and thus continue the Republican ascendency. If they should refuse to thus alter their election laws it would reduce the representatives of the late slave States to about forty-five and render them powerless for evil.

It is plain that this amendment must be consummated before the defunct States are admitted to be capable of State action, or it never can be. . . .

But this is not all that we ought to do before these inveterate rebels are invited to participate in our legislation. We have turned, or are about to turn, loose four million slaves without a hut to shelter them or a cent in their pockets. The infernal laws of slavery have prevented them from acquiring an education, understanding the commonest laws of contract, or of managing the ordinary business of life. This Congress is bound to provide for them until they can take care of themselves. If we do not furnish them with homesteads, and hedge them around with protective laws; if we leave them to the legislation of their late masters, we had better have left them in bondage. Their condition would be worse than that of our prisoners at Andersonville. If we fail in this great duty now, when we have the power, we shall deserve and receive the execration of history and of all future ages. . . .

This Congress owes it to its own character to set the seal of reprobation upon a doctrine which is becoming too fashionable, and unless rebuked will be the recognized principle of our Government. Governor Perry[1] and other provisional governors and orators proclaim that "this is the white man's Government." The whole copperhead party, pandering to the lowest prejudices of the ignorant, repeat the cuckoo cry, "This is the white man's Government." Demagogues of all parties, even some high in authority, gravely shout, "This is the white man's Government." What is implied by this? That one race of men are to have the exclusive right forever to rule this nation, and to exercise all acts of sovereignty, while all other races and nations and colors are to be their subjects, and have no voice in making the laws and choosing the rulers by whom they are to be governed. Wherein does this differ from slavery except in degree? Does not this contradict all the distinctive principles of the Declaration of Independence? When the great and good men promulgated that instrument, and pledged their lives and sacred honors to defend it, it was supposed to form an epoch in civil government. Before that time it was held that the right to rule was vested in families, dynasties, or races, not because of superior intelligence or virtue, but because of a divine right to enjoy exclusive privileges.

Our fathers repudiated the whole doctrine of the legal superiority of families or races, and proclaimed the equality of men before the law. Upon that they created a revolution and built the Republic. They were prevented by slavery from perfecting the superstructure whose foundation they had thus broadly laid. For the sake of the Union they consented to wait, but never relinquished the idea of its final completion. The time to which they looked forward with anxiety has come. It is our duty to complete their work. If this Republic is not now made to stand on their great principles, it has no honest

[1] Benjamin F. Perry of South Carolina, a Unionist rewarded by Johnson with an appointment as provisional governor of the state—ED.

foundation, and the Father of all men will still shake it to its center. If we have not yet been sufficiently scourged for our national sin to teach us to do justice to all God's creatures, without distinction of race or color, we must expect the still more heavy vengeance of an offended Father, still increasing his inflictions as he increased the severity of the plagues of Egypt until the tyrant consented to do justice. And when that tyrant repented of his reluctant consent, and attempted to re-enslave the people, as our southern tyrants are attempting to do now, he filled the Red sea with broken chariots and drowned horses, and strewed the shores with dead carcasses.

Mr. Chairman, I trust the Republican party will not be alarmed at what I am saying. I do not profess to speak their sentiments, nor must they be held responsible for them. I speak for myself, and take the responsibility, and will settle with my intelligent constituents.

This is not a "white man's Government," in the exclusive sense in which it is used. To say so is political blasphemy, for it violates the fundamental principles of our gospel of liberty. This is man's Government; the Government of all men alike; not that all men will have equal power and sway within it. Accidental circumstances, natural and acquired endowment and ability, will vary their fortunes. But equal rights to all the privileges of the Government is innate in every immortal being, no matter what the shape or color of the tabernacle which it inhabits.

If equal privileges were granted to all, I should not expect any but white men to be elected to office for long ages to come. The prejudice engendered by slavery would not soon permit merit to be preferred to color. But it would still be beneficial to the weaker races. In a country where political divisions will always exist, their power, joined with just white men, would greatly modify, if it did not entirely prevent, the injustice of majorities. Without the right of suffrage in the late slave States, (I do not speak of the free States,) I believe the slaves had far better been left in bondage. I see it stated that very distinguished advocates of the right of suffrage lately declared in this city that they do not expect to obtain it by congressional legislation, but only by administrative action, because, as one gallant gentleman said, the States had not been out of the Union. Then they will never get it. The President is far sounder than they. He sees that administrative action has nothing to do with it. If it ever is to come, it must be constitutional amendments or congressional action in the Territories, and in enabling acts.

How shameful that men of influence should mislead and miseducate the public mind! They proclaim, "This is the white man's Government," and the whole coil of copperheads echo the same sentiment, and upstart, jealous Republicans join the cry. Is it any wonder ignorant foreigners and illiterate natives should learn this doctrine, and be led to despise and maltreat a whole race of their fellow-men?

Sir, this doctrine of a white man's Government is as atrocious as the infamous sentiment that damned the late Chief Justice [Roger Taney] to everlasting fame; and, I fear, to everlasting fire.

16.2:   The White South Responds
(1865, 1866, 1874)

White southerners were themselves divided over Reconstruction. In the immediate aftermath of Confederate surrender, many were too stunned to resist the North's dictation. But that mood did not last very long. In a matter of months many southern leaders, including former Confederate officials, had regained their composure and were preparing to salvage what they could from the shambles of defeat. Under the state governments reestablished under President Johnson's auspices, they resisted major changes in relations between the races and refused to express contrition at their section's secessionist past. When Thaddeus Stevens and his Radical allies in Congress imposed more stringent conditions, they fought back even harder.

The first selection below is an example of the Black Codes passed by the conservative southern state governments established under Johnson's 1865 proclamations. These state laws were designed to regularize legal relations between blacks and the dominant white society now that slavery was gone. They accepted the end of slavery, but in most cases they cast blacks as inferior beings, not full citizens, and even placed them in jeopardy of quasi-reenslavement.

Among the harshest of the state Black Codes was that of Mississippi, a state, like South Carolina, with a black majority in its population. What elements of this code implied recognition of the end of the slave system? What provisions suggest that white Mississippians were not willing to accord the freed men and women full equality? Can you see from this document why black leaders and Radical Republicans considered Johnson's Reconstruction policy too lenient?

A substantial minority of native-born white southerners for a time came to terms with the Radical state administrations imposed by Congress when it seized control of Reconstruction policy. Called "scalawags," these Republican voters were particularly numerous in the former nonslaveholding parts of the South and among businessmen of Whig antecedents. To scalawags, the enemy was often the former planter elite that had pulled the South into a disastrous war, not the Republican politicians in Washington. Joining with blacks, newly enfranchised under the Fourteenth and Fifteenth Amendments to the Constitution, and with "carpetbaggers"—northern whites who came South to make their fortunes after 1865—they won control for a time over the state governments established under the Reconstruction Acts.

The second document is by a scalawag. James W. Hunnicutt was a

South Carolina Baptist minister who had originally supported secession and then changed his mind. The selection is his testimony before the congressional Joint Committee on Reconstruction in early 1866. Why does Hunnicutt emphasize the treatment of white unionists in the South? Do you feel that the questioner, Radical Republican Senator Jacob Howard of Michigan, is leading the witness?

The third item in this section represents the position of the "redeemers," the ardent white conservatives who fought to wrest political supremacy from the Radical Republicans who controlled the state Reconstruction governments.

An editorial from the Atlanta News *of September 10, 1874, it charges the Republicans and blacks with barbarism. Were the charges valid? Do you know if the Radical regimes in the South were more corrupt, wasteful, and incompetent than state governments elsewhere during this era? Were the charges based more on race prejudice than on reality? How do you explain the vitriol of the conservative southern attack on the Radical regimes?*

Mississippi Black Code

MISSISSIPPI LEGISLATURE

1. Civil Rights of Freedmen in Mississippi

Sec. 1. *Be it enacted,* . . . That all freedmen, free negroes, and mulattoes may sue and be sued, implead and be impleaded, in all the courts of law and equity of this State, and may acquire personal property, and choses [sic] in action, by descent or purchase, and may dispose of the same in the same manner and to the same extent that white persons may: *Provided,* That the provisions of this section shall not be so construed as to allow any freedman, free negro, or mulatto to rent or lease any lands or tenements except in incorporated cities or towns, in which places the corporate authorities shall control the same. . . .

Sec. 3. . . . All freedmen, free negroes, or mulattoes who do now and have herebefore lived and cohabited together as husband and wife shall be taken and held in law as legally married, and the issue shall be taken and held as legitimate for all purposes; that it shall not be lawful for any freedman, free negro, or mulatto to intermarry with any white person; nor for any white person to intermarry with any freedman, free negro, or mulatto; and any person who shall so intermarry, shall be deemed guilty of felony, and on

Laws of the State of Mississippi Passed at the Regular Session of the Mississippi Legislature, Held in the City of Jackson, October–December, 1865 (Jackson: J. J. Shannon and Company, 1866), pp. 82–93.

conviction thereof shall be confined in the State penitentiary for life; and those shall be deemed freedmen, free negroes, and mulattoes who are of pure negro blood, and those descended from a negro to the third generation, inclusive, though one ancestor in each generation may have been a white person.

Sec. 4. . . . In addition to cases in which freedmen, free negroes, and mulattoes are now by law competent witnesses, freedmen, free negroes, or mulattoes shall be competent in civil cases, when a party or parties to the suit, either plaintiff or plaintiffs, defendant or defendants, and a white person or white persons, is or are the opposing party or parties, plaintiff or plaintiffs, defendant or defendants. They shall also be competent witnesses in all criminal prosecutions where the crime charged is alleged to have been committed by a white person upon or against the person or property of a freedman, free negro, or mulatto: *Provided,* that in all cases said witnesses shall be examined in open court, on the stand; except, however, they may be examined before the grand jury, and shall in all cases be subject to the rules and tests of the common law as to competency and credibility. . . .

Sec. 6. . . . All contracts for labor made with freedmen, free negroes, and mulattoes for a longer period than one month shall be in writing, and in duplicate, attested and read to said freedman, free negro, or mulatto by a beat, city or county officer, or two disinterested white persons of the county in which the labor is to be performed, of which each party shall have one; and said contracts shall be taken and held as entire contracts, and if the laborer shall quit the service of the employer before the expiration of his term of service, without good cause, he shall forfeit his wages for that year up to the time of quitting.

Sec. 7. . . . Every civil officer shall, and every person may, arrest and carry back to his or her legal employer any freedman, free negro, or mulatto who shall have quit the service of his or her employer before the expiration of his or her term of service without good cause; and said officer and person shall be entitled to receive for arresting and carrying back every deserting employe aforesaid the sum of five dollars, and ten cents per mile from the place of arrest to the place of delivery; and the same shall be paid by the employer, and held as a set-off for so much against the wages of said deserting employe: *Provided,* that said arrested party, after being so returned, may appeal to the justice of the peace or member of the board of police of the county, who, on notice to the alleged employer, shall try summarily whether said appellant is legally employed by the alleged employer, and has good cause to quit said employer; either party shall have the right of appeal to the county court, pending which the alleged deserter shall be remanded to the alleged employer or otherwise disposed of, as shall be right and just; and the decision of the county court shall be final. . . .

Sec. 9. . . . If any person shall persuade or attempt to persuade, entice, or cause any freedman, free negro, or mulatto to desert from the legal employment of any person before the expiration of his or her term of service, or shall knowingly employ any such deserting freedman, free negro, or mulatto, or shall knowingly give or sell to any such deserting freedman, free negro, or mulatto, any food, raiment, or other thing, he or she shall be guilty of a misdemeanor, and, upon conviction, shall be fined not less than twenty-five dollars and not more than two hundred dollars and the costs; and if said fine and costs shall not be immediately paid, the court shall sentence said convict to not exceeding two months' imprisonment in the county jail, and he or she shall moreover be liable to the party injured in damages: *Provided,* if any person shall, or shall attempt to, persuade, entice, or cause any freedman, free negro, or mulatto to desert from any legal employment of any person, with the view to employ said freedman, free negro, or mulatto without the limits of this State, such person, on conviction, shall be fined not less than fifty dollars, and not more than five hundred dollars and costs; and if said fine and costs shall not be immediately paid, the court shall sentence said convict to not exceeding six months imprisonment in the county jail. . . .

2. Mississippi Apprentice Law

Sec. 1. . . . It shall be the duty of all sheriffs, justices of the peace, and other civil officers of the several counties in this State, to report to the probate courts of their respective counties semi-annually, at the January and July terms of said courts, all freedmen, free negroes, and mulattoes, under the age of eighteen, in their respective counties, beats or districts, who are orphans, or whose parent or parents have not the means or who refuse to provide for and support said minors; and thereupon it shall be the duty of said probate court to order the clerk of said court to apprentice said minors to some competent and suitable person, on such terms as the court may direct, having a particular care to the interest of said minor: *Provided,* that the former owner of said minors shall have the preference when, in the opinion of the court, he or she shall be a suitable person for that purpose.

Sec. 2. . . . The said court shall be fully satisfied that the person or persons to whom said minor shall be apprenticed shall be a suitable person to have the charge and care of said minor, and fully to protect the interest of said minor. The said court shall require the said master or mistress to execute bond and security, payable to the State of Mississippi, conditioned that he or she shall furnish said minor with sufficient food and clothing; to treat said minor humanely; furnish medical attention in case of sickness; teach, or cause to be taught, him or her to read and write, if under fifteen years old, and will conform to any law that may be hereafter passed for the regulation of the duties and relation of master and apprentice. . . .

Sec. 3. . . . In the management and control of said apprentice, said master or mistress shall have the power to inflict such moderate corporal chastisement as a father or guardian is allowed to inflict on his or her child or ward at common law: *Provided,* that in no case shall cruel or inhuman punishment be inflicted

Sec. 4. . . . If any apprentice shall leave the employment of his or her master or mistress, without his or her consent, said master or mistress may pursue and recapture said apprentice, and bring him or her before any justice of the peace of the county, whose duty it shall be to remand said apprentice to the service of his or her master or mistress; and in the event of a refusal on the part of said apprentice so to return, then said justice shall commit said apprentice to the jail of said county, on failure to give bond, to the next term of the county court; and it shall be the duty of said court at the first term thereafter to investigate said case, and if the court shall be of opinion that said apprentice left the employment of his or her master or mistress without good cause, to order him or her to be punished, as provided for the punishment of hired freedmen, as may be from time to time provided for by law for desertion, until he or she shall agree to return to the service of his or her master or mistress: . . . if the court shall believe that said apprentice had good cause to quit his said master or mistress, the court shall discharge said apprentice from said indenture, and also enter a judgment against the master or mistress for not more than one hundred dollars, for the use and benefit of said apprentice. . . .

3. Mississippi Vagrant Law

Sec. 1. *Be it enacted,* etc., . . . That all rogues and vagabonds, idle and dissipated persons, beggars, jugglers, or persons practicing unlawful games or plays, runaways, common drunkards, common night-walkers, pilferers, lewd, wanton, or lascivious persons, in speech or behavior, common railers and brawlers, persons who neglect their calling or employment, misspend what they earn, or do not provide for the support of themselves or their families, or dependents, and all other idle and disorderly persons, including all who neglect all lawful business, habitually misspend their time by frequenting houses of ill-fame, gaming-houses, or tippling shops, shall be deemed and considered vagrants, under the provisions of this act, and upon conviction thereof shall be fined not exceeding one hundred dollars, with all accruing costs, and be imprisoned at the discretion of the court, not exceeding ten days.

Sec. 2. . . . All freedmen, free negroes and mulattoes in this State, over the age of eighteen years, found on the second Monday in January, 1866, or thereafter, with no lawful employment or business, or found unlawfully assembling themselves together, either in the day or night time, and all white persons so assembling themselves with freedmen, free negroes or mulattoes, or usually associating with freedmen, free negroes or mulattoes, on terms of equality, or living in adultery or fornication with a freed woman, free negro or mulatto, shall be deemed vagrants, and on conviction thereof shall be fined in a sum not exceeding, in the case of a freedman, free negro or mulatto, fifty dollars, and a white man two hundred dollars, and imprisoned at the discretion of the court, the free negro not exceeding ten days, and the white man not exceeding six months. . . .

Sec. 7. . . . If any freedman, free negro, or mulatto shall fail or refuse to pay any tax levied according to the provisions of the sixth section of this act, it shall be *prima facie* evidence of vagrancy, and it shall be the duty of the sheriff to arrest such freedman, free negro, or mulatto or such person refusing or neglecting to pay such tax, and proceed at once to hire for the shortest time such delinquent tax-payer to any one who will pay the said tax, with accruing costs, giving preference to the employer, if there be one. . . .

4. Penal Laws of Mississippi

Sec. 1. *Be it enacted,* . . . That no freedman, free negro or mulatto, not in the military service of the United States government, and not licensed so to do by the board of police of his or her county, shall keep or carry fire-arms of any kind, or any ammunition, dirk or bowie knife, and on conviction thereof in the county court shall be punished by fine, not exceeding ten dollars, and pay the costs of such proceedings, and all such arms or ammunition shall be forfeited to the informer; and it shall be the duty of every civil and military officer to arrest any freedman, free negro, or mulatto found with any such arms or ammunition, and cause him or her to be committed to trial in default of bail.

[Sec.] 2. . . . Any freedman, free negro, or mulatto committing riots, routs, affrays, trespasses, malicious mischief, cruel treatment to animals, seditious speeches, insulting gestures, language, or acts, or assaults on any person, disturbance of the peace, exercising the function of a minister of the Gospel without a license from some regularly organized church, vending spirituous or intoxicating liquors, or committing any other misdemeanor, the punishment of which is not specifically provided for by law, shall, upon conviction thereof in the county court, be fined not less than ten dollars, and not more than one hundred dollars, and may be imprisoned at the discretion of the court, not exceeding thirty days.

Sec. 3. . . . If any white person shall sell, lend, or give to any freedman, free negro, or mulatto any fire-arms, dirk or bowie knife, or ammunition, or any spirituous or intoxicating liquors, such person or persons so offending, upon conviction thereof in the county court of his or her county, shall be fined not exceeding fifty dollars, and may be imprisoned, at the discretion of the court, not exceeding thirty days. . . .

Sec. 5. . . . If any freedman, free negro, or mulatto, convicted of any of the misdemeanors provided against in this act, shall fail or refuse for the space of five days, after conviction, to pay the fine and costs imposed, such person shall be hired out by the sheriff or other officer, at public outcry, to any white person who will pay said fine and all costs, and take said convict for the shortest time.

Johnson's Policies Criticized

JAMES W. HUNNICUTT

Mr. [Jacob] Howard: What is the effect of President Johnson's policy of reconstruction there? [South Carolina]—*A.:* . . . They are all in favor of President Johnson's policy of reconstruction. As soon as they get their ends served by him they would not touch him, but he is their man now. They say that in 1868 the South will be a unit, and that with the help of the copperhead party of the North they will elect a President. They do not care to have slavery back, but they will try and make the federal government pay them for their slaves. A man from Virginia told me today that they would be paid for their Negroes. This gentleman lost forty Negroes. This is their idea; they do not want slavery back, but they want to be paid for their slaves. They say that unless you accept their debt they will repudiate yours. They say they are not interested in this government.

Q.: They would be glad to have Uncle Sam assume the payment of the Confederate debt?—*A.:* Yes, sir, and to pay them for their Negroes and to indemnify them for their loss of property in the war. It is an impression of most of them, men, women, and children, that they are going to be paid for every rail burned, for every stick of timber destroyed, and for every Negro lost. One man told me in my house that as soon as they could get the reins of government in their hands they would undo everything that this administration has done, with an awful adjective prefixed to the word "administration." He said, "We have as much right to undo what the administration has done as they have to destroy the government of the Constitution"—as they claim the administration has done.

Q.: They propose to get back into the Union for the purpose of restoring the Constitution?—*A.:* Yes, sir; and the testimony of the Negroes will not be worth a snap of your finger, and all this is done for policy. A Negro can come and give his testimony, and it passes for what it is worth with the courts. They can do what they please with it; there are the judges, the lawyers, and the jury against the Negro, and perhaps every one of them is sniggering and laughing while the Negro is giving his testimony.

Q.: Has not the liberal policy of President Johnson in granting pardons and amnesties rather tended to soothe and allay their feelings towards the government of the United States?—*A.:* No, sir, not towards the government of the United States nor towards the Union men.

Q.: What effect has it had in that respect?—*A.:* It has made them more impudent. They were once humble and felt that they had done wrong, but this policy has emboldened them, and they are more impudent today, more

Report of the Joint Committee on Reconstruction, (Washington, D.C.: Government Printing Office, 1866) pt. 2, pp. 150–51.

intolerant, and more proscriptive than they were in 1864. They say that we are the traitors and went over to the damned Yankees. Our present mayor [of Fredericksburg] Slaughter, had sixty men of Grant's army, who were wounded in the wilderness and sent to Fredericksburg, forwarded to General [Robert E.] Lee as prisoners-of-war. When Fredericksburg fell into our hands Slaughter made his escape. The federals arrested sixty citizens of Fredericksburg to be held as hostages for these sixty soldiers whom Slaughter had sent to the enemy, and among them was my wife's brother, who was living in Fredericksburg, and yet that same Slaughter was reelected mayor of Fredericksburg last summer after the collapse of the rebellion. Old Tom Barton, the commonwealth's attorney, said in 1861 (and I suppose his feelings are the same still) that all these Union shriekers ought to be hung as high as Haman, and this old man was reelected commonwealth attorney by the people of the county. Every member of the rebel common council was reelected. One of the men who were elected members of the common council from that district stated that none of the Union men who went over to the Yankees during the war should be allowed to return to Fredericksburg; he was also appointed director of a bank there. These are the men we have got over us, and what kind of justice can we expect in the courts?

Q.: You will probably get pretty summary justice?—*A.:* I think so; these are facts.

Q.: Where is Slaughter now?—*A.:* He is now mayor of Fredericksburg and will be reelected next month; we need not run a Union man there; we are disfranchised.

Q.: Is not Slaughter a good Union man?—*A.:* Oh! He has been notoriously Union all the time, as the papers say—notoriously Union! I saw that stated in a Fredericksburg paper; it stated that they had been persecuting Mayor Slaughter, who had been notoriously Union all the time.

Q.: You have not a great deal of confidence in the truthfulness of secession?—*A.:* No, sir; I have not.

Q.: Where their political standing is concerned?—*A.:* I used to have some confidence, not in secession, but in the people; but it seems to me that their whole nature and character has been changed, and that when treason enters a man's heart, every virtue he has departs.

Q.: Could Jefferson Davis be convicted of treason in that part of Virginia?—*A.:* As I went home last Sunday week in the boat, I was in company with a delegation from the Virginia legislature which waited upon President Johnson, and I heard one of them say that there could not be a jury obtained south of the Potomac who would convict Jeff Davis, and that the man who would write down there that Jeff Davis should be punished would be in danger. Jeff Davis cannot be punished down there, and they would elect Lee tomorrow, if there were no difficulty in the way, governor of Virginia. There is no question about that in my mind.

Q.: Do you think of anything that you wish to relate?—*A.:* No, sir; I simply wish to state that I make these remarks conscientiously. I was born and raised in the South; my interests of every kind, social, financial, religious and political, are in the South; my church is in the South, and I am going soon to Richmond to edit a paper. Nothing but the good of the country, my own safety, and the safety of my children, and of Union men and of freedmen, could have induced me to come before you and make this statement. I am a friend of the South. I have written for the South, and I shall write in behalf of the South, but the South is one thing, and traitors and treason in the South are different things.

White People Must Regain Control of Their States

EDITOR, *ATLANTA NEWS*

Let there be White Leagues formed in every town, village and hamlet of the South, and let us organize for the great struggle which seems inevitable. If the October elections which are to be held at the North are favorable to the radicals, the time will have arrived for us to prepare for the very worst. The radicalism of the republican party must be met by the radicalism of white men. We have no war to make against the United States Government, but against the republican party our hate must be unquenchable, our war interminable and merciless. Fast fleeting away is the day of wordy protests and idle appeals to the magnanimity of the republican party. By brute force they are endeavoring to force us into acquiescence to their hideous programme. We have submitted long enough to indignities, and it is time to meet brute-force with brute-force. Every Southern State should swarm with White Leagues, and we should stand ready to act the moment [President Ulysses S.] Grant signs the civil-rights bill.[1] It will not do to wait till radicalism has fettered us to the car of social equality before we make an effort to resist it. The signing of the bill will be a declaration of war against the southern whites. It is our duty to ourselves, it is our duty to our children, it is our duty to the white race whose prowess subdued the wilderness of this continent, whose civilization filled it with cities and towns and villages, whose mind gave it power and grandeur, and whose labor imparted to it prosperity, and whose love made peace and happiness dwell within its homes, to take the gage of battle the moment it is thrown down. If the white democrats of the North are men, they will not stand idly by and see us borne down by northern radicals and half-barbarous negroes. But no matter what they may do, it is time for us to organize. We have been temporizing long enough. Let northern

Walter L. Fleming, ed., *Documentary History of Reconstruction: Political, Military, and Industrial, 1865 to the Present Time* (Cleveland: The Arthur H. Clark Company, 1907), vol. 2, pp. 387–88.
[1] A bill proposed by Charles Sumner in 1870–71 that sought to guarantee blacks non-segregated, equal access to all public accommodations—ED.

radicals understand that military supervision of southern elections and the civil-rights bill mean war, that war means bloodshed, and that we are terribly in earnest, and even they, fanatical as they are, may retrace their steps before it is too late.

16.3: The Black Response (1865, 1868, 1866)

Emancipation and Union victory liberated almost 4 million black Americans from bondage. What role would they now play in the life of their region? Would they be citizens and voters? How would they earn a living? What claim did they have on their communities for education and other services? These and other questions confronted northern policy makers and voters after Confederate defeat.

To educated blacks, many of them former "free people of color," the most important right that the government could confer was that of suffrage, the right to vote. In the first selection below, Frederick Douglass, the prominent black abolitionist, argues for the necessity of giving the vote to the newly freed slaves. What are Douglass's arguments? This address was greeted with applause by his audience, but he was speaking to a Boston abolitionist convention. How do you think white southerners felt about suffrage for blacks? Do you know how most white northerners felt about giving black men the vote at this time—Douglass's Boston audience notwithstanding? Note Douglass's reference to woman suffrage. Why does he believe black males should be given the vote before white women?

The second selection is an excerpt from a debate at the 1868 South Carolina constitutional convention, which was called after Congress refused to accept the state's "Johnson government" and established stricter rules for southern readmission to the Union.

One of the many topics the convention delegates debated was land ownership. If conservative southern whites sought to reestablish a system of near slavery, blacks and some of their Radical defenders wanted what seemed to many contemporaries to be the other extreme: to create a black farm-owner class by redistributing white-owned land. The participants in the selection below are Richard H. Cain, a black minister originally from New York; Francis L. Cardozo, a South Carolinian of mixed race, also a minister; and N. G. Parker and C. P. Leslie, white carpetbaggers. Their debate focuses on a resolution asking the federal Congress to appropriate $1 million to be used to buy small homesteads for South Carolina freed men and women. What are the arguments pro and con? What is the reference to "confiscation"? Congress never made the appropriation.

Can you guess why from the evidence in this debate? What would have been the advantage to the nation at large if ideas such as Cardozo's and Cain's had been enacted?

The third selection adds education to the "wish list" of Southern blacks during Reconstruction. Why were they so eager for education? Did they have access to education in slave days? Was their faith in education as salvation part of the American tradition? Was it misguided or exaggerated?

What the Black Man Wants

FREDERICK DOUGLASS

MR. PRESIDENT,—I came here [to the annual meeting of the Massachusetts Anti-Slavery Society at Boston], as I come always to the meetings in New England, as a listener, and not as a speaker; and one of the reasons why I have not been more frequently to the meetings of this society, has been because of the disposition on the part of some of my friends to call me out upon the platform, even when they knew that there was some difference of opinion and of feeling between those who rightfully belong to this platform and myself; and for fear of being misconstrued, as desiring to interrupt or disturb the proceedings of these meetings, I have usually kept away, and have thus been deprived of that educating influence, which I am always free to confess is of the highest order, descending from this platform. I have felt, since I have lived out West, that in going there I parted from a great deal that was valuable; and I feel, every time I come to these meetings, that I have lost a great deal by making my home west of Boston, west of Massachusetts; for, if anywhere in the country there is to be found the highest sense of justice, or the truest demands for my race, I look for it in the East, I look for it here. The ablest discussions of the whole question of our rights occur here, and to be deprived of the privilege of listening to those discussions is a great deprivation.

I do not know, from what has been said, that there is any difference of opinion as to the duty of abolitionists, at the present moment. How can we get up any difference at this point, or at any point, where we are so united, so agreed? I went especially, however, with that word of Mr. [Wendell] Phillips, which is the criticism of Gen. Banks and Gen. Banks's policy. I hold that that policy is our chief danger at the present moment; that it practically enslaves the negro, and makes the [Emancipation] Proclamation of 1863 a mockery and delusion. What is freedom? It is the right to choose one's own employment. Certainly it means that, if it means any thing; and when any individual or combination of individuals, undertakes to decide for any man

William D. Kelley, Wendell Phillips, and Frederick Douglass, *The Equality of Men before the Law Claimed and Defended* (Boston: n.p., 1865), pp. 36–39.

when he shall work, where he shall work, at what he shall work, and for what he shall work, he or they practically reduce him to slavery. (Applause.) He is a slave. That I understand Gen. Banks to do—to determine for the so-called freedman, when, and where, and at what, and for how much he shall work, when he shall be punished, and by whom punished. It is absolute slavery. It defeats the beneficent intentions of the Government, if it has beneficent intentions, in regard to the freedom of our people.

I have had but one idea for the last three years, to present to the American people, and the phraseology in which I clothe it is the old abolition phraseology. I am for the "immediate, unconditional, and universal" enfranchisement of the black man, in every State in the Union. (Loud applause.) Without this, his liberty is a mockery; without this, you might as well almost retain the old name of slavery for his condition; for, in fact, if he is not the slave of the individual master, he is the slave of society, and holds his liberty as a privilege, not as a right. He is at the mercy of the mob, and has no means of protecting himself.

It may be objected, however, that this pressing of the negro's right to suffrage is premature. Let us have slavery abolished, it may be said, let us have labor organized, and then, in the natural course of events, the right of suffrage will be extended to the negro. I do not agree with this. The constitution of the human mind is such, that if it once disregards the conviction forced upon it by a revelation of truth, it requires the exercise of a higher power to produce the same conviction afterwards. The American people are now in tears. The Shenandoah has run blood—the best blood of the North. All around Richmond, the blood of New England and of the North has been shed—of your sons, your brothers and your fathers. We all feel, in the existence of this Rebellion, that judgments terrible, wide-spread, far-reaching, overwhelming, are abroad in the land; and we feel, in view of these judgments, just now, a disposition to learn righteousness. This is the hour. Our streets are in mourning, tears are falling at every fireside, and under the chastisement of this Rebellion we have almost come up to the point of conceding this great, this all-important right of suffrage. I fear that if we fail to do it now, if abolitionists fail to press it now, we may not see, for centuries to come, the same disposition that exists at this moment. (Applause.) Hence, I say, now is the time to press this right.

It may be asked, "Why do you want it? Some men have got along very well without it. Women have not this right." Shall we justify one wrong by another? That is a sufficient answer. Shall we at this moment justify the deprivation of the negro of the right to vote, because some one else is deprived of that privilege? I hold that women, as well as men, have the right to vote (applause), and my heart and my voice go with the movement to extend suffrage to woman; but that question rests upon another basis than that on which our right rests. We may be asked, I say, why we want it. I will tell you why we want it. We want it because it is our *right*, first of all. (Applause.) No class of men can, without insulting their own nature, be content with any deprivation of their rights. We want it, again, as a means for educating our race. Men are so constituted that they derive their conviction of their own possibilities largely from the estimate formed of them by others. If nothing is expected of a people, that people will find it difficult to contradict that expectation. By depriving us of suffrage, you affirm our incapacity to form an intelligent judgment respecting public men and public measures; you declare before the world that we are unfit to exercise the elective franchise, and by this means lead us to undervalue ourselves, to put a low estimate upon ourselves, and to feel that we have no possibilities like other men. Again, I want the elective franchise, for one, as a colored man, because ours is a peculiar government, based upon a peculiar idea, and that idea is universal suffrage. If I were in a monarchical government, or an autocratic or aristocratic government, where the few bore rule and the many were subject, there would be no special stigma resting upon me, because I did not exercise the elective franchise. It would do me no great violence. Mingling with the mass, I should partake of the strength of the mass; I should be supported by the mass, and I should have the same incentives to endeavor with the mass of my fellow-men; it would be no particular burden, no particular deprivation; but here, where universal suffrage is the rule, where that is the fundamental idea of the Government, to rule us out is to make us an exception, to brand us with the stigma of inferiority, and to invite to our heads the missiles of those about us; therefore, I want the franchise for the black man.

There are, however, other reasons, not derived from any consideration merely of our rights, but arising out of the condition of the South, and of the country—considerations which have already been referred to by Mr. Phillips—considerations which must arrest the attention of statesmen. I believe that when the tall heads of this Rebellion shall have been swept down, as they will be swept down, when the [Jefferson] Davises and [Robert] Toombses and [Alexander] Stephenses, and others who are leading in this Rebellion shall have been blotted out, there will be this rank undergrowth of treason, to which reference has been made, growing up there, and interfering with, and thwarting the quiet operation of the Federal Government in those States. You will see those traitors handing down, from sire to son, the same malignant spirit which they have manifested, and which they are now exhibiting, with malicious hearts, broad blades, and bloody hands in the field, against our sons and brothers. That spirit will still remain; and whoever sees the Federal Government extended over those Southern States will see that Government in a strange land, and not only in a strange land, but in an enemy's land. A post-master of the United States in the South will find himself surrounded by a hostile spirit; a collector in a Southern port will find himself surrounded by a hostile spirit; a United States marshal or United States judge will be surrounded there by a hostile element. That enmity will not die out in a year, will not die out in an age. The Federal Government will be looked upon in those States precisely as the Governments of Austria and France are looked upon in Italy at the present moment. They will endeavor to circumvent, they will endeavor to destroy, the peaceful operation of this

Government. Now, where will you find the strength to counterbalance this spirit, if you do not find it in the negroes of the South? They are your friends, and have always been your friends. They were your friends even when the Government did not regard them as such. They comprehended the genius of this war before you did. It is a significant fact, it is a marvellous fact, it seems almost to imply a direct interposition of Providence, that this war, which began in the interest of slavery on both sides, bids fair to end in the interest of liberty on both sides. (Applause.) It was begun, I say, in the interest of slavery on both sides. The South was fighting to take slavery out of the Union, and the North fighting to keep it in the Union; the South fighting to get it beyond the limits of the United-States Constitution, and the North fighting to retain it within those limits; the South fighting for new guarantees, and the North fighting for the old guarantees;—both despising the negro, both insulting the negro. Yet, the negro, apparently endowed with wisdom from on high, saw more clearly the end from the beginning than we did. When [William] Seward said the status of no man in the country would be changed by the war, the negro did not believe him. (Applause.) When our generals sent their underlings in shoulder-straps to hunt the flying negro back from our lines into the jaws of slavery, from which he had escaped, the negroes thought that a mistake had been made, and that the intentions of the Government had not been rightly understood by our officers in shoulder-straps, and they continued to come into our lines, threading their way through bogs and fens, over briers and thorns, fording streams, swimming rivers, bringing us tidings as to the safe path to march, and pointing out the dangers that threatened us. They are our only friends in the South, and we should be true to them in this their trial hour, and see to it that they have the elective franchise.

I know that we are inferior to you in some things—virtually inferior. We walk about among you like dwarfs among giants. Our heads are scarcely seen above the great sea of humanity. The Germans are superior to us; the Irish are superior to us; the Yankees are superior to us (laughter); they can do what we cannot, that is, what we have not hitherto been allowed to do. But while I make this admission, I utterly deny that we are originally, or naturally, or practically, or in any way, or in any important sense, inferior to anybody on this globe. (Loud applause.) This charge of inferiority is an old dodge. It has been made available for oppression on many occasions. It is only about six centuries since the blue-eyed and fair-haired Anglo-Saxons were considered inferior by the haughty Normans, who once trampled upon them. If you read the history of the Norman Conquest, you will find that this proud Anglo-Saxon was once looked upon as of coarser clay than his Norman master, and might be found in the highways and byways of old England laboring with a brass collar on his neck, and the name of his master marked upon it. *You* were down then! (Laughter and applause.) You are up now. I am glad you are up, and I want you to be glad to help us up also. (Applause.)

The story of our inferiority is an old dodge, as I have said; for wherever men oppress their fellows, wherever they enslave them, they will endeavor to find the needed apology for such enslavement and oppression in the character of the people oppressed and enslaved. When we wanted, a few years ago, a slice of Mexico, it was hinted that the Mexicans were an inferior race, that the old Castilian blood had become so weak that it would scarcely run down hill, and that Mexico needed the long, strong and beneficent arm of the Anglo-Saxon care extended over it. We said that it was necessary to its salvation, and a part of the "manifest destiny" of this Republic, to extend our arm over that dilapidated government. So, too, when Russia wanted to take possession of a part of the Ottoman Empire, the Turks were "an inferior race." So, too, when England wants to set the heel of her power more firmly in the quivering heart of old Ireland, the Celts are an "inferior race." So, too, the negro, when he is to be robbed of any right which is justly his, is an "inferior man." It is said that we are ignorant; I admit it. But if we know enough to be hung, we know enough to vote. If the negro knows enough to pay taxes to support the government, he knows enough to vote; taxation and representation should go together. If he knows enough to shoulder a musket and fight for the flag, fight for the government, he knows enough to vote. If he knows as much when he is sober as an Irishman knows when drunk, he knows enough to vote, on good American principles. (Laughter and applause.)

But I was saying that you needed a counterpoise in the persons of the slaves to the enmity that would exist at the South after the Rebellion is put down. I hold that the American people are bound, not only in self-defence, to extend this right to the freedmen of the South, but they are bound by their love of country, and by all their regard for the future safety of those Southern States, to do this—to do it as a measure essential to the preservation of peace there. But I will not dwell upon this. I put it to the American sense of honor. The honor of a nation is an important thing. It is said in the Scriptures, "What doth it profit a man if he gain the whole world and lose his own soul?" It may be said, also, What doth it profit a nation if it gain the whole world, but lose its honor? I hold that the American government has taken upon itself a solemn obligation of honor, to see that this war—let it be long or let it be short, let it cost much or let it cost little—that this war shall not cease until every freedman at the South has the right to vote. (Applause.) It has bound itself to it. What have you asked the black men of the South, the black men of the whole country, to do? Why, you have asked them to incur the deadly enmity of their masters, in order to befriend you and to befriend this Government. You have asked us to call down, not only upon ourselves, but upon our children's children, the deadly hate of the entire Southern people. You have called upon us to turn our backs upon our masters, to abandon their cause and espouse yours; to turn against the South and in favor of the North; to shoot down the Confederacy and uphold the flag—the American flag. You have called upon us to expose ourselves to all the subtle machinations of their malignity for all time. And now, what do you propose to do when you come to make peace? To reward your enemies, and trample in the dust your friends? Do you intend to sacrifice the very men who have come to the rescue of your banner in the South, and incurred the lasting displeasure of their masters thereby? Do you intend to sacrifice them and reward your enemies? Do you mean to give your enemies the right to vote, and take it away from your friends? Is that wise policy? Is that honorable? Could American honor withstand such a blow? I do not believe you will do it. I think you will see to it that we have the right to vote. There is something too mean in looking upon the negro, when you are in trouble, as a citizen, and when you are free from trouble, as an alien. When this nation was in trouble, in its early struggles, it looked upon the negro as a citizen. In 1776 he was a citizen. At the time of the formation of the Constitution the negro had the right to vote in eleven States out of the old thirteen. In your trouble you have made us citizens. In 1812 Gen. [Andrew] Jackson addressed us as citizens—"fellow-citizens." He wanted us to fight. We were citizens then! And now, when you come to frame a conscription bill, the negro is a citizen again. He has been a citizen just three times in the history of this government, and it has always been in time of trouble. In time of trouble we are citizens. Shall we be citizens in war, and aliens in peace? Would that be just?

I ask my friends who are apologizing for not insisting upon this right, where can the black man look, in this country, for the assertion of this right, if he may not look to the Massachusetts Anti-Slavery Society? Where under the whole heavens can he look for sympathy, in asserting this right, if he may not look to this platform? Have you lifted us up to a certain height to see that we are men, and then are any disposed to leave us there, without seeing that we are put in possession of all our rights? We look naturally to this platform for the assertion of all our rights, and for this one especially. I understand the anti-slavery societies of this country to be based on two principles,—first, the freedom of the blacks of this country; and, second, the elevation of them. Let me not be misunderstood here. I am not asking for sympathy at the hands of abolitionists, sympathy at the hands of any. I think the American people are disposed often to be generous rather than just. I look over this country at the present time, and I see Educational Societies, Sanitary Commissions, Freedmen's Associations, and the like,—all very good: but in regard to the colored people there is always more that is benevolent, I perceive, than just, manifested towards us. What I ask for the negro is not benevolence, not pity, not sympathy, but simply *justice*. (Applause.) The American people have always been anxious to know what they shall do with us. Gen. Banks was distressed with solicitude as to what he should do with the negro. Everybody has asked the question, and they learned to ask it early of the abolitionists, "What shall we do with the negro?" I have had but one answer from the beginning. Do nothing with us! Your doing with us has already played the mischief with us. Do nothing with us! If the apples will not remain on the tree of their own strength, if they are worm-eaten at the core, if they are early ripe and disposed to fall, let them fall! I am not for tying or fastening them on the tree in any way, except by nature's plan, and if they will not stay there, let them fall. And if the negro cannot stand on his own legs, let him fall also. All I ask is, give him a chance to stand on his own legs! Let him alone! If you see him on his way to school, let him alone,—don't disturb him! If you see him going to the dinner-table at a hotel, let him go! If you see him going to the ballot-box, let him alone,—don't disturb him! (Applause.) If you see him going into a work-shop, just let him alone,—your interference is doing him a positive injury. Gen. Banks's "preparation" is of a piece with this attempt to prop up the negro. Let him fall if he cannot stand alone! If the negro cannot live by the line of eternal justice, so beautifully pictured to you in the illustration used by Mr. Phillips, the fault will not be yours, it will be his who made the negro, and established that line for his government. (Applause.) Let him live or die by that. If you will only untie his hands, and give him a chance, I think he will live. He will work as readily for himself as the white man. A great many delusions have been swept away by this war. One was, that the negro would not work; he has proved his ability to work. Another was, that the negro would not fight; that he possessed only the most sheepish attributes of humanity; was a perfect lamb, or an "Uncle Tom;" disposed to take off his coat whenever required, fold his hands, and be whipped by anybody who wanted to whip him. But the war has proved that there is a great deal of human nature in the negro, and that "he will fight," as Mr. Quincy, our President, said, in earlier days than these, "when there is a reasonable probability of his whipping anybody." (Laughter and applause.)

The Ex-Slaves Should Have Land

Mr. [Richard H.] Cain: I offer this resolution with good intentions. I believe that there is need for immediate relief to the poor people of the State. I know from my experience among the people, there is a pressing need of some measures to meet the wants of the utterly destitute. The gentleman [C. P. Leslie] says that it will only take money out of the Treasury. Well, that is the intention. I do not expect to get it anywhere else. I expect to get the money, if at all, through the Treasury of the United States, or some other department. It certainly must come out of the Government. I believe such an appropriation would remove a great many of the difficulties now in the State and do a vast amount of good to poor people. It may be that we will not get it, but that will not debar us from asking. It is our privilege and right. Other Conventions have asked from Congress appropriations. Georgia and

Proceedings of the Constitutional Convention of South Carolina, 1868 (New York: Arno Press, 1968), pp. 378–424.

other States have sent in their petitions. One has asked for $30,000,000 to be appropriated to the Southern States. I do not see any inconsistency in the proposition presented by myself.

Mr. C. P. Leslie: Suppose I should button up my coat and march up to your house and ask you for money or provisions, when you had none to give, what would you think of me.

Mr. Cain: You would do perfectly right to run the chance of getting something to eat. This is a measure of relief to those thousands of freed people who now have no lands of their own. I believe the possession of lands and homesteads is one of the best means by which a people is made industrious, honest and advantageous to the State. I believe it is a fact well known, that over three hundred thousand men, women and children are homeless, landless. The abolition of slavery has thrown these people upon their own resources. How are they to live. I know the philosopher of the New York Tribune says, "root hog or die;" but in the meantime we ought to have some place to root. My proposition is simply to give the hog some place to root. I believe if the proposition is sent to Congress, it will certainly receive the attention of our friends. I believe the whole country is desirous to see that this State shall return to the Union in peace and quiet, and that every inhabitant of the State shall be made industrious and profitable to the State. I am opposed to this Bureau system.[1] I want a system adopted that will do away with the Bureau, but I cannot see how it can be done unless the people have homes. As long as people are working on shares and contracts, and at the end of every year are in debt, so long will they and the country suffer. But give them a chance to buy lands, and they become steady, industrious men. That is the reason I desire to bring this money here and to assist them to buy lands. . . .

I do not desire to have a foot of land in this State confiscated. I want every man to stand upon his own character. I want these lands purchased by the government, and the people afforded an opportunity to buy from the government. I believe every man ought to carve out for himself a character and position in this life. I believe every man ought to be made to work by some means or other, and if he does not, he must go down. . . . I want to have the satisfaction of showing that the freedmen are as capable and willing to work as any men on the face of the earth. This measure will save the State untold expenses. I believe there are hundreds of persons in the jail and penitentiary cracking rock to-day who have all the instincts of honesty, and who, had they an opportunity of making a living, would never have been found in such a place. I think if Congress will accede to our request, we shall be benefited beyond measure, and save the State from taking charge of paupers, made such by not having the means to earn a living for themselves. . . .

---

[1] Cain probably means the work of the Freedmen's Bureau in negotiating labor contracts for the ex-slaves, contracts that were difficult to enforce—ED.

Mr. C. P. Leslie: . . . I assert that time will prove that the petition offered, and the addresses made here to-day, were most inopportune. These address-es have been listened to by a large concourse of spectators, and have held out to them that within a very short time they are to get land. We all know that the colored people want land. Night and day they think and dream of it. It is their all in all. As these men retire from the hall and go home, the first thing they do is to announce to the people "joy on earth, and good will to all mankind." We are all going to have a home. . . . And when I know as they know, that without land a race of people, four millions in number, travelling up and down the earth without a home are suffering, I cannot but denounce those who would, for political purposes, add to their misery by raising expec-tations that could never be realized. . . .

Let us have a little more light upon the subject. Parson French, who, it is well known, has the welfare of the colored people at heart, did go to Washington and portrayed to leading Senators and members of Congress the terrible predicament of the colored people in the State. He said that cot-ton had sold so low that all the people were poverty stricken. The white peo-ple, he told them, were not able to plant, and there being no necessity to employ laborers, the colored people were turned out of house and home, and he begged them to loan the people, or the State, a million of dollars. Their answer was, "Mr. French, for God's sake, send up no petitions for money, for we cannot give one dollar." . . .

Mr. F[rancis] L. Cardozo: . . . The poor freedmen were induced, by many Congressmen even, to expect confiscation. They held out the hope of confis-cation. [Union] General [William Tecumseh] Sherman did confiscate, gave the lands to the freedmen; and if it were not for President Johnson, they would have them now. The hopes of the freedmen have not been realized, and I do not think that asking for a loan of one million, to be paid by a mortgage upon the land, will be half as bad as has been supposed. I have been told by the Assistant Commissioner that he has been doing on a private scale what this petition proposes to do. I say every opportunity for helping the colored man should be seized upon. I think the adoption of this mea-sure will do honor to the Convention. We should certainly vote for some measure of relief for the colored men, as we have to the white men, who mortgaged their property to perpetuate slavery, and whom they have liberat-ed from their bonds.

Mr. N. G. Parker: I am glad that the gentleman who has just taken his seat has distinctly laid down the proposition that any member who votes against this petition votes against the colored man. I am a friend to the colored man, and he knows it. I have a record extending back for twenty years that shows it. . . .

I tell you, Mr. President, that the destitution that prevails this winter in those snow clad [Northern and Western] States is greater than it has ever been before. Thousands, yes millions, are out of employment, and what is the cause of it. I cannot stop now to elaborate the causes, but I will only briefly allude to them. War and its results are directly the cause of it. One of the results of the war, and the principal one, was the overthrow of slavery and tyranny in the Southern States; this was the good result of it; but the expense it caused the nation to do this, and the debt it incurred, and the overthrow of the labor system and consequent disturbance of trade and commerce, was the immediate evils. The burdensome taxation which followed is another principle cause of distress which now prevails in the Northern and Western States. The fact is patent that all the manufacturing States need aid; and let me tell you if the Congress of the United States grants additional aid to any of the unreconstructed States, for anything further than to perfect the reconstruction already half consummated, and the support of the Military and the Freedmen's Bureau, that in my opinion such a howl will go up as never was heard before, and I for one, would despair of success.

Our friends are trembling at Washington to-day, and all over the country, lest New Hampshire should cast a Democratic vote at her approaching election. I am of the opinion that if Congress should pass the appropriation called for just at this particular time, that every State from Maine to California would roll up such a Democrat vote in the coming election that was never heard of, or dreamt of, by the most ardent Democrat in this country. The result of the elections for the last year should not be unheeded.

Where would be our reconstruction if Andrew Johnson and the Democratic party had the handling of us? . . .

The Treasury of the United States has already as many drafts upon it as it can well bear. They have no money to purchase lands in South Carolina to sell on a credit—it is asking too much. Look at the almost overwhelming debt of the nation, and would you colored men, or white men, seek to increase it? For what was it contracted? and what keeps the expenses of Government to-day so large? It was contracted to make you free, and it is continually increased to preserve, protect and defend your freedom.

There never was a more liberal and humane government, nor never one that made such herculian [*sic*] efforts to retrieve the past as she has made and is making. We cannot ask her to do more than she is doing. There is such a thing as disgusting our friends. Do not let us weary them. If she will continue to afford us the protection she has afforded us in the past three years, if she will continue to the end in sustaining the reconstruction she commenced, if she will sustain the Freedmen's Bureau as long as it is a necessity, and give us the military necessary to protect and defend us, in God's name let us be satisfied. . . .

Mr. R. H. Cain: This measure, if carried out, therefore, will meet a want which the Bureau never can meet. A man may have rations to-day and not tomorrow, but when he gets land and a homestead, and is once fixed on that land, he never will want to go to the Commissary again. It is said that I depicted little farms by the roadside, chickens roosting on the fence, and all those poetical beauties. . . . I prefer this to seeing strong men working for the paltry sum of five or ten dollars a month, and some for even three dollars a month. How can a man live at that rate. I hate the contract system as I hate the being of whom my friend from Orangeburg (Mr. [Benjamin F.] Randolph) spoke last week (the devil). It has ruined the people. After fifty men have gone on a plantation, worked the whole year at raising twenty thousand bushels of rice, and then go to get their one-third, by the time they get through the division, after being charged by the landlord twenty-five or thirty cents a pound for bacon, two or three dollars for a pair of brogans that costs sixty cents, for living that costs a mere song, two dollars a bushel for corn that can be bought for one dollar; after I say, these people have worked the whole season, and at the end make up their accounts, they find themselves in debt. . . . I want to see a change in this country. Instead of the colored people being always penniless, I want to see them coming in with their mule teams and ox teams. I want to see them come with their corn and potatoes and exchange for silks and satins. I want to see school houses and churches in every parish and township. I want to see children coming forth to enjoy life as it ought to be enjoyed. This people know nothing of what is good and best for mankind until they get homesteads and enjoy them.

With these remarks, I close. I hope the Convention will vote for the proposition. Let us send up our petition. The right to petition is a jealous right. It was a right guaranteed to the Barons of England. The American people have always been jealous of that right, and regarded it as sacred and inviolate. That right we propose to maintain. It is said here that some high officers are opposed to it. I do not care who is opposed to it. It is none of their business. I do not care whether General [Robert K.] Scott, General [Ulysses S.] Grant or General anybody else is opposed to it, we will petition in spite of them. I appeal to the delegates to pass this resolution. It will do no harm if it does no good, and I am equally confident that some gentleman will catch what paddy gave the drum when they go back to their constituents.

The Ex-Slaves Crave Education

The Desire of the Blacks for Education

Senate Ex. Doc. no. 27, 39 Cong., 1 Sess. Report of J. W. Alvord, Superintendent of Schools for the Freedmen's Bureau

January 1, 1866

A general desire for education is everywhere manifested. In some instances, as in Halifax county [Virginia], very good schools were found taught and paid for by the colored people themselves. Said a gentleman to me, "I constantly see in the streets and on the door-steps opposite my dwelling groups

Walter L. Fleming, ed., *Documentary History of Reconstruction: Political, Military, and Industrial, 1865 to the Present Time* (Cleveland: The Arthur H. Clark Company, 1907), vol. 2, pp. 182–83.

of little negroes studying their spelling-books." . . .

Not only are individuals seen at study, and under the most untoward circumstances, but in very many places I have found what I will call "native schools," often rude and very imperfect, but there they are, a group, perhaps, of all ages, trying to learn. Some young man, some woman, or old preacher, in cellar, or shed, or corner of a negro meeting-house, with the alphabet in hand, or a torn spelling-book, is their teacher. All are full of enthusiasm with the new knowledge the book is imparting to them.

Freedmen's Bureau Schools in North Carolina

Senate Ex. Doc. no. 6, 39 Cong., 2 Sess., p. 104. Report of Gen[eral] John C. Robinson of the Freedmen's Bureau

1866

It is no unfrequent occurrence to witness in the same rooms, and pursuing the same studies, the child and parent—youth and gray hairs—all eagerly grasping for that by which, obtained, they are intellectually regenerated. . . .

As an evidence of the great interest manifested for acquiring knowledge, an instance, probably never before equalled in the history of education, is to be found in one of the schools of this State, where side by side sat representatives of four generations in a direct line, viz.: a child six years old, her mother, grandmother, and great-grandmother, the latter over 75 years of age. All commenced their alphabet together, and each one can read the Bible fluently.

Night schools have met with gratifying success, and are eagerly sought for by those whose labors are of such a character as to prevent their attendance during the day. . . .

Sunday schools have been established at many points where teachers reside. . . . It is evident much good has been accomplished by their establishment, and no estimate can be made of the beneficial results of their full development.

17

An Industrial Nation

During the thirty-five years following the Civil War, the United States became the world's richest and most productive industrial nation. The drive to industrial supremacy was not effortless or untroubled, however. It was accompanied by greed, corruption, and exploitation; it also threatened older patterns of living, degraded the physical environment, and weakened traditional political values.

Yet most Americans of the day probably thought of the sweeping economic and social changes of this era as progress. We today, although we are the beneficiaries of our predecessors' sacrifices, are perhaps more skeptical. Do our greater doubts derive from our ability to see further and clearer than our forebears? Or have we, without knowing what it was really like, romanticized preindustrial rural life?

In the selections below Americans who lived through the late nineteenth-century surge of growth describe their experiences or evaluate the processes that swept them along. In considering what these people said, remember that no one individual could see more than a tiny part of what was a truly massive event. Where some workers may have experienced hardship, for example, others may have found the good life. (In this connection, see if you can determine from the work of economic historians whether income per person in America was growing or declining in this period. You may also want to know what was happening to "real" annual wages, that is, the total buying power of wage earners' yearly wages.)

17.1:   The Industrial Status Quo Defended (1889, 1883)

Among the educated middle class, there was little doubt that the changes underway during the late nineteenth century were an enormous boon to

humankind. Below, two members of this group defend both the achieve-
ment and the way it was accomplished.

    The first document is by David A. Wells, an influential economist,
businessman, and science popularizer. Writing in the late 1880s, he
describes the wonders of recent technological progress. Wells was an
unabashed admirer of laissez faire, the system of unregulated private
enterprise and limited government celebrated by the orthodox economic
thinkers of the day. He talks much of the savings in labor that the new
technology effected. Was there a debit as well as a credit side of this aspect
of technology? Did the gains offset the losses?

    The second selection is by William Graham Sumner, an Episcopal
minister who taught economics and sociology at Yale University. Sumner
was a deeply committed "social Darwinist." His views derived from the
theories of English naturalist Charles Darwin, who believed that the
competition for survival among living things was the mechanism for
increasing biological complexity and ensuring biological advance. In late
nineteenth-century America, Darwin's influential ideas were increasing-
ly applied to validate views that in human society, as in nature, compe-
tition and struggle were the proper vehicles for progress. Any attempt to
soften their effects, said the social Darwinists, was misguided and would
in the end do more harm than good.

    What are the basic precepts of Sumner's views? How might they have
been used to support the economic status quo in late nineteenth-century
America? Is there any validity to Sumner's ideas? Have opinions like his
been used in recent years to support unfettered economic competition? If
so, by whom?

Economic Changes[1]

DAVID A. WELLS

When the historian of the future writes the history of the nineteenth century
he will doubtless assign to the period embraced by the life of the generation
terminating in 1885, a place of importance, considered in its relations to the
interests of humanity, second to but very few, and perhaps to none, of the
many similar epochs of time in any of the centuries that have preceded it;
inasmuch as all economists who have specially studied this matter are substantially agreed that, within the period named, man in general has attained
to such a greater control over the forces of Nature, and has so compassed

---

David A. Wells, *Recent Economic Changes* (New York: D. Appleton and Company, 1899), pp. 27 ff.
[1]Footnotes deleted.

their use, that he has been able to do far more work in a given time, produce far more product, measured by quantity in a ratio to a given amount of labor, and reduce the effort necessary to insure a comfortable subsistence in a far greater measure than it was possible for him to accomplish twenty or thirty years anterior to the time of the present writing (1889). In the absence of sufficiently complete data, it is not easy, and perhaps not possible, to estimate accurately, and specifically state the average saving in time and labor in the world's work of production and distribution that has been thus achieved. In a few departments of industrial effort the saving in both of these factors has certainly amounted to seventy or eighty per cent; in not a few to more than fifty per cent. . . .

The displacement of muscular labor in some of the cotton-mills of the United States, within the last ten years, by improved machinery, has been from thirty-three to fifty per cent, and the average work of one operative, working one year, in the best mills of the United States, will now, according to Mr. [Edward] Atkinson, supply the annual wants of 1,600 fully clothed Chinese, or 3,000 partially clothed East Indians. In 1840 an operative in the cotton-mills of Rhode Island, working thirteen to fourteen hours a day, turned off 9,600 yards of standard sheeting in a year; in 1886 the operative in the same mill made about 30,000 yards, working ten hours a day. In 1840 the wages were $176 a year; in 1886 the wages were $285 a year.

The United States census returns for 1880 report a very large increase in the amount of coal and copper produced during the ten previous years in this country, with a very large comparative diminution in the number of hands employed in these two great mining industries; in anthracite coal the increase in the number of hands employed having been 33·2 per cent, as compared with an increase of product of 82·7; while in the case of copper the ratios were 15·8 and 70·8, respectively. For such results, the use of cheaper and more powerful blasting agents (dynamite), and of the steam-drill, furnish an explanation. And, in the way of further illustration, it may be stated that a car-load of coal, in the principal mining districts of the United States, can now . . . be mined, hoisted, screened, cleaned, and loaded in one half the time that it required ten years previously.

The report of the United States Commissioner of Labor for 1886 furnishes the following additional illustrations:

"In the manufacture of agricultural implements, specific evidence is submitted showing that six hundred men now do the work that, fifteen or twenty years ago, would have required 2,145 men—a displacement of 1,545.

"The manufacture of boots and shoes offers some very wonderful facts in this connection. In one large and long-established manufactory the proprietors testify that it would require five hundred persons, working by hand processes, to make as many women's boots and shoes as a hundred persons now make with the aid of machinery—a displacement of eighty per cent.

"Another firm, engaged in the manufacture of children's shoes, states that the introduction of new machinery within the past thirty years has displaced about six times the amount of hand-labor required, and that the cost of the product has been reduced one half.

"On another grade of goods, the facts collected by the agents of the bureau show that one man can now do the work which twenty years ago required ten men.

"In the manufacture of flour there has been a displacement of nearly three fourths of the manual labor necessary to produce the same product. In the manufacture of furniture, from one half to three fourths only of the old number of persons is now required. In the manufacture of wallpaper, the best evidence puts the displacement in the proportion of one hundred to one. In the manufacture of metals and metallic goods, long-established firms testify that machinery has decreased manual labor $33^1/3$ percent."

In 1845 the boot and shoe makers of Massachusetts made an average production, under the then existing conditions of manufacturing, of 1·52 pairs of boots for each working day. In 1885 each employé in the State made on an average 4·2 pairs daily, while at the present time in Lynn and Haverhill the daily average of each person is seven pairs per day, "showing an increase in the power of production in forty years of four hundred per cent."

The business of making bottles has been arduous and unhealthy, with a waste of about thirty-three per cent of the "melting"; and, although this waste is used afterward, there is a deterioration in its quality from its employment a second time. For many years this specialty of industrial production experienced little improvement; but it finally commenced in the substitution in 1885 of the so-called Siemens "tank" furnace, in place of the old-fashioned "coal" furnace for the melting of glass; one of the former supplanting eight of the latter; requiring four men in place of twenty-eight to feed it, producing 1,000,000 square feet of glass per month, in place of a former product of 115,000 feet, and working continuously, while the coal-furnaces work on an average but eighteen days per month. Such an improvement in the methods of manufacture, as might be expected, revolutionized the former equilibrium, in this department of the glass industry as respects the supply and demand of both labor and product, and occasioned serious riots among the glass-workers of Charleroi, in Belgium, where it was first introduced. The process of producing the bottle by "blowing" was not, however, affected by the above noticed improvement; but within the last year (1888) a practical method of producing bottles is reported as having been invented and practically applied in England, which now bids fair to entirely do away with the process of "blowing," with an accompanying immense increase of daily product and a corresponding reduction in the former cost of labor. . . .

Nothing has had a greater influence in making possible the rapidity with which certain branches of retail business are now conducted, as compared with ten years ago—more especially the sale of groceries—than the cheap and rapid production of paper bags. At the outset, these bags were all made by hand-labor; but now machinery has crowded out the hand-workers, and factories are in existence in the United States which produce millions of paper bags per week, and not unfrequently fill single orders for three millions. Paper sacks for the transportation of flour are now (1889) used to the extent of about one hundred millions per annum; and to this same extent have superseded the use and requirement of cotton sacks and of barrels. With machinery have also come many improvements: square bags that stand up of themselves, and need only when filled from a measure to have the top edges turned over to make the package at once ready for delivery. A purchaser can now also take his butter or lard in paper trays that are brine and grease proof; his vinegar in paper jars that are warranted not to soak for one hour; a bottle of wine wrapped in a corrugated case that would not break if he dropped it on the pavement, and his oysters in paper pails that will hold water overnight. A few years ago, to have furnished gratuitously these packages, would have been deemed extravagance; but now it is found to pay as a matter of business.

The increase in the producing capacity of the United States in respect to the manufacture of paper during the years from 1880 to 1887 inclusive, was also very striking, namely: in number of mills, twenty-five per cent; in product, sixty-seven per cent; in value of product, twenty-seven per cent. The reduction in the prices of paper in the United States under such circumstances has been very great, and since 1872, for all qualities, full fifty per cent.

The *sobriquet* of an apothecary was formerly that of a pill-maker; but the modern apothecary no longer makes pills, except upon special prescriptions; inasmuch as scores of large manufactories now produce pills by machinery according to the standard or other formulas, and every apothecary keeps and sells them, because they are cheaper, better, and more attractive than any that he can make himself.

Certain branches of occupation formerly of considerable importance under the influence of recent improvements seem to be passing out of existence. Previous to 1872, nearly all the calicoes of the world were dyed or printed with a coloring principle extracted from the root known as *madder;* the cultivation and preparation of which involved the use of thousands of acres of land in Holland, Belgium, eastern France, Italy, and the Levant, and the employment of many hundreds of men, women, and children, and of large amounts of capital; the importation of madder into the United Kingdom for the year 1872 having been 28,731,600 pounds, and into the United States for the same year 7,786,000 pounds. To-day, two or three chemical establishments in Germany and England, employing but few men and a comparatively small capital, manufacture from coal-tar, at a greatly reduced price, the same coloring principle; and the former great business of growing and preparing madder—with the land, labor, and capital involved—is gradually becoming extinct; the importations into Great Britain for the year 1887 having declined to 1,934,700 pounds, and into the United States to 1,049,800 pounds.

The old-time business of making millstones—entitled to rank among the first of labor-saving inventions at the very dawn of civilization—is rapidly passing into oblivion, because millstones are no longer necessary or economical for grinding the cereals. The steel roller produces more and better flour in the same time at less cost, and as an inevitable consequence is rapidly taking the place of the millstone in all countries that know how to use machinery. And, as the art of skillfully grooving the surface of a hard, flinty rock for its conversion into a millstone is so laborious, so difficult of accomplishment (four or five years of service being required in France from an apprentice before he is allowed to touch a valuable stone), and to a certain extent so dangerous from the flying particles of steel and stone, humanity, apart from all economic considerations, may well rejoice at its desuetude. . . .

But in respect to no other one article has change in the conditions of production and distribution been productive of such momentous consequences as in the case of wheat. On the great wheat-fields of the State of Dakota, where machinery is applied to agriculture to such an extent that the requirement for manual labor has been reduced to a minimum, the annual product of one man's labor, working to the best advantage, is understood to be now equivalent to the production of 5,500 bushels of wheat. In the great mills of Minnesota, the labor of another one man for a year, under similar conditions as regards machinery, is in like manner equivalent to the conversion of this unit of 5,500 bushels of wheat into a thousand barrels of flour, leaving 500 bushels for seed-purposes; and, although the conditions for analysis of the next step in the way of results are more difficult, it is reasonably certain that the year's labor of one and a half men more—or, at the most, two men—employed in railroad transportation, is equivalent to putting this thousand barrels of flour on a dock in New York ready for exportation, where the addition of a fraction of a cent a pound to the price will further transport and deliver it at almost any port of Europe.

Here, then, we have the labor of three men for one year, working with machinery, resulting in the producing all the flour that a thousand other men ordinarily eat in a year, allowing one barrel of flour for the average consumption of each adult. Before such a result the question of wages paid in the different branches of flour production and transportation becomes an insignificant factor in determining a market; and, accordingly, American flour grown in Dakota, and ground in Minneapolis, from a thousand to fifteen hundred miles from the nearest seaboard, and under the auspices of men paid from a dollar and a half to two dollars and a half per day for their labor, is sold in European markets at rates which are determinative of the prices which Russian peasants, Egyptian "fellahs," and Indian "ryots," can obtain in the same markets for similar grain grown by them on equally good soil, and with from fifteen to twenty cents per day wages for their labor.

On the wheat-farms of the Northwestern United States it was claimed in 1887 that, with wages at twenty-five dollars per month and board for permanent employés, wheat could be produced for forty cents per bushel; while in Rhenish Prussia, with wages at six dollars per month, the cost of production was reported to be eighty cents per bushel.

How much more significantly differences manifest themselves in the results of mechanical production, when long periods of time are taken for comparison, is illustrated by a statement made by Adam Smith in his "Wealth of Nations" (first published in 1776), respecting the manufacture of pins, and which then seemed to him as something extraordinary, and a statement of the present condition of this business, as set forth in an official report to the United States Department of State in the year 1888. . . . In the time of Adam Smith it was regarded as a wonderful achievement for ten men to make 48,000 pins a day, but now three men can make 7,500,000 pins of a vastly superior character in the same time.

A great number of other similar and equally remarkable experiences, derived from almost every department of industry except the handicrafts, might be presented; but it would seem that enough evidence has been offered to prove abundantly, that in the increased control which mankind has acquired over the forces of Nature, and in the increased utilization of such control—mainly through machinery—for the work of production and distribution, is to be found a cause sufficient to account for most if not all the economic disturbance which, since the year 1873, has been certainly universal in its influence over the domain of civilization; abnormal to the extent of justifying the claim of having been unprecedented in character, and which bids fair in a greater or less degree to indefinitely continue. Other causes may and doubtless have contributed to such a condition of affairs, but in this one cause alone (if the influences referred to can be properly considered as a unity) it would seem there has been sufficient of potentiality to account not only for all the economic phenomena that are under discussion, but to occasion a feeling of wonder that the world has accommodated itself so readily to the extent that it has to its new conditions, and that the disturbances have not been very much greater and more disastrous.

We Must Not Help the Weak at the Expense of the Strong

WILLIAM GRAHAM SUMNER

Certain ills belong to the hardships of human life. They are natural. They are part of the struggle with Nature for existence. We cannot blame our fellow-men for our share of these. My neighbor and I are struggling to free ourselves from these ills. The fact that my neighbor has succeeded in this struggle better than I constitutes no grievance for me. Certain other ills are due

William Graham Sumner, *What Social Classes Owe to Each Other* (New York: Harper and Brothers, 1883), pp. 17–27, 138–145.

to the malice of men, and to the imperfections or errors of civil institutions. These ills are an object of agitation, and a subject of discussion. The former class of ills is to be met only by manly effort and energy; the latter may be corrected by associated effort. The former class of ills is constantly grouped and generalized, and made the object of social schemes. We shall see, as we go on, what that means. The second class of ills falls on certain social classes, and reform will take the form of interference by other classes in favor of that one. The last fact is, no doubt, the reason why people have been led . . . to believe that the same method was applicable to the other class of ills. The distinction here made between the ills which belong to the struggle for existence and those which are due to the faults of human institutions is of prime importance. . . .

The question whether voluntary charity is mischievous or not is one thing; the question whether legislation which forces one man to aid another is right and wise, as well as economically beneficial, is quite another question. Great confusion and consequent error is [*sic*] produced by allowing these two questions to become entangled in the discussion. Especially we shall need to notice the attempts to apply legislative methods of reform to the ills which belong to the order of Nature.

There is no possible definition of "a poor man." A pauper is a person who cannot earn his living; whose producing powers have fallen positively below his necessary consumption; who cannot, therefore, pay his way. A human society needs the active co-operation and productive energy of every person in it. A man who is present as a consumer, yet does not contribute either by land, labor, or capital, to the work of society, is a burden. On no sound political theory ought such a person share in the political power of the State. He drops out of the ranks of workers and producers. Society must support him. It accepts the burden, but he must be cancelled from the ranks likewise. About him no more need be said. But he is not the "poor man." The "poor man" is an elastic term, under which any number of social fallacies may be hidden.

Neither is there any possible definition of "the weak." Some are weak in one way, some in another; and those who are weak in one sense are strong in another. In general, however, it may be said that those whom humanitarians and philanthropists call the weak are the ones through whom the productive and conservative forces of society are wasted. They constantly neutralize and destroy the finest efforts of the wise and industrious, and are a dead-weight on the society in all its struggles to realize any better things. Whether the people who mean no harm, but are weak in the essential powers necessary to the performance of one's duties in life, or those who are malicious and vicious, do the more mischief, is a question not easy to answer. . . .

The humanitarians, philanthropists, and reformers, looking at the facts of life as they present themselves, find enough which is sad and unpromising in the condition of many members of society. They see wealth and poverty side by side. They note great inequality of social position and social chances. They eagerly set about the attempt to account for what they see, and to devise schemes for remedying what they do not like. In their eagerness to recommend the less fortunate classes to pity and consideration they forget all about the rights of other classes; they gloss over all the faults of the classes in question, and they exaggerate their misfortunes and their virtues. They invent new theories of property, distorting rights and perpetrating injustice, as any one is sure to do who sets about the re-adjustment of social relations with the interests of one group distinctly before his mind, and the interests of all other groups thrown into the background. When I have read certain of these discussions I have thought that it must be quite disreputable to be respectable, quite dishonest to own property, quite unjust to go one's own way and earn one's own living, and that the only really admirable person was the good-for-nothing. The man who by his own effort raises himself above poverty appears, in these discussions, to be of no account. The man who has done nothing to raise himself above poverty finds that the social doctors flock about him, bringing the capital which they have collected from the other class, and promising him the aid of the State to give him what the other had to work for. In all these schemes and projects the organized intervention of society through the State is either planned or hoped for, and the State is thus made to become the protector and guardian of certain classes. The agents who are to direct the State action are, of course, the reformers and philanthropists. Their schemes therefore, may always be reduced to this type—that A and B decide what C shall do for D. It will be interesting to inquire, at a later period of our discussion, who C is, and what the effect is upon him of all these arrangements. In all the discussions attention is concentrated on A and B, the noble social reformers, and on D, the "poor man." I call C the Forgotten Man, because I have never seen that any notice was taken of him in any of the discussions. When we have disposed of A, B, and D we can better appreciate the case of C, and I think that we shall find that he deserves our attention, for the worth of his character and the magnitude of his unmerited burdens. Here it may suffice to observe that, on the theories of the social philosophers to whom I have referred, we should get a new maxim of judicious living: Poverty is the best policy. If you get wealth, you will have to support other people; if you do not get wealth, it will be the duty of other people to support you.

No doubt one chief reason for the unclear and contradictory theories of class relations lies in the fact that our society, largely controlled in all its organization by one set of doctrines, still contains survivals of old social theories which are totally inconsistent with the former. In the Middle Ages men were united by custom and prescription into associations, ranks, guilds, and communities of various kinds. These ties endured as long as life lasted. Consequently society was dependent, throughout all its details, on status, and the tie, or bond, was sentimental. In our modern state, and in the United States more than anywhere else, the social structure is based on contract, and status is of the least importance. Contract, however, is rational—even rationalistic. It is also realistic, cold, and matter-of-fact. A contract relation is based on a sufficient reason, not on custom or prescription. It is not permanent. It endures only so long as the reason for it endures. In a state based on contract sentiment is out of place in any public or common affairs. It is relegated to the sphere of private and personal relations, where it depends not at all on class types, but on personal acquaintance and personal estimates. The sentimentalists among us always seize upon the survivals of the old order. They want to save them and restore them. Much of the loose thinking also which troubles us in our social discussions arises from the fact that men do not distinguish the elements of status and of contract which may be found in our society.

Whether social philosophers think it desirable or not, it is out of the question to go back to status or to the sentimental relations which once united baron and retainer, master and servant, teacher and pupil, comrade and comrade: That we have lost some grace and elegance is undeniable. That life once held more poetry and romance is true enough. But it seems impossible that any one who has studied the matter should doubt that we have gained immeasurably, and that our farther gains lie in going forward, not in going backward. The feudal ties can never be restored. If they could be restored they would bring back personal caprice, favoritism, sycophancy, and intrigue. A society based on contract is a society of free and independent men, who form ties without favor or obligation, and cooperate without cringing or intrigue. A society based on contract, therefore, gives the utmost room and chance for individual development, and for all the self-reliance and dignity of a free man. That a society of free men, co-operating under contract, is by far the strongest society which has ever yet existed; that no such society has ever yet developed the full measure of strength of which it is capable; and that the only social improvements which are now conceivable lie in the direction of more complete realization of a society of free men united by contract, are points which cannot be controverted. It follows, however, that one man, in a free state, cannot claim help from, and cannot be charged to give help to, another. To understand the full meaning of this assertion it will be worth while to see what a free democracy is. . . .

Social improvement is not to be won by direct effort. It is secondary, and results from physical or economic improvements. That is the reason why schemes of direct social amelioration always have an arbitrary, sentimental, and artificial character, while true social advance must be a product and a growth. The efforts which are being put forth for every kind of progress in the arts and sciences are, therefore, contributing to true social progress. Let any one learn what hardship was involved, even for a wealthy person, a century ago, in crossing the Atlantic, and then let him compare that hardship even with a steerage passage at the present time, considering time and money cost. This improvement in transportation by which "the poor and weak" can be carried from the crowded centres of population to the new land is worth more to them than all the schemes of all the social reformers. An improvement in surgical instruments or in anæsthetics really does more for those who are not well off than all the declamations of the orators and pious wishes of the reformers. Civil service reform would be a greater gain to the laborers than innumerable factory acts and eight-hour laws. Free trade would be a greater blessing to "the poor man" than all the devices of all the friends of humanity if they could be realized. If the economists could satisfactorily solve the problem of the regulation of paper currency, they would do more for the wages class than could be accomplished by all the artificial doctrines about wages which they seem to feel bound to encourage. If we could get firm and good laws passed for the management of savings-banks, and then refrain from the amendments by which those laws are gradually broken down, we should do more for the non-capitalist class than by volumes of laws against "corporations" and the "excessive power of capital." . . .

We each owe it to the other to guarantee rights. Rights do not pertain to *results*, but only to *chances*. They pertain to the *conditions* of the struggle for existence, not to any of the results of it; to the *pursuit* of happiness, not to the possession of happiness. It cannot be said that each one has a right to have some property, because if one man had such a right some other man or men would be under a corresponding obligation to provide him with some property. Each has a right to acquire and possess property if he can. It is plain what fallacies are developed when we overlook this distinction. Those fallacies run through *all* socialistic schemes and theories. If we take rights to pertain to results, and then say that rights must be equal, we come to say that men have a right to be equally happy, and so on in all the details. Rights should be equal, because they pertain to chances, and all ought to have equal chances so far as chances are provided or limited by the action of society. This, however, will not produce equal results, but it is right just because it will produce unequal results—that is, results which shall be proportioned to the merits of individuals. We each owe it to the other to guarantee mutually the chance to earn, to possess, to learn, to marry, etc., etc., against any interference which would prevent the exercise of those rights by a person who wishes to prosecute and enjoy them in peace for the pursuit of happiness. If we generalize this, it means that All-of-us ought to guarantee rights to each of us. But our modern free, constitutional States are constructed entirely on the notion of rights, and we regard them as performing their functions more and more perfectly according as they guarantee rights in consonance with the constantly corrected and expanded notions of rights from one generation to another. Therefore, when we say that we owe it to each other to guarantee rights we only say that we ought to prosecute and improve our political science.

If we have in mind the value of chances to earn, learn, possess, etc., for a man of independent energy, we can go one step farther in our deductions about help. The only help which is generally expedient, even within the limits of the private and personal relations of two persons to each other, is that which consists in helping a man to help himself. This always consists in opening the chances. A man of assured position can, by an effort which is of no appreciable importance to him, give aid which is of incalculable value to a man who is all ready to make his own career if he can only get a chance. The truest and deepest pathos in this world is not that of suffering but that of brave struggling. The truest sympathy is not compassion, but a fellow-feeling with courage and fortitude in the midst of noble effort.

Now, the aid which helps a man to help himself is not in the least akin to the aid which is given in charity. If alms are given, or if we "make work" for a man, or "give him employment," or "protect" him, we simply take a product from one and give it to another. If we help a man to help himself, by opening the chances around him, we put him in a position to add to the wealth of the community by putting new powers in operation to produce. It would seem that the difference between getting something already in existence from the one who has it, and producing a new thing by applying new labor to natural materials, would be so plain as never to be forgotten; but the fallacy of confusing the two is one of the commonest in all social discussions. . . .

Instead of endeavoring to redistribute the acquisitions which have been made between the existing classes, our aim should be to *increase, multiply, and extend the chances.* Such is the work of civilization. Every old error or abuse which is removed opens new chances of development to all the new energy of society. Every improvement in education, science, art, or government expands the chances of man on earth. Such expansion is no guarantee of equality. On the contrary, if there be liberty, some will profit by the chances eagerly and some will neglect them altogether. Therefore, the greater the chances the more unequal will be the fortune of these two sets of men. So it ought to be, in all justice and right reason. The yearning after equality is the offspring of envy and covetousness, and there is no possible plan for satisfying that yearning which can do aught else than rob A to give to B; consequently all such plans nourish some of the meanest vices of human nature, waste capital, and overthrow civilization. But if we can expand the chances we can count on a general and steady growth of civilization and advancement of society by and through its best members. In the prosecution of these chances we all owe to each other good-will, mutual respect, and mutual guarantees of liberty and security. Beyond this nothing can be affirmed as a duty of one group to another in a free state.

17.2: The Industrial Worker (1885, 1878)

Although real wages had been rising for American wage earners in the half-century following the Civil War, they remained low compared to the incomes of the professional and business classes. That gap in itself would undoubtedly have produced social resentment, but there were other aspects of wage earners' lives that also created discontent. The work day was long and mind-deadening, on-the-job health conditions were poor, industrial accidents were frequent, unemployment was common. Laboring people at times responded to these conditions by strikes and riots. Some also turned to trade unionism to solve their difficulties. A small but significant minority even questioned the validity of private property rights and the basic assumptions of capitalism.

The first selection below is the testimony of a New York tailor, Conrad Carl, to a U.S. Senate committee investigating the conditions of labor and the relations of capital and labor in 1885. Carl's work experience bridged the important change from hand to machine labor in the garment industry. He obviously was not happy about the change. Why not? Does his description allow, however, for the possibility that the changes were good for consumers or the economy as a whole, although not necessarily for Carl's fellow garment workers? Were the circumstances of the garment workers typical of labor in this period?

The second selection is from the constitution of the Knights of Labor, a trade union organization of national scope that flourished for a time in the 1880s. The Knights were not a modern trade union. Their goals went beyond the higher wages, shorter hours, and improved working conditions demanded by such "pure and simple" trade unions as the American Federation of Labor. Still, the selection expresses eloquently the yearnings of wage earners exposed to the hazards and challenges of post–Civil War industrial life. What vision of society is implicit in the document below? Does it seem to foreshadow later reform movements? How do you explain the Knights' reluctance to employ strikes?

How Changes in the Garment Industry Have Harmed Labor

CONRAD CARL

CONRAD CARL sworn and examined.
  By Mr. PUGH:

Question: How long have you resided in this city?—*Answer.:* Nearly thirty years.

Q.: What has been your profession or occupation?—*A.:* I have been a tailor since boyhood.

Q.: Are you an employé or an employer?—*A.:* An employé.

Q.: Have you been an employé during the whole time you have been in the business?—*A.:* The whole time.

Senate Committee on the Relations between Capital and Labor (Washington, DC: Government Printing Office, 1885), vol. 2, pp. 413–21.

Q.:   Please give us any information that you may have as to the relation existing between the employers and the employés in the tailoring business in this city, as to wages, as to treatment of the one by the other class, as to the feeling that exists between the employers and the employed generally, and all that you know in regard to the subject that we are authorized to inquire into?

A.:   During the time I have been here the tailoring business is altered in three different ways. Before we had sewing-machines we worked piece-work with our wives, and very often our children. We had no trouble then with our neighbors, nor with the landlord, because it was a very still business, very quiet; but in 1854 or 1855, and later, the sewing-machine was invented and introduced, and it stitched very nicely, nicer than the tailor could do; and the bosses said: "We want you to use the sewing-machine; you have to buy one." Many of the tailors had a few dollars in the bank, and they took the money and bought machines. Many others had no money, but must help themselves; so they brought their stitching, the coat or vest, to the other tailors who had sewing-machines, and paid them a few cents for the stitching. Later, when the money was given out for the work, we found out that we could earn no more than we could without the machine; but the money for the machine was gone now, and we found that the machine was only for the profit of the bosses; that they got their work quicker, and it was done nicer.

Q.:   How about the average wages?—*A.:*   The average wages before the [Civil] war (that marks an epoch, you know) was [*sic*] from $8 to $10 a week for a man working with his wife.

Q.:   Is the work graded in any way? Do certain employés do certain kinds of work? Is the work classified in the shop?—*A.:*   At that time it was divided among vest-makers, pants-makers, and coat-makers.

Q.:   You have cutters, I suppose?—*A.:*   The cutter was in the shop, in the boss's shop. We worked at home in our rooms. We had to buy fuel to heat the irons for pressing, and light in the winter; and we worked very deep in the night. The hours of working at that time were about fifteen to twenty hours a day.

Q.:   You worked by the day then, and not by the piece?—*A.:*   Piece-work, only piece-work, in our own rooms.

Q.:   Was working that length of time voluntary, or was it required by the employer?—*A.:*   He had no place to put us in. He would not pay out the money to hire a large room or hall to put his tailors in to make the coats or vests, and the tailor himself had to give his room for the business and had to buy coal and furnish the light to do the work for the boss.

Q.:   And then the tailors bought sewing-machines to do the work?—*A.:*   Yes.

Q.:   You say they worked from fifteen to eighteen hours a day before the war; how is it now?—*A.:*   Now they have to work quicker, because they cannot work so long. The machine makes too much noise in the place, and the neighbors want to sleep, and we have to stop sewing earlier; so we have to work faster. We work now in excitement—in a hurry. It is hunting; it is not work at all; it is a hunt.

Q.:   You turn out two or three times as much work per day now as you did in prior times before the war?—*A.:*   Yes, sir; two or three times as much; and we have to do it, because the wages are two-thirds lower than they were five or ten years back. . . .

Q.:   How much wages were paid a day after the war?—*A.:*   From 1864 to 1873, . . . they ran from $20 to $25 a week for a tailor and his wife. A tailor is nothing without a wife, and very often a child. If the child is old enough, about twelve or fourteen years, it is employed in the tailor's business; but the children often go out into the factories to earn something.

Q.:   How much did you make after the war, from 1864 to 1873?—*A.:*   I made boys' fine fancy jackets and could get from $2 to $3.50 or $4 apiece for them.

Q.:   Was that for the jacket, or for the making of it?—*A.:*   For the making of it.

Q.:   How much are you paid for making a vest of the same sort now?—*A.:* The highest is $1.

Q.:   For what sort of a vest?—*A.:*   Not vests—jackets.

Q.:   How much were you paid for pants from 1864 to 1873?—*A.:*   From five shillings to a dollar or nine shillings apiece.[1]

Q.:   Now how much is paid?—*A.:*   It is from 15 to 28 cents.

Q.:   On what sort of material do you work?—*A.:*   All wool.

Q.:   What was paid for making a coat, from 1864 to 1873?—*A.:*   From 12 shillings to three or four dollars.

Q.:   How much is paid now?—*A.:*   From 40 cents to a dollar.

Q.:   You state, then, that there has been a reduction of two-thirds in the pay for some kinds of work?—*A.:*   Yes, sir.

By Mr. GEORGE:

Q.:   Is that owing to the change from hand work to machine work, or is it a reduction from the prices paid for machine work before the war?—*A.:* From machine work to machine work. Hand work was before the war.

[1] A "shilling," as money of account, was about 10 cents—ED.

By the CHAIRMAN:

Q.:   Are the machines on which the work is done now the same as those that were used formerly?—*A.*:   They have better machines now—quicker.

Q.:   Did you do that fast work of which you have told us from 1864 to 1873?—*A.*:   No, sir; the fast work began about five or six years ago, when the wages lowered.

Q.:   You, of course, make more pieces in a given time than you did by hand; what is the difference between the amount of work that you can turn out with a machine and the amount you could turn out by hand?—*A.*:   I have to make now four jackets a day, with my wife and daughter's assistance.

Q.:   You do that with the machine?—*A.*:   All machine work.

Q.:   Working by hand, how many could you turn out?—*A.*:   Oh, with the hand I could make only one.

Q.:   Have you any idea of the number of tailors, men and women, who are engaged in that work in this city?—*A.*:   You mean in the clothing business—in the custom trade? That is another part of the business.

Q.:   I understand that. How many do you think there are?—*A.*:   I don't know; eighteen or twenty thousand.

Q.:   What proportion of them are women and what proportion men, according to your best judgment?—*A.*:   I guess there are many more women than men.

Q.:   The pay of the women is the same as the pay of the men for the same quantity of work, I suppose?—*A.*:   Yes; in cases where a manufacturer—that is, a middleman—gets work from the shop and brings it into his store and employs hands to make it, women get paid by the piece also. If the manufacturer gets 25 cents for a piece, he pays for the machine work on that piece so many cents to the machine-worker, he pays so many cents to the presser, so many cents to the finisher, and so many to the button-sewer—so much to each one—and what remains is to pay his rent and to pay for the machinery.

Q.:   What is your knowledge as to the amount that workers of that class are able to save from their wages?—*A.*:   I don't know any one that does save except those manufacturers.

Q.:   As a class, then, the workers save nothing?—*A.*:   No.

Q.:   What sort of house-room do they have? What is the character, in general, of the food and clothing which they are able to purchase with what they can make by their labor?—*A.*:   They live in tenement houses four or five stories high, and have two or three rooms.

Q.:   What is the character of their clothing?—*A.*:   They buy the clothing that they make—the cheapest of it.

Q.:   What about the character of food that they are able to provide for themselves?—*A.*:   Food? They have no time to eat dinner. They have a sandwich in the middle of the day, and in the evening when they go away from work it is the same, and they drink lager or anything they can get.

Q.: They are kept busy all the time and have but little opportunity for rest?—*A.:* Yes.

Q.: What is the state of feeling between the employers and their employés in that business? How do you workingmen feel towards the people who employ you and pay you?—*A.:* Well, I must say the workingmen are discouraged. If I speak with them they go back and don't like to speak much about the business and the pay. They fear that if they say how it is they will get sent out of the shop. They hate the bosses and the foremen more than the bosses, and that feeling is deep.

Q.: Why do they feel so towards the foremen?—*A.:* They know that they do a wrong onto them; they know that.

Q.: Do not the foremen act under the instruction of the bosses?—*A.:* Well, it seems so.

Q.: Could not the boss correct the wrong that the foreman does, if it is a wrong?—*A.:* Well, when we complain that the foreman is so and so, the boss says, "Oh, I have nothing to do with it; I don't know; go to the foreman; it is the foreman's business." Then when we go to the foreman he says, "Oh, I can't pay more; these are my rules; if you don't like it, go to the boss."

Q.: And when you do go to the boss he sends you back to the foreman?—*A.:* Yes; he says, "I have nothing to do with this; that is my foreman's business; go to him." Therefore the workmen hate them both.

Q.: But can you explain why they hate the foremen, as you say they do, more than the bosses, when the bosses keep the foremen there and could discharge them and get better ones in the places if they desired?—*A.:* Gentlemen, if I say all this here—if it is made public I come out of work.

By Mr. Pugh:

Q.: Then you are testifying here under the apprehension of punishment for what you have stated?—*A.:* Well, I have no fear for any one, you know, and if you think it is better that I say it, I do so.

Q.: What is your feeling of restraint in testifying? What injury would you be subjected to for telling the truth? Would the workingmen in your business testify under a fear of being punished by their employers for telling the truth?—*A.:* Yes. It is nothing but fear.

By Mr. George:

Q.: Can you state the average wages per diem of the tailors in this city at the present time? How much do they make per day on an average, working as you say they do work, by the piece?—*A.:* A man may earn from eight to nine dollars a week.

Q.: How much can the best hands earn?—*A.*: It will not be more than that. I think there is not much difference between the best and the worst. If a piece comes from the machine to the presser it has to be done just as quick as the other ones. One has to work as quick as the other. They all are good workers and have to work together; one wheel goes onto the other wheel and they have all to run together.

Q.: How much can the women earn? About the same as the men?—*A.*: No. A machine-girl gets from eight to nine dollars a week—just as much and sometimes more as a presser; and one who sews or finishes, puts the buttons on jackets, pants or vests, makes from three to four dollars.

Q.: Then a woman who works the machine can make as much as a man can, but a woman who sews, who does the work that cannot be done by the machine, makes only three or four dollars a week?—*A.*: Yes.

Q.: How much did the average tailor make per week before the invention of machines?—*A.*: They made from eight to ten dollars a week. But at that time I could buy for $10 more provisions and clothes than I can buy now for $20.

Q.: You get about the same wages, then, about the same amount of money, but it was worth twice as much to you then because it had double the purchasing power of your present wages. Is that the idea?—*A.*: Yes, sir.

Q.: How many hours do you work to make eight or nine dollars a week?— *A.*: From sunrise to sunset; and my wife works also. I can't say that I earn that amount of money; my wife earns part of it.

Q.: What do you say are the average earnings?—*A.*: Well, a family of three (we are three at home) will make from sixteen to eighteen dollars a week.

Q.: How many hours do the tailors generally work now?—*A.*: From sunrise to sunset.

Q.: That produces them eight or nine dollars a week?—*A.*: Yes.

By the CHAIRMAN:

Q.: What are the hours of work in winters?—*A.*: They make a light in the morning and they have a light burning until 9 or 10 o'clock in the evening. . . .

Q.: Are not the tailors the hardest-worked and poorest-paid class of laborers in the city?—*A.*: The hardest worked, the longest hours, and the poorest paid.

Q.: What proportion of them belong to labor unions? Do all or most of them belong to the unions?—*A.*: No. They are all dispersed—they are all discouraged; they have no union at all.

Q.: To what do you attribute that? What is the reason of it?—*A.*: Well, they have not had success in getting higher wages. As often as they came together or went on a strike, they lost, always.

Q.:   And their wages, you say, have been gradually reduced?—*A.*:   Yes, and some of them that have houses, they are hungrier than the others; they corrupt the foremen, give them money, and get more work for themselves, and take it home and employ poor men and women.

Q.:   You say there is no separate union of the tailors?—*A.*:   No. It was, but it is not now.

Q.:   There are, you say, between eighteen and twenty thousand working tailors in this city?—*A.*:   Yes. I was very glad when the act of the legislature came that cigar-making in tenement houses is forbidden.

Q.:   What is your idea of the value of strikes as a means of remedying your troubles?—*A.*:   It is not always of great value, but it is a necessity. It springs from necessity, and the sooner the workingman will go on strike when he cannot remain on the work—so poor as the workingmen are, they cannot carry that on—the burden is too great.

Preamble to the Constitution of the Knights of Labor[1]

The recent alarming development and aggression of aggregated wealth, which, unless checked, will invariably lead to the pauperization and hopeless degradation of the toiling masses, render it imperative, if we desire to enjoy the blessings of life, that a check should be placed upon its power and upon unjust accumulation, and a system adopted which will secure to the laborer the fruits of his toil; and as this much-desired object can only be accomplished by the thorough unification of labor, and the united efforts of those who obey the divine injunction that "In the sweat of thy brow shalt thou eat bread," we have formed the————with a view of securing the organization and direction, by co-operative effort, of the power of the industrial classes; and we submit to the world the objects sought to be accomplished by our organization, calling upon all who believe in securing "the greatest good to the greatest number" to aid and assist us:

    I.   To bring within the folds of organization every department of productive industry, making knowledge a stand-point for action, and industrial and moral worth, not wealth, the true standard of individual and national greatness.

    II.   To secure to the toilers a proper share of the wealth that they create; more of the leisure that rightfully belongs to them; more societary advantages; more of the benefits, privileges, and emoluments of the world; in a word, all those rights and privileges necessary to make them capable of enjoying, appreciating, defending, and perpetuating the blessing of good government.

    III.   To arrive at the true condition of the producing masses in their educational, moral, and financial condition, by demanding from the various governments the establishment of bureaus of Labor and Statistics.

Terence V. Powderly, *Thirty Years of Labor* (Columbus: Excelsior Publishing House, 1889), pp. 243–45.
[1]Footnotes deleted.

IV.   The establishment of co-operative institutions, productive and distributive.

V.   The reserving of the public lands—the heritage of the people—for the actual settler; not another acre for railroads or speculators.

VI.   The abrogation of all laws that do not bear equally upon capital and labor, the removal of unjust technicalities, delays, and discriminations in the administration of justice, and the adopting of measures providing for the health and safety of those engaged in mining, manufacturing, or building pursuits.

VII.   The enactment of laws to compel chartered corporations to pay their employes weekly, in full, for labor performed during the preceding week, in the lawful money of the country.

VIII.   The enactment of laws giving mechanics and laborers first lien on their work for their full wages.

IX.   The abolishment of the contract system on national, State, and municipal work.

X.   The substitution of arbitration for strikes, whenever and wherever employers and employes are willing to meet on equitable grounds.

XI.   The prohibition of the employment of children in workshops, mines and factories before attaining their fourteenth year.

XII.   To abolish the system of letting out by contract the labor of convicts in our prisons and reformatory institutions.

XIII.   To secure for both sexes equal pay for equal work.

XIV.   The reduction of the hours of labor to eight per day, so that the laborers may have more time for social enjoyment and intellectual improvement, and be enabled to reap the advantages conferred by the labor-saving machinery which their brains have created.

XV.   To prevail upon governments to establish a purely national circulating medium, based upon the faith and resources of the nation, and issued directly to the people, without the intervention of any system of banking corporations, which money shall be legal tender in payment of all debts, public or private.

17.3:   Labor Rejects Capitalism (1912)

Disenchantment with the existing industrial regime led some wage earners to disavow capitalism itself. During the last years of the old century and the opening years of the new, socialist parties were usually the medium through which such root discontent expressed itself. The largest and most durable of these organizations was the Socialist Party of America (SPA), formed in 1901 from an amalgamation of several older socialist groups. For much of its early life the SPA was headed by the eloquent and magnetic Eugene V. Debs, a native-born trade union leader who had led the railroad workers' Pullman Strike in 1894, been jailed, and later become a socialist.

The following is the text of the SPA's platform of 1912, when, with Debs as its presidential candidate, it won almost 900,000 votes. The document embraces a theory of history. What is this theory? Do the Socialists anywhere in this platform endorse the use of force and violence? In what ways did the SPA's specific demands overlap those of lib-

eral political groups that accepted capitalism? What evidence is there in the platform that the Socialists were radicals, interested in fundamental social change? Clearly the Socialists spoke in the name of the wage-earner class. Did they also receive wide wage-earner support? Which groups in contemporary America supported socialist ideas?

Socialist Party Platform of 1912

The Socialist party declares that the capitalist system has outgrown its historical function, and has become utterly incapable of meeting the problems now confronting society. We denounce this outgrown system as incompetent and corrupt and the source of unspeakable misery and suffering to the whole working class.

Under this system the industrial equipment of the nation has passed into the absolute control of a plutocracy which exacts an annual tribute of hundreds of millions of dollars from the producers. Unafraid of any organized resistance, it stretches out its greedy hands over the still undeveloped resources of the nation—the land, the mines, the forests and the water powers of every State of the Union.

In spite of the multiplication of labor-saving machines and improved methods in industry which cheapen the cost of production, the share of the producers grows ever less, and the prices of all the necessities of life steadily increase. The boasted prosperity of this nation is for the owning class alone. To the rest it means only greater hardship and misery. The high cost of living is felt in every home. Millions of wage-workers have seen the purchasing power of their wages decrease until life has become a desperate battle for mere existence.

Multitudes of unemployed walk the streets of our cities or trudge from State to State awaiting the will of the masters to move the wheels of industry.

The farmers in every state are plundered by the increasing prices exacted for tools and machinery and by extortionate rents, freight rates and storage charges.

Capitalist concentration is mercilessly crushing the class of small business men and driving its members into the ranks of propertyless wage-workers. The overwhelming majority of the people of America are being forced under a yoke of bondage by this soulless industrial despotism.

It is this capitalist system that is responsible for the increasing burden of armaments, the poverty, slums, child labor, most of the insanity, crime and prostitution, and much of the disease that afflicts mankind.

Under this system the working class is exposed to poisonous conditions, to frightful and needless perils to life and limb, is walled around with court

Kirk Harold Porter, ed., *National Party Platforms* (New York: The Macmillan Company, 1924), pp. 361–68.

decisions, injunctions and unjust laws, and is preyed upon incessantly for the benefit of the controlling oligarchy of wealth. Under it also, the children of the working class are doomed to ignorance, drudging toil and darkened lives.

In the face of these evils, so manifest that all thoughtful observers are appalled at them, the legislative representatives of the Republican and Democratic parties remain the faithful servants of the oppressors. Measures designed to secure to the wage-earners of this Nation as humane and just treatment as is already enjoyed by the wage-earners of all other civilized nations have been smothered in committee without debate, the laws ostensibly designed to bring relief to the farmers and general consumers are juggled and transformed into instruments for the exaction of further tribute. The growing unrest under oppression has driven these two old parties to the enactment of a variety of regulative measures, none of which has limited in any appreciable degree the power of the plutocracy, and some of which have been perverted into means of increasing that power. Anti-trust laws, railroad restrictions and regulations, with the prosecutions, indictments and investigations based upon such legislation, have proved to be utterly futile and ridiculous.

Nor has this plutocracy been seriously restrained or even threatened by any Republican or Democratic executive. It has continued to grow in power and insolence alike under the administration of [Presidents] Cleveland, McKinley, Roosevelt and Taft.

We declare, therefore, that the longer sufferance of these conditions is impossible, and we purpose to end them all. We declare them to be the product of the present system in which industry is carried on for private greed, instead of for the welfare of society. We declare, furthermore, that for these evils there will be and can be no remedy and no substantial relief except through Socialism under which industry will be carried on for the common good and every worker receive the full social value of the wealth he creates.

Society is divided into warring groups and classes, based upon material interests. Fundamentally, this struggle is a conflict between the two main classes, one of which, the capitalist class, owns the means of production, and the other, the working class, must use these means of production, on terms dictated by the owners.

The capitalist class, though few in numbers, absolutely controls the government, legislative, executive and judicial. This class owns the machinery of gathering and disseminating news through its organized press. It subsidizes seats of learning—the colleges and schools—and even religious and moral agencies. It has also the added prestige which established customs give to any order of society, right or wrong.

The working class, which includes all those who are forced to work for a living whether by hand or brain, in shop, mine or on the soil, vastly outnumbers the capitalist class. Lacking effective organization and class solidarity, this class is unable to enforce its will. Given such a class solidarity and effective organization, the workers will have the power to make all laws and control all industry in their own interest. All political parties are the expression of economic class interests. All other parties than the Socialist party represent one or another group of the ruling capitalist class. Their political conflicts reflect merely superficial rivalries between competing capitalist groups. However they result, these conflicts have no issue of real value to the workers. Whether the Democrats or Republicans win politically, it is the capitalist class that is victorious economically.

The Socialist party is the political expression of the economic interests of the workers. Its defeats have been their defeats and its victories their victories. It is a party founded on the science and laws of social development. It proposes that, since all social necessities to-day are socially produced, the means of their production and distribution shall be socially owned and democratically controlled.

In the face of the economic and political aggressions of the capitalist class the only reliance left the workers is that of their economic organizations and their political power. By the intelligent and class conscious use of these, they may resist successfully the capitalist class, break the fetters of wage slavery, and fit themselves for the future society, which is to displace the capitalist system. The Socialist party appreciates the full significance of class organization and urges the wage-earners, the working farmers and all other useful workers to organize for economic and political action, and we pledge ourselves to support the toilers of the fields as well as those in the shops, factories and mines of the nation in their struggles for economic justice.

In the defeat or victory of the working class party in this new struggle for freedom lies the defeat or triumph of the common people of all economic groups, as well as the failure or triumph of popular government. Thus the Socialist party is the party of the present day revolution which makes the transition from economic individualism to socialism, from wage slavery to free co-operation, from capitalist oligarchy to industrial democracy.

Working Program

As measures calculated to strengthen the working class in its fight for the realization of its ultimate aim, the co-operative commonwealth, and to increase its power against capitalist oppression, we advocate and pledge ourselves and our elected officers to the following program:

Collective Ownership

1. The collective ownership and democratic management of railroads, wire and wireless telegraphs and telephones, express service, steamboat lines, and all other social means of transportation and communication and of all large scale industries.
2. The immediate acquirement by the municipalities, the states or the federal government of all grain elevators, stock yards, storage warehouses, and other distrib-

uting agencies, in order to reduce the present extortionate cost of living.

3. The extension of the public domain to include mines, quarries, oil wells, forests and water power.
4. The further conservation and development of natural resources for the use and benefit of all the people: . . .
5. The collective ownership of land wherever practicable, and in cases where such ownership is impracticable, the appropriation by taxation of the annual rental value of all the land held for speculation and exploitation.
6. The collective ownership and democratic management of the banking and currency system.

Unemployment

The immediate government relief of the unemployed by the extension of all useful public works. All persons employed on such works to be engaged directly by the government under a work day of not more than eight hours and at not less than the prevailing union wages. The government also to establish employment bureaus; to lend money to states and municipalities without interest for the purpose of carrying on public works, and to take such other measures within its power as will lessen the widespread misery of the workers caused by the misrule of the capitalist class.

Industrial Demands

The conservation of human resources, particularly of the lives and well-being of the workers and their families:

1. By shortening the work day in keeping with the increased productiveness of machinery.
2. By securing for every worker a rest period of not less than a day and a half in each week.
3. By securing a more effective inspection of workshops, factories and mines.
4. By the forbidding the employment of children under sixteen years of age.
5. By the co-operative organization of the industries in the federal penitentiaries for the benefit of the convicts and their dependents.
6. By forbidding the interstate transportation of the products of child labor, of convict labor and of all uninspected factories and mines.
7. By abolishing the profit system in government work and substituting either the direct hire of labor or the awarding of contracts to co-operative groups of workers.
8. By establishing minimum wage scales.
9. By abolishing official charity and substituting a non-contributary system of old age pensions, a general system of insurance by the State of all its members against unemployment and invalidism and a system of compulsory insurance by employers of their workers, without cost to the latter, against industrial diseases, accidents and death.

Political Demands

1. The absolute freedom of press, speech and assemblage.
2. The adoption of a graduated income tax and the extension of inheritance taxes, graduated in proportion to the value of the estate and to nearness of kin—the

proceeds of these taxes to be employed in the socialization of industry.
3. The abolition of the monopoly ownership of patents and the substitution of collective ownership, with direct rewards to inventors by premiums or royalties.
4. Unrestricted and equal suffrage for men and women.
5. The adoption of the initiative, referendum and recall and of proportional representation, nationally as well as locally.
6. The abolition of the Senate and of the veto power of the President.
7. The election of the President and Vice-President by direct vote of the people.
8. The abolition of the power usurped by the Supreme Court of the United States to pass upon the constitutionality of the legislation enacted by Congress. National laws to be repealed only by act of Congress or by a referendum vote of the whole people.
9. Abolition of the present restrictions upon the amendment of the constitution, so that instrument may be made amendable by a majority of the voters in a majority of the States.
10. The granting of the right of suffrage in the District of Columbia with representation in Congress and a democratic form of municipal government for purely local affairs.
11. The extension of democratic government to all United States territory.
12. The enactment of further measures for the conservation of health. The creation of an independent bureau of health, with such restrictions as will secure full liberty to all schools of practice.
13. The enactment of further measures for general education and particularly for vocational education in useful pursuits. The Bureau of Education to be made a department.
14. The separation of the present Bureau of Labor from the Department of Commerce and Labor and its elevation to the rank of a department.
15. Abolition of all federal districts courts and the United States circuit court of appeals. State courts to have jurisdiction in all cases arising between citizens of several states and foreign corporations. The election of all judges for short terms.
16. The immediate curbing of the power of the courts to issue injunctions.
17. The free administration of the law.
18. The calling of a convention for the revision of the constitution of the U. S.

Such measures of relief as we may be able to force from capitalism are but a preparation of the workers to seize the whole powers of government, in order that they may thereby lay hold of the whole system of socialized industry and thus come to their rightful inheritance.

18

The Last West

During the half-century following the Civil War, the huge expanse of territory between the Missouri River and the Pacific slope was absorbed into the national economy. This was a region of wide deserts and rugged mountains, fertile plains and valleys, dense timber stands, and rich mineral deposits. In 1865 it was thinly peopled by scores of Native American tribes living primarily as nomadic hunters and foragers who relied on the teeming herds of bison (buffalo) for the food and materiel of their lives.

White Americans, regarded the "last West," as previous "Wests," as a land of opportunity to be conquered and exploited by the plow, the cow, the spade, and the ax. The Indians seemed an impediment to be swept aside or forced to yield to "civilization."

The documents that follow reflect the views of Americans, whites and Indians, of the settlement and exploitation of the trans-Missouri region after 1865. They represent disparate responses to a vast land of diverse terrain, climate, and resources. When you read these selections, as before, see if you can detect the preconceptions and values that informed the views expressed.

18.1: The Mining Frontier (1864)

Among the trans-Missouri West's most coveted resources were its minerals, especially its precious metals, silver and gold. These were a powerful magnet that drew thousands from the East and from foreign lands. The lure of gold, particularly, set off a succession of pell-mell "rushes" that overnight created flourishing and vibrant communities in the mining regions. Most of these boom towns were mushroom growths that withered in a matter of months. A few, however, became the seeds of permanent cities like Denver, Helena, Tucson, and Boise.

The following account captures many of the qualities of the typical Rocky Mountain mining community. Its author is Granville Stuart, who, along with his brother, James, struck gold in 1863 at Alder Gulch in Montana, near the headwaters of the Missouri River. The brothers' efforts to keep their strike secret failed, and in a matter of months the rush of miners to the Gulch had created the community of Virginia City with 4,000 inhabitants. In the next few years the miners extracted $30 million of gold dust and nuggets from the region.

How do you explain the special characteristics of Virginia City? How did such a community govern itself? There is at most only an oblique mention of women in Stuart's account. Do you suppose there were any in Virginia City? What roles might they have served in such a community?

Gold Rush Days

GRANVILLE STUART

The winter of 1863–64 was a mild one, building and mining operations were carried on with but little interruption all winter and before spring every branch of business was represented. Gold was coming out in large quantities. The district extended from the foot of Old Baldy to twelve miles down the creek. The bed of the creek and the bars on both sides were uniformly rich; the bed rock being literally paved with gold. The Alder gulch diggings were the richest gold placer diggings ever discovered in the world.

Freight teams from Salt Lake arrived until late in the fall, bringing in supplies; and while we were not provided with luxuries there was no suffering from food shortage. Molasses was considered by us, a great delicacy and it was both scarce and dear. Sam Hauser hit upon a plan all his own whereby he kept the only one gallon of molasses in our mess all to himself. Returning home one evening tired and hungry, we found Sam sitting at the table holding a mouse suspended by the tail: the little animal had every appearance of having been drowned in the molasses. Sam didn't say that he had taken the mouse from the molasses, we just reached that conclusion by inference and immediately lost our fondness for molasses—not so with Hauser—he continued to spread molasses on his bread every meal until it was all gone. One day, in an inquiring mood, he asked us why we all quit on molasses. James replied that he liked molasses but not well enough to eat it after a mouse had drowned in it: whereupon Hauser informed us that he had killed the mouse and smeared it with molasses later just to see how we would take it.

There was a great number of saloons and each dispenser of liquid refresh-

Granville Stuart, *Forty Years on the Frontier as Seen in the Journals and Reminiscences of Granville Stuart,* Paul C. Phillips, ed. (Cleveland: The Arthur H. Clark Company, 1925), vol. 1, pp. 264–72.

ments had the formula for making "tanglefoot:"—a quantity of boiled mountain sage, two plugs tobacco steeped in water, box cayenne pepper, one gallon water; so if any one got low in whiskey he promptly manufactured more. Saloons, gambling houses, public dance halls (hurdy gurdies) ran wide open and here, as in California, gold dust flowed in a yellow stream from the buckskin bags of the miners into the coffers of the saloons, dance halls, and gambling dens. Gold dust was the sole medium of exchange and it was reckoned at $18.00 an ounce. Every business house had gold scales for weighing the dust. If a man was under the influence of liquor, the bar keepers were not averse to helping themselves liberally to the man's dust, when paying himself for drinks he more often took $1.00 for a drink than the going price of twenty-five cents. A dance at one of the hurdy gurdies cost one dollar and as each dance wound up with an invitation to visit the bar where drinks for self and partner were expected, the cost of a waltz, schottische, or quadrille was usually $1.50. Dances kept up all night long but were usually orderly. If a man was found to be getting too much under the influence of liquor, some obliging friend would expel him from the hall. Every sort of gambling game was indulged in and it was no uncommon thing to see one thousand dollars staked on the turn of a monte card. The miner who indulged in gambling usually worked six days, then cleaned up his dust; and placing it in a buckskin sack hied himself to the nearest gambling house where he remained until he had transferred the contents of the sack to the professional gambler. If he played in luck he could usually stay in the game twenty-four hours. He would then return to his "diggins" without money and often with little grub; a sadder but no wiser man, for he would repeat the same thing over and over as long as his claim lasted and would then start out, blankets on his back, in search of new "diggins" . . . .

About the middle of January, 1864, a regular stampede craze struck Virginia City. The weather had been quite cold and work in the mines was temporarily suspended. A large number of idle men were about town and it required no more than one man with an imaginative mind to start half the population off on a wild goose chase. Somebody would say that somebody said, that somebody had found a good thing and without further inquiry a hundred or more men would start out for the reported diggings.

One report of a discovery on Gallatin river started a large party out in that direction. Every horse that could be found fit to ride was made ready. We had some horses on a ranch near town and brought them in and in less than an hour we had sold them all for about twice what they would have sold for at any other time. Four hundred men left town in mid-winter, with the ground covered with snow, for some place on the Gallatin river; no one seemed to know exactly where they were going, but most of them brought up at Gallatin City. Many, who could not get horses, started on foot. The first night out brought them to a realization of the futility of such a trip and they turned back.

Late in the evening on January 22, a rumor started that a big discovery had been made on Wisconsin creek, a distance of thirty miles from Virginia

City. The report said that as much as one hundred dollars to the pan had been found; and away the people flew all anxious to be first on the ground, where they could "just shovel up gold." Virginia City was almost deserted: men did not stop for horses, blankets, or provisions, the sole aim was to get there first and begin to shovel it out at the rate of one hundred to the pan. Fortunately the distance was not great and the weather was mild. Robert Dempsey had a ranch nearby and the stampeders got a supply of beef from him to last them back to town. It is needless to say that they found no diggings and all returned to Virginia in a few days.

The next great excitement was caused by a rumor of new rich discoveries on Boulder creek, a branch of the Jefferson. We sold every horse that we would spare at about three times its real value. Reece Anderson was among those taken with the fever and he joined the expedition. He had a good saddle and pack horses and plenty of food and blankets. There were so many in this stampede who started with little or nothing that those who had good outfits were obliged to share food with those who had none to keep them from starving and in the long run those with good outfits did not fare much better than those who started with none. Our friend, Reece Anderson, returned in about two weeks without having found any big thing in the way of gold mines, but he had accumulated quite a valuable stock of experience and got his nose, ears, and fingers badly frost-bitten.

The next big excitement started right in town. Somebody reported a "find" at the edge of town and in the morning claims were being staked off the main streets and on the rear of all of our lots. One enthusiastic man began to sink a hole in the street, just above the store and it began to look like we would be dug up and washed out without ceremony. Of course there was no gold found and mining operations in the streets and back yards was soon suspended.

A grand stampede to the Prickley Pear valley in which more than six hundred people took part was the last of the season. Away they went, crossing the hills into Boulder valley. They found the snow very deep, but fortunately not cold. Some good mines had been discovered on one bar about six hundred feet long, but all good ground had been taken when the stampeders arrived. The little army of disappointed men turned around and returned home once more.

18.2:   The Buffalo Destroyed (1876–77)

Much of the trans-Missouri region was too rugged or too dry for conventional agriculture, but in many places it produced an annual crop of short grass that provided forage for grazing animals. Before the arrival of white people the eastern half of the region, the high Plains, supported enormous herds of buffalo, and these in turn provided the Indian tribes with food (their flesh), clothing (their hides), rope (their sinews), and

*fuel (their droppings). By the late 1870s most of the buffalo were gone,
leaving the land for domestic cattle and depriving the Indians of a basic
necessity.*

*The destruction of the buffalo is not a pretty page in our history. In
the following selection a professional buffalo hunter describes his occupation during the late 1870s. What were the hunter's motives? What part
might the transcontinental railroads have played in the destruction of
the buffalo herds? Some scholars believe that the slaughter of the buffalo
was part of a deliberate policy designed to "tame" the nomadic Plains
Indians. Was it?*

The Destruction of the Plains Buffalo

W. SKELTON GLENN

There was several methods to kill [buffalos] and each [hunter] adopted his
own course and plan. They would get together and while one gained a point
from another, he, in turn, would gain a point from him. One method was to
run beside them, shooting them as they ran. Another was to shoot from the
rear, what was termed tail shooting: [always shooting] the hindmost buffalo
and when a day's hunt was done, they would be strung on the ground for a
mile or more, from ten to fifteen yards apart.

We first noticed that the buffaloes always went around a ravine or gulch,
unless going for water straight down a bluff; and as the buffalo always followed these trails a man on foot by a mere cut-off of a hundred yards could
cut him off. That is why they was so far apart in tail-hunting, as it was called.

. . . .

Another method of hunting was to leave your horse out of sight after you
had determined the direction and course of the wind, and then get as near
as possible. If the herd was lying at rest, he would pick out some buffalo that
was standing up on watch and shoot his ball in the side of him so that it
would not go through, but would lodge in the flesh; as on many times it had
been proven by men [who were] well hid and the wind taking the sound of
the gun and the whizz of the bullet off, [that] if a ball passed through a buffalo the herd would stampede and run for miles. A buffalo shot in this manner would merely hump up his back as if he had the colic and commence to
mill round and round in a slow walk. The other buffalo sniffing the blood
and following would not be watching the hunter, and he would continue to
shoot the outside cow buffalo; if there were old cows they would take them
as there would be some two or three offsprings following her. If she would
hump up, he would know that he had the range, and in this way hold the

Rex W. Strickland, ed., "The Recollections of W. S. Glenn, Buffalo Hunter," *Panhandle Plains
Historical Review*, vol. 22 (1949), pp. 20–26.

herd as long as they acted in this way as well as the well trained cowpuncher would hold his herd, only the hunter would use his gun. This was termed mesmerising the buffalo so that we could hold them on what we termed a stand, which afterwards proved to be the most successful way of killing the buffalo.

It was not always the best shot but the best hunter that succeeded, that is, the man who piled his buffalo in a pile so as to be more convenient for the skinner to get at and not have to run all over the country.

.   .   .   .

The hunter was hired by the piece: if robe hides were worth $3.00, [he was] given twenty-five cents for every one that he killed and was brought in by the skinners—was tallied up at camp. It was the camp rustler's business to keep tally of the number of hides killed each day. If the hides were worth $2.50, he [the hunter] got 20 cents; $2.00, he got 15 cents; $1.50, he got 10 cents; and $1.00, he got 5 cents.

.   .   .   .

I have seen their bodies so thick after being skinned, that they would look like logs where a hurricane had passed through a forrest [*sic*]. If they were lying on a hillside, the rays of the sun would make it look like a hundred glass windows. These buffalo would lie in this way until warm weather, drying up, and I have seen them piled fifty or sixty in a pile where the hunter had made a stand. As the skinner commenced on the edge, he would have to roll it out of the way to have room to skin the next, and when finished they would be rolled up as thick as saw logs around a mill. In this way a man could ride over a field and pick out the camps that were making the most money out of the hunt.

These hides, like all other commodities would rise and fall in price and we had to be governed by the prices [in the] East. This man, J. R. Loganstein, that run the hunt, has known them to be shipped to New York, then to Liverpool and back again in order to raise the price or corner the market. . . .

We will now describe a camp outfit. They would range from six to a dozen men, there being one hunter who killed the buffalo and took out the tongues, also the tallow. As the tallow was of an oily nature, it was equal to butter; [it was used] for lubricating our guns and we loaded our own shells, each shell had to be lubricated and [it] was used also for greasing wagons and also for lights in camp. Often chunks as large as an ear of corn were thrown on the fire to make heat. This [i.e., the removal of the tallow] had to be done while the meat was fresh, the hunter throwing it into a tree to wind dry; if the skinner forgot it, it would often stay there all winter and still be good to eat in the spring and better to eat after hanging there in the wind a few days.

We will return to the wagon man. [There were] generally two men to the wagon and their business was to follow up the hunter, if they were not in

The Last West   353

sight after the hunter had made a killing, he would proceed in their direction until he had met them, and when they would see him, he would signal with his hat where the killing was. If they got to the buffalo when they were fresh, their duty was to take out all the humps, tongues and tallow from the best buffalo. The hunter would then hunt more if they did not have hides enough to make a load or finish their day's work.

A remarkable good hunter would kill seventy-five to a hundred in a day, an average hunter about fifty, and a common one twenty-five, some hardly enough to run a camp. It was just like in any other business. A good skinner would skin from sixty to seventy-five, an average man from thirty to forty, and a common one from fifteen to twenty-five. These skinners were also paid by the hide[,] about five cents less than the hunter was getting for killing, being furnished with a grind stone, knives and steel and a team and wagon. The men were furnished with some kind of a gun, not as valuable as Sharp's rifle, to kill cripples with, also kips and calves that were standing around. In several incidents [instances?] it has been known to happen while the skinner was busy, they would slip up and knock him over. Toward the latter part of the hunt, when all the big ones were killed, I have seen as many as five hundred up to a thousand in a bunch, nothing but calves and have ridden right up to them, if the wind was right.

18.3:   The Cattle Kingdom (1866, 1888)

Domestic cattle were introduced into the southern Plains well before 1860. At the end of the Civil War, Texas found itself with a tremendous excess of animals, and in 1866 Texas cattlemen began to drive their herds northward in the spring to the east-west railroads that were beginning to inch across the Plains.

These drives were hard and hazardous. Cowboys and trail bosses often had to fend off unfriendly Indians and irate farmers while dealing with the uncertainties of weather and skittish cattle, prone to stampedes. Arriving at railhead—a succession of "cow towns" along the Missouri Pacific, Kansas Pacific, and Santa Fe railroads—the drivers sold their animals to merchants specializing in cattle marketing. The cowhands were then paid, and, typically, after a wild spree in the dance halls, saloons, and bawdy houses, returned home to prepare for the following spring drive.

The first selection is from the 1866 diary of George C. Duffield, boss of one of the early Texas cattle drives. Hollywood has made the drives seem romantic. Does Duffield's description fit the Hollywood mold? What were some of the hazards of driving Texas cattle to railhead in this early period? Why do we consider the drives romantic?

In the 1870s, after the railroads had pushed beyond the Missouri, the cattle industry spread to the northern Plains. There—in Montana, Wyoming, Idaho, and the Dakotas—enterprising cattlemen established ranches stocked with hardy longhorns imported from Texas. The ranchers had few expenses. The cattle grazed on public land and did not require shelter, even in winter. In the spring they were rounded up, and the new-born calves were branded with each rancher's characteristic mark. They were then sold to buyers and shipped east to the feedlots of the Corn Belt or the slaughterhouses of Chicago and St. Louis.

For a time the Plains cattle industry drew entrepreneurs and capital from the East and even from Europe. Beef prices were high; costs were low; profits inevitably were good. Moreover, the life of a rancher was exciting and glamorous.

One easterner attracted to the ranching life was Theodore Roosevelt. A New Yorker from an elite Knickerbocker family, Roosevelt went to Dakota Territory in 1884 and established the Elkhorn ranch on the Little Missouri River. In the selection below he describes the way the cattle business was conducted in the mid-1880s, with special emphasis on the roundup. the centerpiece of the ranchers' year.

Do you have any sense while reading Roosevelt's account that he is engaged in special pleading? Does his description seem to be romanticized? Would an account written by one of the ranch hands who earned forty dollars a month be as positive as that of the rancher himself? Do you think Roosevelt was ever a real rancher, or was he only an "eastern dude" "who played at the business?"

Diary of a Cattle Drover

GEORGE C. DUFFIELD

March 20th. Struck out to make a trade   crossed the Cherokee and stopped for the night at a Mr. Barbers   contracted for 1000 Head of Beeves at 12$ p. head.

26th.   started at 8 A.M. for Galveston via Buffalo Bayou Brazos Colorado R R   Arrived at Richmond for Dinner and to Harrisburg at 2 PM distance 80 Miles. From Alleytown to Richmond on the Brazos River the Road ran through the Most beautiful Prairie that I ever laid eyes on. Pasture was abundant and the Prairie was literally covered with tens of thousands of cattle Horses and Mules. . . . From Rich to this place the country is Level   good grass and thousands of cattle . . . Left at 3 for Galveston and arrived at 7 P.M. Country level. put at Island City Hotel   Fare 5$ gold pr day.

Originally published as "Driving Cattle from Texas to Iowa, 1866," by George C. Duffield, *Annals of Iowa* 14 (1924): 241–262. Copyright 1924 State Historical Society of Iowa. Reprinted by permission of the publisher.

April 5th.   Started for Sansaba with two wagons and 5 yoke Oxen and Seven hands   Travelled 12 Miles and camped. Rained hard during the night

15th.   Returned to Camp   found 4 new hands had come to Camp Making 20 in all. It Rained hard while we were gone and the River rose. great sport and Men wet crossing.

16th.   Lay round Camp   had two Horse races   won two bits on each went in swimming   fishing and had a gay day   all the Fish to eat we want.

21.   Rode to Mr. Harrells where Boys were hearding Cattle for Him. slept by cattle pen   cattle stampeded and 150 got away.

23rd.   Packed up for off   Travelled six Miles to first pen and camped Rode 15 More to Mr. Montgomerys.

24th.   back over the mountains to Camp at Harrels   Recd 241 cattle and finished Branding Pen   hearded *all* night.

27th. finished Branding   Started for Salt Creek with 835 Beeves   Landed safe.

May 1st.   Travelled 10 miles to Corryell co   Big Stamped   lost 200 head of cattle

2ond.   Spent the day hunting and found but 25 Head   it has been Raining for three days   these are dark days for me.

3rd.   day Spent in hunting cattle   found 23   hard rain and wind   lots of trouble.

4th.   Continued the hunt   found 40 head   day pleasant   Sun shone once more. Heard that the other Herd has stampeded and lost over 200.

5.   Cloudy damp Morning   rode 16 Miles and back to see the other Boys   found them in trouble with cattle all scattered over the country.

7th.   Hunt cattle is the order of the day   found most of our Cattle and drove 12 miles and camped on a large creek in Bosque Co.

8th.   All 3 heards are up and ready to travel off together for the first time   travelled 6 miles   rain pouring down in torrents and here we are on the banks of a creek with 10 or 12 ft water and raising   crossed at 4 Oclock and crossed into the Bosque Bottom   found it 20 ft deep   Ran my Horse into a ditch and got my Knee badly sprained—15 Miles.

9th. Still dark and gloomy   River up   everything looks *Blue* to me   no crossing to day   cattle behaved well.

13th. Big Thunder Storm last night   Stampede lost 100 Beeves   hunted all day   found 50   all tired. Every thing discouraging.

14th. Concluded to cross Brazos   swam our cattle and Horses and built Raft and Rafted our provisions and blankets &c over   Swam River with rope and then hauled wagon over   lost Most of our Kitchen furniture such as camp Kittles Coffee Pots Cups Plates Canteens &c &c.

15. back at River bringing up wagon   Hunting Oxen and other *lost* property. Rain poured down for one Hour. It does nothing but rain   got all our *traps* together that was not lost and thought we were ready for off   dark rainy night   cattle all left us and in morning not one Beef to be seen.

16th. Hunt Beeves is the word—all Hands discouraged and are determined to go   200 Beeves out and nothing to eat.

18th. Everything gloomey   four best hands left us   got to Buchanon at noon and to Rock Creek in Johnston Co   distance 14 [miles].

20th. Rain poured down for two hours   Ground in a flood Creeks up— Hands leaving   Gloomey times as ever I saw   drove 8 miles with 5 hands (359 Head)   passed the night 6 miles S.W. from Fort Worth in Parker Co.

22nd. This day has been spent in crossing the West Trinity and a hard and long to be remembered day to me   we swam our cattle and Horses. I swam it 5 times   upset our wagon in River and lost Many of our cooking utencils again   drove 3 miles and camped.

23rd. Travelled 10 Miles over a beautiful Prairie country such as I expected to see before I came here   stopped for dinner on Henrietta Creek and then on to Elisabeth Town and creek and stopped for the night—Hard rain that night and cattle behaved very bad—ran all night—was on my Horse the whole night and it raining hard.

24th. Glad to see Morning come   counted and found we had lost none for the first time—feel very bad. travelled 14 miles   crossed Denton Creek.

29th. Moved up to River and after many difficulties got all my Drove over but 100.

30th. worked in River all day and 50 Beeves on this side of River yet—am still in Texas.

31st. Swimming Cattle is the order   We worked all day in the River and at dusk got the last Beefe over—and am now out of Texas—This day will long be remembered by men—There was one of our party Drowned to day (Mr Carr) and several narrow escapes and I among the no.

June [1]st. Stampede last night among 6 droves and a general mix up and loss of Beeves. Hunt cattle again   Men all tired and want to leave. am in the Indian country   am annoyed by them   believe they scare the Cattle to get pay to collect them—Spent the day in separating Beeves and Hunting—Two men and Bunch Beeves lost—Many men in trouble. Horses *all* give out and Men refused to do anything.

2ond. Hard rain and wind Storm   Beeves ran and had to be on Horse back all night   Awful night. wet all night   clear bright morning. Men still lost   quit the Beeves and go to Hunting Men is the word—4 P.M. Found our men with Indian guide and 195 Beeves 14 Miles from camp. almost starved not having had a bite to eat for 60 hours   got to camp about 12 M *Tired*

5th. Oh! what a night—Thunder Lightning and rain—we followed our Beeves *all* night as they wandered about—put them on the road at day break   found 90 beeves of an other mans Herd   travelled 18 Miles over the worst road I ever saw and come to Boggy Depot and crossed 4 Rivers   It is well Known by that name   We hauled cattle out of the Mud with oxen half the day

8th. traveled 4 miles and camped for the day to [wait] for 12 Beeves that is in another Heard. this is another gloomey evening and I tremble for the result of this night—Thunder and rain all night   was in the saddle until day light   am almost dead for sleep.

10th. Feel much refreshed this morning and am ready for the duties of the day   crossed Elk and Canion Creeks and camped near S. Fork of Canadian.

12th. Hard Rain and Wind   Big stampede and here we are among the Indians with 150 head of Cattle gone   hunted all day and the Rain pouring down with but poor success   Dark days are these to me   Nothing but Bread and Coffee   Hands all Growling and Swearing—every thing wet and cold   Beeves gone   rode all day and gathered all but 35   Mixed with 8 other Herds   Last night 5000 Beeves stampeded at this place and a general mix up was the result

14th. Last night there was a terrible storm   Rain poured in torrents *all* night and up to 12 M today   our Beeves left us in the night but for *once* on the whole trip we found them *all* together near camp at day break. *all* the other droves as far as I can hear are scattered to the four winds   our Other Herd was all gone. We are now 25 Miles from Ark River and it is Very High   we are water bound by two creeks and but Beef and Flour to eat. am not Homesick but Heart sick.

18th. Nice day   went to Ft Gibson   got some coffee and Beefe. River very High but falling. Gloomey prospect   out of Money and provisions got back to camp and found the Indians had been there and claimed and tried to take some of our cattle   The Indians are making trouble stampeeding cattle here. We expect it. Cook dinner under a tree on the A K River Bank with two Ladies

19th. Good day   15 Indians come to Herd and tried to take some Beeves. Would not let them. Had a big muss   One drew his Knife and I my revolver. Made them leave but fear they have gone for others   they are the Seminoles.

23rd. worked all day hard in the River trying to make the Beeves swim and did not get one over. Had to go back to Prairie   Sick and discouraged. Have *not* got the *Blues* but am in *Hel of a fix.* Indians held High Festival over stolen Beef all night. lost 2 Beeves mired and maby more.

25th. We hired 20 Indians to help us cross. We worked from Morning until 2 Oclock and finally got them over with a loss of 5 and camped near the *old* Mission between the Ark River and the Verdigris.

27th. Beautiful Bright Morn   appearance of warm day   My Back is Blistered badly from exposure while in the River and I with two others are Suffering very much   I was attacked by a Beefe in the River and had a very narrow escape from being hurt by Diving   this day has been very warm   travelled 10 Miles and rested.

July 9th. Still cloudy followed a man that drove off one of My Beeves and got him. Other Herd came up and went on. it camped 1$^1/_2$ Miles from us and that night at 9 Oclock it stampeded and ran one Mile and over. the next Morning.

18th. Spent the day trying to settle up with partners preparitory to starting around Kansas to get Home   Horse stolen last night.

23rd. finished our settlement and divided our Beeves—drove 3 Miles and camped for the night   Made a contract with Mr. Bumbarger of Honey Grove Fanin Co Texas and Mr. Augustus Goff of Paris Lamar Co Texas who had 300 Stock cattle—to go through together and join Herds—

29th. Sunday   Excitement in camp   thought our Horses and oxen were stolen but found them   after many troubles we got down the Mountain and across the Creek   weather very *Hot*   Travelled 8 miles   Lost my coat and went back after it. Osages visited our camp   Are great Beggars.

30th. Drove 6 Miles and crossed Verdigris   had to give the Indians a Beefe for the right of way. Indians saucy   Went Bathing   5 miles in afternoon and camp.

August 1st. No trouble last night but lost a Cow   have travelled about 10 Miles today and while I sit here in the grass in the Broad prairie the Rear of the Herd is coming up   Weather pleasant and no flies.

3rd. All right but 2 men one down with Boils and one with Ague Travelled about 10 Miles over high Rocky Peaks and 2 creeks with fine grass.

8th. Come to Big Walnut   cattle stampeded and ran by 2 farms and the People were very angry but we made it all right   was visited by Many Men   was threatened with the Law but think we are all right now (Plenty of vegetables)

10. Separating cattle is the business of the day. Appearances of rain (no rain).

22nd. We have travelled about 20 miles today and camped on Mill Creek   I am on herd tonight   it is now 11 oclock   a beautiful moonlight night but cool. I have to stand half the night   the day was *cold* and some rain—There is but little timber in all this country   none only on the water courses   there are some fine springs   I have a severe pane in my neck

31st. Last night was one of those old fashioned rainy stormey thundering nights just such as we used to have in Texas   was up with the cattle all night   They travelled where they pleased but we stuck too them until morning. Today we crossed Big Muddy and camped on North fork of Nimehah It commenced raining at dark and rained all night   was up with cattle until midnight and then went to bed   found them all in the morning.

October 3rd. Taylor and I left the Herd and started for Home.

A Round-up on the Plains

THEODORE ROOSEVELT

Cattle-ranching can only be carried on in its present form while the population is scanty; and so in stock-raising regions, pure and simple, there are usual-

Theodore Roosevelt, "Ranch Life in the Far West," *Century Magazine*, vol. 35 (February–April 1888), pp. 500, 850–55.

ly few towns, and these are almost always at the shipping points for cattle. . . .

A true "cow town" is worth seeing,—such a one as Miles City, for instance, especially at the time of the annual meeting of the great Montana Stock-rais- ers' Association. Then the whole place is full to overflowing, the importance of the meeting and the fun of the attendant frolics, especially the horse- races, drawing from the surrounding ranch country many hundreds of men of every degree, from the rich stock-owner worth his millions to the ordinary cowboy who works for forty dollars a month. It would be impossible to imag- ine a more typically American assemblage, for although there are always a certain number of foreigners, usually English, Irish, or German, yet they have become completely Americanized; and on the whole it would be diffi- cult to gather a finer body of men, in spite of their numerous shortcomings. The ranch-owners differ more from each other than do the cowboys; and the former certainly compare very favorably with similar classes of capitalists in the East. Anything more foolish than the demagogic outcry against "cattle kings" it would be difficult to imagine. Indeed, there are very few businesses so absolutely legitimate as stock-raising and so beneficial to the nation at large; and a successful stock-grower must not only be shrewd, thrifty, patient, and enterprising, but he must also possess qualities of personal bravery, hardihood, and self-reliance to a degree not demanded in the least by any mercantile occupation in a community long settled. Stockmen are in the West the pioneers of civilization, and their daring and adventurousness make the after settlement [*sic*] of the region possible. The whole country owes them a great debt.

The stock-growers of Montana, of the western part of Dakota, and even of portions of extreme northern Wyoming,—that is, of all the grazing lands lying in the basin of the Upper Missouri,—have united, and formed them- selves into the great Montana Stock-growers' Association. Among the count- less benefits they have derived from this course, not the least has been the way in which the various round-ups work in with and supplement one another. At the spring meeting of the association, the entire territory mentioned above, including perhaps a hundred thousand square miles, is mapped out into round-up districts, which generally are changed but slightly from year to year, and the times and places for the round-ups to begin refixed so that those of adjacent districts may be run with a view to the best interests of all. . . .

The captain or foreman of the round-up, upon whom very much of its efficiency and success depends, is chosen beforehand. He is, of course, an expert cowman, thoroughly acquainted with the country; and he must also be able to command and to keep control of the wild rough-riders he has under him—a feat needing both tact and firmness.

At the appointed day all meet at the place from which the round-up is to start. Each ranch, of course, has most work to be done in its own round-up district, but it is also necessary to have representatives in all those surround- ing it. A large outfit may employ a dozen cowboys, or over, in the home dis- trict, and yet have nearly as many more representing its interest in the various ones adjoining. Smaller outfits generally club together to run a wagon and send outside representatives, or else go along with their stronger neighbors, they paying part of the expenses. A large outfit, with a herd of twenty thousand cattle or more, can, if necessary, run a round-up entirely by itself, and is able to act independently of outside help; it is therefore at a great advantage compared with those that can take no step effectively without their neighbors' consent and assistance.

If the starting-point is some distance off, it may be necessary to leave home three or four days in advance. Before this we have got everything in readiness; have overhauled the wagons, shod any horse whose forefeet are tender,—as a rule, all our ponies go barefooted,—and left things in order at the ranch. Our outfit may be taken as a sample of every one else's. We have a stout four-horse wagon to carry the bedding and the food; in its rear a mess-chest is rigged to hold the knives, forks, cans, etc. All our four team-horses are strong, willing animals, though of no great size, being originally just "broncos," or unbroken native horses, like the others. The teamster is also cook: a man who is a really first-rate hand at both driving and cooking—and our present teamster is both—can always command his price. Besides our own men, some cowboys from neighboring ranches and two or three representatives from other round-up districts are always along, and we generally have at least a dozen "riders," as they are termed,—that is, cowboys, or "cow-punchers," who do the actual cattlework,—with the wagon. Each of these has a string of eight or ten ponies; and to take charge of the saddle-band, thus consisting of a hundred odd head, there are two herders, always known as "horse-wranglers"—one for the day and one for the night.

At the meeting-place there is usually a delay of a day or two to let every one come in; and the plain on which the encampment is made becomes a scene of great bustle and turmoil. The heavy four-horse wagons jolt in from different quarters, the horse-wranglers rushing madly to and fro in the endeavor to keep the different saddle-bands from mingling, while the "riders," or cowboys, with each wagon jog along in a body. The representatives from outside districts ride in singly or by twos and threes, every man driving before him his own horses, one of them loaded with his bedding. Each wagon wheels out of the way into some camping-place not too near the others, the bedding is tossed out on the ground, and then every one is left to do what he wishes, while the different wagon bosses, or foremen, seek out the captain of the round-up to learn what his plans are.

There is a good deal of rough but effective discipline and method in the way in which a round-up is carried on. The captain of the whole has as lieutenants the various wagon foremen and in making demands for men to do some special service he will usually merely designate some foreman to take charge of the work and let him parcel it out among his men to suit himself. The captain of the round-up or the foreman of a wagon may himself be a ranchman; if such is not the case, and the ranchman nevertheless comes along, he works and fares precisely as do the other cowboys.

There is no eight-hour law in cowboy land: during round-up time we often count ourselves lucky if we get off with much less than sixteen hours; but the work is done in the saddle, and the men are spurred on all the time by the desire to outdo one another in feats of daring and skillful horsemanship. There is very little quarreling or fighting; and though the fun often takes the form of rather rough horse-play, yet the practice of carrying dangerous weapons makes cowboys show far more rough courtesy to each other and far less rudeness to strangers than is the case among, for instance, Eastern miners, or even lumbermen. When a quarrel may very probably result fatally, a man thinks twice before going into it.

The method of work is simple. The mess-wagons and loose horses, after breaking camp in the morning, move on in a straight line for some miles, going into camp again before midday; and the day herd, consisting of all the cattle that have been found far off their range, and which are to be brought back there, and of any others that it is necessary to gather, follows on afterwards. Meanwhile the cowboys scatter out and drive in all the cattle from the country round about, going perhaps ten or fifteen miles back from the line of march, and meeting at the place where camp has already been pitched. The wagons always keep some little distance from one another, and the saddle-bands do the same, so that the horses may not get mixed.

The speed and thoroughness with which a country can be worked depends, of course, very largely upon the number of riders. Ours is probably about an average round-up as regards size. The last spring I was out, there were half a dozen wagons along; the saddle-bands numbered about a hundred each; and the morning we started, sixty men in the saddle splashed across the shallow ford of the river that divided the plain where we had camped from the valley of the long winding creek up which we were first to work.

In the morning the cook is preparing breakfast long before the first glimmer of dawn. As soon as it is ready, probably about 3 o'clock, he utters a long-drawn shout, and all the sleepers feel it is time to be up on the instant, for they know there can be no such thing as delay on the round-up, under penalty of being set afoot. . . . The meal is not an elaborate one; nevertheless a man will have a hurry if he wishes to eat it before hearing the foreman sing out, "Come, boys, catch your horses"; when he must drop everything and run out to the wagon with his lariat. When all are saddled, many of the horses bucking and dancing about, the riders from the different wagons all assemble at the one where the captain is sitting, already mounted. He waits a very short time—for laggards receive but scant mercy—before announcing the proposed camping-place and parceling out the work among those present. If, as is usually the case, the line of march is along a river or creek, he appoints some man to take a dozen others and drive down (or up) it ahead of the day herd, so that the latter will not have to travel through other cattle; the day herd itself being driven and guarded by a dozen men detached for that purpose. The rest of the riders are divided into two bands, placed under men who know the country, and start out, one on each side, to bring in every head for fifteen miles back. The captain then himself rides down to the new camping-place, so as to be there as soon as any cattle are brought in.

Meanwhile the two bands, a score of riders in each, separate and make their way in opposite directions. The leader of each tries to get such a "scatter" on his men that they will cover completely all the land gone over. This morning work is called circle riding, and is peculiarly hard in the Bad Lands on account of the remarkably broken, rugged nature of the country. The men come in on lines that tend to a common center—as if the sticks of a fan were curved. As the band goes out, the leader from time to time detaches one or two men to ride down through certain sections of the country, making the shorter, or what are called inside, circles, while he keeps on; and finally, retaining as companions the two or three whose horses are toughest, makes the longest or outside circle himself, going clear back to the divide, or whatever the point may be that marks the limit of the round-up work, and then turning and working straight to the meeting-place. Each man, of course, brings in every head of cattle he can see.

When the men on the outside circle have reached the bound set them,— whether it is a low divide, a group of jagged hills, the edge of the rolling, limitless prairie, or the long, waste reaches of alkali and sage brush,—they turn their horses' heads and begin to work down the branches of the creeks, one or two riding down the bottom, while the others keep off to the right and the left, a little ahead and fairly high up on the side hills, so as to command as much of a view as possible. . . . All the cattle are carried on ahead down the creek; and it is curious to watch the different behavior of the different breeds. A cowboy riding off to one side of the creek, and seeing a number of long-horned Texans grazing in the branches of a set of coulees, has merely to ride across the upper ends of these, uttering the drawn-out "ei-koh-h-h," so familiar to the cattle-men, and the long-horns will stop grazing, stare fixedly at him, and then, wheeling, strike off down the coulees at a trot, tails in air, to be carried along by the center riders when they reach the main creek into which the coulees lead. . . . Every little bunch of stock is thus collected, and all are driven along together. At the place where some large fork joins the main creek another band may be met, driven by some of the men who have left earlier in the day to take one of the shorter circles; and thus, before coming down to the bottom where the wagons are camped and where the actual "round-up" itself is to take place, this one herd may include a couple of thousand head; or, on the other hand, the longest ride may not result in the finding of a dozen animals. As soon as the riders are in, they disperse to their respective wagons to get dinner and change horses, leaving the cattle to be held by one or two of their number. If only a small number of cattle have been gathered, they will all be run into one herd; if there are many of them, however, the different herds will be held separate.

As soon as, or even before, the last circle riders have come in and have snatched a few hasty mouthfuls to serve as their mid-day meal, we begin to work the herd—or herds, if the one herd would be of too unwieldy size. The animals are held in a compact bunch, most of the riders forming a ring outside, while a couple from each ranch successively look the herds through and cut out those marked with their own brand. It is difficult, in such a mass of moving beasts,—for they do not stay still, but keep weaving in and out among each other,—to find all of one's own animals: a man must have natural gifts, as well as great experience, before he becomes a good brand-reader and is able to "clean up a herd"—that is, be sure he has left nothing of his own in it.

All this time the men holding the herd have their hands full, for some animal is continually trying to break out, when the nearest man flies at it at once and after a smart chase brings it back to its fellows. As soon as all the cows, calves, and whatever else is being gathered have been cut out, the rest are driven clear off the ground and turned loose, being headed in the direction contrary to that in which we travel the following day. Then the riders surround the next herd, the men holding cuts move them up near it, and the work is begun anew.

As soon as all the brands of cattle are worked, and the animals that are to be driven along have been put in the day herd, attention is turned to the cows and calves, which are already gathered in different bands, consisting each of all the cows of a certain brand and all the calves that are following them. If there is a corral, each band is in turn driven into it; if there is none, a ring of riders does duty in its place. A fire is built, the irons heated, and a dozen men dismount to, as it is called, "wrestle" the calves. The best two ropers go in on their horses to catch the latter; one man keeps tally, a couple put on the brands, and the others seize, throw, and hold the little unfortunates.

Every morning certain riders are detached to drive and to guard the day herd, which is most monotonous work, the men being on from 4 in the morning till 8 in the evening, the only rest coming at dinner-time, when they change horses.

From 8 in the evening till 4 in the morning the day herd becomes a night herd. Each wagon in succession undertakes to guard it for a night, dividing the time into watches of two hours apiece, a couple of riders taking each watch. This is generally chilly and tedious; but at times it is accompanied by intense excitement and danger, when the cattle become stampeded, whether by storm or otherwise. The first and the last watches are those chosen by preference; the others are disagreeable, the men having to turn out cold and sleepy, in the pitchy darkness, the two hours of chilly wakefulness completely breaking the night's rest.

But though there is much work and hardship, rough fare, monotony, and exposure connected with the round-up, yet there are few men who do not look forward to it and back to it with pleasure. The only fault to be found is that the hours of work are so long that one does not usually have enough time to sleep. The food, if rough, is good: beef, bread, pork, beans, coffee or tea, always canned tomatoes, and often rice, canned corn, or sauce made from dried apples. The men are good-humored, bold, and thoroughly interested in their business, continually vying with one another in the effort to see which can do the work best. It is superbly health-giving, and is full of excitement and adventure, calling for the exhibition of pluck, self-reliance, hardihood, and dashing horsemanship; and of all forms of physical labor the easiest and pleasantest is to sit in the saddle.

18.4:   The Native Americans (1877, 1881)

The most resistant barrier to white exploitation of the "last West" were the Native American peoples who, until the 1850s, occupied the Great Plains as "One Big Reservation." These were formidable mounted warriors capable of firing a shower of deadly arrows at a target while riding their ponies at full gallop. Yet in the end, they could not stand up to the superior organization and numbers of the whites who coveted their lands.

Beginning in the 1850s the federal government, responding to the demands of western farmers, miners, and railroad promoters, began to force the Plains tribes into smaller and smaller reservations. Using bribery, deception, and threats, the federal government strong-armed the Indians into treaties that reduced their lands to ever-more limited tracts, often arid and rugged terrain that no one else wanted. The Indians resisted, and between 1866 and 1890 the Plains tribes and the U.S. Army fought a series of wars in which the Indians often gave as good as they got. In 1866 the Sioux killed 82 soldiers under the command of Captain W. J. Fetterman; in 1876, commanded by Chiefs Sitting Bull and Crazy Horse, they were again victorious, killing all 265 men under the command of the foolhardy army General George Custer, at the Little Big Horn River.

The first selection below is Sitting Bull's account of the battle on the Little Big Horn as given to a New York newspaper reporter. Why, according to Sitting Bull, were the Indians able to destroy Custer's force? What does the chief's description reveal of Indian values? Do you know if Custer and his men were badly outnumbered? Why, do you think, past generations romanticized Custer? Is he still considered a tragic hero?

The second selection is a portion of President Chester A. Arthur's 1881 State of the Union Address in which Arthur, an easterner, says that the government must cease to treat the Indians as collective members of separate, autonomous nations, and deal with them instead as individuals to be absorbed into mainstream American life. In what way can Arthur's approach be considered generous and enlightened for the day? Is there any significance in the fact that Arthur was an easterner? (The "severalty" proposal for land ownership by individual families, as contrasted with the former communal ownership by tribes, was finally enacted by Congress in 1887 as the Dawes Act.)

Do you know if the Indians benefited or lost under the new policy? What is the significance of Arthur's suggestion concerning education for the Indians? What sort of education, do you suppose, he had in mind?

Sitting Bull Tells How He Defeated Custer

SITTING BULL

"When the fight commenced here," I asked, pointing to the spot where Custer advanced beyond the Little Big Horn, "what happened?"

"Hell!"

"You mean, I suppose, a fierce battle?"

"I mean a thousand devils."

"The village was by this time thoroughly aroused?"

"The squaws were like flying birds; the bullets were like humming bees."

"You say that when the first attack was made, up here on the right of the map, the old men and the squaws and children ran down the valley toward the left. What did they do when this second attack came from up here toward the left?"

"They ran back again to the right, here and here," answered Sitting Bull, placing his swarthy finger on the place where the words "Abandoned Lodges" are.

"And where did the warriors run?"

"They ran to the fight—the big fight."

"So that, in the afternoon, after the fight, on the right hand side of the map was over, and after the big fight toward the left hand side began, you say that the squaws and children all returned to the right hand side, and that the warriors, the fighting men of all the Indian camps, ran to the place where the big fight was going on?"

"Yes."

"Why was that? Were not some of the warriors left in front of these intrenchments on the bluffs, near the right side of the map? Did not you think it necessary—did not your war chiefs think it necessary—to keep some of your young men there to fight the troops who had retreated to those intrenchments?"

"No."

"Why?"

"You have forgotten."

"How?"

"You forget that only a few soldiers were left by the Long Hair[1] on those bluffs. He took the main body of his soldiers with him to make the big fight down here on the left."

"So there were no soldiers to make a fight left in the intrenchments on the right hand bluffs?"

"I have spoken. It is enough. The squaws could deal with them. There were none but squaws and pappooses in front of them that afternoon."

"Well then," I inquired of Sitting Bull, "Did the cavalry, who came down and made the big fight, fight?"

Again Sitting Bull smiled.

"They fought. Many young men are missing from our lodges. But is there an American squaw who has her husband left? Were there any Americans left to tell the story of that day? No."

"How did they come on to the attack?"

"I have heard that there are trees which tremble."

"Do you mean the trees with trembling leaves?"

"Yes."

"They call them in some parts of the western country Quaking Asps; in the eastern part of the country they call them Silver Aspens."

"Hah! A great white chief, whom I met once, spoke these words 'Silver Aspens,' trees that shake; these were the Long Hair's soldiers."

"You do not mean that they trembled before your people because they were afraid?"

"They were brave men. They were tired. They were too tired."

"How did they act? How did they behave themselves?"

At this Sitting Bull again arose. I also arose from my seat, as did the other persons in the room, except the stenographer.

"Your people," said Sitting Bull, extending his right hand, "were killed. I tell no lies about deadmen. These men who came with the Long Hair were as good men as ever fought. When they rode up their horses were tired and they were tired. When they got off from their horses they could not stand firmly on their feet. They swayed to and fro—so my young men have told me—like the limbs of cypresses in a great wind. Some of them staggered under the weight of their guns. But they began to fight at once; but by this time, as I have said, our camps were aroused, and there were plenty of warriors to meet them. They fired with needle guns. We replied with magazine guns—repeating rifles. It was so (and here Sitting Bull illustrated by patting his palms together with the rapidity of a fusilade). Our young men rained lead across the river and drove the white braves back."

"And then?"

"And then, they rushed across themselves."

"And then?"

---

[1]Custer, who wore his hair down his back—ED.

"And then they found that they had a good deal to do."

"Was there at that time some doubt about the issue of the battle, whether you would whip the Long Hair or not?"

"There was so much doubt about it that I started down there (here again pointing to the map) to tell the squaws to pack up the lodges and get ready to move away."

"You were on that expedition, then, after the big fight had fairly begun?"

"Yes."

"You did not personally witness the rest of the big fight? You were not engaged in it?"

"No. I have heard of it from the warriors."

"When the great crowds of your young men crossed the river in front of the Long Hair what did they do? Did they attempt to assault him directly in his front?"

"At first they did, but afterward they found it better to try and get around him. They formed themselves on all sides of him except just at his back."

"How long did it take them to put themselves around his flanks?"

"As long as it takes the sun to travel from here to here" (indicating some marks upon his arm with which apparently he is used to gauge the progress of the shadow of his lodge across his arm, and probably meaning half an hour. An Indian has no more definite way than this to express the lapse of time).

"The trouble was with the soldiers," he continued; "they were so exhausted and their horses bothered them so much that they could not take good aim. Some of their horses broke away from them and left them to stand and drop and die. When the Long Hair, the General, found that he was so outnumbered and threatened on his flanks, he took the best course he could have taken. The bugle blew. It was an order to fall back. All the men fell back fighting and dropping. They could not fire fast enough, though. But from our side it was so," said Sitting Bull, and here he clapped his hands rapidly twice a second to express with what quickness and continuance the balls flew from the Henry and Winchester rifles wielded by the Indians. "They could not stand up under such a fire," he added.

"Were any military tactics shown? Did the Long Haired Chief make any disposition of his soldiers, or did it seem as though they retreated all together, helter skelter, fighting for their lives?"

"They kept in pretty good order. Some great chief must have commanded them all the while. They would fall back across a *coulee* and make a fresh stand beyond on higher ground. The map is pretty nearly right. It shows where the white men stopped and fought before they were all killed. I think that is right—down there to the left, just above the Little Big Horn. There was one part driven out there, away from the rest, and there a great many men were killed. The places marked on the map are pretty nearly the places where all were killed."

"Did the whole command keep on fighting until the last?"

"Every man, so far as my people could see. There were no cowards on either side."

The Indians Must Be Assimilated

CHESTER A. ARTHUR

Prominent among the matters which challenge the attention of Congress at its present session is the management of our Indian affairs. While this question has been a cause of trouble and embarrassment from the infancy of the Government, it is but recently that any effort has been made for its solution at once serious, determined, consistent, and promising success.

It has been easier to resort to convenient makeshifts for tiding over temporary difficulties than to grapple with the great permanent problem, and accordingly the easier course has almost invariably been pursued.

It was natural, at a time when the national territory seemed almost illimitable and contained many millions of acres far outside the bounds of civilized settlements, that a policy should have been initiated which more than aught else has been the fruitful source of our Indian complications.

I refer, of course, to the policy of dealing with the various Indian tribes as separate nationalities, of relegating them by treaty stipulations to the occupancy of immense reservations in the West, and of encouraging them to live a savage life, undisturbed by any earnest and well-directed efforts to bring them under the influences of civilization.

The unsatisfactory results which have sprung from this policy are becoming apparent to all.

As the white settlements have crowded the borders of the reservations, the Indians, sometimes contentedly and sometimes against their will, have been transferred to other hunting grounds, from which they have again been dislodged whenever their new-found homes have been desired by the adventurous settlers.

These removals and the frontier collisions by which they have often been preceded have led to frequent and disastrous conflicts between the races.

It is profitless to discuss here which of them has been chiefly responsible for the disturbances whose recital occupies so large a space upon the pages of our history.

We have to deal with the appalling fact that though thousands of lives have been sacrificed and hundreds of millions of dollars expended in the attempt to solve the Indian problem, it has until within the past few years seemed scarcely nearer a solution than it was half a century ago. But the Government has of late been cautiously but steadily feeling its way to the adoption of a policy which has already produced gratifying results, and

James D. Richardson, ed., *A Compilation of the Messages and Papers of the Presidents* (New York: Bureau of National Literature, 1897), vol. 10, pp. 4641–43.

which, in my judgment, is likely, if Congress and the Executive accord in its support, to relieve us ere long from the difficulties which have hitherto beset us.

For the success of the efforts now making to introduce among the Indians the customs and pursuits of civilized life and gradually to absorb them into the mass of our citizens, sharing their rights and holden to their responsibilities, there is imperative need for legislative action.

My suggestions in that regard will be chiefly such as have been already called to the attention of Congress and have received to some extent its consideration.

First. I recommend the passage of an act making the laws of the various States and Territories applicable to the Indian reservations within their borders and extending the laws of the State of Arkansas to the portion of the Indian Territory not occupied by the Five Civilized Tribes.

The Indian should receive the protection of the law. He should be allowed to maintain in court his rights of person and property. He has repeatedly begged for this privilege. Its exercise would be very valuable to him in his progress toward civilization.

Second. Of even greater importance is a measure which has been frequently recommended by my predecessors in office, and in furtherance of which several bills have been from time to time introduced in both Houses of Congress. The enactment of a general law permitting the allotment in severalty, to such Indians, at least, as desire it, of a reasonable quantity of land secured to them by patent, and for their own protection made inalienable for twenty or twenty-five years, is demanded for their present welfare and their permanent advancement.

In return for such considerate action on the part of the Government, there is reason to believe that the Indians in large numbers would be persuaded to sever their tribal relations and to engage at once in agricultural pursuits. Many of them realize the fact that their hunting days are over and that it is now for their best interests to conform their manner of life to the new order of things. By no greater inducement than the assurance of permanent title to the soil can they be led to engage in the occupation of tilling it.

The well-attested reports of their increasing interest in husbandry justify the hope and belief that the enactment of such a statute as I recommend would be at once attended with gratifying results. A resort to the allotment system would have a direct and powerful influence in dissolving the tribal bond, which is so prominent a feature of savage life, and which tends so strongly to perpetuate it.

Third. I advise a liberal appropriation for the support of Indian schools, because of my confident belief that such a course is consistent with the wisest economy.